Learn Java™ on the Macintosh®

Barry Boone

with Dave Mark

ADDISON-WESLEY DEVELOPERS PRESS

Reading, Massachusetts • Menlo Park, California • New York • Don Mills, Ontario
Harlow, England • Amsterdam • Bonn • Sydney • Singapore • Tokyo
Madrid • San Juan • Paris • Seoul • Milan • Mexico City • Taipei

Library of Congress Cataloging-in-Publication Data

Boone, Barry
      Learn Java on the Macintosh / Barry Boone with Dave Mark.
            p.   cm.
      Includes index.
      ISBN 0-201-19157-1
      1. Macintosh (Computer)—Programming.   2. Java (Computer program language)   I. Mark, Dave.   II. Title.
      QA76.8.M3B663   1996
      005.13'3—dc20   96-20303
                                                                                          CIP

A-W Developers Press is a division of Addison-Wesley Publishing Company, Inc.

Sponsoring Editor: Kim Fryer
Project Manager: John Fuller
Production Assistant: Melissa Lima
Cover design: Andrew M. Newman
Text design: Wilson Graphics and Design (Kenneth J. Wilson)
Set in 10-point Palatino by Octal Publishing, Inc.

1 2 3 4 5 6 7 8 9–MA–0099989796
First printing, July 1996

Thanks to the usual suspects—Mary, Kim, Keith, and Dylan—for their insight, patience, and support. Thanks also to Kevin Raulerson of Metrowerks, whose insightful comments improved this book; and Jim Trudeau, also of Metrowerks, who contributed generously to Appendix D.

—B.B.

Thanks to Deneen, Daniel, and Kelley—LFUEMINM,OK?

—D.M.

Contents

Chapter 1

Welcome Aboard

Welcome to *Learn Java on the Macintosh*. By picking up this book, you have taken the first step toward learning the Java programming language. You're about to learn the most powerful and exciting computer language in wide use today.

What's in This Package?

Learn Java on the Macintosh is a book/CD-ROM package. The book is filled with diagrams, explanations, examples, and exercises designed to teach people new to programming the basics of how to program in Java. This book is tailor-made for people who do not have a programming background but want to learn Java as their first programming language. We'll start by explaining what programming is all about and then move into the specifics of programming in Java and building Java applets (Java programs that run over the Web). By working through the examples and exercises, you can use this book as a self-study guide to build a solid foundation for your explorations of the Java language.

In the back of the book, you'll find a compact disc (CD-ROM) that includes a customized version of Metrowerks CodeWarrior, one of the most popular development environments for the Macintosh. The CD-ROM also contains all of the sample code explored in this book, as well as the answers to all of the exercises. You'll use the CodeWarrior development environment to work with the example Java programs shown in this book and to write your own Java programs.

Also, where appropriate, this book will put the Java language in perspective by mentioning what came before it and by easing you into what you'll experience on the road to becoming a Java programmer.

Why Learn Java?

Java is fast becoming the standard in software development primarily because it is transforming the World Wide Web. While Java is a relatively new language in the evolution of programming, Java is already talked about and used everywhere. There are many good reasons for this, and you'll gain strong insights into these reasons as you progress through this book. By the time you reach the final chapter, you'll be ready to take part in the community of knowledgeable Java programmers, and you'll be able to make the Web come alive by writing applets of your own.

What Should You Know to Get Started?

First of all, you *do not* already need to know how to program in some other language to learn Java. Java is a simpler language than other programming languages in use today, including C and C++. However, though the language itself is simple, there are a few concepts to get straight before you dive in and start writing code. Chapters 3 and 4 ease you into the Java mind-set before you begin learning the language in Chapter 5. So hang through the introductory chapters; we'll get to the good stuff soon.

Second, to use the CD-ROM effectively, you *do* need to know how to use a Macintosh and how to use the mouse to make selections and open and close windows. Do you know how to double-click an application to start it up? Do the scrolling list and other user interface controls in Figure 1.1 look familiar? Do you know how to drag and drop icons? If you use the Macintosh to run programs and edit documents, you have all the skills you need to get started learning Java. And if you have a desire to learn a programming language, you have the only prerequisite you need!

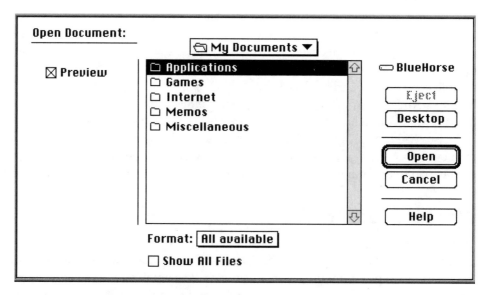

Figure 1.1   Scrolling through a list of documents.

Third, it's helpful to be familiar with the various kinds of applications available for your Mac. The more familiar you are with what modern graphical applications look like—such as word processors, drawing programs, games, personal finance software, and so on—the better sense you'll have for what your own applets should look like as well.

Finally, it's important to have had experience using the Web. This book assumes you already have used browsers to tour the Web and are up-to-date on the latest browsers that incorporate Java. For more information on Web browsers that incorporate Java, turn to Appendix G. Also, check out the Sun, Netscape, and Microsoft home pages.

What Equipment Will You Need?

Although you can learn the basic concepts of Java just by reading this book, you'll get the most out of *Learn Java on the Macintosh* if you run each example program as you read how it works. To do this, you'll need a Macintosh with a 68020, 68030, 68040, or PowerPC processor; at least 8 megabytes of memory; System 7.1 or a newer version (for 68K-based Macintosh computers) or System 7.1.2 or a newer version (for Power Macintosh computers); and, of course, a CD-ROM drive so that you can install your new programming environment. If you already have Metrowerks CodeWarrior, you'll still want a CD-ROM drive to install the sample code and exercises contained on the CD-ROM. (If you are using a version of the Mac OS before System 7.5, you must also obtain and install Apple's Thread Manager extension into your extensions folder. Appendix G contains references for where to look for this software and how to find other information relating to Java and CodeWarrior.)

The Lay of the Land

There are 15 chapters in this book, plus 7 appendixes. Chapter 1 (this chapter) provides an introduction to what you'll find in this book and what this book covers.

Chapter 2 introduces you to the CD-ROM portion of the book/CD-ROM package. You'll learn about CodeWarrior, the Java programming environment that you'll use to run all of the programs in this book. This chapter explains how to install the software that is on the CD-ROM (you'll use this software to develop your own Java applets and to learn the Java language) and how to test CodeWarrior to ensure it's working properly.

Chapter 3 offers an overview of programming for the World Wide Web and shows you how Java fits into the Web picture. Just how does a Web browser arrange a Web page? And what does the browser do when it encounters a Java applet in a Web page?

Chapter 4 begins the exploration of concepts central to Java programming. It's always a good idea to design a program as thoroughly as you can before you begin writing code; this chapter suggests four questions you should try to answer before you turn to writing your software. This chapter also introduces three terms you may have already heard people mention in relation to Java: *class*, *object*, and *method*. You'll explore these terms by working through a detailed example, without yet writing any code, that illustrates how to design Java applets.

Chapter 5 introduces the steps you'll follow when you develop a Java applet. By creating the simplest possible Java applet, you'll learn how to work with CodeWarrior to create a new program, edit a file to write your own Java program, get your Java program ready to run, and then execute your program.

Chapter 6 explores the basics of most programming languages, including Java: variables and operators. When you finish this chapter, you'll have tasted your first morsels of real programming. You'll know how to declare a variable and how to use operators to store data in your variables. In particular, you'll learn about ways to refer to numbers inside your program. You'll even learn a little bit about programming with style!

Chapter 7 provides an introduction to defining and invoking methods (chunks of code that accomplish a specific task). You'll also learn how to hook into the communication that takes place between the browser and your own Java applet to start to customize your applet.

Chapter 8 moves into the true potential of programming languages by discussing flow control. You'll learn how to use Java programming constructs, such as `if`, `while`, and `for` loops, to control the direction of your program and indicate when to execute certain sets of instructions instead of others.

Chapter 9 explores how to create and use objects that are based on your classes. You'll keep track of data by using objects, and you'll provide behavior for your objects by writing methods. Once you've completed this chapter, you'll know many of the concepts central to Java.

Chapter 10 introduces you to lots of classes provided for you by Java that you can use in your own applets. You'll learn how to extend Java's classes to add your own data and behavior to what Java provides by default.

Chapter 11 discusses what it means to create a graphical user interface in Java. You'll learn the necessary steps for creating your own windows, buttons, and text input fields, and you'll learn how to paint pictures in your applet's window. Creating a graphical user interface will enable your Java applets to become part of the World Wide Web. You'll also learn how to respond to mouse clicks and keyboard entry to create truly interactive applets.

Chapter 12 returns to variables and data types to cover some more ways to store data in your classes, objects, and methods. These include floating-point values, characters, strings, collections of data called *arrays*, and minidatabases called *vectors* and *hash tables*.

Chapter 13 dives into a few advanced topics that can help you write even more powerful programs. For example, you'll learn how you can get into the act of creating new objects from your own classes by defining constructors and how to respond to error conditions by handling exceptions. You'll also learn how your HTML (Hypertext Markup Language) pages can pass data to your applets.

Chapter 14 provides an overview of how you can create stand-alone Java applications in addition to the applets you've developed to run on the Web. Stand-alone applications offer almost all of the features of applets without requiring your computer to be connected to the Internet at all.

Chapter 15 offers a path for further exploration since you will have surveyed the basics of the Java language and have achieved a solid grasp of how to program in Java. This chapter shows you where to look to learn more about Java's advanced topics, such as using threads to make more than one thing occur at the same time.

Appendix A is a glossary of the technical terms used in this book.

Appendix B contains a listing of all of the programs discussed in this book. You might find this appendix particularly useful if you're looking for an example of some Java code in action, such as how to define a method, how to create a new object, or how to write a `for` loop.

Appendix C provides a summary for the syntax of each of the Java statements and keywords introduced in this book. Need an exact specification of a `switch` statement? It's right here in Appendix C.

Appendix D provides some more details about the version of Metrowerks CodeWarrior included on the CD-ROM. It also describes the differences between the version of CodeWarrior provided here and the commercial version.

Appendix E presents exercises for each chapter that you can use to turn this book into a self-study guide.

Appendix F provides answers to the exercises.

Appendix G points the way to other books and resources on the Internet for learning more about programming in Java.

Conventions Used in This Book

As you read this book, you'll encounter a few standard conventions that make the book easier to read. For example, technical terms appearing for the first time are in **boldface**. You'll find most of these terms in the glossary in Appendix A.

All of the source code examples in this book are presented using a special font, known as the `code font`. This font is also used for source code fragments that appear in the middle of running text. Menu items, or items you'll click on, appear in **Chicago font**.

By the Way

> Occasionally, you'll come across a block of text set off in a box, like this. These blocks are called *tech blocks* and are intended to add technical detail to the subject currently being discussed. Each tech block fits into one of five categories: "By the Way," "Style," "Detail," "Definition," and "Warning." "By the Way" tech blocks are intended to be informative but not crucial. "Style" tech blocks contain information relating to your Java programming style. "Detail" tech blocks offer more detailed information about the current topic. "Definition" tech blocks contain the definition of an important Java term. "Warning" tech blocks are usually trying to caution you about some potential programming problem, so pay attention!

Review

This book provides an introduction to Java for new programmers. By using the Java development environment available on the CD-ROM included with this book, you'll be able to work through all of the syntax, grammar, and concepts required to begin mastering the Java language.

What's Next?

You're ready to roll! In Chapter 2, you'll install the software that is on the CD-ROM and explore the CodeWarrior environment so that you can begin running the samples in this book and writing your own Java programs.

Chapter 2

Installing and Testing CodeWarrior Lite

Tucked into the back of this book is a CD containing a special, limited version of CodeWarrior, one of the leading Macintosh programming environments. This special version is CodeWarrior Lite, and it provides you with all the tools you'll need to work with the programming examples presented in this book.

This chapter will guide you through installing and testing CodeWarrior Lite. We'll run an applet here that writes "Hello, world!" in its window, but we'll skim over the details concerning how the applet actually makes this occur. The rest of this book covers this kind of thing in detail, but before we dive into the deep ocean of Java programming, let's get CodeWarrior Lite up and running.

Installing CodeWarrior Lite

When you insert the *Learn Java* CD into your CD-ROM drive, the main *Learn Java* CD window will appear on your desktop. (If this window does not appear automatically, double-click the CD icon that appears on your desktop.) In the center of that window is the CodeWarrior Lite Installer icon (Figure 2.1). Double-click that icon to launch the installer.

Figure 2.1   The CodeWarrior Lite Installer icon.

By the Way

> If you already own version 9.0 or higher of CodeWarrior, you may want to skip the installation of CodeWarrior Lite. If that is the case, just drag the Learn Java Projects folder from the top level of the CD onto your hard drive or choose "Custom Install" and only select the option labeled Learn Java on the Macintosh Projects. If you do run into problems, try removing the full CodeWarrior from your hard drive (do this only if you have a backup or the original installation CD around, however) and install CodeWarrior Lite instead.

When you start the installer, you'll be presented with a list of possible installation configurations (Figure 2.2). The simplest way to go is to use the "Easy Install," which will require about 15 megs of free hard drive space. If you've got the space, click the **Install** button. Otherwise, click **Quit** and go make some room.

After the installation is complete, you will no longer need the CD (though you might want to keep it as a backup). Also, if the installer suggests you restart your Mac, make sure you do so before proceeding with the rest of this chapter.

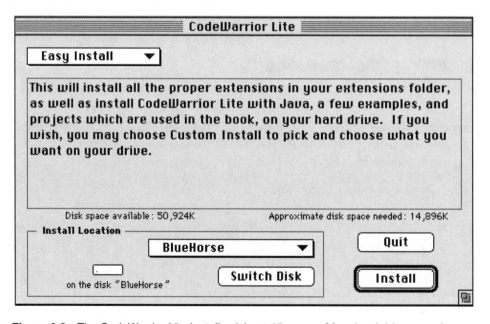

Figure 2.2 The CodeWarrior Lite installer (about 15 megs of free hard drive space).

Testing CodeWarrior Lite

Now that CodeWarrior Lite is installed, let's take it for a spin. Open the Learn Java Projects folder on your hard drive; then open the subfolder named 02.01 - hello, world. You should see a window similar to the one shown in Figure 2.3. The three files in this window contain the ingredients you'll use to build your first Java applet.

Double-click the file HelloWorld.μ. A window just like the one shown in Figure 2.4 should appear.

This window is called the **project window**. It contains information about the files used to build a Java applet. Since this information is stored in the file HelloWorld.μ, this file is also known as a **project file**. A file that ends in the characters .μ is likely to be a project file. (You can type a 'μ' (the Greek letter *mu*) on the Mac by holding down the option key and typing the letter *m*.)

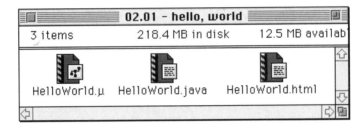

Figure 2.3 The 02.01 - hello, world subfolder.

Figure 2.4 The HelloWorld.μ project window.

Warning

> If you got a message telling you that the document HelloWorld.μ could not be opened, restart your Mac and try again. If this still doesn't work, try rebuilding your desktop. To do this, restart your Mac and then press the command and option keys simultaneously. Keep holding both keys down until the Mac asks you if you'd like to rebuild your desktop. Click **OK** and go watch MTV for a few minutes until it's done.

If some other window appears instead of the one shown in Figure 2.4, you double-clicked the wrong file. That's no problem; quit CodeWarrior and try double-clicking the file HelloWorld.μ again.

The project window shown in Figure 2.4 is split into two groups. The first group, titled "Java Source," lists the files that contain the Java **source code** for your application. Source code is a set of instructions that determine what your application will do and when it will do it. The HelloWorld project contains two Java source files. The first file, HelloWorld.java, contains the specific Java instructions that define the applet that will make the words "Hello, world!" appear in the applet. The second file, classes.zip, identifies a file containing code supplied by Java that gets combined into all your applets.

The second group, titled "HTML files," contains a single Hypertext Markup Language (HTML) file called HelloWorld.html. Let's take a look at this HTML file before looking at the Java source code. Double-click this file name in the project window. This will open a window displaying the contents of the HTML file (Figure 2.5). (HTML is the language used to define Web pages.)

This simple HTML file specifies two things. First, it specifies the name of a file containing the applet to run and where to find it. This file name is given as HelloWorld.class (as specified by code=), and its location is given as the folder named HelloWorld (as specified by codebase=). Second, it specifies the size of the area in which the applet will appear. This size is given as 250 pixels wide by 50 pixels high.

Figure 2.5 The contents of the HelloWorld.html file.

Even though the HTML file specifies that the applet is contained in a file named `HelloWorld.class`, you would not find a file named `HelloWorld.class` if you did a search of your Mac hard drive right now. Not to worry: Creating `.class` files is what CodeWarrior is all about! We'll create this file in just a moment.

You can display this HTML file using a Web browser that supports Java to run your applet. Another way to run an applet in CodeWarrior is to drop an HTML file that references your applet onto Metrowerks Java, an application supplied with CodeWarrior. Doing this launches Metrowerks Java, which then runs the applet referenced by the HTML file.

Before we run the applet, we have to create the file named `HelloWorld.class`. Let's start by taking a look at the source code in `HelloWorld.java`. Double-click the label `HelloWorld.java` in the project window. A source code window will appear containing the source code in the file `HelloWorld.java` (Figure 2.6). This is your first Java program.

The HelloWorld program tells the computer to display the text "Hello, world!" inside the applet's window. Don't worry about how this works right now. We'll get into the details later on. For now, let's create the applet and crank it up.

Go to the **Project** menu and select **Make** (alternatively, you can hold down the command key and type the letter *m*). CodeWarrior now does two things. First, it creates the folder named HelloWorld. Second, it creates the file named `HelloWorld.class` and places this file into the HelloWorld folder. These will show up in the same folder that contains your source code and are shown in Figure 2.7.

`HelloWorld.class` is the file referenced from `HelloWorld.html`. This file is known as a **compiled class file**. The compiled class file contains the definition for your applet that is ready to run in a Web page. This is what CodeWarrior does: It turns your Java source files into files that can be run as part of the Web.

Open the folder named `HelloWorld` to take a look at the icon for the file `HelloWorld.class`. This file will appear as in Figure 2.8.

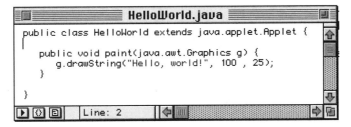

Figure 2.6 The source code window with the source code from the file `HelloWorld.java`.

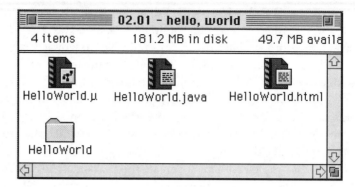

Figure 2.7 The subfolder 02.01 - hello, world with the addition of the HelloWorld folder.

Figure 2.8 The compiled class file generated by CodeWarrior, called HelloWorld.class.

By the Way

> Who's the funny-looking cartoon character that appears on the Java class file icon and in other places relating to Java? The guy's name is Duke, and he's the unofficial mascot of the Java language. (Most programming languages do not have mascots, but you're in luck with Java.) You'll run across him in various places as you pursue your investigations into Java.

You can close the HelloWorld folder once you've seen the compiled class file. Now for the good part: Run the applet by dragging and dropping the icon for the HTML file that is in your HelloWorld project folder onto the Metrowerks Java application icon. You'll find the Metrowerks Java application icon in your Metrowerks CodeWarrior folder. (Figure 2.9 shows what these folders and application icons look like. Also, check out Figure 2.11 for pictures of what's happening here.)

The very first time you try to run an applet using Metrowerks Java, a window may appear that informs you that you are about to run a Java applet. Metrowerks Java presents this message mainly because Java makes an incredible effort to ensure that no applets do damage to your Mac (or to any other computer on which you run the applet). This message is perfectly normal. To acknowledge that you

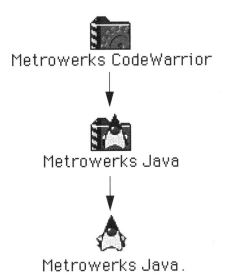

Figure 2.9 The Metrowerks CodeWarrior folder contains the Metrowerks Java folder, which contains the Metrowerks Java application.

wish to run Java applets, which is what you'll do throughout this book, click the **Accept** button at the bottom of the information window.

Once you drop the HTML file onto the Metrowerks Java application and indicate you wish to run the applet, two windows will appear.

By the Way

We'll use the drag-and-drop method in this book to run applets, but there might be other ways to run applets by the time the CodeWarrior development environment is complete for Java. (Of course, you can always run the applet in a Java-enabled Web browser.) Check the documentation with your development environment for more information on other ways to run your applets. (One convenient technique is to make an alias for Metrowerks Java and place this somewhere easily accessible on your desktop.)

The first window is titled "Java Output." The Java Output window will look like the one shown in Figure 2.10. This window provides a place for the Metrowerks Java application as well as for applets themselves to display information to the developer.

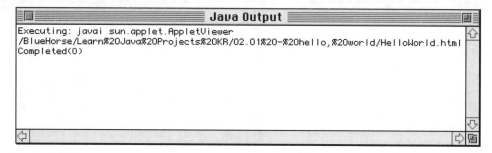

Figure 2.10 The Java Output window with messages from the Metrowerks Java application and from the applet itself.

By the Way

> You may notice the words BlueHorse at the start of the path that indicates where the .html file is located on the Mac. These screen shots reflect the particular Mac on which they were made (on this Mac, the hard disk was named BlueHorse). This name will vary, of course, from Mac to Mac. When run on your particular computer, the Java Output window will display the name of your hard disk instead.

Looking at the Java Output window, you can see that Metrowerks Java provides some information so that you can tell what's happening behind the scenes. Metrowerks Java then reads in the class file referenced by the HTML file. This is known as **loading** the class.

By the Way

> Various messages appear in the Java Output window when the default for the Applet Viewer is "verbose." Check the documentation that comes with your environment to see how you might be able to adjust this setting in CodeWarrior.

After the class is loaded, Metrowerks Java starts up the Applet Viewer. The Applet Viewer is the second window that appears when you drop the HTML file onto the Metrowerks Java icon. When you do so, Metrowerks Java starts up the Applet Viewer. The Applet Viewer is CodeWarrior's way of simulating a Web browser so that you can work with your applets from within the Metrowerks Java environment (that is, without turning away from CodeWarrior and starting up a full browser application). The Applet Viewer knows how to display the applet referenced by the HTML file, although it will not display any other information defined by the HTML file. Metrowerks Java runs the applet in the Applet Viewer. As you can see from Figure 2.11, the applet simply displays the words "Hello, world!" in the center of the window.

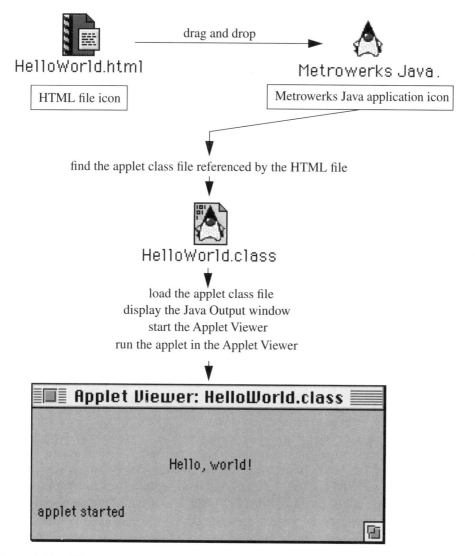

Figure 2.11   What happens when you run an applet.

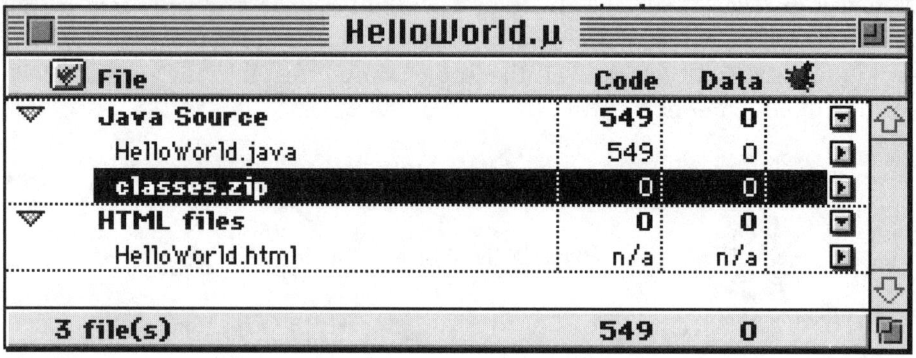

Figure 2.12 The project window showing the size of the program in bytes now that the applet has been created.

Once you are done admiring this amazing applet, select **Quit** from the **File** menu. This will quit Metrowerks Java and the Applet Viewer, and you'll be back in CodeWarrior Lite.

Before we leave, check out the project window again (you can reopen it by double-clicking the file HelloWorld.μ if you've already closed the project window). If you look closely, you'll see that numbers appear in each row of the project window, where before there were only 0s (Figure 2.12). These numbers indicate the size of the resulting applet code in bytes.

We're all done for now. You can quit CodeWarrior Lite if you'd like to. If you're asked if you want to save the results of your program, select **Don't Save**, and let's move on. (If you click the **Save** button, the results produced by your program are saved as a text file, which you can then open by using CodeWarrior or your favorite word processor.)

Congratulations! You've just built and run your first Java applet!

Review

You've installed the CodeWarrior Lite development environment and even created and run your first Java applet. You've poked around the CodeWarrior environment a little, exploring the project file, the HTML file, and the Java source file. You may have some questions relating to what you've seen. Rest assured: These will all be answered soon enough. For now, with CodeWarrior up and running, you're all set to forge ahead!

What's Next?

The next two chapters provide a context for understanding Java. Chapter 3 looks at Java in relation to the Web. You'll learn the important concepts behind Web programming and why Java is a great language to use for writing programs that run over the Web. We'll also touch on some concepts that will help you understand the files you created when you compiled the HelloWorld Java applet in this chapter. Chapter 4 introduces programming concepts you should know before you begin writing Java programs. Once you understand these core concepts, we'll ease into Java programming in Chapter 5.

Chapter 3

Web Programming Basics

Before we dive into Java programming, let's put this endeavor into context. You probably know that Java programs can be run over the Web, but what does this mean exactly? How do Web browsers arrange elements on a Web page, and what does it mean to add a software application to a Web page? Software applications are created by writing computer programs. What does it even mean to write a computer program in the first place?

This chapter will answer these questions and more. You'll also learn how Java meshes with HTML and why Java is a perfect programming language for writing software applications that run over the Web. With these concepts under your belt, you'll be able to turn to the specifics of Java in Chapter 4 and learn how to design your own Java applets.

Web Content

Web pages can contain almost anything: pictures, text, links to other Web pages, tables, charts, sound, animation, and more. These diverse multimedia elements allow people to create very sophisticated Web pages. However, until recently, Web pages were limited in that they could not incorporate software applications. With Java, this is no longer the case. Java allows complete applications—drawing programs, spreadsheets, word processors, games, and, in fact, any kind of application at all—to be included as part of a Web page.

Definition

We'll often use the terms *application* and *applet* interchangeably. Throughout this book, you will be writing applications in the traditional software sense, but an **applet** (the "official" Java term invented by Sun Microsystems, the company that developed the Java language) is a Java application that runs over the Web.

Before we look at how to add a software application to a Web page, let's review how Web browsers work. This will allow you to understand how a Web browser displays a traditional document containing text and formatting instructions in HTML and what a Web browser does when it encounters a software application.

What Traditional Web Browsers Do

Web browsers do three things very well. First, they download files from other computers connected to the Internet (Figure 3.1).

Typically, these files contain instructions written in HTML that tell the Web browser what the Web page should look like.

Second, after downloading the file, the Web browser arranges the text in this file and downloads and arranges any images referenced by this file. These elements are positioned according to formatting instructions also found in the file (Figure 3.2).

The third thing browsers do is display connections to other Web pages. These other Web pages can be located anywhere on the Internet—that is to say, anywhere in the world. In many Web browsers, these connections, or links, between Web pages are displayed in blue and are underlined. The HTML document itself indicates where these links to other pages should appear. The browser's job is to know when the user has clicked on a link and then to retrieve the document (the file) on the Internet, and then format and display the elements in the document so that they appear in the Web browser.

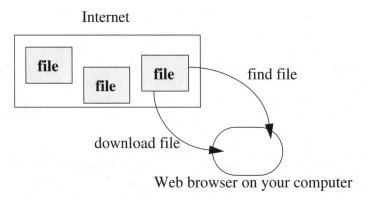

Figure 3.1 Downloading a file found on the Internet.

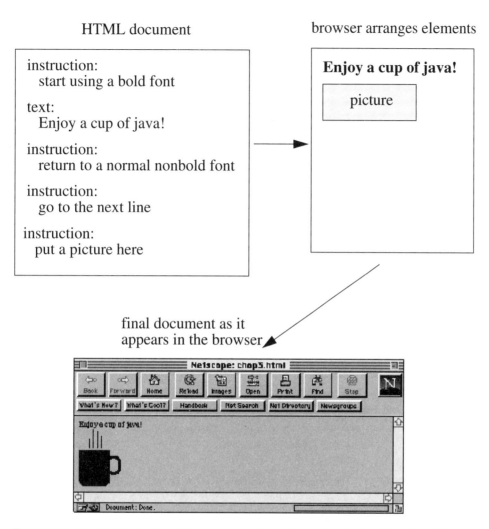

Figure 3.2 Positioning text and images according to formatting instructions found in an HTML file.

How Traditional Web Browsers Work

If you've ever looked at the source document for a Web page or have created Web pages yourself, you know that Web pages are defined using HTML. These HTML documents contain the text to display in a Web page. Sprinkled in with this text are special formatting instructions written in HTML. These formatting instructions are placed between left and right angle brackets, like this:

```
<a formatting instruction would go here>
```

For example, in the file shown in Listing 3.1, we placed HTML formatting statements around the text "Enjoy a cup of java!" so that this text appeared in bold.

Listing 3.1   A simple HTML file.

```
<bold>
Enjoy a cup of java!
</bold>
<br>
<img src="coffee.gif">
```

Images are kept in separate files from the HTML document. To indicate that a picture should appear in a Web page, the Web page creator can indicate where the Web browser should look to find the computer on the Web that contains the image and what file this image is in. Earlier, the image was on the same computer and in the same directory as the HTML document itself. That allowed us simply to name the file containing the picture. The Web browser then knew where to look. If we wanted to indicate that the picture existed on a different computer, we would need to supply the address for that computer, like this, for example:

```
<img src="http://www.bluehorse.com/mypics.gif">
```

By the Way

Knowing how to write HTML documents is not strictly necessary for programming in Java. In fact, a thorough discussion of using HTML to design Web pages is beyond the scope of this book. However, if you are unfamiliar with HTML and would like to know more, many books are available to help you get started with HTML. We humbly recommend *Learn HTML on the Macintosh,* by Dave Mark and David Lawrence. There are also a number of sites on the Web that explain what HTML is all about. Check out Appendix G for a listing of these sites.

As the Web browser reads through the downloaded file containing the formatting instructions and the text to display, the browser sets aside enough space on the screen to display the elements in the document. The browser leaves enough room to draw the images and flows the text around these images; the browser spaces the lines of the text far enough apart to accommodate the appropriate font; the browser leaves enough room in the display for tables; and the browser takes care of arranging any other elements as appropriate (Figure 3.3).

Once the Web browser arranges the images, text, and links, all the user can do is view the document. The elements just sit there, passively, until the user clicks a

Web page

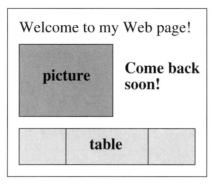

Figure 3.3 Schematic of a Web page with a variety of elements arranged by the Web browser according to the HTML instructions in the document and with enough space for each element.

link and the browser displays a new page. While this is actually quite a feat, such a Web page still lacks the interactivity that people have come to expect from using a computer.

Interactivity

Recently, Web browsers have become capable of handling another type of element: a software application. Just as it sets aside a region of the screen to display images and text, a Web browser can now also set aside a region of the screen in which to display the user interface for an application. With an application, a Web page is no longer passive but can offer any type of capability you're used to from the desktop.

For example, as the comet Hyakutake recently made its (mostly fuzzy) appearance in the nighttime sky, a number of excellent Web pages showed diagrams of the comet's path through the Solar System and through the backdrop of stars as seen from the earth. While this was informative, a Web page created using Java could have made such pages come alive. Rather than showing printouts of plots made with desktop-bound software applications, a software application written in Java could have been inserted into a Web page. This would have allowed any Web user to make his or her own plots, animate the flight of the comet, simulate how the comet would appear if it increased or decreased in magnitude, and so on. In other words, Java applications on the Web can provide the immediacy, interactivity, excitement, and power you've come to expect from the software applications sitting on your own Mac's hard drive.

What does it mean to include a software application in a Web page? In many ways, the software application referenced by an HTML document is treated just like any other element on a Web page. As with images, software applications are kept in separate files. The Web page creator indicates that a software application should be part of the Web page by using an HTML tag called `applet`. Here's an example (the specifics of this `applet` tag will be explained in much greater detail later in this book):

```
<applet code=HelloWorld.class width=250 height=50> </applet>
```

The name of the file containing the application to run is given after the words `code=` and, in this example, is named `HelloWorld.class`. When the Web browser encounters an `applet` tag, it downloads the file containing the application referenced by this tag from the Internet (Figure 3.4).

As with other Web page elements, the browser sets aside enough space on the screen to display the user interface for the Java application. The amount of space required by the application is initially provided in the `applet` tag. (That's what the width and height keywords specify.) The browser flows the text and the other Web page elements around this application as necessary to format the rest of the Web page (Figure 3.5).

Web browsers that are capable of running software applications written in Java are said to be **Java-enabled**. Java-enabled Web browsers include Netscape Navigator 2.0 and Sun's HotJava, and soon all Web browsers are likely to incorporate support for Java applications.

When a traditional Web browser has downloaded an HTML document and formatted the display, that's the end of the story. However, once a Java-enabled Web browser has downloaded a Java application, that's only the beginning! After the Java application is downloaded, the Web browser runs the Java program—just

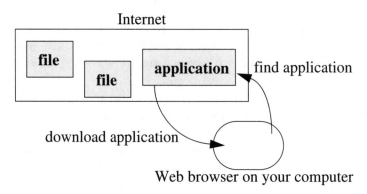

Figure 3.4 Downloading a Java application found on the Internet.

Web page

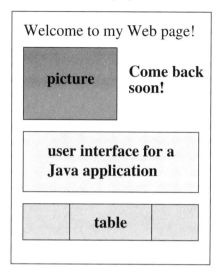

Figure 3.5 An application's user interface as part of a Web page.

as if you, the end user, started a program by double-clicking an icon on the Mac. So, now you can interact with the application that is part of the Web page just as if you had installed the application on your Mac's hard drive. Just as a store-bought application can be anything at all, so, too, can a Java application be whatever the programmer has imagined.

Jazzing Up Your Web Page

In addition to writing full-fledged applications, there are also other ways for adding pizzazz to your Web page. Some of these ways include using extensions to Web browsers that allow you to create animation (such as with a product called Shockwave). Some extensions allow you to perform simple tasks such as finding the average of a set of numbers (by using a scripting language such as JavaScript or VisualBasic Script).

Some of these options make a Web page more interactive; some only provide a "special effect"—which is nice, but that's as far as these options go. While these Web page elements have their places and, in some situations, may do the job just fine, it's important to know that these other approaches are not programming languages. Only Java is a complete programming language for the Web. The next section explains why this distinction is so important.

Reasons for Programming

People have long dreamed of achieving what today's computer technology makes possible. Back in the 1800s, mathematicians and inventors theorized about machines that could perform complex calculations and follow instructions to solve problems. Since the 1940s and 1950s, when modern computers were first invented, people have written programs to perform tasks that would have been impossible without these computers and the programs that controlled them. These tasks range from landing a man on the moon to creating feature-length movies with computer-generated astronauts and cowboys.

You might have a more pressing need to write a program than space exploration or moviemaking. You might want to find a simple way to calculate your mortgage payments. You might want to maintain your favorite recipes in a home-grown database. You might want to create a nifty computer game you've dreamed up. Or you might want to promote your company on the Web by creating a software application that illustrates and perhaps even sells your company's products or services.

All of these examples require that you control the computer to make it do the things you want. To control the computer, you need to write a program. If you want to write a spreadsheet application, adventure game, drawing program, or any other software application, there is no other way to do it. If you're new to programming, you'll find that writing programs and making the computer do what you tell it to do can be a fun-filled, exciting, and rewarding experience.

What Is a Program?

A **program** defines the exact steps that a computer must follow to perform some action. For example, if you wanted to explain to a person (rather than to a computer) how to call for help in an emergency, you might say

- First, pick up a telephone handpiece.
- Then, dial 911.

These instructions are concise and explicit. You need to do the same kind of thing when you write computer programs.

For a more computer-oriented example, check out the following. If you wanted to add some numbers, it would be nice to be able to create a file for the computer that read

```
Hi, Computer!
Do me a favor. Ask me for five numbers, add them, then
tell me the sum.
```

These instructions are understandable to an English-speaking person. Computers, however, don't understand English. Instead, computers understand something called, naturally enough, **machine language**. So, if you want to tell a computer what to do, you need to tell it what to do in machine language.

Unfortunately, machine language is difficult for people to speak and understand. Machine language is written using only 1s and 0s, and people don't usually want to communicate using only 1s and 0s. They want to use words. So, instead, programmers perform the following steps.

First, they use a programming language, such as C, Pascal, or Java, to write out words that describe how the program should work. Learning a computer language is somewhat analogous, in its objective, to learning to speak a foreign language. For example, if you want to communicate effectively when you are in Rome, you need to learn Italian. Similarly, if you want to communicate instructions to your computer, you need to learn a programming language.

After a programmer has used a programming language to describe how a program should work, the programmer must **compile** the program. To compile a program means to turn the C, Pascal, or Java instructions into machine language. A **compiler** knows how to perform this translation from words to 1s and 0s. Compilers save you, the programmer, from needing to speak in 1s and 0s yourself.

By writing in a programming language, programmers bridge the gap between people and computers (Figure 3.6). Programmers can write in a combination of English and special words and symbols to tell computers what to do. This book will teach you all about writing in the Java programming language. When you write Java programs, you'll be telling the computer exactly what to do!

Note that even though Figure 3.6 shows part of a program written as if it were in English, this is not quite how Java programs look. You'll see soon what programs do look like when you start programming in Java in Chapter 5.

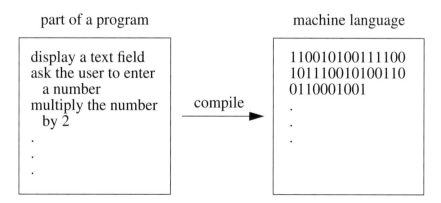

Figure 3.6 Bridging the gap between people and computers: Programmers write in a programming language; compilers translate this to 1s and 0s.

How Is Java Different from HTML?

If you're familiar with HTML, you may be saying to yourself, "I've written HTML documents that also tell the computer what to do—how to format text, how to lay out a table, and more. Is a software application just a glorified HTML document?"

Not quite. Computer languages such as Java address a different need than HTML. HTML is tailored to one specific task—page formatting. However, you cannot use HTML to store data, perform calculations, or communicate with other parts of your computer or network. For example, it would be impossible to use HTML, and only HTML, to perform even simple tasks such as calculating the area of a triangle, drawing a squiggly line as the user moves the mouse across the screen, or creating a game of Tetris. In Java, these things are easy. Some of these objectives are easier to achieve than others, of course—Tetris being a little more difficult than calculating the area of a triangle. The point is that these examples are *impossible* to accomplish in HTML but are quite natural to implement in Java.

Other Programming Languages

Java is not the first programming language to come along. The most popular languages of the recent past include BASIC, FORTRAN, Pascal, C, and C++. Each of these languages was developed with particular objectives in mind, and each was quite successful in achieving these objectives.

For example, BASIC (Beginner's All-purpose Symbolic Instruction Code) was designed in the 1960s and, as its name implies, was meant to be a simple language for people new to programming. While the original BASIC language is not used much today, there are quite a few people programming in a Microsoft variant of BASIC called Visual Basic. (The main reason for this is that Microsoft Chairman Bill Gates *loves* BASIC.)

FORTRAN (FORmula TRANslation) was invented in the 1950s and is adept at manipulating and displaying large values and writing mathematical equations. Engineers and scientists still use FORTRAN a lot for solving problems in their fields.

Pascal was named in honor of the 17th-century French mathematician Blaise Pascal. The goal behind Pascal was to create a language that encouraged computer science students to write good structured programs. Pascal was introduced in the 1970s, and it was hot for a time. It's still in use today, although it's not as popular as it once was.

Developed at AT&T, C was named (believe it or not) from the third attempt at creating a language. (The first was named A; the second was named B.) C provides a kind of combination of being able to program at a high level while still being able to get down to the details of machine language and manipulate 1s and

0s directly. C is good for writing system software, and the Unix operating system, for example, is usually implemented in C.

All of these programming languages basically encourage the programmer to write a big list of instructions for the computer to follow. This approach works fine for simple programs. Over the years, however, programmers began to realize that while these languages were powerful, they did not always work well when writing large or complex programs.

In the 1980s, a new way of thinking about software began to emerge. Programmers found a better way to program complicated applications such as drawing programs, spreadsheets, scientific simulations, and so on. This better way was to think of the application not as one big list of instructions, but as a collection of *objects*. The next chapter gets into the details of what objects are. For now, here's a simple example. Suppose you want to write a program that represents something in the real world—say, the flow of traffic through your city. Your program will have streets, cars, traffic lights, drawbridges, and everything else that affects the flow of traffic. If you were using a program that supported objects, each of these real-world elements—the streets, cars, and so on—would be represented by an object in your program.

C++ is a language that uses objects. (It was named C++ as a way of indicating it was incrementally better than C.) While C++ was not the first language to use objects, many programmers have used C++ in recent years because they already knew C, and C++ is based on C. It was therefore easier for experienced programmers to figure out C++ than to learn a new language altogether.

Developing Software Using These Other Languages

There are many other programming languages than the five just mentioned, and you may have some background in one of these other languages. The basic characteristics of just about any language that came before Java are the same, however. Almost all of the pre-Java languages (including BASIC, FORTRAN, Pascal, C, and C++) were built for a world in which the application that resulted from compiling a program would run on one (and only one!) type of computer. If you wanted to run the application on a different type of computer, you would have to recompile the program for that type of computer. This fact is crucial to understanding one of the primary reasons for Java's existence.

Every computer is based on a particular chip. In fact, chips are so central to a computer that computers are often identified by the kind of chip they contain: People talk about a "386," a "486," or a "Pentium," for example. However, chips know nothing about C, Pascal, or any other language; they understand only machine language. What's more, each type of chip speaks its own brand of machine language.

With each type of chip speaking a different machine language, a programmer must compile the same program separately for each type of chip on which the application will run. Sometimes, the programmer must even change the program a little to get it to run correctly on a new type of chip. This process is known as **porting**.

Now, so far, by talking about computer chips, we've just been considering the hardware side of things. If you've used both Windows and the Mac, you'll notice there are many differences, both large and small, in how applications look. For example, the symbols along the top of the windows are different. Windows 95 reacts to two mouse buttons, while the Mac reacts to only one. And, if you've ever programmed in these different environments, you know that the way you create a window on the Mac, for example, is nothing like how you create one in Windows 95. Your code looks completely different. This means that the code that creates your **user interface** (the way in which the user interacts with the application by using windows, buttons, checkboxes, and so on) must be rewritten and compiled every time you port your application to a new operating environment (Figure 3.7).

By the Way

Windows 95, Windows NT, the Mac OS, Solaris, OS/2, Linux, and DOS are all examples of operating environments. Pentiums, SPARCs, 486s, and Power-PCs are examples of computer chips.

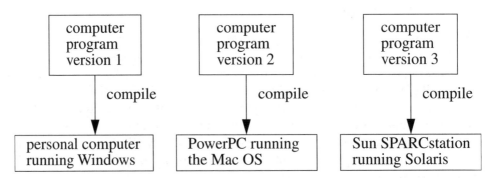

Figure 3.7 Compiling different programs for different types of chips and operating environments.

Why Java Is Perfect for the Web

While other languages were created with the intent that programs written in those languages would be developed for one type of chip and one operating environment, the Java language was developed with a different idea in mind. Java's creators envisioned the same Java program running on many different types of computer chips and in many different operating environments—without modification.

While writing a program expressly for one type of chip and one type of operating environment works great when you know what kind of computer the end user has, this is not a good solution for the World Wide Web. On the Web, everybody is using a different computer. If you develop an application and place it on your Web page, you have no way of knowing who will access this page and its corresponding application. Will they be Windows NT users? Mac users? Unix users? OS/2 users? Box users? The list goes on and on! In fact, all of these users will likely access your Web page, and all will want to run your application.

If you develop your application using a traditional language, you'll have to create different versions of this program and compile these different versions for different computers. By contrast, the same compiled Java program runs on any hardware and software combination (Figure 3.8). This is perfect for the Web, and this is one reason why Java is so hot. Applications written in Java work on the Web regardless of the computer that accesses them. Applications written in other languages do not have this capability.

There are also a number of other reasons why Java is perfect for the Web. Here are two:

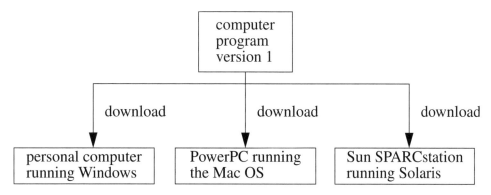

Figure 3.8 Downloading the same Java application for different chips and operating environments.

1. It is virtually impossible to write a computer virus in Java. This is much more crucial on the Web than it is for shrink-wrapped products. When you buy a program in a store, there is some accountability; you know where you purchased it and who was responsible for the software. When you encounter a program on the Web, you're much less sure of who wrote it, why they wrote it, and what the program will do. It's great to know that a Java program that you encounter on the Web will never wreak havoc with your computer.

2. Java programs are small compared with programs written in other languages. This is important when programs are transferred over the Web. Users don't want to spend a lot of time waiting for a program to appear on their computers. Java helps make this waiting time as small as possible.

By the Way

> What's the history of Java? Java was invented at Sun Microsystems in the early 1990s. The developers' original intent was to create a language that was safe to run (impossible for viruses and easy for programmers to write error-free software) and that could run on any type of computer. When the Web came along, people began to realize that Java was perfect for the Web. When Sun built Java into a Web browser and showed the world what was possible, Web aficionados were hooked!
>
> You may be wondering where the name Java came from. Depending on which story you hear, the name was either hit upon at a favorite cafe frequented by the development team of this new language or at a brainstorming meeting where they were trying to think of a name that would "wake up" the Web.

Runtime Environments

By now you might be asking, "How is it possible to run the same Java program on different types of chips and operating environments when other programs can't do the same thing? If different types of chips speak different machine languages, and if different operating environments have different types of user interfaces, what makes Java programs so special that they don't care what chip or environment they run on?"

The key to making the same Java program work on different computers with different types of chips and environments is the **Java interpreter**. What actually happens is as follows. You write a Java program and compile it, just as you do with any program written in any language. However, the Java compiler does not convert your program to machine language specific to the computer on which you want to run. Instead, the Java compiler converts your program to machine language that runs on a *theoretical* machine. This theoretical machine speaks its

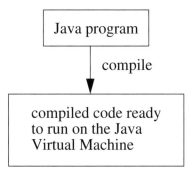

Figure 3.9 How Java bridges the gap between people and machine: Java programs are compiled for the Java Virtual Machine.

own brand of machine language. This theoretical machine is called, appropriately enough, the Java Virtual Machine (JVM). Figure 3.9 shows this part of the picture.

So where is this Java Virtual Machine? Where does it exist on your Mac? All you have is the Mac hardware, right? Right! The Java Virtual Machine is implemented in *software*. It runs as a program—the Java interpreter. Figure 3.10 takes Figure 3.9 one step further.

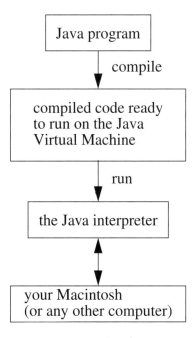

Figure 3.10 Why Java can run on any computer: Java programs run in the Java interpreter, which implements the Java Virtual Machine on your Mac.

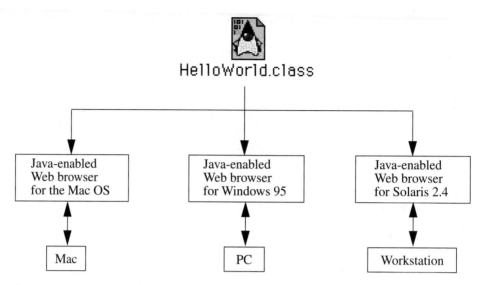

Figure 3.11   Running the same class file on multiple platforms.

The Java interpreter is what is different from chip to chip and operating environment to operating environment. It's the Java interpreter that translates between the Java Virtual Machine's machine language and the machine language spoken by your computer. There's a Java interpreter for Windows 95; there's a Java interpreter for the Mac (for CodeWarrior, it's the one supplied by Metrowerks called Metrowerks Java); and so on.

The different Java interpreters allow the same Java program you write to run on different machines. In fact, you can take the same HTML file you used in Chapter 2 and the same compiled class file generated by CodeWarrior, and you can run them on Windows 95, Windows NT, Solaris, and anywhere else that a Web browser with a Java interpreter exists. This is depicted in Figure 3.11.

Figure 3.11 shows the same thing as Figure 3.10 but with the Hello-World.class file being loaded into a Java-enabled browser. You'll work on the Macintosh while using this book, but all of the Java programs presented here, as well as all of the Java programs you write, will run just fine on any other computer.

Review

By writing a program, you can tell a computer exactly what steps to perform. You can make the computer do anything at all. This allows you to create very exciting Web pages. With Java, Web pages can contain software applications, and browsing the Web becomes a much more interactive and rewarding experience.

Why use Java to write Web applications? Why not use a language that came before Java, such as BASIC or C? Java is a programming language that is perfect for the Web. Java is an **interpreted language**, which means that it can run on any computer that has a Java interpreter. Java interpreters have been built directly into new Web browsers, which allows their browsers to run Java applets. Java is a modern language that uses objects. It is also impossible to write a virus using Java that can be downloaded over the Web.

What's Next?

You now have an understanding of how Java fits into the overall Web programming picture. In the next chapter, we'll look at a programming problem and find a solution for it that's tailored to Java. You'll learn how to approach Java development so that the solutions you plan before you begin writing your programs are easy to implement in Java.

Chapter 4

Problem Solving in Java

Writing a computer program is a lot like solving a puzzle. You have to understand your objective. Often, it's helpful to be creative. And, perhaps most important, you need a strategy for solving the problem at hand.

When you program in Java, it's important to know how to solve the problem in front of you in such a way that you can implement your solution in Java easily. Put more concretely, Java is the tool at your disposal; it's important to know how to use this tool most efficiently.

This chapter will explain how to solve programming problems in a way that makes it easy to write Java programs. We'll introduce three terms that you'll become quite familiar with by the time you've written a few Java programs. These three terms are *object*, *class*, and *method*. You don't know yet what these words mean as far as Java is concerned, but you'll have a pretty good idea by the end of this chapter.

While introducing these terms, we'll also cover a few Java keywords so that you can begin to see how to program in Java. However, we won't compile any of these programs until the next chapter.

Before we examine how to solve problems in Java and discuss what objects, classes, and methods are, let's consider what you'll experience as a programmer.

What It's Like to Be a Programmer

Programming is an extremely rewarding experience. When you program, you find ways to structure your ideas that are both logical and creative. Even though both the programs and the computers that programs run on are based on logic, that does not mean that programming is a science.

An important part of programming is recognizing that there is not necessarily a "right" or "wrong" way to write a program. Many times, the right way simply means that the program behaves as you expect it to. However, while this is often the case, you'll come to realize that some Java programs are "better" than others in terms of how easy they are to maintain, how fast they run, and how efficiently they use the resources of the computer on which they run. This book is filled with examples that help show you how to write fast, efficient programs that are easy to maintain. Keep in mind, however, that your primary concern is always going to be whether the program does what you intend it to do.

Why learn how to approach Java programs before you learn the language? Why not just jump in and start programming? One of the most crucial lessons to learn in programming is that the better prepared you are, the more quickly and easily you'll be able to write your programs. Examples abound in real life with regard to other activities. For example, architects create blueprints before the construction crew begins erecting the building. Pilots plot their courses before they take to the skies. Doctors plan out an operation before they place the patient under anesthesia. So, too, as a programmer, you should plan your application before you start writing code. In addition to teaching the Java language, this book will teach you how to plan your programs before you begin clicking away at your keyboard.

Let's discuss the programming process and learn how to plan your programs.

The Programming Process

One way to plan out your program is to answer four questions, as follows.

- Question 1: What will the program do?

For some programs, this might seem like a simple question to answer, but there is more to this question than first meets the eye. Answering this question involves clarifying your objectives for the program and considering what your program will look like to the user when your program runs.

Definition

> What your program looks like when it runs and how users interact with your program is referred to as a program's **user interface**. If the program takes advantage of graphical elements, such as windows, buttons, and pictures, the user interface is called a **graphical user interface** (GUI, pronounced "gooey"). Programs that don't use a GUI, but instead write characters to the screen without taking advantage of any graphics capabilities, use a **character-mode user interface**.

- Question 2: What are the different parts of your program?

Answering this question means first thinking about how your program will be put together. You might have parts of the program that perform calculations;

you might have parts of the program that display text fields in which the user enters numbers; other parts of your program might draw windows that display results calculated by the program.

- Question 3: What is the sequence of tasks your program will perform?

All programs perform a sequence of tasks. It's important to write out this sequence of tasks before you get involved in writing Java code so that you'll know what code you need to write in the first place.

- Question 4: What data will your program need?

Most programs you write will need to keep track of certain data. Once you know what your program will do and how it will do it, you can think about what data you'll need to keep track of.

This chapter will explain what each of these questions means and how you can go about answering them. Once you have answered these four questions, you will be ready to actually write your program. Starting with the next chapter, we'll begin to write working applets using Java.

Let's look at a few examples to see how you can go about answering these four questions.

Designing Your Program

You can tinker with an applet called SimpleDraw by going to the Learn Java Projects folder. Open the SimpleDraw folder and drag and drop the file named `SimpleDraw.html` onto the Metrowerks Java icon. You can create squares and circles in different colors by selecting the shape to draw and the colors in which to draw them and then clicking in the applet to create a shape at that location. Figure 4.1 shows a typical SimpleDraw session.

Let's look at this applet from the programmer's perspective. There is a lot going on here, and this little applet illustrates lots of Java features, including user interface elements, user interaction, drawing, and managing data. (We'll return to this applet often throughout this book.) How would you go about designing this applet? If you're unsure, you can always start at question 1 listed earlier, and see where that takes you. As we work through each of the four questions in the sections that follow, you'll learn all about objects, classes, and methods, which are the building blocks for all Java programs.

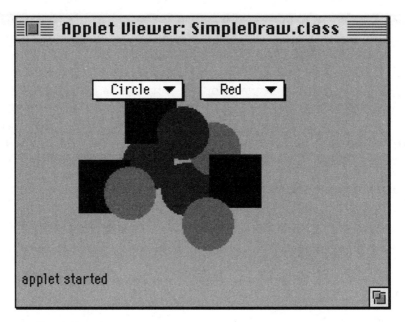

Figure 4.1 SimpleDraw in action.

Question 1: What Will the Program Do?

If you had a chance to experiment with this applet, you'll be able to formulate a description of this applet that goes something like this: The user interacts with this simple drawing applet by first indicating which shape to draw. The user has a choice of drawing a circle or a square. The user can also indicate which color to use when drawing the shape: red, green, or blue. To select the shape to draw and the color to use, the user picks from a list of possible options. The user then clicks in the applet window, and the applet draws the indicated shape at the location of the mouse click.

Question 2: What Are the Different Parts of Your Program?

Once you can describe the things you expect your program to do, you can start to plan out how your program will do them. In Java, your program will consist of a collection of different parts, and each of these parts will have a different task. Here are the three examples:

1. A spreadsheet applet might consist of cells and formulas. The cells' task would be to display numbers, and the formulas' task would be to calculate the numbers to display.

2. An applet used by NASA (the National Aeronautics and Space Administration) to send an unmanned space probe to Jupiter might consist of a number of parts, including the space probe, Jupiter, Jupiter's moons, and the earth. This applet would maintain space flight information with the probe itself, and it would use the other parts of the program to calculate the effects of the planets and moons on the path of the probe.

3. A payroll program might consist of a collection of employees as well as a variety of graphical user interface elements. The parts representing the employees would maintain data specific to each employee, and the graphical user interface elements would allow a user to interact with the employees.

Here's how we might think of these three applets:

Table 4.1 The parts of three sample programs and their tasks.

	Part	*Task*
Spreadsheet	cells	display number
	formulas	calculate number to display
Jupiter Mission	space probe	maintain space flight information
	Jupiter	have an effect on the space probe's flight
	Jupiter's moons	have an effect on the space probe's flight
	the earth	have an effect on the space probe's flight
Payroll	employees	keep track of employee data
	graphical user interface elements	interact with the employees

Let's introduce one word of terminology at this point. Instead of saying that we want to identify the "parts of the program," let's use an official term. In Java, each of these parts is called an **object**.

Objects

Objects represent "real-world" or conceptual parts of whatever it is you are trying to program. Everything in your Java applet will be represented by an object. You will always create at least one object for every applet you write because your applet itself is defined as an object. Objects include all the items in a graphical user interface, such as the windows that appear on the screen, the buttons the user can click with the mouse, and text fields that allow the user to type in characters. For our examples given earlier, each cell in the spreadsheet and each formula would be an object, each moon and planet in the Solar System would be an object, and each employee and user interface element in the payroll program would be an object.

Objects Equal Data and Behavior

When you use objects, these objects "know" how to take care of themselves. We alluded to this when we mentioned that each part, or object, had a task. There is no overall part of your program that controls everything. For example, for the spreadsheet program, a cell object might use its formula object to determine what it should display. The formula object would know how to use the data it stores to calculate the number to display. The cell object would know how to display this number. For the payroll program, each employee object might know its hourly wage and how many hours the employee worked that month. The employee object would know how to use the values it keeps for the hourly wage and number of hours worked to calculate the employee's earned income for that month.

These examples imply that objects consist of two parts: data and behavior. Figure 4.2 provides a high-level schematic of an object.

Objects equal data and behavior combined; an object's data and behavior allow it to carry out its task. As for data, objects need to keep track of the information that makes each object unique. For example, each employee object in the payroll program might have a different hourly wage. For the simple drawing program, each shape that the user draws is an object, and each circle and square

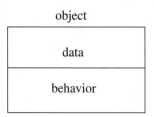

Figure 4.2 An object: data and behavior.

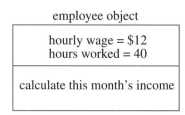

Figure 4.3 A specific employee object.

might have a different position on the screen. As for behavior, objects can do things with their data. What an object can do with its data defines its behavior. For example, the space probe object in the NASA program might know its current speed and direction and could calculate where it will be at some future time. Employee objects in the payroll program could calculate their earned income. Figure 4.3 illustrates how you might think of a specific employee object. This object would maintain data for a particular employee's hourly wage and hours worked this month, and it would provide behavior for calculating the employee's earned income for the month based on its data. (In this case, it could multiply the hourly wage by the hours worked to arrive at the earned income for the month.)

Classes

While answering question 2, what are the different parts of your program, you've been introduced to objects. You might notice, thinking over some of the candidates for objects provided so far, that some objects are very similar to one another. For example, for the payroll program, you probably don't have to provide a separate definition for each employee object. Employees differ only by the data they contain. Suppose you have 100 employees in your company. Each employee maintains an hourly wage and the number of hours worked. Each employee knows how to calculate his or her income for the month. Employees are all likely to look pretty similar. Employee objects could all be considered to be part of the same group.

For the NASA program, all the planets are pretty similar, too, when it comes down to it. They all obey Kepler's, Newton's and Einstein's laws. They differ only in their mass, rotation, distance from the sun, current position, and so on. That is, they have the same behavior, just different data. All of the planet objects could be said to belong to the same group, or class, of objects.

In Java, when objects have similar definitions and differ only by the data they contain, they all belong to the same **class**. In fact, objects are defined by their classes.

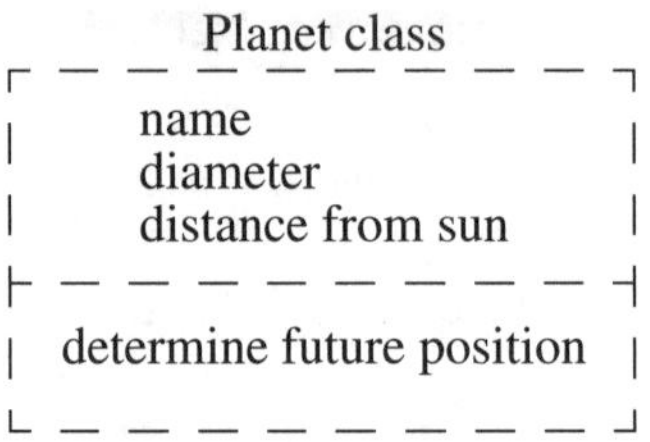

Planet class

```
┌  ─  ─  ─  ─  ─  ─  ─  ─  ┐
│      name                  │
│      diameter              │
│      distance from sun     │
├  ─  ─  ─  ─  ─  ─  ─  ─  ┤
│   determine future position │
└  ─  ─  ─  ─  ─  ─  ─  ─  ┘
```

Figure 4.4 The Planet class, which defines a planet in a general way by specifying the data it will maintain and the behavior it will have.

Here are some examples of classes. For the spreadsheet application mentioned earlier, we would have two classes: a Cell class and a Formula class. For the NASA program, we would have a Probe class, a Planet class, and maybe a separate Moon class. For the payroll program, we would have an Employee class.

Classes define objects in a general way. A class definition in a Java program might say something like, "I am an Employee class. All employee objects will maintain two pieces of data: their hourly wage and the number of hours worked. All employees will know how to calculate their earned income by multiplying their hourly wage by the number of hours they worked." Another class definition might say, "I am a Planet class. Each planet object will maintain its name, diameter, and distance from the sun. Each planet can determine where it will be at some future time given its current data and the laws of astronomy." A schematic for a Planet class is illustrated in Figure 4.4 (we'll discuss the Employee class later in this book when we actually implement the payroll applet).

Classes are central to Java programs. Classes define the data your objects will maintain. Classes also specify the behavior for your objects. You will base all of your objects on a class that either you define or that comes predefined as part of Java. Figure 4.5 shows that when planet objects are created, they are based on the Planet class. Each planet object maintains its own unique data and has access to the behavior defined by its class.

What's in Your Java Source File?

You've learned that everything in your program is represented by an object, and objects are defined using classes. In fact, your entire application will consist of a collection of class definitions. For example, you might have a Java program that implements the spreadsheet application. This program could be contained in a file on your Mac. This file would define the classes that you need. First, the file would contain the definition for the Applet class (all applets contain a definition for an Applet class); after this, the file would contain a definition for the Cell class;

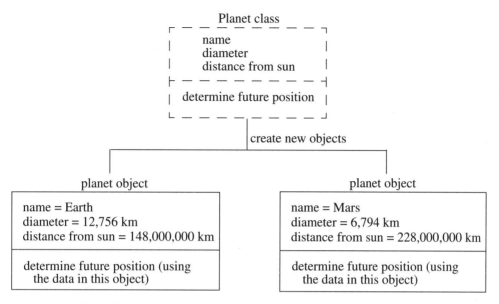

Figure 4.5 Using the Planet class to create individual planet objects.

following this, the file would contain the definition for the Formula class. A simplified outline of this file would be

```
start definition for the Applet class
   Java code that describes the objects created from this class
end definition for the Applet class

start definition for the Cell class
   Java code that describes the objects created from this class
end definition for the Cell class

start definition for the Formula class
   Java code that describes the objects created from this class
end definition for the Formula class
```

How you write these classes is what Java programming is all about. In fact, it's time to look at your first piece of Java code! Here's how you define a class, devoid of Java code that describes the objects created from this class:

```
class YourClassName {

}
```

45

You replace *YourClassName* with the name of the class you want.

Let's put this into action. How would you define a class for a Romulan War Bird? You would write the following:

```
class RomulanWarBird {


}
```

As you might surmise from these two examples of a class definition, Java uses one symbol to indicate where a class begins and another similar symbol to indicate where a class ends. These symbols are called *curly braces:*

- The left curly brace, {, indicates where a class begins.
- The right curly brace, }, indicates where a class ends.

All of the Java code that describes these classes would be placed between the left curly brace ({) and the right curly brace (}) for each class. Even empty classes would compile, but they wouldn't do much because they don't have any Java code between their left and right curly braces.

Let's return to SimpleDraw, identify the classes and objects that will be part of this program, and define them. As with most programs, this one can be divided into two broad areas: the user interface and the rest of it. What are the elements of the user interface? To answer that, we can examine what we said the program will do. We need a way to select the shape to draw, and we need a way to select the color to use for the shape. We can use a class defined by Java called a Choice and create two objects out of it. We can click on the applet itself to draw a shape there. We will also define an Applet class. What about the rest of it? We need a definition for two shapes to draw: the circle and the square. Figure 4.6 points out where the objects are in the SimpleDraw applet as well as which classes they came from.

There are three custom classes defined by this program: the applet, the circle, and the square. Let's start by looking at the shapes. We can create classes for these—and you already know how to start to define classes:

```
class Circle {
}

class Square {
}
```

The class that will define our applet is an interesting animal, so let's take a moment to see what an applet's class definition looks like. We'll create a class

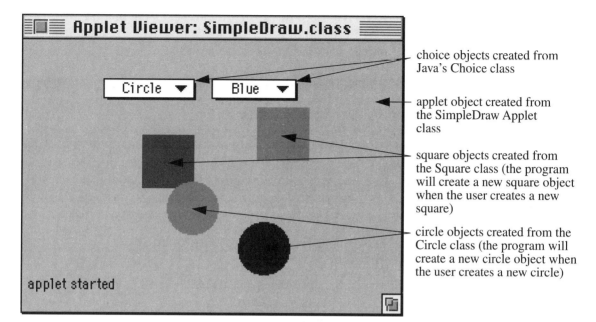

Figure 4.6 The objects in the SimpleDraw applet.

called SimpleDraw that will take on the roles and responsibilities of being the Applet class. Here's how we can define this class:

```
public class SimpleDraw extends java.applet.Applet {
}
```

In addition to what you saw already for defining classes, this class definition introduces two new keywords: `public` and `extends`. The `public` keyword indicates that this class can be referenced by any other class (not all classes can be referred to by any other class, as you'll see in Chapter 10). The `extends` keyword indicates what roles, responsibilities, and default behavior the class will take on (as you'll also learn more about in Chapter 10). For now, it's enough to know this is how you define an Applet class.

Let's think about what we have so far. You know that you need to identify the parts of your application. Each part of your application will be an object. You create objects based on class definitions. We've even looked at some empty class definitions. We defined a class called Circle and a class called Square. We also defined an Applet class called SimpleDraw. Do these classes do anything yet?

No. Not yet. You have to tell them what to do. That's the programmer's job. So, what do you need to do to create a full-fledged class that does things? You need to tell the class two things:

1. What tasks the objects based on the class will perform.

2. What data the objects will need to keep track of.

From these two items, you can see how answering our four questions is leading us along in Java development. In fact, we're now up to question 3. Now, in addition to defining classes, you'll learn about methods and more about creating objects.

Question 3: What Is the Sequence of Tasks Your Program Will Perform?

We've already determined a great deal from answering question 1, What will the program do? Based on what we've said so far, there are two parts to the simple drawing program: the user interface and the rest of it. Each part has its sequence of tasks, and these tasks do not require more than a few steps each.

Making a Task List

First, the simple drawing program will need to arrange its user interface—that is,

1. Display selections for shape types and color.

2. Make the applet's window big enough to draw in.

Second, when the user clicks in the applet, the program will

1. Determine the shape type to draw and color in which to draw it.

2. Create a new shape object for the appropriate shape type.

3. Draw this new shape object at the location clicked in the proper color.

Defining Behavior with Methods

How do we define an object's behavior? To do this, we tell the class the approach, or method, its objects will use to perform a particular task. We describe behavior by writing out a sequence of instructions. In Java, this sequence of instructions that define a particular task that an object will perform is officially called a **method**. For now, all you need to know concerning methods is that they define an object's behavior.

Creating Objects

Step 3 in the task list just given provides a good illustration of where and when a program creates objects. The following three screenshots show a typical user's progression through the simple drawing application.

Take a look at what's going on, starting in Figure 4.7. When the user draws a new square by clicking on the applet, the simple drawing program creates a new object based on the Square class. The program fills in the data for the Square class (its position and color) and draws it on the applet.

As shown in Figure 4.8, the user next clicks on the applet with the circle choice selected. The program creates a circle object based on the Circle class, fills in the circle object's data (position and color), and draws it on the screen.

The user can continue on indefinitely. Figure 4.9 shows the user creating a second square. The program now creates a second square object based on the Square class. This second square object will contain the data that makes it unique and different from the first square object. It will have a different position on the screen, maybe a different color. And the user can keep on going. In fact, the user can create as many shapes as he or she desires!

Thus, the Square and Circle classes act like templates or rubber stamps to "stamp out" shapes when the user draws on the applet. Notice that the same

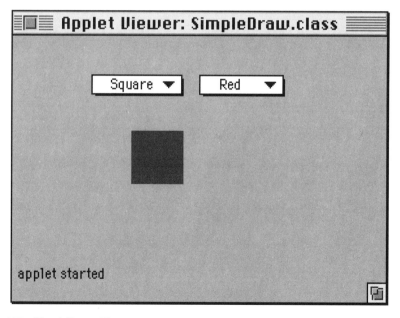

Figure 4.7 SimpleDraw: The user has just drawn one square by selecting "square" from the shape selection choice and clicking on the applet.

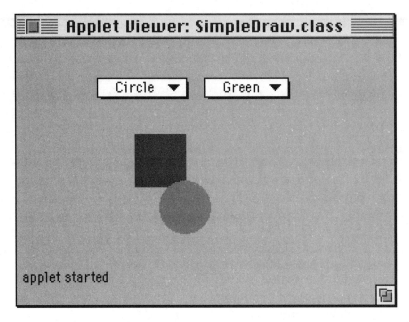

Figure 4.8 SimpleDraw: The user has now selected "circle" and has drawn a circle by clicking on another location on the applet.

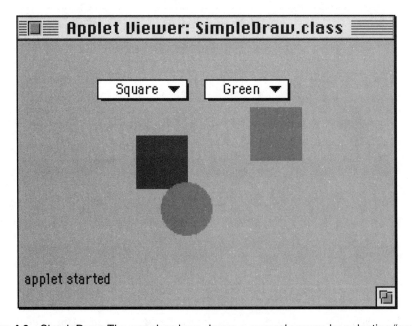

Figure 4.9 SimpleDraw: The user has here drawn a second square by selecting "square" from the shape selection choice and then clicking on the applet.

shape classes are used again and again to stamp out different objects. Another analogy would be a cookie cutter. You wouldn't use a cookie cutter once and then throw it away! Instead, you would use the same cookie cutter over and over, creating as many cookies as you wanted (or, at least, as many cookies as you had the dough for!). Each cookie would be decorated a little differently, blue sprinkles on one, red sprinkles on a second, green on a third, but each cookie would be essentially the same.

With our drawing program, our Square class and our Circle class act like cookie cutters. Since classes are like cookie cutters, we can use them to create as many squares and circles as we need. In particular, we can stamp out a new square or a new circle every time the user draws a new shape by clicking on the applet.

Each object will look to its class for its behavior. Each object will also look to its class to see what data it should keep track of. This is illustrated in Figure 4.10.

This diagram shows what's happening conceptually with classes and objects, but what's going on in the computer with classes and objects? Here's the basic idea: Classes are part of your application; you define classes using Java code. This is shown in Figure 4.11.

When you create objects, you are asking the computer to set aside some memory to hold the data for those objects. For a circle object created from the Circle class, that data might include the circle's position on the screen and its color. The computer would set aside the appropriate amount of memory to hold this data, based on what the class indicated every object needed to keep track of. This is shown in Figure 4.12. (This figure contains a slightly simplified diagram. While both your application and the data created by your application are maintained in

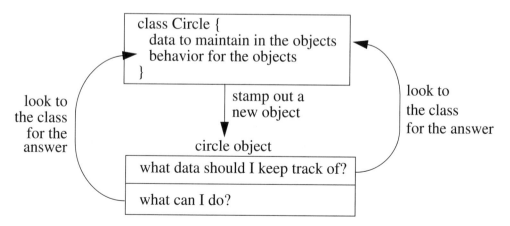

Figure 4.10 What happens conceptually: Objects look to their classes for their behavior and to see what data they should maintain.

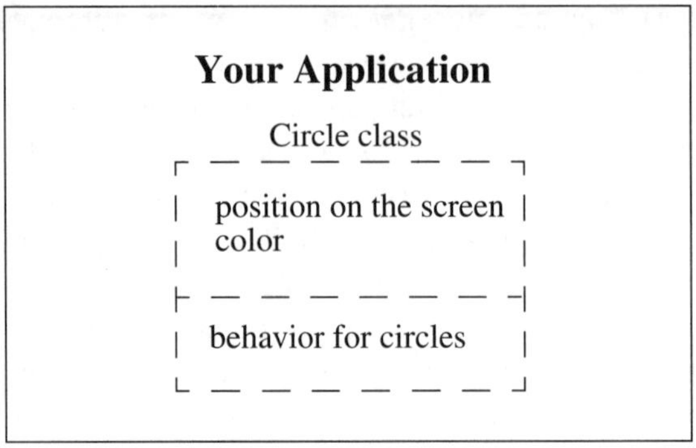

Your Application

Circle class

position on the screen
color

behavior for circles

Figure 4.11 Diagram showing that classes are defined in your application.

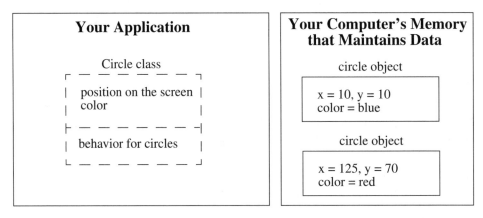

Figure 4.12 What goes on in the computer: Objects are created in your computer's memory.

your computer's memory, they are maintained in separate regions of memory.) Note that your application can fill up memory with as many objects as it needs.

Some programs are simple enough that they never need to define a class other than an Applet class. In these cases, the applet itself can handle all the details of the program. The HelloWorld applet that you saw in Chapter 2 is an example of an applet that does not use any additional classes or objects.

To recap, here's what you know so far: You need to define classes. Your classes will be used like cookie cutters to stamp out objects. Each object will maintain data that makes it unique. Your classes will provide the instructions that tell objects how to behave. These instructions will be contained in methods.

You also know that objects keep track of the data that makes them unique. This leads us to question 4.

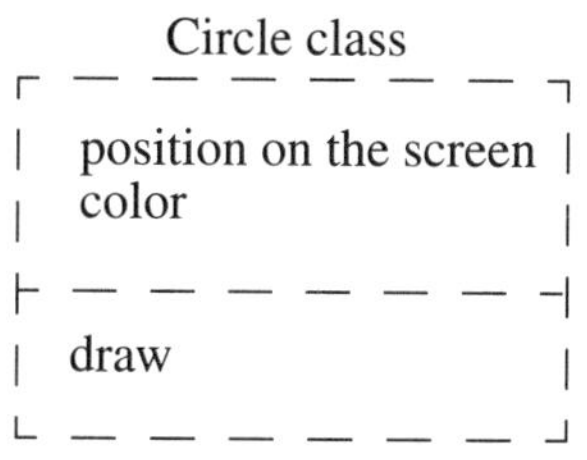

Circle class

| position on the screen |
| color |

| draw |

Figure 4.13 The Circle class.

Question 4: What Data Will Your Program Need?

Based on our discussion of question 3, we need to know two pieces of information:

1. The color to use for the shape of the object.
2. The location where the user clicked.

The Circle class, for example, might look like what is shown in Figure 4.13. This class would specify that a circle object should maintain two pieces of data: its color and where it should appear on the screen (that is, where the user clicked). The circle object's behavior, as supplied by the class, includes being able to draw itself at the proper location and in the proper color. The Square class would be similar to this, but it would draw differently.

Let's also give a bit of thought to the Applet class. Remember, each applet contains at least one Applet class definition. Based on what we said the simple drawing application would do, the Square class and Circle class provide only part of the functionality for this application. The rest must be supplied by the applet class. For example, Figure 4.14 shows a possible Applet class.

As you can see, the applet will need to work with the shape classes to make the program work. This is typical in a Java application, where different classes implement their own parts of the program and work together to get the job done.

The Final Result

The outcome of answering the four questions of what your program will do, what the different parts of it are, what tasks it will accomplish, and what data it needs is a game plan for writing your Java program. Once you know where you're going, you can get there much more easily!

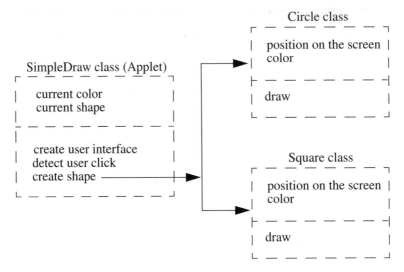

Figure 4.14 An Applet class for the simple drawing program that interacted with the Square and Circle classes.

Review

This chapter opened by comparing writing a computer program to solving a puzzle. You now have an understanding of how to go about solving a programming puzzle. Before you begin writing your Java applet, it's a good idea to plan out your program. One way to proceed is to answer the following four questions:

- *Question 1: What will the program do?* Answering this question involves determining what users will see when they run your program.

- *Question 2: What are the different parts of your program?* Answering this question leads to determining the classes you'll define for your program and what objects they will create when the user runs your program.

- *Question 3: What is the sequence of tasks your program will perform?* Answering this question leads to finding the methods for your classes. Methods contain the instructions the computer must follow to make your applet do the things you want it to do.

- *Question 4: What data will your program need?* Answering this question helps you plan out what data you'll keep track of in your objects.

Let's review some terminology before moving on:

- *Objects* describe the different parts of your application. Each object maintains data that makes it unique and has access to behavior that enables the object to perform calculations and do things.

- *Classes* act like cookie cutters and stamp out objects. Classes define what data an object should maintain and what behavior it has.

- *Methods* are sequences of instructions that give your objects behavior. You'll learn much more about methods in upcoming chapters.

You've also learned a small but highly important bit of Java syntax and grammar: You now know how to define a class (albeit an empty class). You know how to design objects, thinking through the data they should contain and the behavior they'll have. (You'll see more examples throughout this book to get you into the swing of things.) You define classes in your program by writing the word `class` followed by your class name, and you indicate the start and end of the class using a left and right curly brace. You place all your Java code that describes what data the object should keep track of and what behavior it has between the left and right curly braces.

All of your Java applets will be a collection of some number of classes—at least one since you always need a class that takes on the roles and responsibilities of an applet (you'll learn what some of these roles and responsibilities are in the next chapter, and you'll learn more as you progress). You might have one Applet class that defines your entire program; more complicated programs might define many additional classes.

What's Next?

Once you plan out your program, you're all set to write Java code. In fact, it's time to take off the gloves and really get to it! In the next chapter, you'll take a look at how to write, edit, and test a Java program by implementing the simplest applet possible and learning what the Java development cycle is all about. You'll also learn how to write messages to the Java Output window so that you can see what's going on as your program runs. In other words, you're about to write your first applet!

Chapter 5

The Development Cycle

Now you're all set to go. You know how to approach the design of your applet. You know to first answer four basic questions, starting with determining what your applet will do. You've been introduced to the terms *class*, *object*, and *method*. You've learned that your applet consists of classes, that classes define sets of instructions called methods, and that classes can be used as templates to create objects. Objects maintain data that make individual objects unique, and they look to their classes for their behavior.

Once you've planned out your applet, the next step is to write the program. This means programming in Java by defining classes, creating objects, and writing methods.

This chapter will introduce you ever so gently to Java programming and the Java development cycle. We'll write a simple program by defining three empty classes. In fact, we'll start so simply that, at first, our three classes will not even define any behavior or data. You'll learn how to begin a program, edit a program, compile it, and run it; and you'll see what happens when the compiler complains about your program due to typos. You'll also learn how to write a simple message to the Java Output window to help you see how your program is working.

An Overview

Having passed the planning stage, you are ready to write the program. You'll find that you iterate through a particular cycle with every program you write. Programmers refer to this cycle as the "development cycle."

A **development cycle** is made up of the steps required to develop a Java applet. These steps include creating a file to hold your program, editing the file to create your classes and methods, running and testing your program, and making changes to your program as necessary.

The reason that developing in Java (or in any programming language, for that matter) involves a development *cycle* is that programs rarely, if ever, work correctly on a programmer's first attempt. Programs are usually too complex to write all in one shot and get working the very first time. That is, instead of a one-time

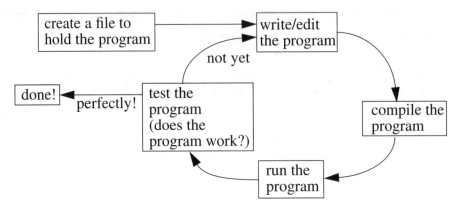

Figure 5.1 The development cycle in action.

progression that involves writing the program, compiling it, running it, and then distributing thousands of copies, programmers repeat these development steps as often as necessary, rewriting and editing the program, compiling again, running again, and then—you guessed it—editing, compiling, and so on, until it all works as intended. Figure 5.1 shows this cycle in action.

As we've already covered, the more you plan out your program, the better off you'll be because you'll increase your chances of having your program work in fewer attempts. This, in turn, will save you hours of programming time and confusion. The less debugging you have to do, the happier you'll be as a programmer.

Definition

> **Debugging** is the process of removing the "bugs," or problems, in a program. The term comes from the early days of computers when problems arose because of actual bugs (ants, spiders, and so on) that got into the big, room-sized computers that scientists and engineers then used. In those days, when you said you were debugging your program, you weren't kidding!

Organizing Your Files

Before you write your first program, let's take a moment to consider what files you'll need.

Source File

Your Java program will be contained in a text file that you'll work with directly. You'll open this file and type in your Java program. If you want to change the program, you'll edit this file.

The file that contains your Java program is called your **source file**. The Java instructions contained in this file are referred to as your **source code**. (The main purpose of this book is to teach you how to write Java source code—that is, what to put inside your Java source files.) All of your Java source files will end in the file extension .java.

Project File

Since your program can be contained in more than one file, CodeWarrior provides a way for organizing your different source files into one **project**. You'll need to create a project for your Java program when using CodeWarrior, even if your program is contained within one file. (You've already seen project files in Chapter 2, and this chapter will review how they work.)

HTML File

To run your applet, you need to define a Hypertext Markup Language (HTML) file to invoke your applet. This can be a very simple one- or two-line file that uses the <applet> and </applet> tags, as we'll explain.

Compiled Class File

Once you've written your Java source code and defined a project file for CodeWarrior, you can compile your program. As discussed in Chapter 3, compiling a Java program means generating instructions that are ready for the Java interpreter to execute on your computer.

When you compile your program, the compiler creates a new file that ends in the extension .class. The compiler will create one .class file for each of the classes you've defined, even if you have defined multiple classes within the same .java file. For example, suppose you have a Java source file named MyClass.java that contains two class definitions, one for a class named MyClass and another for a class named YourClass. When you compile this program in CodeWarrior, the compiler will create two new files (or will overwrite these files if they already exist). The first file the compiler will create is a file named MyClass.class, and the second is a file named YourClass.class. Figure 5.2 diagrams this example. The files generated by the compiler that end in the extension .class are known, as you might expect, as **class files** or **compiled class files**.

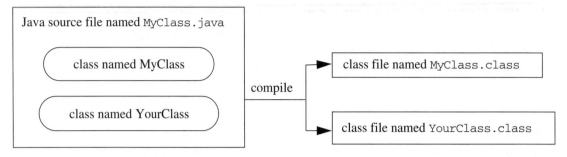

Figure 5.2   Creating compiled class files.

Detail

You might hear some Java programmers talking about "bytecodes." **Bytecodes** refer to the instructions in the compiled classes. These are the machine language instructions contained in the files that end in .class.

An Example: The Simplest Applet

Let's take everything we've learned so far and proceed through the development of a simple Java program that displays a window on the screen. For this first example, you'll go step-by-step through each word and symbol. By the end, you'll have written your first applet.

First, let's answer the questions set forth in the previous chapter. This will allow us to plan out our applet.

Question 1: What will the program do? The program will display a window on the screen.

Question 2: What are the different parts of your program? All we have to do is display a window, so the only part of the program we need to think about is the part that does this one thing. We already know that every program is made up of at least one class: an Applet class. One of the things that an applet can do by default is display a window on the screen. This makes our task quite straightforward. All we need to do, then, is create an Applet class. We'll call our Applet class SimplestApplet. This program is also simple enough that we do not need to create any objects.

Question 3: What is the sequence of tasks your program will perform? There is only one task: display a window.

Question 4: What data will your program need? This program will not need any data.

So, how do we create a class? You already know how to do this first step from the previous chapter. To define a class in Java, you write the word class followed by the name of the class. We can call our class anything we want to, but, as mentioned, we'll call our class SimplestApplet. We'll also indicate we're creating an applet by using the keywords introduced in Chapter 4: `public` and `extends`. (Just what these keywords are doing will be explained in Chapter 10. For now, it's enough to know this is what you do when you define a class that will take on the roles and responsibilities of an applet.)

Style

> A word about naming classes and methods: In this example, the name SimplestApplet is an arbitrary name. We could also call our class Hello, FirstExample, or Fred. It doesn't matter. While it might be funnier to call the class Fred, such a name would not be very descriptive. Someone else reading your code would have no idea what this class was all about. Therefore, you should always take a stab at naming the class in such a way that it provides a clue to its existence.

Defining an Applet class named SimplestApplet, we have

```
public class SimplestApplet extends java.applet.Applet {

}
```

Although our SimplestApplet class does not contain any Java code between the curly braces, it will compile and run just fine. The Java compiler will understand that we are defining a class that's an applet, even though we have not yet provided any code for this class. We can always change this file later.

Let's create a file that contains this simple class definition for an applet. Here are the steps you can follow:

1. Normally, you would create a new project file and a new Java source file in CodeWarrior to hold your new program. While the full version of CodeWarrior obviously allows you to do this, the version of CodeWarrior Lite on the CD restricts this functionality. (Metrowerks can't just give away their crown jewels, after all.) So, if you do not have the full-blown version of CodeWarrior and instead are using the version of CodeWarrior Lite found on the CD, we have supplied a project file with an empty Java source file that you can use for this exercise. To find this empty project, go to the Learn Java Projects folder and open the file `05.01 - empty project`. Double-click `SimplestApplet.μ` to start up CodeWarrior Lite if it's not already running. Open the file to edit by double-clicking `SimplestApplet.java` in the project window.

2. Once the empty source window named `SimplestApplet.java` (Figure 5.3) appears, type the following two lines into this window (Figure 5.4):

```
public class SimplestApplet extends java.applet.Applet {
}
```

3. Compile this Java source file. Select the **Make** command from the **Project** menu (just be certain you have opened the project `SimplestApplet.μ` to enable this menu option). Executing this command creates the type of folder and file you've seen before: The folder is named SimplestApplet, and the compiled class file within this folder is named `SimplestApplet.class` (Figure 5.5).

To execute this applet, you have to supply an HTML file to drop onto the Metrowerks Java application icon. Once you perform this drag-and-drop operation, your applet will load and run automatically. We've already supplied an

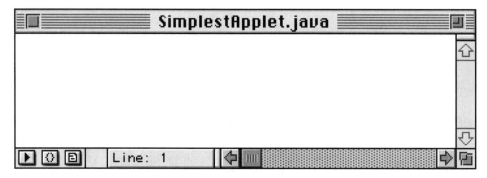

Figure 5.3   The empty Java source file, ready for your code.

Figure 5.4   The `SimplestApplet.java` window after you've entered the empty class definition.

Figure 5.5 The files in your project's folder after you've compiled your Java source code.

HTML file in the SimplestApplet project for you to use. (For testing purposes, you'll often create HTML files for your new projects by cutting and pasting from existing HTML files and changing the name of the Applet class referred to by the HTML file.) Take a look at the HTML file now by double-clicking the file `SimplestApplet.html` in the project window (Figure 5.6).

There are two lines in this file. The first line begins the applet definition:

```
<applet codebase="SimplestApplet" codebase="SimplestApplet"
code="SimplestApplet.class" width=250 height=50>
```

(While this book's page width forces us to break this HTML code into two lines, you can see from the screenshot in Figure 5.6 that this code really requires only one line in the HTML file.) This line of HTML code does the following two things:

1. It identifies which class defines the applet through the use of the keyword `code=`. The name of the compiled class file that contains the applet is supplied

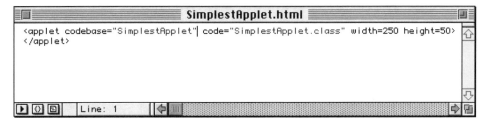

Figure 5.6 The `SimplestApplet.html` file.

in quotes. It also identifies where to find this compiled class. It is in the folder named SimplestApplet, which is identified by the keyword `codebase=`.

2. It provides an initial size for the applet. If the applet were running in a Web browser rather than in a special window for testing that's supplied by Metrowerks Java, then the browser would be able to arrange the other elements in the Web page around the applet because the browser would know how much room the applet needed. The keywords `width=` and `height=` indicate that the applet should be sized to the values provided.

The second line ends the applet definition:

```
</applet>
```

This, my friends, is a perfectly valid applet and HTML file! What's more, since an applet automatically displays a window and since we've set the size for this window in the HTML file, we're done.

The SimplestApplet class should compile fine. If, for some reason, a window appears indicating that something went wrong, close this window and look over your `SimplestApplet.java` file very carefully. Be sure you've typed in everything exactly as shown in this book. Remember, Java, like all programming languages, is very picky about what letters and symbols you type and will become confused if you don't follow the rules of the language *exactly*. (At the end of this chapter, we'll look at how error messages identify where something went wrong.)

Once your applet compiles, you can run the applet. Just as you did in Chapter 2, drag the icon for the HTML file called `SimplestApplet.html` from the folder `05.01 - empty project` and drop it onto the Metrowerks Java application icon. When you do, the Java interpreter (Metrowerks Java) will start and run your applet. Figure 5.7 shows what this will look like.

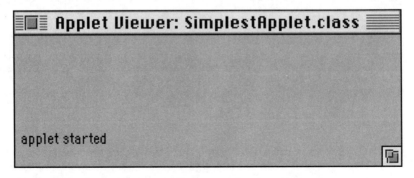

Figure 5.7 SimplestApplet as it appears when run on a Mac.

We've created an actual working applet, even though it's not doing much yet. Starting in Chapter 6, you'll begin to write some Java code for real. For now, just think about the steps that are occurring when you create, compile, and run a Java applet. Think about launching the Java interpreter and Applet Viewer (Metrowerks Java) by dropping the HTML file icon onto the Metrowerks Java application icon; how Metrowerks Java loads the class referred to in the HTML file; and how it sizes the window according to the dimensions in the HTML file. Notice that the Applet class knows how to display a window on the screen without your doing anything. All you have to do is tell it its default size.

Editing the Source File

Now you get to see how the development cycle works. In the next few sections, you'll edit the source file, add some classes, and even generate some syntax errors so that you can see what to do when something unexpected happens at compile time.

Let's start by adding a couple of new classes to SimplestApplet. Return to the source file for the SimplestApplet project. (The source file is named `Simplest-Applet.java`.) Open this file if it is not already open by double-clicking the file icon or by double-clicking the file name in the `SimplestApplet.µ` project window.

Let's add a class definition for a Circle class and a Square class. You already know how to create a simple empty class definition. For these two classes, you can write

```
class Circle {
}

class Square {
}
```

Put these definitions after the definition for the Applet class called Simplest-Applet. Figure 5.8 shows what your source file will look like after you've added these two classes.

Now, recompile the SimplestApplet project (select **Make** from the **Project** menu). If you run the applet again, you'll find it hasn't changed. By compiling, you will have created two new class files, however. Each of these class files will be named based on the new classes you defined: `Circle.class` and `Square.class`. You'll find these in the folder containing your project—the folder named `05.01-empty project`.

```
┌──────────────────────────────────────────────────────────┐
│ ▣  ═══════════ SimplestApplet.java ═══════════        ▣  │
├──────────────────────────────────────────────────────────┤
│ public class SimplestApplet extends java.applet.Applet {⬆ │
│ }                                                        ▤ │
│                                                            │
│ class Circle {                                             │
│ }                                                          │
│                                                            │
│ class Square {                                             │
│ }|                                                       ⬇ │
├──────────────────────────────────────────────────────────┤
│ ▶ ◇ ▣  │ Line: 8 │  ◀ ▥▥             ▶ ▣ │
└──────────────────────────────────────────────────────────┘
```

Figure 5.8 `SimplestApplet.java` after you've added two new empty classes.

From this basic skeleton of three classes, you can start defining the rest of the SimplestApplet program, eventually turning it into the SimpleDraw applet. That would include things like adding graphical user interface elements to your applet window to allow the user to draw, making new circle and square objects out of the Circle class and Square class when the user clicked in the applet, and defining the appropriate data and behavior needed by the circles and squares in this application. You'll learn how to do all of these things very soon. By adding to the outline to the applet we've started here, you'll learn how to keep track of data, how to define methods, how to create objects, how to interact with the user, and much more.

Syntax Errors

Sometimes, you'll find that your program won't compile, even though you thought you typed in your program as it should appear. When this occurs, you're most likely dealing with a **syntax error**.

What Are Syntax Errors?

You'll generate a syntax error when you try to compile if you use the wrong word or symbol in your program. For example, if you forget to use a closing right curly brace (}) to end a class definition and compile, you'll generate a syntax error. If you misspell a word and compile, you'll generate a syntax error. Sometimes, when you're just starting out, you'll stare at a program and be convinced you've typed it in correctly, yet the compiler will still complain about syntax errors. How annoying! When that occurs, it's very likely you've used a keyword or a symbol incorrectly and the compiler really is right after all. You can browse through the appendixes to find examples of how to use Java's keywords and symbols if you do get stuck.

Generating Syntax Errors

Let's generate a syntax error so that you can see what happens (in case you haven't run into one already!). Our SimplestApplet program currently contains six lines of code (counting the lines with the single closing right curly brace, but not counting the blank lines). If we leave off the first left curly brace in this file, the program will appear as in Listing 5.1.

Listing 5.1   A program that will not compile.

```
class SimplestApplet extends java.applet.Applet
}

class Circle {
}

class Square {
}
```

Go ahead and attempt to compile this program now (select **Make** from the **Project** menu). What happens? You get a syntax error! Figure 5.9 shows what a syntax error looks like.

Not only did the Java compiler find that there was a problem, but it also identified what the problem was and where it occurred. You can open the file and jump right to the line that contains the error by double-clicking the syntax error. You'll notice a little arrow identifies the line where the compiler thought there was a problem (Figure 5.10). To fix the error, all you have to do is enter the left curly brace as appropriate and recompile.

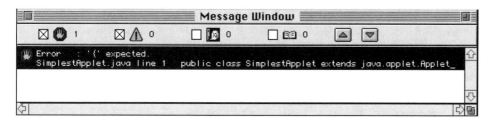

Figure 5.9   Syntax error generated because of a problem with the source code.

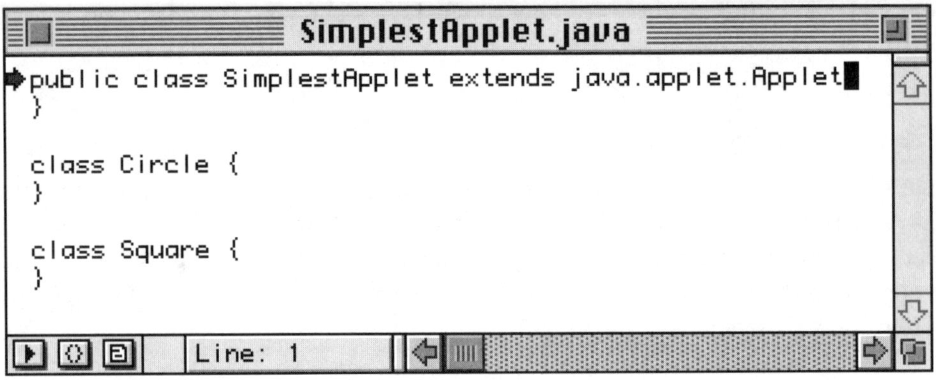

Figure 5.10 Arrow indicating where the compiler has identified a syntax error.

Warning

The messages indicating a syntax error has occurred will not *always* correctly identify where the error exists, though it will usually be close by (within a line or so). The reason this can happen is that the compiler must make a guess as to what went wrong while it was looking over your program; since it doesn't always know what you were trying to do, it sometimes makes assumptions. If the line identified by the compiler does not look incorrect, try checking out the line above it before pulling your hair out.

Displaying Messages

Even though we won't start displaying things inside the applet's window until Chapter 11, our programs are still capable of displaying messages. You can do this by writing to the Java Output window. (Remember, the Java Output window is always displayed by Metrowerks Java when you run your applet.)

Definition

The Java Output window plays the role of the **standard output** when running applets using Metrowerks Java. In the old days of writing software, computer terminals didn't have such things as windows, menus, and so on. They only displayed characters. Back then, programmers didn't have to worry about where text they displayed would end up—as long as they wrote to the standard output, it would end up on the device being used to interact with the computer. That device might be a screen or even a line printer, but there wasn't any possibility of its being displayed in some window floating on the screen; there simply weren't any windows!

In these modern times, things are more complicated, but new languages still retain the concept of writing text to the standard output. Even in a sophisticated language like Java, this idea is still around. CodeWarrior allows you to write to the standard output by supplying the Java Output window.

The Java Output Window

Even if you don't write anything to the Java Output window yourself, Metrowerks Java still writes its own messages to this window. As you saw in Chapter 2, this includes messages indicating that a particular Applet class is loading and running.

To make a message appear in this Java Output window (that is, the standard output) from your own program, you use a command that looks like this:

```
System.out.println("Your message goes here.");
```

This cryptic-looking line of code contains a few aspects of Java that will be fully explained later. Until then, it's best to just accept that this works when we use it in our own sample programs. This code will display the following line of text in the Java Output window:

```
Your message goes here.
```

You can put almost anything between the parentheses and quotes and have it appear in the Java Output window. As another example, to write the message "I like Java in the springtime," you could write a line of code like this:

```
System.out.println("I like Java in the springtime");
```

As you might guess, this code makes the line:

```
I like Java in the springtime
```

appear in the Java Output window.

Static Initializers

Now, where do we put these lines of code? We can put them in two places: in methods and in static initializers. We haven't learned how to define our own methods quite yet; that's to be covered in Chapter 7. So for now, let's turn our attention to **static initializers**.

When you drop your HTML file onto the Metrowerks Java icon, Metrowerks Java starts up. It loads the Applet class listed after the code= keyword in your HTML file. When your class loads, Java looks to see whether the class has defined a static initializer. If it has, then Metrowerks Java executes this code.

The way you define a static initializer is by using the static keyword and an opening and closing curly brace, like this:

```
public class StaticInit extends java.applet.Applet {

    static {
        System.out.println("I like Java in the springtime");
    }

}
```

As indicated, the code between the opening and closing curly braces after the keyword static is executed when this class is loaded. Hey—this means we have written a Java program that actually does something! To see this work, drag and drop the StaticInit.html file icon onto the Metrowerks Java application icon. You can find this HTML file in the folder named 05.02 – static located in Learn Java Projects. When it runs, you'll see that, as before, the applet window itself is blank. However, our new message appears in the Java Output window. Figure 5.11 shows what the Java Output window looks like when this static initializer code is added to an otherwise empty Applet class definition.

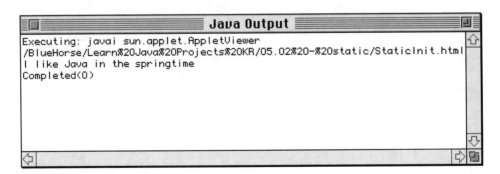

Figure 5.11   A static initializer message in the Java Output window.

Each line of Java code that actually *does* something is referred to as a **statement**. Each statement must always end in a semicolon (;), similar to the way that most English sentences end in a period. Notice the semicolon at the end of the line

```
System.out.println("I like Java in the springtime");
```

You would receive a syntax error from the compiler without this ending semicolon. Look for the semicolon in the lines of code that follow in this chapter and throughout the rest of this book to become familiar with it.

What if you wanted to write a second message in addition to singing about Java in the spring? How could you also write out a message about preferring another drink in the summer? You could write another line of code right after the first, like this:

```
static {
    System.out.println("I like Java in the springtime");
    System.out.println("I like iced tea in the summer");
}
```

Notice that each line of code ends in a semicolon. You can write as many lines of code as you'd like. Just put them all between the starting left curly brace and the ending right curly brace and you'll be fine.

With Metrowerks Java and the Applet Viewer, if you want to make a change to your Java source code and rerun your applet, you should not drag and drop the HTML file onto the Metrowerks Java icon again. As long as Metrowerks Java is still running, you should select **Reload** from the **Applet** menu.

More Complicated Messages

You must place all the text you'd like to appear in the Java Output window within quotes. In addition to writing text, you can also write other types of information. For example, you can display a number like this:

```
System.out.println(99);
```

You can even combine text and numbers by using the plus sign (+), like this:

```
System.out.println("My agent number is " + 99 + "!");
```

This code would display the line

```
My agent number is 99!
```

In the next chapter, you'll see how you can take advantage of this technique to write even more sophisticated messages to the Java Output window.

Review

This chapter outlined the development cycle for programming in Java. You'll always follow these basic steps when writing your Java programs: Create and edit a file to contain your Java source code, compile this code, and run your program. When you want to make changes, repeat these steps, starting with editing the file that contains your Java source code. You now know how to write code in your `.java` files and compile them to create `.class` files. You even know how to fix syntax errors should you ever see these beasts.

This chapter stepped through the simplest possible Java applet. You are probably beginning to get a sense that applets know how to do some things by default. For example, your Applet class knew how to put a window up on the screen all by itself. You also learned how to make messages appear in a window on the screen. Soon, you'll be displaying messages in the applet window itself, adding graphical user interface elements and more. In the upcoming chapters, you'll gain insights into these as well as other mysteries of Java programming.

What's Next?

In the next chapter, our first formal programming chapter, you'll learn how to work with data. Chapter 6 discusses how to maintain data in your program by using variables and how to use operators to change the values in those variables. This will provide the basis for all of the programming chapters that follow.

Chapter 6

Variables and Operators

Congratulations on reaching Chapter 6! You're on the verge of becoming a Java programmer. Let's take stock of where you stand right now.

You're beginning to get comfortable with the CodeWarrior environment. In particular, you know how to open a project and edit a project's source code. You know how to run a Java program, and you've run a number of Java programs as you progressed through the first five chapters. You created a very simple applet in Chapter 5, having learned the stages of the development cycle and one or two Java keywords relating to applets. You even know what to do if you run into any syntax errors, and you've experienced how to go about fixing them.

You've learned a little about what it's like to develop a program using Java, including how to think through your program's design by answering four questions. You've also put together classes that will become the framework for your application. You know how to write messages to the Java Output window. You know that each line of code is a statement and that each statement ends in a semicolon.

Doesn't all this sound like you're on the road to becoming a programmer? Now it's time to go a little further.

One of the primary tasks of a program is to work with data. Programs work with just about every type of data you can imagine, ranging from a person's hourly wage in a personnel file, to a bank balance in a checking account, to a flight path for a space probe, to the colors of circles and squares. To write programs, then, you need to know how to work with the data required by the program. So far, we've hinted at how to begin *planning* to work with data, but we haven't gotten into the details. This chapter will show you what you need to know to work with data using Java.

This chapter uses parts of Chapter 5 from the second edition of *Learn C on the Macintosh*, written by Dave Mark and published by Addison-Wesley. The C language was a direct predecessor to Java, so the approaches for maintaining and manipulating data are quite similar between C and Java. We took advantage of this situation to present text that has already been tested in production, as it were, and run through the gamut by tens of thousands of readers of Dave's other book. Where necessary, we updated this text to take into account the differences with Java.

An Introduction to Variables

A large part of the programming process involves working with data. In Java, data is represented by using **variables**. Variables can be thought of as containers for your program's data. Imagine three containers on a table. Each container has a label: "cup1," "cup2," and "cup3." Now imagine that you have three pieces of paper. Write a number on each piece of paper and place one piece inside each of the three containers. Figure 6.1 shows what this might look like.

Now imagine asking a friend to reach into the three cups, pull out the number in each one, and add the three values. You can ask your friend to place the sum of the three values in a fourth container created just for this purpose. The fourth container is labeled "sum" and is shown in Figure 6.2.

This is exactly how variables work. Variables are containers for your program's data. You create a variable and place a value in it. You then ask the computer to do something with the value in your variable. You can ask the computer to add three variables and place the result in a fourth variable. You can even ask the computer to take the value in a variable, multiply it by 2, and place the result back into the original variable.

Getting back to our example, now imagine that you changed the values in cup1, cup2, and cup3. Once again, you could call on your friend to add the three values, updating the value in the container sum. You've reused the same variables using the same formula to achieve a different result. Here's the Java version of the formula:

```
sum = cup1 + cup2 + cup3;
```

Every time you execute this line of source code, you place the sum of the variables cup1, cup2, and cup3 into the variable named sum. At this point, it's not important to understand exactly how this line of Java code works. What is important to understand is the basic idea behind variables. Each variable in your program is

Figure 6.1 Placing a number in each of three cups.

sum

Figure 6.2 Adding three numbers and placing the result in a container labeled "sum."

like a container with a value in it. This chapter will teach you how to create variables and how to place a value in a variable.

Working with Variables

Variables come in a variety of **types**. A variable's type determines the kind of data that can be stored in that variable. You determine a variable's type when you create the variable. (We'll discuss creating variables in just a second.) Some variable types are useful for working with numbers. Other variable types are designed to work with text. Still others are good for maintaining true/false values. In this chapter, we'll discuss only one type of variable. This will be the variable of type int (int stands for "integer"). A variable of type int can hold a numerical value, such as 27 or –589.

Working with variables is a two-stage process. First, you create a variable; then, you use a variable. In Java, you create a variable by declaring it. Declaring a variable tells the compiler, "Create a variable for me. I need a container in which to place a piece of data." When you declare a variable, you have to specify both the variable's type and its name. In our earlier example, we created four containers, or cups, each having a label. In the Java world, this would be the same as creating four variables with the names cup1, cup2, cup3, and sum. In Java, if we want to use the value stored in a variable, we use the variable's name. (You'll see how to do this later in the chapter.)

Here's an example of a variable declaration:

```
int   myVariable;
```

This declaration tells the compiler to create a variable of type int (remember, an int is designed to work with numbers) with the name myVariable. The type of the variable (in this case, int) is extremely important. As you'll see, a variable type determines the kind and range of values a variable can be assigned.

75

Variable Names

Here are two rules to follow when you create your own variable names:

1. Variable names must always start with an uppercase or lowercase letter (A, B,..., Z or a, b,..., z) or with an underscore (_).

2. The remainder of the variable name must be made up of uppercase or lowercase letters, numbers (0, 1,..., 9), or the underscore.

These two rules yield such variable names as `myVariable`, `THIS_NUMBER`, `VaRiAbLe_1`, and `A1234_4321`. Note that a Java variable may never include a space or a character such as `&` or `*`. These two rules *must* be followed.

On the other hand, these rules do leave a fair amount of room for inventiveness. Over the years, different groups of programmers came up with additional guidelines (also known as *conventions*) that made variable names more consistent and a bit easier to read.

Macintosh programmers tend to use the following two conventions (which we'll also use throughout this book):

1. We'll form our variable names from lowercase letters and numbers, always starting with a lowercase letter. This yields variable names like `number` and `digit33`.

2. When we create a variable with more than one word, we'll start the variable name with a lowercase letter and each successive word in the variable name with an uppercase letter. This yields variable names like `myVariable` and `howMany`.

Java is a **case-sensitive language**, which means that it distinguishes between uppercase and lowercase letters. The compiler will cough out an error if you sometimes refer to `myVariable` and other times refer to `myvariable`. Adopt a naming convention and stick with it: Be consistent!

By the Way

Many times, programmers use a variable named `i` or `j` to keep track of integers. In fact, this book uses these names for some of its variables as well. Why `i` and `j`? Why not `a` and `b` or `q` and `z`? Actually, `a` and `b` (and any other letter—or any other word, for that matter) are just as valid as `i` and `j`. Using `i` and `j` is just a convention.

The reason this convention arose has to do with the computer languages that come before Java. In particular, at one time, FORTRAN was one of the most popular computer languages around. FORTRAN is designed for math, and, in earlier versions of FORTRAN, the way the variables were named determined what types of values they could hold. In particular, all variables that began with the letters *i* through *n* could hold an integer value (*i* and *n* being the first two letters of *int*eger). So, whenever FORTRAN programmers needed a simple integer, they would use i. If they needed another integer and i was already in use, they would use j, and so on. This convention has stayed with programmers and is still used all the time today.

The Size of a Type

When you declare a variable, the compiler reserves a section of memory for the exclusive use of that variable. When you assign a value to a variable, you are modifying the variable's dedicated memory to contain that value. The amount of memory assigned to a variable is determined by the variable's type.

For example, the following variable declaration reserves memory for the exclusive use of the variable myInt:

```
int    myInt;
```

If you later assign a value to myInt, that value is stored in the memory allocated for myInt. If you ever refer to the value of myInt, you'll be referring to the value stored in this memory.

Operators

One way to assign a value to a variable is to use the = operator, also known as the **assignment operator**. An operator is a special character (or set of characters) representing a specific computer operation. The assignment operator tells the computer to compute the value to the right of the = and to assign that value to the variable on the left of the =.

Take a look at this line of source code:

```
myInt = 237;
```

This statement causes the value 237 to be placed in the memory allocated for myInt. In this line of code, myInt appears on the left side of the = operator. A variable makes a fine left-hand side of an assignment. A number (like 237) makes a terrible left-hand side. Why? Because values are copied *from the right side to the left side* of the = operator. For example, the following line of code asks the compiler to copy the value in `myInt` to the number 237:

```
237 = myInt;
```

Since you can't change the value of a number, the compiler will report an error when it encounters this line of code (the error message will complain about an "Invalid left-hand side of assignment").

By the Way

As we just illustrated, you can use numerical constants (such as 237) directly in your code. In the programming world, these constants are called **literals**. Just as there are different types of variables, there are also different types of literals. You'll see more on this topic later in this book.

Look at this example code placed into a static initializer for an Applet class:

```
public class Sample0601 extends java.applet.Applet {

    static {
        int    myInt, anotherInt;

        myInt = 503;
        anotherInt = myInt;
    }
}
```

Notice that two variables are declared in this program. One way to declare multiple variables is to separate the variables by a comma (,), as is done here. There's no limit to the number of variables you can declare using this method. (Just be sure to end this line with a semicolon.)

These variables could also have been declared by using two separate statements:

```
int    myInt;
int    anotherInt;
```

Either way is fine. As you'll see, Java is an extremely flexible language. For example, you can declare variables pretty much anywhere in your program. Consider this example:

```
public class Sample0602 extends java.applet.Applet {

    static {
        int    myInt;

        myInt = 503;

        int    anotherInt;
        anotherInt = myInt;
    }
}
```

This code will work perfectly; the only issue is a matter of style. Some programmers like to place all the variable declarations at the start of the method so that they are easy to find. Some programmers like to declare variables just before they're used. In this book, we'll declare all the variables at the start of the method, which is what the majority of programmers do, especially those who have programmed in less flexible languages that required all variables to be declared first. You should pick a style you like and be consistent.

Let's take a look at the static initializer for this program. This static initializer starts by declaring an int:

```
int    myInt;
```

Next, this program assigns the value 503 to myInt:

```
myInt = 503;
```

Then, the program declares another variable:

```
int    anotherInt;
```

Finally, the value in myInt is copied into anotherInt:

```
anotherInt = myInt;
```

After this last statement, the variable anotherInt also contains the value 503.

Now that you know how to declare a variable and use the assignment operator to set it to a value, let's look at some of the other operators in Java. Many of these operators have to do with arithmetic operations (such as addition, subtraction, and so on). We'll look at these operators in this chapter. Other operators are useful for comparing two values and determining things like whether one is greater or less than another. We'll look at these operators later in the book.

Arithmetic Operators

The +, –, ++, and –– Operators

The + and – operators each take two values and reduce them to a single value. For example, the following statement will first resolve the right side of the = by adding the numbers 5 and 3:

```
myInt = 5 + 3;
```

Once that's done, the resulting value (8) is assigned to the variable on the left side of the =. This statement assigns the value 8 to the variable `myInt`. Assigning a value to a variable means copying the value into the memory allocated to that variable.

Here's another example:

```
myInt = 10;
anotherInt = 12 - myInt;
```

The first statement assigns the value 10 to `myInt`. The second statement subtracts 10 from 12 to get 2 and then assigns the value 2 to `anotherInt`.

The ++ and –– operators operate on a single value only. The ++ operator **increments** (raises) the value by 1, and the –– operator **decrements** (lowers) the value by 1. Take a look:

```
myInt = 10;
myInt++;
```

The first statement assigns `myInt` a value of 10. The second statement changes the value of `myInt` from 10 to 11. Here's an example with ––:

```
myInt = 10;
-- myInt;
```

This time, the second line of code leaves `myInt` with a value of 9. You may have noticed that the first example shows the ++ following `myInt`, whereas the second example shows the –– preceding `myInt`.

The position of the ++ and -- operators determines when their operation is performed in relation to the rest of the statement. Placing the operator to the right of a variable or an expression (this is called **postfix notation**) resolves all values before performing the increment (or decrement) operation. Placing the operator to the left of the variable (this is called **prefix notation**) performs the increment (or decrement) first, and then the evaluation continues. The following examples should make this point clear.

First, consider this code:

```
myInt = 10;
anotherInt = myInt--;
```

The first statement assigns myInt a value of 10. In the second statement, the -- operator is to the right of myInt. This use of postfix notation assigns myInt's value to anotherInt before decrementing myInt. This example leaves myInt with a value of 9 and anotherInt with a value of 10.

Now, here's the same example, written using prefix notation:

```
myInt = 10;
anotherInt = -- myInt;
```

This time, the -- is to the left of myInt. In this case, the value of myInt is decremented before being assigned to anotherInt. The result? Both myInt and anotherInt are left with a value of 9.

The += and -= Operators

In Java, you can place the same variable on both the left and right sides of an assignment statement. For example, the following statement increases the value of myInt by 10:

```
myInt = myInt + 10;
```

The same result can be achieved using the += operator:

```
myInt += 10;
```

In other words, the preceding statement is the same as

```
myInt = myInt + 10;
```

In the same way, the -= operator can be used to decrement the value of a variable. The following statement decrements the value of myInt by 10:

```
myInt -= 10;
```

The *, /, *=, and /= Operators

The * and / operators each take two values and reduce them to a single value, much the same as the + and - operators do. The following statement multiplies 3 by 5, leaving myInt with a value of 15:

```
myInt = 3 * 5;
```

The following statement divides 5 by 2 and, if myInt is declared as an int (or any other type designed to hold whole numbers), assigns the integral (truncated) result to myInt:

```
myInt = 5 / 2;
```

The number 5 divided by 2 is 2.5. Since myInt can hold only whole numbers, the value 2.5 is truncated, and the value 2 is assigned to myInt.

Detail

> Math alert! Numbers like –37, 0, and 22 are known as **whole numbers**, or **integers**. Numbers like 3.14159, 2.5, and .0001 are known as **fractional numbers** or **floating-point numbers**.

The *= and /= operators work much the same as their += and -= counterparts. The following two statements are identical:

```
myInt *= 10;
myInt = myInt * 10;
```

The following two statements are also identical:

```
myInt /= 10;
myInt = myInt / 10;
```

The / operator doesn't perform its truncation automatically. The accuracy of the result is limited by the data type of the operands. As an example, if the division is performed using ints, the result will be an int and is truncated to an integer value. Several data types (such as float, introduced shortly) support floating-point division, using the / operator.

Operator Order

Sometimes, the expressions you create can be evaluated in many ways. For example,

```
myInt = 5 + 3 * 2;
```

You can add 5 and 3 and then multiply the result by 2 (giving 16). Alternatively, you can multiply 3 by 2 and add 5 to the result (giving 11). Which is correct?

Java has a set of built-in rules for resolving the order of operators. As it turns out, the * operator has a higher precedence than the + operator, so the multiplication will be performed first, yielding a result of 11.

Although it helps to understand the relative precedence of the Java operators, it is difficult to keep track of them all. That's where parentheses come in. Use parentheses in pairs to define the order in which you want your operators performed. The following statement will leave myInt with a value of 16:

```
myInt = ( 5 + 3 ) * 2;
```

The following statement will leave myInt with a value of 11:

```
myInt = 5 + ( 3 * 2 );
```

You can use more than one set of parentheses in a statement, as long as they occur in pairs—one left parenthesis associated with each right parenthesis. The following statement will leave myInt with a value of 16:

```
myInt = ( ( 5 + 3 ) * 2);
```

Bitwise Operators

There are a few special operators that work with the individual bits in a variable or number. These are most often used only as advanced programming techniques, but we'll mention them here because you will run across them in your travels, especially when combining variables that define properties and styles. For example, we'll use these operators in Chapter 11 when specifying a font style. For now, here's what you need to know.

The **bitwise operators**, (which are operators that work on bits rather than taking into account the number as a whole, are listed in Table 6.1.

Table 6.1   Bitwise operators.

Operator	Description
>>>	Shifts the bits in a variable to the right and fills the vacated bits with 0s.
		Performs a logical OR, which results in 1 if either of the bits is on and 0 if both bits are off.
^	Performs a logical AND, which results in 1 only if both bits are on and 0 otherwise.
<<	Shifts the bits in a variable to the left.
>>	Shifts the bits in a variable to the right.

You can check out Dave Mark's book *Learn C on the Macintosh* for an explanation of the equivalent bitwise operators in C and for a thorough discussion of bits, bytes, and binary arithmetic. In Chapter 11 when we define a font's style, we'll show how you can use this logical OR operator to combine values.

Sample Programs

Starting with this chapter, we will include a section that steps through sample code, line by line, that illustrates the programming concepts you learned about in the chapter.

So far in this chapter, we've discussed variables (mostly of type int) and operators (mostly arithmetic). The program examples on the following pages combine variables and operators into useful Java statements.

Opening Operator.µ

Our first program, maintained by the project file Operator.µ, provides a testing ground for some of the operators covered in the previous sections. Operator.java declares a variable (myInt) and uses a series of statements to change the value of

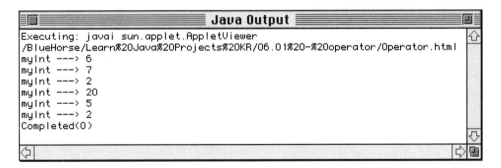

Figure 6.3 The Operator.µ project window.

the variable. By including a System.out.println() after each of these statements, Operator.java makes it easy to follow the variable, step-by-step, as its value changes.

Start up CodeWarrior by double-clicking on the project file Operator.µ inside the Learn Java Projects folder, in the subfolder named 06.01 - operator. The project window for Operator.µ should appear as in Figure 6.3.

Compile this applet by selecting **Make** from the **Project** menu. Once the code compiles, drag and drop the HTML file icon from the folder 06.01 - operator onto the Metrowerks Java application icon. Metrowerks Java will launch the Applet Viewer and run the program, displaying the output from the program in the Java Output window. Compare your output to that shown in Figure 6.4. They should be the same (except, of course, for differences in the hard disk name and folder name where you installed CodeWarrior and the Learn Java Projects folder).

```
Executing: javai sun.applet.AppletViewer
/BlueHorse/Learn%20Java%20Projects%20KR/06.01%20-%20operator/Operator.html
myInt ---> 6
myInt ---> 7
myInt ---> 2
myInt ---> 20
myInt ---> 5
myInt ---> 2
Completed(0)
```

Figure 6.4 The output generated by the Operator applet.

Stepping Through the Source Code

Before we step through the source code in Operator.java, you might want to bring the source code up on your screen (double-click the name Operator.java in the project window or select **Open** from the **File** menu and then double-click the file name operator.java). A new window will appear, listing the source code in the file Operator.java.

The file Operator.java starts off by defining a new class, just as you learned about in the previous chapter. This program defines an Applet class called Operator.

We've placed a whole bunch of Java statements inside a static initializer. These statements set a value for a variable, change the value, and then display the new results.

The static initializer starts out by declaring an int variable named myInt:

```
int    myInt;
```

At this point in the program, myInt is equal to 0. We haven't set it to any particular value, but Java always makes sure your variables contain some known value.

The next line of code uses the * operator to calculate a value of 6 and the = operator to assign this new value to myInt. Following that, we use System.out.println() to display the value of myInt in the Java Output window:

```
myInt = 3 * 2;
System.out.println("myInt ---> " + myInt);
```

The next line of Operator.java increments myInt from 6 to 7 and prints the new value in the Java Output window:

```
myInt += 1;
System.out.println("myInt ---> " + myInt);
```

The next line decrements myInt by 5 and prints its new value, 2, in the Java Output window:

```
myInt -= 5;
System.out.println("myInt ---> " + myInt);
```

Next, myInt is multiplied by 10, and its new value, 20, is printed in the Java Output window:

```
myInt *= 10;
System.out.println("myInt ---> " + myInt);
```

Next, `myInt` is divided by 4, resulting in a new value, 5:

```
myInt /= 4;
System.out.println("myInt ---> " + myInt);
```

Finally, `myInt` is divided by 2. Since 5 divided by 2 is 2.5 (not a whole number), a truncation is performed, and `myInt` is left with a value of 2:

```
myInt /= 2;
System.out.println("myInt ---> " + myInt);
```

Opening `Postfix.μ`

Our next program demonstrates the difference between postfix and prefix notation (the ++ and -- operators defined earlier in the chapter). In the Finder, go into the Learn Java Projects folder, then into the `06.02 - postfix` subfolder, and double-click the project file `Postfix.μ`. CodeWarrior will close the project file `Operator.μ` and open `Postfix.μ`.

Take a look at the source code in the file `Postfix.java` and try to predict the result of the two `System.out.println()` statements before you run the program. Careful, this example is tricky! (This file is displayed in Figure 6.5.) Remember, you can open a source code listing for `Postfix.java` by double-clicking the name `Postfix.java` in the project window.

Once your guesses are locked in, select **Make** from the **Project** menu to compile the applet and then drop the HTML file in the `06.02 - postfix` folder onto the Metrowerks Java application. How'd you do? Compare your two guesses with the output in Figure 6.6. Let's look at the source code.

Stepping Through the Source Code

The first half of `Postfix.java` is what you've seen before. The variable `myInt` is declared to be of type `int` inside a static initializer. Then, `myInt` is assigned a value of 5:

```
int  myInt;
myInt = 5;
```

The tricky part comes next. The first call to `System.out.println()` has an expression embedded in it. This is another feature of the Java language. Where

```
Postfix.java

public class Postfix java.applet.Applet {

    static {

        int        myInt;

        myInt = 5;

        System.out.println("myInt ---> " + myInt++);

        System.out.println("myInt ---> " + ++myInt);

    }
}

Line: 2
```

Figure 6.5 The file Postfix.java.

there's room for a variable, there's often room for an entire expression. This allows you to perform two actions in the same line of code so that

```
System.out.println("myInt ---> " + myInt++);
```

performs two different tasks. First, the message myInt ---> 5 is printed to the Java Output window. (That is, at the time the message is printed, myInt has a value of 5.) Second, myInt is incremented by 1. By the time this line of code is finished executing, myInt has a value of 6. Two things for the price of one!

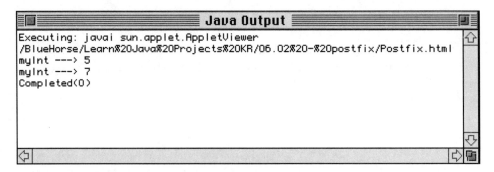

```
Java Output

Executing: javai sun.applet.AppletViewer
/BlueHorse/Learn%20Java%20Projects%20KR/06.02%20-%20postfix/Postfix.html
myInt ---> 5
myInt ---> 7
Completed(0)
```

Figure 6.6 The output generated by the program Postfix.

The use of postfix notation in the preceding line of code ensures the increment by 1 occurs after the value for `myInt` is printed. Check out the next line of code:

```
System.out.println("myInt ---> " + ++myInt);
```

This line of code uses prefix notation. This ensures that `myInt` is incremented first, which makes `myInt` take on the value of 7. Then, the message is printed to the Java Output window.

By the Way

Can you break each of these `System.out.println()` statements into two separate ones?

The first `System.out.println()` looks like this:

```
System.out.println("myInt ---> " + myInt++);
```

Give it a try and then read on. . . .Here's the two-statement version:

```
System.out.println("myInt --> " + myInt);
myInt++;
```

Notice that the statement incrementing `myInt` was placed after the `System.out.println()`. Do you see why? The postfix notation makes this necessary. Run through both versions and verify this for yourself.

The second `System.out.println()` looks like this:

```
System.out.println("myInt ---> " + ++myInt);
```

Here's the two-statement version:

```
++myInt;
System.out.println("myInt ---> " + myInt);
```

This time, the statement incrementing `myInt` came before `System.out.println()`. It's the prefix notation that makes this necessary. Again, go through both versions and verify this for yourself.

The purpose of demonstrating the complexity of the postfix and prefix operations is twofold. On the one hand, it's extremely important that you understand exactly how these operators work from all angles. This will allow you to write code that works and will aid you in making sense of other programmers' code. On the other hand, embedding prefix and postfix operators within statements that also perform other tasks may save you a line of code but, as you can see, may force you to take more time to unravel the logic.

Programming with Style

You've now learned enough about Java that it's time to say a few words about style. As your programs become more complicated, one danger you must always guard against is writing code that is difficult to understand and maintain. With that in mind, let's look at some approaches for making sure your code is clear, is easy to read, and is written in a style that most programmers use in their own code.

Writing Comments

One great technique for explaining your program to other programmers is to use comments. Comments are written directly in English and are mixed right into your source code. When you add a comment, you first tell the Java compiler you're beginning a comment. This way, the compiler knows that it should skip over your comment before it begins to compile again.

There are two basic types of comments you can add to your code. The first type is created by using two forward slashes, like this:

```
// This is a comment.
```

Here's an example of this type of comment:

```
public class PieEaters extends java.applet.Applet {

    static {
        int numPieces;   // Number of pieces of pie left

        numPieces = 8;   // We started with 8 pieces

        numPieces--;       // Marge had a piece
        numPieces--;       // Lisa had a piece
        numPieces -= 2; // Bart had two pieces!!
        numPieces -= 4; // Homer had the rest!!!

        System.out.println("Slices left = " + numPieces); // no more
    }

}
```

Everything starting from the `//` that's on the same line is ignored by the compiler. Comments that use the double forward slashes should appear after all the other code on a line. They can also appear on lines all by themselves.

The other type of comment is better suited to larger and more involved comments. You can indicate the start of a comment by using `/*` (forward-slash star) and the end of a comment by using `*/` (star forward-slash). Everything between the `/*` and `*/` is ignored by the compiler. For example, here is this type of comment in action:

```
public class PieEaters extends java.applet.Applet {

    static {
        int numPieces;   // Number of pieces of pie left

        numPieces = 8;   // We started with 8 pieces

        numPieces--;     // Marge had a piece

    /* This program charts the progress of a bunch of pie eaters.
       Even if we put valid Java code within the comment, this code
       is ignored.

        numPieces--;     // Lisa had a piece
        numPieces -= 2;  // Bart had two pieces!!
        numPieces -= 4;  // Homer had the rest!!!

        This is the end of the comment. */

        System.out.println("Slices left = " + numPieces); // 7 left
    }

}
```

Formatting

As your programs grow more and more complicated, it becomes increasingly important to use good programming style and format to help keep your code readable. Nothing is more frustrating than trying to figure out someone else's code that is difficult to read and is not well documented. Well, maybe there is one thing more frustrating—having this experience with your own code! You'll find that when you return to look over your own code the next day, the next week, or longer, you'll be glad you took a few moments to make your code easy to read and understand. Here are a few simple techniques you can use to help you find a programming style you're comfortable with.

Inserting White Space

You'll notice that the sample code in this book intersperses lots of white space in the form of blank lines and indentations. The Java compiler does not care how much white space you insert into your code. The compiler will simply ignore this white space. Check out the following program and compare it to the PieEaters program shown earlier:

```
public class PieEaters extends java.applet.Applet { static { int
numPieces; numPieces = 8;  numPieces--; numPieces--;
numPieces -= 2; numPieces -=
4; System.out.println("Slices left = " + numPieces); }
}
```

Even this simple example shows that your program can start to look pretty hairy when it's not nicely formatted. As you can see, the original looks much better!

Lining Up the Curly Braces

Notice, in the original PieEaters applet, how the closing right curly brace always aligns with the line that begins with the corresponding left curly brace. This makes it easy to see where related chunks of code begin and end. All the statements within a block of code delineated by curly braces are first indented by three or four spaces or by a tab stop (it doesn't matter, just be consistent) and then aligned within that block. And, as was already pointed out, each closing right curly brace is placed on its own line.

You'll find lots of other examples of indentation and white space usage in the appendixes at the back of this book and in the sample programs on the CD-ROM. Of course, these styling and formatting techniques are not requirements of the language. You might want to find your own programming style, but keep in mind the style shown here is what most Java programmers use when they develop software.

Review

This chapter introduced the concepts of variables and operators. You've learned how to declare a variable and assign a value to it. You've also learned how to perform arithmetic operations, such as addition, subtraction, multiplication, and division, and you've learned about the operators +=, -=, *=, and /=.

The only types of variables you've worked with so far have been `ints`, which hold whole numbers, or integers. Soon, you'll be introduced to other data types that are more appropriate to use for floating-point or fractional values. You'll also learn about operators that answer questions such as, Is one variable greater than another? Are two variables equal?

You've also considered programming style. You can use comments, white space (blank lines and indentations), and curly brace alignment to help make certain you can decipher your own code when you return to it at a later date.

What's Next?

Now that you've seen how to use variables, it's time to discuss how you can implement behavior. This means creating methods. In Chapter 7, you'll be introduced to the basics of creating methods. In Chapter 8, you'll learn how to write methods that do some very sophisticated things, such as make decisions and "loop" through a sequence of statements. In Chapter 9, you'll see how to associate the same methods and variables you're learning about now with your own custom objects.

Chapter *7*

Introduction to Methods

Now we turn our attention to making our applets *do* something! In order to reach that point, we have to journey across one more bridge to the land of methods. The first part of this chapter will describe how to create and work with methods. In the second part, we'll use this knowledge to start programming our applets.

Creating a Method

Methods are one of the building blocks of objects and classes. All of the behavior associated with your Applet class and with the classes used by your Applet class is defined by methods.

A **method** is a chunk of source code that accomplishes a specific task. Methods identify themselves by names. For example, you might have a method that contains the set of instructions describing what should appear in an applet's window. You might call this method `paint()`. Or you might write a method for the circle objects we discussed earlier that would calculate the circle's area. This method might be called `calculateArea()`. A NASA space shuttle program, a tic-tac-toe program, and a business program might have methods called `fireThrusters()`, `determineNextMove()`, and `calculatePayroll()`, respectively. Each of these methods would contain the instructions necessary to perform its specific task.

Detail

> Throughout this book, we'll refer to methods by placing a pair of parentheses after their names. This will help to distinguish between method names and variable names. For example, `radius()` would refer to a method, while `radius` would refer to a variable.

Each method defines a chunk of code that performs a specific task. Methods work together so that a method handling a certain task can ask another method to perform a subtask. After the other method **executes**, it **returns control** back to the first method.

Let's look at a simple example before studying the details. Here's a set of instructions that displays the colors of the rainbow in the Java Output window, one line at a time:

```
System.out.println("red");
System.out.println("orange");
System.out.println("yellow");
System.out.println("green");
System.out.println("blue");
System.out.println("indigo");
System.out.println("violet");
```

This code will work fine, especially if we'll only run through this code in one spot in our program. If our program needs to write out the colors of the rainbow in two different places, we would end up duplicating this code. That would be wasteful in terms of space and programming effort. It would be much better to group these seven statements together into one bundle and execute this chunk of code whenever we need to.

We can do that exact thing by turning these seven lines of code into their own method. Here's an example of a method that writes out the seven colors of the rainbow:

```
void writeColors() {
    System.out.println("red");
    System.out.println("orange");
    System.out.println("yellow");
    System.out.println("green");
    System.out.println("blue");
    System.out.println("indigo");
    System.out.println("violet");
}
```

We'll refer to this method as writeColors(). The method definition starts with the keyword void, which we'll cover in just a moment. You can see the method name, writeColors, is followed by a left and a right parenthesis, which we'll go over also. Then, a left curly brace indicates the start of the method. All of the statements that make up the method follow this left curly brace. After all the method's statements, the method indicates where it ends by using a right curly brace.

Now, whenever you want to write all the colors of the rainbow to the Java Output window, you can **invoke** this method from someplace in your code. Invoking a method means executing its instructions. You can invoke a method in Java by writing

```
writeColors();
```

This single line makes all seven statements in the `writeColors()` method execute, which makes the Java Output window fill up with rainbow color names.

Invoking a Method

As Figure 7.1 shows, invoking `writeColors()` is straightforward. Your method turns control over to the method named `writeColors()`. When `writeColors()` is done executing its statements, it returns control back to the spot in your method where you invoked `writeColors()`.

For example, look at these three lines of code:

```
System.out.println("Here are the colors of the rainbow:");
writeColors();
System.out.println("When was the last time you saw a rainbow?");
```

These three statements would write the following to the Java Output window:

```
Here are the colors of the rainbow:
red
orange
yellow
green
blue
indigo
violet
When was the last time you saw a rainbow?
```

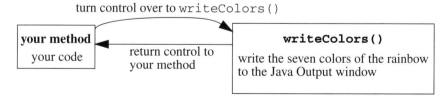

Figure 7.1 Invoking `writeColors()`.

97

Using Variables

Just as you used variables in a static initializer in the previous chapter, you can also use variables in your methods. Here's an example of a method that finds the area of a triangle:

```
void triangleArea() {
    int area;
    int base;
    int height;

    base = 10;
    height = 20;

    area = (base * height) / 2;
}
```

This method, named `triangleArea()`, uses the variables `base` and `height` to hold the triangle's data and `area` to hold the result of the calculation.

Variable Scope

In Java, every variable is said to have a **scope**, or range. A variable's scope defines where in the program you have access to a variable. In other words, if a variable is declared inside one method, can another method refer to the same variable? The answer is no!

Java defines variable scope as follows. A variable declared inside a method is **local** to that method and may be referenced only inside that method. (If you ever hear programmers referring to a local variable, this is what they mean most often: a variable declared inside a method and accessible only inside that method.)

That is, outside the method that defines the variable, the variable doesn't appear to exist! This means you cannot declare a variable inside one method and then refer to that same variable inside another method. Here's an example that will never compile:

```
public class Triangle extends java.applet.Applet {

    void displayArea() {
        int area;
        int base;
        int height;
```

```
    base = 5;
    height = 6;
    findArea();

    System.out.println("The area is " + area);
}

void findArea() {
    area = (base * height) / 2; // Does not compile!
}
```

This code *would* compile fine if the variables declared inside the method displayArea() were accessible to the method findArea(). However, they are not. Since findArea() knows nothing about variables declared in another method, the compiler will complain about undeclared variables if you do attempt to compile this.

If you do declare variables named area, base, and height inside findArea(), these would be considered different variables altogether. A variable named base in displayArea(), for example, would know nothing about a variable named base in findArea(). That is, changing base in findArea() would not affect base in displayArea(), and each method could use its own local variable named base independently of the other.

Communicating Between Methods

So, then, how can methods communicate with each other? How can one method tell another method to use a particular value in a calculation? How can a method return the result of a calculation to the method that invoked it? Java, of course, provides a way to do this. Instead of sharing local variables, you pass data between methods.

Some methods require you to supply them with data when you invoke them. Whether you have to supply data or not depends on how the method is defined. Methods require data when they need help performing a particular task. Values you might provide include numbers to be used in calculations or messages that should appear on the screen. In the preceding example, findArea() could be defined as taking the values for the area and height. That would enable display-Area() to pass findArea() the values to use in the calculation.

Some methods return a result to the code that invoked it. Again, whether a method returns a result or not depends on how it is defined. Results returned by a method might include the value of a calculation or whether the method was successful or not in carrying out its task. In our triangle example, findArea() could return the area it calculated back to displayArea(). That would enable display-Area() to use findArea() to perform the calculation and display the result provided by findArea().

In the case of writeColors(), this method does not return a value, nor does it need any values from the code invoking it to write out the seven rainbow colors. This is a simple method, but we left unanswered the meaning of the keyword void as well as the empty parentheses after the method name. Now that we've gotten our feet wet, let's start looking at the details of invoking and writing methods.

Whether you supply any data to the method you invoke or whether the method returns a result depends on how the method you invoke has been defined. If you do supply some data to the method and if the method does return a result, invoking a method could be diagrammed as in Figure 7.2.

For another example, you might have a method that finds the average of two numbers called findAverage(). This type of method would be quite different from writeColors(). First, it would be useful to be able to supply findAverage() with the two numbers for which you want to find the average. Second, it would be great if findAverage() returned the result of this calculation back to the method that invoked it.

To perform the calculation that finds the average of two numbers, you would use variables and operators very similar to those in the triangle example, like this:

```
int average;
average = (num1 + num2) / 2;
```

This code does not yet show the variables num1 and num2 being defined and assigned values, but we'll get to that in a moment. For now, just know they are int values that have been initialized to the values for which we want to find the average.

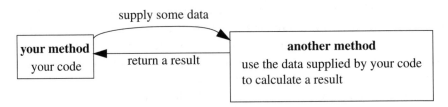

Figure 7.2 Invoking a method that uses some data you supply to calculate and return a result.

To turn this code into its own method, you can wrap this code in a method definition. Here's an outline of what the method definition might look like (we'll turn this into Java code in a moment):

```
define a method that returns an int and accepts two ints {
    calculate the average of the two ints
    return the average
}
```

At any time, you can find the average of two numbers by invoking this method. This would occur as depicted in Figure 7.3.

Take a look at how you would invoke this method in Java. In this example, we're finding the average for two numbers, 10 and 20:

```
int average = findAverage(10, 20);
```

As you can see, we're supplying two numbers to `findAverage()`. We supply the values to `findAverage()` inside the parentheses, separating the values by using a comma (,). Remember, when we invoked `writeColors()` previously, like this,

```
writeColors();
```

we just used an empty set of parentheses because `writeColors()` did not take any values. That is, `writeColors()` was self-sufficient; it had all the information it needed to write out the colors of the rainbow. However, `findAverage()` needs to know which values it should use in its calculation.

Somehow, `findAverage()` is calculating the average of these two numbers (but notice our own code does not need to concern itself with how this is accomplished). Once the average is determined, `findAverage()` returns this value. We assign the value it returns—in this case, 15—to our own variable, which we've

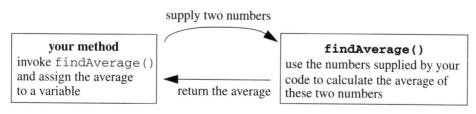

Figure 7.3   Invoking a method to find the average of two numbers.

named average. We do this assignment using the assignment operator, =, just as if we were assigning a number instead of invoking a method. That is,

```
int average = 15;
```

and

```
int average = findAverage(10, 20);
```

are both perfectly valid statements in Java, as long as findAverage() returns an int value.

Defining Parameters and Return Values

Now let's write the method that finds the average. We already know what the **body** of the method will be—that is, what the chunk of code will look like that performs the calculation. We've already written this code, here it is again:

```
int average;
average = (num1 + num2) / 2;
```

The Keyword return

The way that we return a value from a method is to use the keyword return followed by the value we would like to return. So, to return the value contained in the variable named average, we would write

```
return average;
```

To return a number directly, we can just write out the number. For example, this code shows the value 0 being returned:

```
return 0;
```

If findAverage() did *not* receive any data when it was invoked, it would be defined like this:

```
int findAverage() {

    int average;

    average = (num1 + num2) / 2; // Does not compile!
    return average;
}
```

As with `writeColors()`, all of the method's statements are contained between a left curly brace and a right curly brace. The method definition indicates that it returns an `int` value, as you can tell by the keyword `int` preceding the method name. With `writeColors()`, we used the keyword `void` to indicate `writeColors()` did not return a value at all.

Parameters

This would be a complete method definition, except for one thing: We have not yet declared or initialized the variables `num1` and `num2`. If `findAverage()` did not provide a way to set `num1` and `num2`—for example, if it always used the same values, such as 10 and 30—then we could write our `findAverage()` method as follows:

```
int findAverage() {

    int num1 = 10;
    int num2 = 30;
    int average;

    average = (num1 + num2) / 2;
    return average;
}
```

This code would compile and run just fine. However, this would not make `findAverage()` particularly flexible or useful.

Rather, we would prefer to invoke `findAverage()` as we did in the previous section, supplying the values for `num1` and `num2` ourselves, not leaving them "hard-coded" to 10 and 30 in the `findAverage()` method itself. To accomplish this, we place the variable definitions between the parentheses after the method name, like this:

```
int findAverage(int num1, int num2) {

    int average;

    average = (num1 + num2) / 2;
    return average;
}
```

Now, this method definition indicates that it accepts two int values when it is invoked and that it also returns a value of type int. You can see how this definition matches up to an invocation of this method, such as

```
int result = findAverage(10, 20);
```

The value 10 is assigned to the variable num1, and the value 20 is assigned to the variable num2. Inside findAverage(), the calculation for the average of these two numbers takes place, and the result is assigned to the variable named average. Then, the value of average—in this case, 15—is returned by findAverage(). The calling code assigns this returned value to the variable it named result.

Detail

> Notice that we have defined the variable result and used it in a statement all on one line. This is perfectly valid in Java. Also, we have not yet learned what to do with values that are fractional other than truncating them. For example, if we found the average of 1 and 2, the calculation would yield 1.5. We'll learn how to deal with these types of values in Chapter 12.

You must always be certain to match up the way you invoke a method with the method's definition. If the method takes three values (or **parameters** in programmer parlance), you should supply these three parameters whenever you invoke the method. Anything else would cause the compiler to complain and not compile your program. For example, given a method like this,

```
int findAverage(int num1, int num2, int num3) {
    int average = (num1 + num2 + num3) / 3;
    return average;
}
```

you would need to supply three values when you invoked it, like this:

```
int result = findAverage(10, 20, 30);
```

That is, if findAverage() took three parameters, invoking it by

```
int result = findAverage(10, 20);
```

wouldn't cut it.

Ways to Use return

There are several ways to use `return`. If your method does not require you to re-turn a value, you can exit a method immediately by using this statement:

```
return;
```

This statement returns control back to the code that invoked this method right away, without executing the rest of the method's code after the `return` statement.

You should only use this type of `return` statement, without a value, if your method is declared as not returning a value—that is, if it is declared as `void`. You'll receive an error from the compiler if you try to use this plain `return` statement in a method that indicates it returns a value, as in a method declared as

```
int addTheseNumber(int num1, int num2) {
    int sum = num1 + num2;
    return;
}
```

This definition for `addTheseNumbers()` indicates it will return a value of type `int`—but then the method forgets to return a value with the `return` statement! The compiler will complain about this.

Here are two versions of valid `return` statements for `addTheseNumbers()`. The first is

```
return (num1 + num2);
```

This statement first adds `num1` to `num2` and returns the result, without the need for declaring a variable named `sum`. You can also write the same thing like this:

```
return num1 + num2;
```

Notice that the second version does not include any parentheses. Either of these forms is fine.

Designing with Methods

What's the advantage of creating methods? With methods, you can create chunks of code that perform specific tasks. This is a great help to software development because it enables you to think about parts of your programs in high-level sections rather than always thinking in terms of the details.

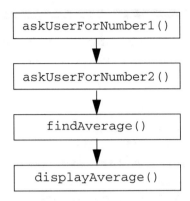

Figure 7.4 One method invoking each of these four other methods in turn, one after the other.

You might be beginning to see how you can use methods in your own programs. If you wanted to ask the user for two numbers, find the average for these two numbers, and then display the result, you could segment your own program into four methods, each performing a particular task. This is diagrammed in Figure 7.4. Here is the code:

```
askUserForNumber1();
askUserForNumber2();
findAverage();
displayAverage();
```

You could also segment this further. For example, the two methods askUserForNumber1() and askUserForNumber2() are probably very similar. Rather than duplicating code between them, you can collect the similar code into a single method, perhaps called getInput(). Now, askUserForNumber1() and askUserForNumber2() can each invoke getInput() to handle the common details. Figure 7.5 expands on Figure 7.4 to take this into account.

Taking Part in Your Applet's Life Cycle

So, you've slogged through the first part of this chapter and learned the basics of methods. You've learned how to write methods and how to invoke them, how to pass parameters to them and how to return values. Now it's time for the payoff. In this section, you'll learn how to tap into the dialog that takes place between your applet and the Web browser. (We'll talk about the browser in this chapter, but we mean the environment in which your applet is running, which will be an Applet Viewer if you are developing in CodeWarrior.)

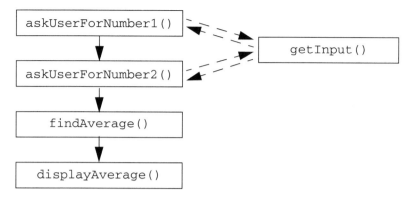

Figure 7.5 Creating a method called `getInput()` shared by two other methods.

What does the browser say to the applet? What can you (and should you) do when the browser talks to your applet? The short answer is that the browser controls what happens in the life of your applet, and you should do the things appropriate to a particular event in your applet's life. The way that a browser informs an applet of a particular stage of its life is by invoking a method. Aha! This is why we needed to understand methods before we got to this point!

Applets have a life. It's true. It's just that their lives are lived out in the computer. Applets are born; applets live; they awaken; they sleep; and they pass on. Before we step through the applet's life cycle, however, there is one detail about applets that we haven't covered yet and that it's time for you to know about.

Applet Classes and Instances

When we created our applets so far, we made them like this:

```
public class MyApplet extends java.applet.Applet {
}
```

Working with this class definition makes it appear that when we run an applet, we are working with the Applet class. This is true, but only up to a point. What's happening is this. First, the class is loaded into the browser. Then, any static initializer code is executed, as we've seen. Next, and most important, the browser *creates an object based on your Applet class*. That is, the browser **instantiates** (creates an **instance** of) your Applet class. At this point, your applet is born. Once this is accomplished, the browser begins trying to invoke **instance methods** for your applet object. This is illustrated in Figure 7.6.

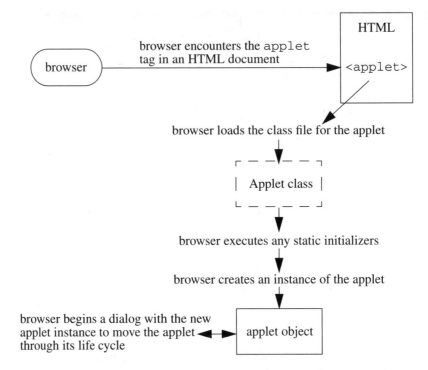

Figure 7.6 Diagram showing how the browser (or Applet Viewer) creates an instance of your Applet class and begins to interact with this object.

There is a different instance method corresponding to each stage of an applet's life. If you don't supply a method for a particular applet phase in life, that's fine. The browser doesn't care; it goes on its merry way. However, supplying a method is your big chance to insert your own behavior into your applet and make your applet unique.

The Applet Life Cycle

Here is the sequence of events that make up the life cycle of an applet:

1. First, an applet is born. This occurs when the applet is loaded into the browser and instantiated. As soon as the applet has been instantiated, the browser invokes the applet's init() method.

2. After the applet has been initialized, the browser starts it going. The browser invokes the applet's start() method.

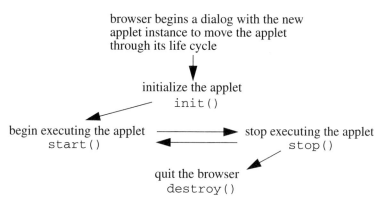

Figure 7.7 The life cycle of an applet.

3. If the user changes to a Web page other than the one that contains the applet, the applet goes to sleep. The browser invokes the applet's `stop()` method when this occurs. If the user turns back to the original Web page that did contain the applet, the applet wakes up. The browser invokes its `start()` method again when this occurs.

4. Finally, at some point when the applet is no longer needed, it goes away. This would occur if the user quit the browser, for example. At this point, the browser invokes the applet's `destroy()` method.

Figure 7.7 shows the life cycle of an applet.

Hooking In

You don't have to be a mere spectator to these events. Remember, you define your own Applet class. All you have to do to respond to these method invocations is to supply the appropriate method, defined as Java expects it to be defined. Here are the method definitions for each of the four life cycle methods just discussed:

```
public void init() {
}

public void start() {
}

public void stop() {
}

public void destroy() {
}
```

109

As you can see by these method definitions, the methods do not take any values as parameters and do not return a value. They must be declared as `public`. Since the Applet class as well as these methods are declared as `public`, these methods are able to be invoked from anywhere. (As you'll see in Chapter 10, only methods defined like this can be invoked from anywhere; other methods have restrictions.) For these four life cycle methods, this ability to be invoked from anywhere enables the browser to invoke these methods when it needs to tell the applet to enter a new phase in life.

You can decide to implement any of these, none of these, or all of these, according to the needs of your applet. Mix and match as you please. As earlier examples have shown, you don't need to supply any of these methods for your applet if you don't want to.

What should you do with `init()`? Or `start()`? Or any of them? Here are some things that you might think about doing with each of these four methods:

- `init()`: This method is invoked only once in the applet's life—the very first time the user runs the applet. You might want to initialize your applet's user interface by creating windows, buttons, and other graphical elements. For example, the SimpleDraw applet provides an `init()` method to create the shape and color selection choices. `init()` is probably the method you'll use the most.

- `start()`: This method is invoked every time the browser starts up your applet. For example, if the user turns to the Web page containing this applet, `start()` will be invoked. If the user then turns to another page and then turns back, `start()` will be invoked again. This is different from `init()`, which is invoked only the very first time. If you are performing any animation or playing any sounds, you might want to start these going inside the `start()` method.

- `stop()`: This method is invoked every time the browser stops your applet. There will be one `stop()` invocation for every `start()`. You can take this time to halt any animation or sound that you might have begun in `start()`.

- `destroy()`: This method is invoked only once—at the very end of an applet's life. There will be one `destroy()` invocation for every `init()`. When the browser unloads the applet—for example, if the user quits the browser—this method will be invoked. You might take this time to free any resources you've allocated in the system. It's very likely that you'll hardly ever write a `destroy()` method.

There are a number of other methods that you can write for your applet that will be invoked in other situations. These include methods that let you know things like when the user clicked the mouse, when the user resized your applet, or when the user typed in text from the keyboard. You'll see a number of these other applet methods as you progress.

Sample Programs

The following three sample programs illustrate the basics of methods that we've covered in this chapter.

LifeCycle.µ

Let's take a look at the applet's life cycle as it unfolds when we run an applet. When you run an applet in a browser, the applet might bounce back and forth between the methods `start()` and `stop()`. If the user turns away from the Web page containing the applet, the browser will invoke the applet's `stop()` method. However, the browser will not yet destroy the applet. If the user turns back to the Web page containing the applet, the browser will invoke the applet's `start()` method again. Only when the user quits the browser (or the browser unloads the applet for some reason of its own) will the applet ever receive `destroy()`.

Since we're running the applet in the Applet Viewer, we can't simulate this behavior of stopping the applet and restarting it, but we can come close. At least, we can see the progression from `init()` to `start()` when we run the applet and then on to `stop()` and `destroy()` when we shut it down.

To see this, go to the subfolder `07.01 - life cycle` in the Learn Java Projects folder. Make this applet in the usual way (double-clicking the project file Life-Cycle.µ then selecting **Make** from the **Project** menu). Drop the file Life-Cycle.html onto the Metrowerks Java icon. The applet will start up inside the Applet Viewer, and you'll see messages in the Java Output window indicating that the browser did indeed invoke `init()` and `start()`. This is shown in Figure 7.8.

Now, close the Applet Viewer. This will end the LifeCycle application. The Applet Viewer will invoke the applet's `stop()` and `destroy()` methods. You can see these messages appear in the Java Output window, as shown in Figure 7.9.

Check out the source code by opening LifeCycle.java. The LifeCycle applet provides a method for each of the four stages in the applet's life. It implements `init()`, `start()`, `stop()`, and `destroy()`. All that the LifeCycle applet does with these methods is write a line to the Java Output window to let you know that they were invoked. Of course, you can do much more complicated things in these methods, from creating sophisticated user interfaces to starting animation and other multimedia effects. All we do here, however, is indicate that the Applet Viewer is in fact communicating with the applet to let it know what stage in life it has reached.

111

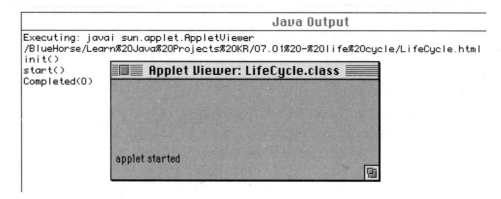

Figure 7.8 The LifeCycle applet after it has started running. (Notice that the Applet Viewer is still running, so the applet has not yet received `stop()` and `destroy()`.)

Figure 7.9 Closing the Applet Viewer so that the applet goes away. (The applet completes the rest of its life cycle methods by invoking `stop()` and `destroy()`.)

InitMethod.μ

By using the life cycle methods as hooks into your applet, you can customize your applet by invoking other methods. Go to the subfolder `07.02 - init` in the Learn Java Projects folder and double-click the project file `InitMethod.μ` to see an applet that illustrates this.

The applet defined here provides an `init()` method to invoke its own custom methods. The progression from the `init()` method to the custom methods is illustrated in Figure 7.10.

Make the applet. Then drop the HTML file in this folder onto the Metrowerks Java application, and you'll see the Java Output window reflect the progression of methods shown in Figure 7.10. Let's take a quick look at the source code to see how these methods are implemented.

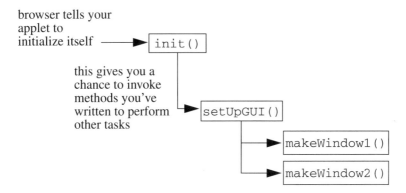

Figure 7.10 Executing your own methods from one of the life cycle methods.

Stepping Through the Source Code

The intent of this applet is to illustrate how you might combine your own methods with methods invoked for you by Java. For example, when you prepare a user interface by creating windows, text fields, buttons, and so on, you only want to create these user interface objects once and then just hang onto them for the life of the applet. The `init()` method is a good place to create a user interface since `init()` is executed only once during the life of an applet.

Open up the file `InitMethod.java` to browse the source code. Looking at this applet, you can see that it defines an `init()` method. The `init()` method invokes `setUpGUI()` after writing a message to the Java Output window:

```
public void init() {
    System.out.println("init()");
    setUpGUI();
}
```

The `setUpGUI()` method relies on two other methods, called `makeWindow1()` and `makeWindow2()`. These custom methods all write messages to the Java Output window, but they don't do anything else yet. You can see, however, how you can invoke your own methods at different times in the applet's life—in this case, when the applet is first loaded into the system. You'll use this technique all the time when writing your own applets.

Average.µ

You learned about parameters and return values in this chapter, so let's take a look at an applet that uses methods that take parameters and return values. Go to the subfolder named 07.03 - average in the Learn Java Projects folder. Make the applet and drop the file Average.html onto the Metrowerks Java icon. You'll see three lines appear in the Java Output window as illustrated in Figure 7.11. This applet uses a method that finds the average of three numbers. We've invoked this method three times and used System.out.println() each time to show the returned value in the Java Output window. Let's take a look at the source code.

Stepping Through the Source Code

Open Average.java to view the Java source code. Take a look at the top four lines of the start() method:

```
public void start() {

    int average;

    average = findAverage(10, 20, 30);
    System.out.println(average);
```

After declaring an int variable, start() invokes findAverage(). findAverage() takes three parameters, and these values are supplied as 10, 20, and 30. Since find-Average() returns an int value, the result of this method invocation is assigned to the variable average. The next line displays this result in the Java Output window.

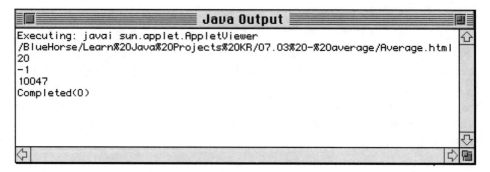

Figure 7.11 Displaying the average of three sets of numbers in the Java Output window.

After this, `start()` invokes `findAverage()` two more times, each time passing it a different set of parameters. `findAverage()` responds each time by performing the calculation for the average based on the parameters supplied to it and returns the result. Each time, the new result is assigned to `average` and displayed in the Java Output window:

```
average = findAverage(-400, 182, 213);
System.out.println(average);

average = findAverage(9901, 20201, 41);
System.out.println(average);
```

```
}
```

The method `findAverage()` is defined as follows:

```
int findAverage(int num1, int num2, int num3) {
    return (num1 + num2 + num3)/3;
}
```

`findAverage()`'s three `int` parameters are declared as `num1`, `num2`, and `num3`. From the method declaration, you can see that `findAverage()` returns an `int` value. This means it must provide a `return` statement that returns an `int`. `findAverage()` uses some of the arithmetic operators you saw in Chapter 6 to calculate the average for the three parameters. It then returns the result of this calculation.

The first time `start()` invokes `findAverage()`, `num1` is equal to 10, `num2` is equal to 20, and `num3` is equal to 30. The second time `start()` invokes `findAverage()`, `num1` is equal to −400, `num2` is equal to 182, and `num3` is equal to 213. And the third time? You can probably guess by now by looking back at the `start()` method and seeing how it was invoked; `num1` is equal to 9901, `num2` is equal to 20201, and `num3` is equal to 41.

Review

This chapter explained how to define and invoke methods. You've learned that methods often invoke other methods and that methods can communicate with each other by passing parameters and returning values.

You've also seen what happens when the browser (or Applet Viewer) loads your Applet class and begins to run your applet. The browser creates an instance (that is, an object) based on your Applet class. The browser then tries to invoke its life cycle methods (`init()`, `start()`, `stop()`, and `destroy()`) so that the applet can do things like arrange its user interface or shut down when it is no longer on the screen. By supplying these methods for your applet, you can make your applet do the things you want it to do, when you want it to do them.

What's Next?

Now that you know how to write chunks of code called methods, let's next turn our attention to making these methods control what your program does. This means writing methods that make decisions, choose to execute one block of code over another block, and repeat certain statements to perform more complex operations. Chapter 8 covers these topics by looking at flow control. Armed with this knowledge, you'll be able to add sophisticated behavior to your objects in Chapter 9.

Chapter 8

Controlling Your Program's Flow

The previous chapter showed you how to write and invoke methods—methods that so far have followed a straightforward, sequential progression: The computer executed the first statement, then the second, then the third, and so on; and when it reached the end of the method, it returned.

There's much more to writing methods than that! One powerful feature of all programming languages is the ability to control the flow through your program. For example, you can write code that will execute only if a certain condition is met. You can write code that loops back to an earlier statement and begins again. You can write all sorts of fancy programs by using flow control. That's what this chapter will cover.

Boolean Values

Before we proceed, there's one more data type that we need to cover because we'll start to make reference to it here. This is data type `boolean`. A **Boolean value** can take only one of two values: true or false. Here's an example:

```
boolean javaIsFun;

javaIsFun = true;
```

You might also say

```
javaIsFun = false;
```

With Boolean values, there are no other possibilities, such as "sometimes" or "occasionally." It's either true or false. That's it. (In Java, the values `true` and `false` are part of the language.)

If you don't set the Boolean to anything, its value is false, as in

```
boolean dinosaursArePurple;
```

At this point, `dinosaursArePurple` has the value of false (which *is* the case, isn't it?).

You'll soon see that Boolean values have many uses in Java. This simple data type allows for the creation of some very sophisticated programs!

By the Way

What kind of word is *Boolean* anyway? This term was derived from the name of a 19th-century mathematician named George Boole. Boole determined the rules involving operands that could only take the values of true or false. It was more than a century later before his rules were applied to the field of computer science, where they were found to be crucial to computer and software design. Hence, from Boole, we have Boolean values represented by the data type `boolean`.

In preceding chapters, we've written a number of simple methods; now it's time to go further. Here, you'll learn a few advanced ways to implement your methods that draw upon the computer's abilities to test for certain conditions. After the computer has performed a test—say, by testing whether one number is less than another number—the computer can execute different steps depending on the outcome of that test.

This chapter borrows heavily from Chapter 6 of *Learn C on the Macintosh*, by Dave Mark. The two chapters are not identical, however, since there are a number of differences between C and Java. Legions of C programmers have successfully learned all about flow control with *Learn C on the Macintosh*, so who are we to tinker with success?

Flow Control

The programs you've written so far have all consisted of a straightforward series of statements, one right after the other. Every statement is executed in the order it occurred.

Flow control is the ability to define the order in which your program's statements are executed. Java provides several keywords you can use in your program to control your program's flow. One of these is the keyword `if`.

The `if` Statement

The keyword `if` allows you to choose among several options in your program. In English, you might say something like this:

```
If it's raining outside, I'll bring my umbrella; otherwise, I won't.
```

In the previous sentence, you're using the word *if* to choose between two options. Depending on the weather, you'll do one of two things: You'll bring your umbrella, or you won't bring your umbrella.

Java's `if` statement gives you this same flexibility. Here's an example:

```
public class Tester extends java.applet.Applet {

    public void init() {

        int myInt = 5;

        if (myInt == 0)
            System.out.println("myInt is equal to zero.");
        else
            System.out.println("myInt is not equal to zero.");
    }
}
```

This applet, named Tester, defines an `init()` method. This method declares `myInt` to be of type `int` and sets the value of `myInt` to 5. Next, we use the `if` statement to test whether `myInt` is equal to 0. If `myInt` is equal to 0 (which we know is not true), we'll print one string; otherwise, we'll print a different string. As expected, this program prints the string

```
myInt is not equal to zero
```

Forms of the `if` Statement

An `if` statement can come in two forms. The first, known as plain `if`, fits this pattern:

```
if ( boolean expression )
    statement
```

An `if` statement will always consist of the keyword `if`, a left parenthesis, a *boolean expression*, a right parenthesis, and a *statement*. (We'll define what an expression is and what a statement is in a minute.) This first form of `if` executes the statement if the Boolean expression in parentheses is true. An English example of the plain `if` might be

```
If it's raining outside, I'll bring my umbrella.
```

Notice that this statement tells us what will happen only if it's raining outside. No particular action will be taken if it isn't raining.

The second form of `if`, known as `if-else`, fits this pattern:

```
if ( boolean expression )
    statement
else
    statement
```

An `if-else` statement will always consist of the keyword `if`, a left parenthesis, a *boolean expression*, a right parenthesis, a *statement*, the keyword `else`, and a second *statement*. This form of `if` executes the first statement if the Boolean expression is true and executes the second statement if the Boolean expression is false. An English example of an `if-else` statement might be

```
If it's raining outside, I'll bring my umbrella; otherwise, I won't.
```

Notice that this example tells us what will happen if it's raining outside (I'll bring my umbrella) and if it isn't raining outside (I won't bring my umbrella).

The example programs presented later in the chapter demonstrate the proper use of both `if` and `if-else`. Our next step at this point is to define our terms.

Expressions

In Java, an **expression** is anything that has a value. Two kinds of expressions are: **numeric expressions**, which have numeric values, and **Boolean expressions**, which can only have the values of true or false.

Numeric Expressions

Variables that represent numbers, such as variables of type `int`, are a type of numeric expression since a variable will always have a value. (Remember, Java initializes your numeric variable to 0 for you if you don't assign it a value.) Here are some examples of numeric expressions:

```
myInt + 3

(myInt + anotherInt) * 4

myInt++
```

An assignment statement is also an expression. Can you guess the value of an assignment statement? The value of an assignment statement is the value of its left side after the assignment. Check out the following code fragment:

```
myInt = 5;
myInt += 3;
```

Both of these statements qualify as expressions. The value of the first expression is 5. The value of the second expression is 8 (because we added 3 to `myInt`'s previous value).

Boolean Expressions

Earlier, we defined the `if` statement as follows:

```
if ( boolean expression )
    statement
```

We then said that the statement gets executed if the expression is true. Let's look at Java's concept of truth.

Everyone has an intuitive understanding of the difference between true and false. We would all agree that the following statement is false:

```
5 equals 3
```

We would also agree that the following statement is true:

```
5 and 3 are both greater than 0
```

This intuitive grasp of true and false carries over into the Java language. So, a Boolean expression is an expression that can be evaluated in terms of truth or falsehood. Note that Boolean expressions are different from numeric expressions. You cannot write Java code like this:

```
int myInt = 27;

if ( myInt )   // this won't work!
    System.out.println("myInt is not equal to 0");
```

This code is not allowed in Java, and the compiler will tell you in no uncertain terms. The compiler will complain that myInt in the line of code

```
if ( myInt )
```

is a numeric expression. The Java compiler requires the expression in the if statement to evaluate to true or false. Before we see how to turn this line of code into a Boolean statement that Java will accept, let's take a look at comparative operators.

Comparative Operators

Java has a special set of operators called **comparative operators**. A comparative operator compares its left side with its right side and produces a value of either true or false, depending on the relationship of the two sides.

For example, the operator == determines whether the expression on the left is equal in value to the expression on the right. In the following, the expression evaluates to true if myInt is equal to 5 and to false if myInt is not equal to 5:

```
myInt == 5
```

Here's an example of the == operator at work:

```
if (myInt == 5)
    System.out.println("myInt is equal to 5");
```

If myInt is equal to 5, the Boolean expression myInt == 5 evaluates to true and System.out.println() gets executed. If myInt isn't equal to 5, the Boolean expression evaluates to false and System.out.println() is skipped. Just remember, the key to triggering an if statement is a Boolean expression that evaluates to true.

Table 8.1 shows some other comparative operators. You'll see some of these operators in the example programs later in this chapter.

Table 8.1   Some comparative operators.

Operator	Resolves to true if...
==	left side is equal to right.
<=	left side is less than or equal to right.
>=	left side is greater than or equal to right.
<	left side is less than right.
>	left side is greater than right.
!=	left side is not equal to right.

Back in the last section, we saw some code that would not compile in Java because the expression in the `if` statement was not a Boolean expression:

```
int myInt = 27;

if ( myInt )   // this won't work!
    System.out.println("myInt is not equal to 0");
```

Knowing what we now know about the comparative operators, how can we fix this code? One way to make this work is instead of writing

```
if ( myInt )
```

you can write

```
if ( myInt != 0 )
```

The expression `myInt != 0` is now a Boolean expression that has a true or false value: Either `myInt` is equal to 0 or it is not. The operator `!=` means "is not equal to."

Logical Operators

Our next set of operators, collectively known as **logical operators**, is modeled on the mathematical concept of truth tables. If you don't know much about truth tables (or are just frightened by mathematics in general), don't panic. Everything you need to know is outlined in the next few paragraphs.

The first of the set of logical operators is the ! operator. The ! operator turns true into false and false into true. Table 8.2 shows the truth table for the ! operator.

Table 8.2 Truth table for the ! operator.

(boolean expression)	(!boolean expression)
true	false
false	true

If the Boolean expression is true, applying the ! operator to the same expression yields the value false. If the expression is false, applying the ! operator to the same expression yields the value true. The ! operator is commonly referred to as the NOT operator; !A is pronounced "Not A."

Here's a piece of code that demonstrates the ! operator:

```
boolean  myFirstBoolean, mySecondBoolean;

myFirstBoolean = false;
mySecondBoolean = !myFirstBoolean;
```

In this code, we first declare two Booleans. We then assign the value `false` to the first Boolean, use the ! operator to turn the `false` into a `true`, and assign it to the second Boolean. This is very important. Take another look at Table 8.2. The ! operator converts true into false and false into true.

The previous chunk of code translated `mySecondBoolean` from `false` to `true`. Now, if we encounter the code

```
if (mySecondBoolean)
   System.out.println("mySecondBoolean must be true");
```

`System.out.println()` will get executed, and the message

```
mySecondBoolean must be true
```

will appear on the screen.

Now take a look at this piece of code:

```
if (!mySecondBoolean)
    System.out.println("mySecondBoolean must be false");
```

This time, `System.out.println()` will get executed if `mySecondBoolean` is false. Do you see why? If `mySecondBoolean` is false, then `!mySecondBoolean` must be true.

The `!` operator is a **unary** operator. Unary operators operate on a single expression (the expression to the right of the operator). The other two logical operators, `&&` and `||`, are **binary** operators. Binary operators, such as the `==` operator and all the other comparative operators presented earlier, operate on two expressions, one on the left side and one on the right side of the operator.

The `&&` operator is commonly referred to as the AND operator. The result of an `&&` operation is true if, and only if, both the left side and the right side are true.

Here's an example:

```
boolean  hasCar, hasTimeToGiveRide;

hasCar = true;
hasTimeToGiveRide = true;

if (hasCar && hasTimeToGiveRide)
    System.out.println("Hop in - I'll give you a ride!");
else
    System.out.println("I've either got no car, no time, or neither");
```

This example uses two variables. One indicates whether the program has a car; the other, whether the program has time to give us a ride to the mall. All philosophical issues aside (Can a program have a car?), the question of the moment is, Which `System.out.println()` statement will fire? Since both sides of the `&&` were set to `true`, the first `System.out.println()` will be invoked. If either one (or both) of the variables were set to `false`, the second `System.out.println()` would be invoked. Another way to think of this is that we'll get a ride to the mall only if our friendly program has a car *and* has time to give us a ride. If either of these is not true, we're not getting a ride. By the way, notice the use here of the second form of `if`: the `if-else` statement.

The || operator is commonly referred to as the OR operator. The result of an || operation is true if either the left side or the right side, or both sides, of the || are true. Put another way, the result of an || is false if, and only if, both the left side and the right side of the || are false.

Here's an example:

```
boolean   nothingElseOn, newEpisode;

nothingElseOn = true;
newEpisode = true;

If (newEpisode || nothingElseOn)
   System.out.println("Let's watch Star Trek!");
else
   System.out.println("Something else is on and I've seen this one.");
```

This example uses two variables to decide whether we should watch "Star Trek" (your choice: Classic Trek, TNG, DS9, or Captain Kate). One variable indicates whether anything else is on right now, and the other tells you whether this episode is a rerun. If this is a brand-new episode *or* if nothing else is on, we'll watch "Star Trek."

Here's a slight twist on the previous example:

```
boolean   nothingElseOn, itsARerun;

nothingElseOn = true;
itsARerun = false;

if ( (!itsARerun) || nothingElseOn )
   System.out.println("Let's watch Star Trek!");
else
   System.out.println("Something else is on and its a rerun");
```

This time, we've replaced the variable newEpisode with its exact opposite, itsARerun. Look at the logic that drives the if statement (you don't need to be Spock or Tuvok to figure it out!). We're combining itsARerun with the ! operator. Before, we cared whether the episode was a new episode. This time, we are concerned that the episode is not a rerun.

Both the && and the || operators are summarized in Table 8.3. If you look in the folder Learn Java Projects, you'll find a subfolder named 08.01 - truth tester. The file truthTester.java contains the three examples we just went through. Take some time to play with the code. Take turns changing the variables from `true` to `false` and back again. Use this code to get a good feel for the `!`, `&&`, and `||` operators.

Table 8.3 Truth table for the `&&` and `||` operators.

expression A	expression B	expression A `&&` expression B	expression A `||` expression B
true	true	true	true
true	false	false	true
false	true	false	true
false	false	false	false

Detail

There's another operator supplied by Java that affects flow control. This operator is not used very often, but you might see it around. This operator is written as `?:` (yes, you're reading that right: "question-mark colon"), and it allows your program to do one of two things, depending on a Boolean expression. Here's the format:

```
boolean expression ? action if true : action if false
```

This is somewhat the same as

```
if ( boolean expression )
    action if true
else
    action if false
```

except that the `?:` operator can be a little more compact at times.

One thing this operator is particularly useful for is assigning a value to a variable based on a Boolean expression. For example, you can assign a string object to a new string instance, depending on the result of a Boolean expression, like this:

(continued)

127

```
int i = 5;
String s = i < 3 ? new String ("i < 3") : new String ("i >= 3");
```

In this case, the string s would hold the text "i >= 3" at the end of these two statements. Check out examples on the Web at JavaSoft's site and turn to the Java Language Specifications for more information. You can also look in Dave Mark's *Learn C on the Macintosh* for some good examples and advice concering this operator.

Compound Expressions

All of the examples presented so far have consisted of relatively simple expressions. Here's an example that combines several operators:

```
int   myInt;

myInt = 7;

if ( (myInt >= 1) && (myInt <= 10) )
    System.out.println("myInt is between 1 and 10");
else
    System.out.println("myInt is not between 1 and 10");
```

This example tests whether a variable is in the range between 1 and 10.
    The key here is the expression

```
(myInt >= 1) && (myInt <= 10)
```

This expression lies between the if statement's parentheses and uses the && operator to combine two smaller expressions. Notice that the two smaller expressions are each surrounded by parentheses to avoid any ambiguity.

Statements

Near the beginning of the chapter, we defined the if statement as

```
if ( boolean expression )
    statement
```

We've covered expressions quite thoroughly. Now, we'll turn our attention to statements.

At this point in the book, you probably have a pretty good intuitive model of the statement. You would probably agree that this is a statement:

```
myInt = 7;
```

But is the following one statement or two?

```
if (isCold)
    System.out.println("Put on your sweater!");
```

The previous code fragment is a statement within another statement. The `System.out.println()` resides within a larger statement, the `if` statement.

The ability to break your code out into individual statements is not a critical skill. Getting your code to compile, however, *is* critical. As we introduce new types of statements, pay attention to the statement syntax. And pay special attention to the examples. Where do the semicolons go? What distinguishes this type of statement from all other types?

As you build up your repertoire of statement types, you'll find yourself using one type of statement within another. That's perfectly acceptable in Java. In fact, every time you create an `if` statement, you'll use at least two statements, one within the other. Take a look at this example:

```
if (myVar >= 1)
    if (myVar <= 10)
        System.out.println("myVar is between 1 and 10");
```

This example uses an `if` statement as the statement for another `if` statement. It invokes `System.out.println()` if both `if` expressions are true—that is, if myVar is greater than or equal to 1 and less than or equal to 10. You could have accomplished the same result with this piece of code:

```
if ( (myVar >=1) && (myVar <=10) )
    System.out.println("myVar is between 1 and 10");
```

Take a look at another example:

```
if (myVar != 0)
    if ((1/myVar) < 1)
        System.out.println("myVar is in range");
```

One thing you don't want to do in Java is divide an `int` value by 0. Any `int` divided by 0 will cause Java to halt your program. (Actually, dividing by 0 would cause Java to "throw an exception," which would, by default, halt your program. You'll learn about exceptions later in this book.) In the preceeding example, the first expression tests to make sure that `myVar` is not equal to 0. If `myVar` is equal to 0, the second expression won't even be evaluated! The sole purpose of the first `if` is to make sure that the second `if` never tries to divide by 0.

Java is pretty smart about what to evaluate. Imagine what would happen if we wrote the code this way:

```
if ( (myVar != 0) && ((1 / myVar) < 1) )
    System.out.println("myVar is in range");
```

As it turns out, the left half of the `&&` operator evaluates to false, the right half of the expression will *never be evaluated*, and the entire expression will evaluate to false. Why? Because if the left operand is false, it doesn't matter what the right operand is; true or false, the expression will evaluate to false. Be aware of this as you construct your expressions.

Detail

> While `int` values will cause Java to stop your program if you divide them by 0, this is not true with floating-point values! In Java, floating-point values reflect the mathematical concept that division by zero is equal to infinity. Floating-point values understand the concept of infinity, and it is perfectly legal to divide Java's floating-point values by 0. You'll learn more about floating-point values soon.

Curly Braces Revisited

Earlier, you learned about the curly braces ({ }) that delimit the beginning and ending of classes and methods. These braces also play an important role in statement construction. Just as parentheses can be used to group terms of an expression together, curly braces can be used to group multiple statements together. Here's an example:

```
boolean lightIsOn;
lightIsOn = true;

if (lightIsOn) {
    System.out.println("turn off");
    lightIsOn = false;
}
```

In the example, if `lightIsOn` is true, both of the statements in curly braces will be executed. A pair of curly braces can be used to combine any number of statements into a single superstatement, also known as a **block**. You can use this technique anywhere a statement is called for.

Curly braces can be used to organize your code, much as you would use parentheses to ensure that an expression is evaluated properly. This concept is especially appropriate when dealing with nested statements. Consider this code, for example:

```
if (myInt >= 0)
    if (myInt <= 10)
        System.out.println("myInt is between 0 and 10");
else
    System.out.println("myInt is negative");
```

Do you see the problem with this code? It's tricky, but think about this: Which `if` does the `else` belong to? As written (and as formatted, which makes it tricky), the `else` looks as though it belongs to the first `if`. That is, if `myInt` is greater than or equal to 0, the second `if` is executed; otherwise, the second `System.out.println()` is invoked. Is this right?

Nope. As it turns out, an `else` belongs to the `if` closest to it (the second `if`, in this case). Here's a slight rewrite:

```
if (myInt >= 0)
    if (myInt <= 10)
        System.out.println("myInt is between 0 and 10");
    else
        System.out.println("myInt is not between 0 and 10");
```

One point here is that formatting is nice, but it won't fool the compiler. More important, this example shows how easy it is to make a mistake. Check out this version of the code:

```
if (myInt >= 0) {
    if (myInt <= 10)
        System.out.println("myInt is between 0 and 10");
} else
    System.out.println("myInt is negative");
```

Do you see how the curly braces help? In a sense, they act to hide the second if inside the first `if` statement. There is no chance for the `else` to connect to the hidden `if`.

Curly braces (as well as parentheses) are great for clarifying your code, and you should feel free to use them wherever it helps make your code more readable. No one we know ever got fired for using too many parentheses or too many curly braces.

Where to Place the Semicolon

So far, the statements we've seen fall into two categories. The first category is simple statements, and the second is compound statements.

Simple Statements

Method invocations, such as

```
addTheseNumbers(10, 20);
```

and assignment statements, such as

```
myBoolean = true;
```

are examples of **simple statements**. Always place a semicolon at the end of a simple statement, even if it is broken over several lines, like this:

```
System.out.println("Connect the dots using only four lines:

                    *    *    *
                    *    *    *
                    *    *    *");
```

Compound Statements

Statements made up of several parts—including, possibly, other statements—are called **compound statements**. Compound statements obey some pretty strict rules of syntax. The `if` statement, for example, always looks like this:

```
if ( boolean expression )
    statement
```

Notice there are no semicolons in this definition. The statement part of the `if` can be a simple statement or a compound statement. If the statement is simple, follow the semicolon rules for simple statements by placing a semicolon at the end of the statement:

```
if (x == 3)
    y = 4;
```

If the statement is compound, follow the semicolon rules for that particular type of statement:

```
if (x == 3)
    if (y == 2)
        z = 1;
```

The Loneliest Statement

A single semicolon qualifies as a statement, albeit a somewhat lonely one. For example,

```
if (bored)
    ;
```

is a code fragment that is a legitimate (and thoroughly useless) `if` statement. If `bored` is true, the semicolon statement gets executed. The semicolon by itself doesn't do anything but fill the bill where a statement was needed. There are times where the semicolon by itself is exactly what you need.

The while Statement

The `if` statement uses the value of an expression to decide whether to execute or to skip over a statement. If the statement is executed, it is executed just once. Another type of statement, the `while` statement, repeatedly executes a statement as long as a specified expression is true. The `while` statement follows this pattern:

```
while ( boolean expression )
    statement
```

The `while` statement is also known as a `while` **loop** because after the statement is executed, the `while` loops back to reevaluate the expression (Figure 8.1). If the result of the expression is true, the statement is executed, and then the

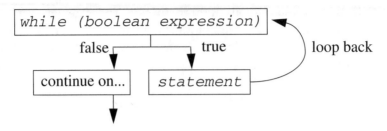

Figure 8.1 A diagram of the `while` loop.

expression is evaluated again. If the expression is false, the statement is skipped, and the program continues on.

Here's an example of the `while` loop in action:

```
int i;

i = 0;

while (++i < 3)
    System.out.println("Looping: " + i);

System.out.println("We are past the while loop");
```

This example starts by declaring a variable, i, to be of type int; i is then initialized to 0. Next comes the `while` loop. The first thing the `while` loop does is evaluate its expression. The `while` loop's expression is

```
++i < 3
```

Before this expression is evaluated, i has a value of 0. The prefix notation used in the expression (++i) increments the value of i to 1 before the remainder of the expression is evaluated. The evaluation of the expression results in true since 1 is less than 3. Since the expression is true, the `while` loop's statement, a single `System.out.println()` statement, is executed. Here's the output after the first pass through the loop:

```
Looping: 1
```

Next, the `while` loops back and reevaluates its expression. Once again, the prefix notation increments i, this time to a value of 2. Since 2 is less than 3, the expression evaluates to true, and the `System.out.println()` is executed again. Here's the output after the second pass through the loop:

```
Looping: 1
Looping: 2
```

Once the second `System.out.println()` completes, it's back to the top of the loop to reevaluate the expression. Will this never end? Once again, i is incremented, this time to a value of 3. Aha! This time, the expression evaluates to false since 3 is not less than 3. Once the expression evaluates to false, the `while` loop ends. Control passes to the next statement, the second `System.out.println()` in our example:

```
System.out.println("We are past the while loop");
```

The `while` loop was driven by three factors: **initialization**, **modification**, and **termination**. Initialization is any code that affects the loop but occurs before the loop is entered. In our example, the critical initialization occurred when the variable i was set to 0.

Style

In a loop, you'll frequently use a variable that changes value each time through the loop. In our example, the variable i was incremented by 1 each time through the loop. The first time through the loop, i had a value of 1. The second time, i had a value of 2. Variables that maintain a value based on the number of times through a loop are known as **counters**.

Traditionally, programmers have given counter variables simple names, such as i, j, and k (as mentioned earlier, this is an old FORTRAN convention). In the interest of clarity, some programmers use such names as `counter` or `loopCounter`. The nice thing about names like i, j, and k is that they don't get in the way; they don't take up a lot of space on the line. On the other hand, your goal should be to make your code as readable as possible, so it would seem that a name like `counter` would be better than the uninformative i, j, or k.

Once again, pick a style you are comfortable with and stick with it!

Within the loop, modification is any code that changes the value of the loop's expression. In our example, the modification occurred within the expression itself when the counter i was incremented.

Termination is any condition that causes the loop to end. In our example, termination occurs when the expression has a value of false. This occurs when the counter i has a value that is not less than 3. Take a look at this example:

```
int i;

i = 1;

while (i < 3) {
    System.out.println("Looping: " + i);
    i++;
}

System.out.println("We are past the while loop");
```

This example produces the same results as the previous example. This time, however, the initialization and modification conditions have changed slightly. In this example, i starts with a value of 1 instead of 0. In the previous example, the ++ operator was used to increment i at the *top of the loop*. This example modifies i at the *bottom of the loop*.

Both of these examples show different ways to accomplish the same end. The expression "There's more than one way to eat an Oreo" sums up the situation perfectly. There will always be more than one solution to any programming problem. Don't be afraid to do things your own way. Just make sure that your code works properly and is easy to read.

The for Statement

Another way to control loops in your program is by using the for statement. The for statement is similar to the while statement, following the basic model of initialization, modification, and termination. Here's the pattern for the for statement:

```
for ( initialization expression; test expression; modification
expression )
    statement
```

The first expression represents the for statement's initialization. Typically, this expression consists of an assignment statement, setting the initial value of a counter variable. This first expression is evaluated once, at the top of the loop.

The second expression is identical in function to the expression in a `while` statement, providing the termination condition for the loop. This expression is evaluated and tested each time through the loop, before the statement is executed.

Finally, the third expression provides the modification portion of the `for` statement. This expression is evaluated at the bottom of the loop, immediately following execution of the statement.

Warning

All three of these expressions are optional and may be left out entirely. For example, here's a `for` loop that leaves out all three expressions:

```
for ( ; ; )
    doSomethingForever();
```

Since this loop has no terminating expression, it is known as an **infinite loop**. Infinite loops are generally considered bad form and should be avoided like the plague!

The `for` loop can also be described in terms of a `while` loop:

```
initialization expression;
while ( test expression ) {
    statement
    modification expression;
}
```

By the Way

Since you can always rewrite a `for` loop as a `while` loop, why introduce the `for` loop at all? Sometimes, a programming idea fits more naturally into the pattern of a `for` statement. If the `for` loop makes the code more readable, why not use it? As you write more and more code, you'll develop a sense of when to use the `while` and when to use the `for`.

Here's an example of a `for` loop:

```
int i;

for (i = 1; i < 3; i++)
    System.out.println("Looping: " + i);

System.out.println("We are past the for loop");
```

This example is identical in functionality to the `while` loops presented earlier.

Note the three expressions on the first line of the `for` loop. Before the loop is entered, the first expression is evaluated:

```
i = 1
```

Once the expression is evaluated, `i` has a value of 1. We are now ready to enter the loop. At the top of each pass through the loop, the second expression is evaluated:

```
i < 3
```

If the expression evaluates to true, the loop continues. Since `i` is less than 3, we can proceed. Next, the statement is executed:

```
System.out.println("Looping: " + i);
```

Here's the first line of output:

```
Looping: 1
```

Having reached the bottom of the loop, the `for` evaluates its third expression:

```
i++
```

This changes the value of `i` to 2. Back to the top of the loop we go to evaluate the termination expression:

```
i < 3
```

Since `i` is still less than 3, the loop continues. Once again, the `System.out.println()` does its thing. The Java Output window looks like this:

```
Looping: 1
Looping: 2
```

Next, the `for` evaluates the third expression:

```
i++
```

The value of `i` is incremented to 3. Back to the top of the loop we go again to evaluate the termination expression:

```
i < 3
```

Lo and behold! Since `i` is no longer less than 3, the loop ends, and the second `Sys-tem.out.println()` in our example is executed:

```
System.out.println("We are past the for loop");
```

As was the case with `while`, `for` can take full advantage of a pair of curly braces:

```
for (i = 0; i < 10; i++) {
    doThis();
    doThat();
    danceALittleJig();
}
```

In addition, both `while` and `for` can take advantage of the loneliest statement, the lone semicolon:

```
for (i = 0; i < 1000; i++)
    ;
```

This example does nothing 1000 times but does take some time to execute. The initialization expression is evaluated once, and the modification and termination expressions are each evaluated 1000 times. Here's a `while` version of the loneliest loop:

```
i = 0;

while (i++ < 1000)
    ;
```

LoopTester.μ

Interestingly, there is an important difference between the `for` and `while` loops you just saw. Take a minute to look back and try to predict the value of `i` the first time through each loop and *after* each loop terminates. Were the results the same for the `while` and `for` loops? Hmmm.... You might want to take another look.

Here's a sample program that should clarify the difference between these two loops. Look in the subfolder `08.02 - loop tester` in the Learn Java Projects folder. Compile the project by using the **Make** command, and then run the applet by dropping the file `LoopTester.html` onto the Metrowerks Java icon. The Java Output window will display output from a variety of loops, as shown in Figure 8.2.

Open the file `LoopTester.java` to view the source code for this applet. The LoopTester applet starts off in `init()` by defining a counter variable, i. It then sets i to 0 and enters a `while` loop:

```
while (i++ < 4)
    System.out.println("while: i=" + i);
```

The loop executes four times, resulting in this output:

```
while: i=1
while: i=2
while: i=3
while: i=4
```

Do you see why? If not, go through the loop yourself, calculating the value for i each time through the loop. Remember, since we are using postfix notation (i++), i gets incremented *after* the test is made to see whether it is less than 4. The test and the increment happen at the top of the loop, before the loop is entered.

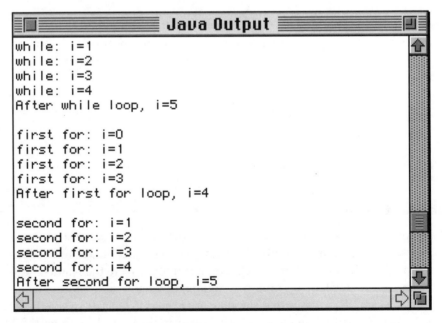

Figure 8.2 The output from `LoopTester.μ`, showing the output from three different loops.

Once the loop completes, we print the value of i again:

```
System.out.println("After while loop, i=" + i);
```

Here's the result:

```
After while loop, i=5
```

Here's how we got that value. The last time through the loop (with i equal to 4), we go back to the top of the while loop, test to see whether i is less than 4 (it no longer is), and then do the increment of i, bumping it from 4 to 5.

OK, one loop down, two to go. This next loop looks as if it should accomplish the same thing. The difference is that we don't do the increment of i until the bottom of the loop, until we've been through the loop once already:

```
for (i = 0; i < 4; i++)
    System.out.println("first for: i=" + i);
```

As you can see by the output, i ranges from 0 to 3 instead of from 1 to 4:

```
first for: i=0
first for: i=1
first for: i=2
first for: i=3
```

After we drop out of the for loop, we once again print the value of i:

```
System.out.println("After first for loop, i=" + i);
```

Here's the result:

```
After first for loop, i=4
```

As you can see, the while loop ranged i from 1 to 4, leaving i with a value of 5 at the end of the loop. The for loop ranged i from 0 to 3, leaving i with a value of 4 at the end of the loop. So how do we fix the for loop so that it works the same way as the while loop? Take a look at our third loop example:

```
for (i = 1; i <= 4; i++)
    System.out.println("second for: i=" + i);
```

141

This `for` loop starts i at 1 instead of 0, and it tests to see whether i is *less than or equal to* 4 instead of just less than 4. We could also have used the terminating expression i < 5 instead. Either one will work. Here's the output from this loop:

```
second for: i=1
second for: i=2
second for: i=3
second for: i=4
```

Once again, we print the value of i at the end of the loop:

```
System.out.println("After second for loop, i=" + i);
```

Here's the last piece of output:

```
After second for loop, i = 5
```

This second `for` loop is the functional equivalent of the `while` loop. Take some time to play with this code. You might try to modify the `while` loop to match the first `for` loop.

The `while` and `for` statements are by far the most common types of Java loops. For completeness, however, we'll cover the remaining loop, a little-used gem called the `do` statement.

The `do` Statement

The `do` statement is a `while` statement that evaluates its expression at the bottom of its loop instead of at the top. Here's the pattern a `do` statement must match:

```
do
    statement
while ( expression );
```

Here's an example:

```
i = 1;

do {
    System.out.println(i);
    i++;
} while (i < 3);

System.out.println("We are past the do loop");
```

The first time through the loop, i has a value of 1. System.out.println() prints a 1 in the Java Output window, and then the value of i is bumped to 2. It's not until this point that the expression i < 3 is evaluated. Since 2 is less than 3, a second pass through the loop occurs.

During this second pass, System.out.println() prints 2 in the Java Output window, and then the value of i is bumped to 3. Once again, the expression i < 3 is evaluated. Since 3 is not less than 3, we drop out of the loop to the second System.out.println().

The important thing to remember about do loops is this: Since the expression is not evaluated until the bottom of the loop, the body of the loop (the statement) is always executed at least once. Since for and while loops both check their expressions at the top of the loop, it's possible for either to drop out of the loop before the body of the loop is executed.

Let's move on to a completely different type of statement, known as the switch.

The switch Statement

The switch statement uses the value of an expression to determine which of a series of statements to execute. Here's an example that should make this concept a little clearer:

```
switch (theYear) {
    case 1066:
        System.out.println("Battle of Hastings");
        break;
    case 1492:
        System.out.println("Columbus sailed the ocean blue");
        break;
    case 1776:
        System.out.println("Declaration of Independence");
        System.out.println("A very important document!");
        break;
    default:
        System.out.println("Don't know what happened this year");
}
```

The switch is constructed of a series of case statements, each based on a specific value of theYear. If theYear has a value of 1066, execution continues with the statement following that case's colon—in this example, the line

```
System.out.println("Battle of Hastings");
```

143

Execution continues, line after line, until either the bottom of the `switch` (the right curly brace) or a `break` statement is reached. In this sample code, the next line is a `break` statement.

The `break` statement comes in handy when you are working with `switch` statements and loops. The `break` tells the computer to jump immediately to the next statement after the end of a loop or `switch`.

Continuing with the example, if `theYear` has a value of 1492, the `switch` jumps to the lines

```
System.out.println("Columbus sailed the ocean blue");
break;
```

A value of 1776 jumps to the lines

```
System.out.println("Declaration of Independence");
System.out.println("A very important document!");
break;
```

Notice that this `case` has two statements before the `break`. There is no limit to the number of statements a `case` can have: One is OK; 653 is OK. You can even have a `case` with no statements at all.

This example also contains a `default`. If the `switch` can't find a `case` that matches the value of its expression, the `switch` looks for a `default`. If the `default` is present, its statements are executed. If no `default` is present, the `switch` completes without executing any of its statements.

Here's the pattern for the `switch` statement:

```
switch ( expression ) {
   case constant:
      statements
   case constant:
      statements
   default:
      statements
}
```

Detail

Why would you want a case with no statements? Here's an example:

```
switch (myVar) {
    case 1:
    case 2:
        doSomething();
        break;
    case 3:
        doSomethingElse();
}
```

In this example, if myVar has a value of 1 or 2, the method doSomething() is invoked. If myVar has a value of 3, the method doSomethingElse() is invoked. If myVar has any other value, nothing happens. Use a case with no statements when you want two different cases to execute the same statements.

Think about what happens with this example:

```
switch (myVar) {
    case 1:
        doSometimes();
    case 2:
        doFrequently();
    default:
        doAlways();
}
```

If myVar is 1, all three functions get called. If myVar is 2, doFrequently() and doAlways() get called. If myVar has any other value, doAlways() gets called all by itself. This is a good example of a switch without breaks.

At the heart of each switch is its test expression. Most switches are based on single variables, but assignments and other types of expressions make perfectly acceptable test expressions.

Each case is based on a **constant**. Numbers (such as 47 or –12,932) are valid constants. Variables, such as myVar, are not. As you'll see later, single characters (such as 'a' or '$') are also valid constants. However, runs of characters (such as "Gummy-bear"), called **strings**, are not.

If your switch uses a default, make sure that you use it as shown in the pattern described. Don't include the keyword case before the keyword default.

`break` Statements in Loops

The `break` statement has other uses besides the `switch` statement. Here's an example of a `break` used in a `while` loop:

```
i = 1;

while ( i <= 9 ) {

    playAnInning( i );
    if ( itIsRaining() )
        break;
    i++;
}
```

This example tries to play nine innings of baseball. As long as the method `itIsRaining()` returns with a value of `false`, the game continues uninterrupted. If `itIsRaining()` returns a value of `true`, the `break` statement is executed, and the program drops out of the loop, interrupting the game.

The `break` statement allows you to construct loops that depend on multiple factors. The termination of the loop depends on the value of the expression found at the top of the loop, as well as on any outside factors that might trigger an unexpected `break`.

Detail

The most common way to use the `break` statement is in halting loops, and this is how you'll use it most often. Here's an example:

```
int i = 0;
while (i < 10) {
    if (haltLoop())
        break;
    System.out.println("i = " + i);
    i++;
}

System.out.println("We're out of the loop");
```

If `haltLoop()` ever returns `true`, the `break` statement will execute, and the message "We're out of the loop" will be the next message to appear in the Java Output window.

What happens if you have a **nested loop** (a loop inside another loop)? What does the break statement do then? Here's an example of a nested loop:

```
int i = 0;
while (i < 10) {

    int j = 0;
    while (j < 10) {
        if (haltLoop())
            break;
        j++;
    }

    i++;
}
```

At first, i equals 0, and j goes from 0 through 9, falling out of the inner while loop when j reaches 10. We're still inside the while loop controlled by i, however, so we go back to the top of this while loop. This time, i equals 1, and we enter the inner loop controlled by j once more. Again, j ranges from 0 to 9, falling out of the loop when j equals 10. Since we're still inside the i loop, we go back to the top of the i loop; now, i equals 2; and so on. We'll continue on until i equals 10 and we fall out of the outer while loop controlled by i.

In this example, if haltLoop() ever returns true, we only break out of the inner loop, controlled by j. We fall back into the i loop and continue on with the i loop, incrementing i and entering the j loop again. How can we break out of both the j loop *and* the i loop?

The way this is done is by giving a name, or **label**, to the statement that defines the i loop. Then, you can use the break statement to request a break to the loop indicated by that label. Here's a way to break out of both the inner loop and the outer loop:

```
int i = 0;

iLoop: while (i < 10) {
```

```
    int j = 0;
    while (j < 10) {
        if (haltLoop())
            break iLoop;
        j++;
    }


    i++;
}
```

Notice this time we gave the outer loop the label iLoop, and the break statement referenced this name. While the default behavior for the break statement is to break out of the immediate loop in which it is embedded, in this example, the break statement would break out of the loop that was named, which happened to be the outer loop. If haltLoop() ever returns true in this example, we would fall out of both the j loop and the i loop right away and would move on with the rest of the code.

For more information and examples, check out *Java Essentials for C and C++ Programmers*, Barry Boone's book published by Addison-Wesley, which describes a variety of sample programs that use break statements to control the flow through a program.

Sample Programs

IsOdd.µ

This program combines for and if statements to tell you whether the numbers 1 through 20 are odd or even and whether they are an even multiple of 3. The program also introduces a brand-new operator: the % operator. Go into the Learn Java Projects folder and then into the 08.03 - is odd subfolder. Open the project IsOdd.µ.

Compile and run IsOdd.µ by selecting **Make** from the **Project** menu and dropping the HTML file IsOdd.html onto the Metrowerks Java icon. You should see something like the Java Output window shown in Figure 8.3.

You should see a line for each number from 1 through 20. Each of the numbers will be described as either odd or even. Each of the multiples of 3 will have additional text describing them as such. Here's how the program works.

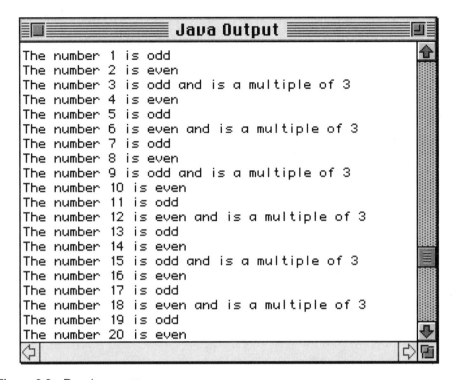

Figure 8.3 Running IsOdd.µ.

Stepping Through the Source Code

This program starts off with the usual class definition for an applet. This class, IsOdd, defines an init() method to try out some of the flow control keywords we learned in this chapter. init() begins by declaring a counter variable named i:

```
public class IsOdd extends java.applet.Applet {
    public void init() {
        int i;
```

Our goal here is to step through each of the numbers from 1 to 20. For each number, we want to check to see whether the number is odd or even. We also want to check whether the number is evenly divisible by 3. Once we've analyzed a number, we'll use System.out.println() to display a description of the number in the Java Output window.

As you might expect, the next step is to set up a for loop, using i as a counter initialized to 1. The loop will keep running as long as the value of i is less than or equal to 20. This is the same as saying that the loop will exit as soon as the value

149

of i is found to be greater than 20. Every time the loop reaches the bottom, the third expression, i++, will be evaluated, incrementing the value of i by 1. This is a classic for loop:

```
for (i = 1; i <= 20; i++) {
```

Now we're inside the for loop. Our goal is to display a single line for each number—that is, one line each time through the for loop. If you check back to Figure 8.3, you'll notice that each line starts with the phrase

```
The number x is
```

In this phrase, x is the number being described. That's the purpose of using System.out.print() rather than System.out.println(). With the System.out.print() version, rather than System.out.println(), the output does not skip to the next line after it is displayed in the Java Output window; this means we can keep on displaying text to the Java Output window, and it will be placed on the same line as before:

```
System.out.print("The number " + i + " is ");
```

Notice that this System.out.print() statement was not part of an if statement. We want this System.out.print() to display its message every time through the loop. The next sequence of System.out.print() statements is a different story altogether.

The next chunk of code determines whether i is even or odd and then uses System.out.print() to display the appropriate word in the Java Output window. Because the last message was written using System.out.print() rather than System.out.println(), the word "even" or "odd" will appear in the window on the *same line* as and immediately following

```
The number x is
```

The next chunk of code introduces the operator %, which is a binary operator that returns the remainder when the left operand is divided by the right operand. For example, i % 2 divides 2 into i and returns the remainder. If i is even, this remainder will be 0; if i is odd, this remainder will be 1:

```
if ((i % 2) == 0)
    System.out.print("even");
else
    System.out.print("odd");
```

In the expression i % 3, the remainder will be 0 if i is evenly divisible by 3; otherwise, i will be either 1 or 2:

```
if ((i % 3) == 0)
   System.out.print(" and is a multiple of 3");
```

If i is evenly divisible by 3, we'll add the following phrase to the end of the current line:

```
and is a multiple of 3
```

Finally, we display a blank and prepare for the next number in the loop by making the display start at the next line:

```
        System.out.println("");
     }
   }
}
```

The loop ends with a right curly brace.

NextPrime.μ

In our next program, we focus on the mathematical concept of **prime numbers**. A prime number is any number whose only factors are 1 and itself. For example, 6 is not a prime number because its factors are 1, 2, 3, and 6. The number 5 is prime because its factors are limited to 1 and 5. The number 12 isn't prime because its factors are 1, 2, 3, 4, 6, and 12.

The next program finds the next prime number greater than a specified number. For example, if we set our starting point to 14, the program will find the next prime, 17. We have the program set up to check for the next prime after 19. Know what that is?

Go into the Learn Java Projects folder and then into the 08.04 - next prime subfolder. Open the project NextPrime.μ. Compile NextPrime.java by selecting **Make** from the **Project** menu, and then run the applet by dropping Next-Prime.html onto the Metrowerks Java icon. You should see something like the Java Output window shown in Figure 8.4.

As you can see, buried at the end of the verbose messages in the Java Output window is the line "The next prime after 19 is 23." Here's how the program works.

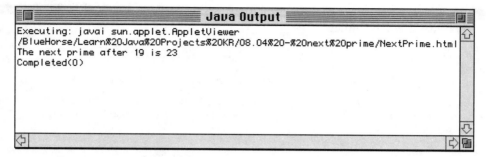

Figure 8.4 Running NextPrime.μ.

Stepping Through the Source Code

As with the other recent applets, this applet defines an init() method to perform our test of the language:

```
public class NextPrime extends java.applet.Applet {
    public void init() {
```

We're going to need a boatload of variables. The first four are defined as ints. The fifth, isPrime, is a Boolean that is used to keep track of whether we've found a prime or not:

```
int     startingPoint, candidate, last, i;
boolean isPrime;
```

We'll start at 19:

```
startingPoint = 19;
```

You can set startingPoint to whatever you'd like to and recompile and rerun this program to find other primes. The variable candidate will hold the current candidate we are considering. Is candidate the lowest prime number greater than startingPoint? By the time we are done, it will be!

Since 2 is the lowest prime number, if startingPoint is less than 2, we know that the next prime is 2. By setting candidate to 2, our work is done:

```
if ( startingPoint < 2 ) {
    candidate = 2;
}
```

If `startingPoint` is 2, the next prime is 3, and we'll set `candidate` accordingly:

```
else if ( startingPoint == 2 ) {
   candidate = 3;
}
```

If we got this far, we know that `startingPoint` is greater than 2. Since 2 is the only even prime number and since we've already checked for `startingPoint` being equal to 2, we can now limit our search to odd numbers only. We'll start `candidate` at `startingPoint` and then make sure that `candidate` is odd. If it isn't, we'll decrement `candidate`. Why decrement instead of increment? If you peek ahead a few lines, you'll see that we're about to enter a do loop and that we bump `candidate` to the next odd number at the top of the loop. By decrementing `candidate` now, we're preparing for the bump at the top of the loop, which will take `candidate` to the next odd number greater than `startingPoint`:

```
else {

   candidate = startingPoint;
   if (candidate % 2 == 0)     /* Test only odd numbers */
      candidate--;
```

This loop will continue stepping through consecutive odd numbers until we find a prime number. We'll start `isPrime` off as `true` and then check the current `candidate` to see whether we can find a factor. If we do find a factor, we'll set `isPrime` to `false`, forcing us to repeat the loop:

```
do {

   isPrime = true; // Assume glorious success
   candidate += 2; // Bump to the next number to test
```

Now we'll check to see whether `candidate` is prime. This means verifying that `candidate` has no factors other than 1 and `candidate`. To do this, we'll check the numbers from 3 to the square root of `candidate` to see whether any of them divides evenly into `candidate`. If not, we know we've got ourselves a prime!

The way we find the square root of a number in Java is to use a class method defined by the Math class (the Math class is supplied by Java, which you'll learn more about in Chapter 10). This method actually returns a floating-point number (naturally enough, since the square root of any given number may not be an integer). However, we only want an integer since we are finding the last number to check for a factor. What we want is to truncate the floating-point number, dropping any fractional portion, and simply to use the integer portion.

The way we achieve this in Java is by **casting**. We want to change the floating-point value to an integer. We can do this by writing (int) in front of the expression for the floating-point number (you'll learn much more about floating-point numbers and casting in Chapter 12):

```
last = (int)Math.sqrt( candidate );
```

By the Way

So why don't we check from 2 up to candidate - 1? Why start with 3? Since candidate will never be even, we know that 2 will never be a factor. For the same reason, we know that no even number will ever be a factor.

Why stop at the square root of candidate? Good question! To help understand this approach, consider the factors of 12, other than 1 and 12. They are 2, 3, 4, and 6. The square root of 12 is approximately 3.46. Notice how this fits nicely in the middle of the list of factors. Each of the factors less than the square root will have a matching factor greater than the square root. In this case, 2 matches with 6 (2 * 6 = 12) and 3 matches with 4 (3 * 4 = 12). This will always be true. If we don't find a factor by the time we hit the square root, there won't be a factor, and the candidate is prime.

Take a look at the top of the for loop. We start i at 3. Each time we hit the top of the loop (including the first time through the loop), we'll check to make sure that we haven't passed the square root of candidate and that isPrime is still true. If isPrime is false, we can stop searching for a factor since we've just found one! Finally, each time we complete the loop, we bump i to the next odd number:

```
/* Loop through odd numbers only */
for ( i = 3; (i <= last) && isPrime; i += 2 ) {
```

Each time through the loop, we'll check to see whether i divides evenly into candidate. If so, we know that it is a factor, and we can set isPrime to false:

```
        if ( (candidate % i) == 0 )
            isPrime = false;
    }
```

```
      } while ( !isPrime );
}
```

Once we drop out of the `do` loop, we use a `System.out.println()` statement to display both the starting point and the first prime number greater than the starting point:

```
    System.out.println( "The next prime after " + startingPoint
+ " is " + candidate);


    }
}
```

If you are interested in prime numbers, play around with this program. See whether you can modify the code to display all the prime numbers from 1 to 100. How about the first 100 prime numbers?

Review

This chapter covered many of the details of implementing your methods. You've learned how to branch based on certain conditions, how to execute one set of statements instead of others, and how to loop through your code. Mastering the information in this chapter involves learning many new Java keywords and new ways of thinking about problems.

The comparative operators covered here that you'll use most often include <, >, ==, and !=. (As you learned, these are the less than, greater than, equal to, and not equal to operators, respectively.) You now know you can use these operators in conjunction with keywords to control the flow through your program. The keywords you learned in this chapter include `if`, `else`, `for`, `while`, `do`, `switch`, `case`, and `break`. Take the time to make sure you understand how each of these works. If you would like some more examples, check out the appendixes for more references and example code.

What's Next?

You've covered many of the important aspects of creating a method (storing data in variables, branching, looping, and working with operators). In Chapter 9, we'll take all this to the next level by creating objects from our classes. You'll see all your effort to learn about variables and methods pay off with objects. You'll create objects to implement the different parts of your application. You'll define variables for your objects and give your objects specific values that make each object unique, and you'll give your objects behavior using methods.

Chapter 9

Objects

So far, the applets in this book did not need to create their own objects. We're about to change all that. Starting with this chapter, we'll create objects based on our classes and use these objects in our applets.

Even though you haven't created any objects yourself, you have been working with objects all along. In particular, as you have learned, the browser makes an instance of your Applet class when it runs your applet. We'll also explore methods and variables in much more depth here by learning how to make methods and variables part of your objects.

The Purpose of Objects

Let's review what the purpose of an object is before diving into the details of an object. Objects represent the different parts of your application. You create new objects based on classes. By defining classes and creating objects, you can write programs that reflect the "real world" and model the problem at hand.

For example, remember our payroll program discussion from Chapter 4? You might create objects to represent the employees in your program. Each employee object might keep track of three pieces of information: an employee number, the employee's hourly wage, and the number of hours the employee has worked so far this month. You would create an Employee class that defined what each employee object looked like. This is depicted in Figure 9.1.

In your program, you could create a specific **instance**, or object, based on this Employee class to hold the particular values for a given employee. For example, if

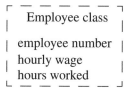

Figure 9.1 A schematic of a class called Employee.

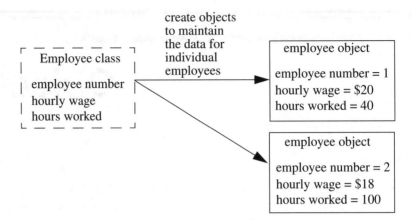

Figure 9.2 A schematic of two specific instances, or objects, created from the Employee class.

your company had two employees, employee number 1 might have an hourly wage of $20 and might have worked 40 hours so far this month. Employee number 2 might have an hourly wage of $18 and might have worked 100 hours so far this month. This is depicted in Figure 9.2.

Figure 9.2 shows that the Employee class specifies the data that each employee object will have, but it does not provide any values. Instead, the individual employee objects maintain the values that make each employee unique. As your company grows, you can create new employee objects from the Employee class, using the Employee class like a template or a cookie cutter, as we covered in Chapter 4. Once you create a new employee object, you can fill in the values that make that employee unique. For example, a new employee just joining the company would need an object dedicated to the new employee. This would be the third employee object we created so far. This new object would maintain its own unique values, such as employee number 3, an hourly wage of $10, and 0 hours worked this month.

One of the great things about classes is that, in addition to specifying the *data* that objects will hold, they also specify the *behavior* that objects will have. Often, an object's behavior involves manipulating an object's data in some way, perhaps by performing a calculation. For example, we could create a method that allowed employee objects to calculate the employee's income for the month. In the Java program, this new method would be defined in the class definition. Remember, from Chapter 4, that objects look to their classes to see what behavior they are capable of. Our new method might be called earnedIncome(). This method might multiply the number of hours worked by the employee's hourly wage to arrive at the earned income for a given employee for that month.

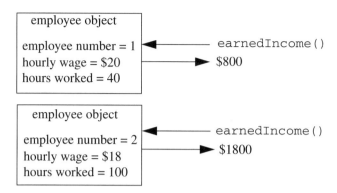

Figure 9.3 A schematic of employee objects responding to a method invocation.

Now, if we invoked employee number 1's `earnedIncome()` method, `earned-Income()` would access the data for employee number 1. It would find that the hourly wage was equal to 20 and that hours worked so far this month were equal to 40. Then, `earnedIncome()` would perform the multiplication and return a value of 800. If we invoked employee number 2's `earnedIncome()` method, `earnedIncome()` would access the instance variables for employee number 2. It would find that the hourly wage was equal to 18 and that hours worked so far this month were equal to 100. In this case, `earnedIncome()` would perform the multiplication using employee 2's own unique data and return a value of 1800. This is depicted in Figure 9.3.

The purpose of objects, then, is to allow you to design and implement your programs in a way that models the real world as much as possible. Here, for example, employees maintain their own data and can determine how much they should be paid each month. Your applets will become a collection of objects that store data and know how to behave. What's more, your objects will sometimes create other objects and interact with them to get the job done. For example, an applet that acted as a payroll program would create employee objects and interact with them to keep track of the employees in the company. As another example, the SimpleDraw program you saw earlier is an applet that creates circle and square objects.

Since you'll often need to create new objects when writing your own applets, it's high time you learned how to create new objects based on your classes. Let's turn to this topic next.

How to Create Objects

To create a new object from a class, you use a command called new. Here's an example. Let's say you have an empty class, called Circle, defined like this:

```
class Circle {
}
```

To create an instance of this class, you could write a line of code like this:

```
new Circle();
```

This statement returns a new object. This might remind you a little bit of a method invocation, except for the keyword new preceding Circle(). Typically, you would assign this new object to a variable.

To declare a variable that can hold an object of a particular type, you use the class name as the data type of the variable. For example, to declare a variable called myCircle that will hold an object that is an instance of class Circle, you would write

```
Circle myCircle;
```

Then, when you create the new object, you would assign it to the variable myCircle, like this:

```
myCircle = new Circle();
```

You could also declare the variable, create the object, and assign the new object to the new variable all in one line, like this:

```
Circle myCircle = new Circle();
```

Definition

What you are doing with the code new Circle() is invoking a class's **constructor**. A constructor is a special method that initializes an object. Java provides a default constructor for your classes, so you don't have to define one yourself to create objects based on your classes. However, you can if you want to, and Chapter 13 explains how you would go about doing this. Creating your own constructor allows you to initialize an object when it is first created.

Just as some methods take parameters, some constructors take parameters, too. Sometimes, you'll pass parameters to a constructor to initialize the object when you create it. For example, Java supplies a type of class called a String. A string object maintains some text, such as "Goodbye Yellow Brick Road" or "This is Green leader, over." You can create a new string instance like this:

```
String s = new String();
```

This statement declares a variable named s that will hold a string object. It then creates a new string object using the new command and invokes the String class's default constructor. The resulting object is assigned to s.

This creates a perfectly good string, except for one thing: This string wouldn't contain any text. Yet, that's the whole point of strings! Instead of creating a string without any text, you almost always will want to supply this text to the string's constructor. You supply this data as a parameter to the constructor, just as you supply parameters to methods. You would supply the text for the string when you create the string like this:

```
String s = new String("What I Did on my Summer Vacation");
```

As you can see, you just place the constructor's parameter between the parentheses following the constructor invocation. As with methods, if there's more than one parameter, you separate the parameters using commas.

Now that you know how to create new objects, let's look at how to use them in your applets.

Defining Instance Variables

As you learned in the previous three chapters, variables allow you to keep track of the data used in your methods. For example, to define a method that finds the perimeter of a triangle, you could write

```
int findPerimeter() {
    int side1 = 5;
    int side2 = 12;
    int side3 = 13;

    return (side1 + side2 + side3);
}
```

This method defines three variables. The variables side1, side2, and side3 hold the length of each side of a specific triangle. This method returns the length of the triangle's perimeter. This example shows how variables can be used inside a method to store data, as you've seen already.

To store data inside an *object*, you can do the same kind of thing. That is, like methods, objects can define variables to keep track of their own data.

Here's an example of a Triangle class that defines three variables for its instances:

```
class Triangle {
    int side1;
    int side2;
    int side3;
}
```

When you create an instance of this class, you set aside enough memory to store the three int values named side1, side2, and side3 that are listed in the class definition. Figure 9.4 shows how a triangle object based on the Triangle class is created.

At first, the three instance variables will have the value 0. (This is the default value for int variables.) However, you can access these variables, assign values to them, and retrieve their values whenever you want to. This lets you create a triangle object, for example, and then immediately assign values to it, such as side1 = 3, side2 = 4, and side3 = 5. The next section shows you how. We'll cover how to access instance variables by also discussing instance methods.

Defining Instance Methods

We wrote methods in the preceding two chapters for an applet. These methods started out as the applet life cycle methods init(), start(), stop(), and destroy(). We also showed how init() could invoke a method we wrote ourselves called setUpGUI() and how to define our own method called findAverage() that

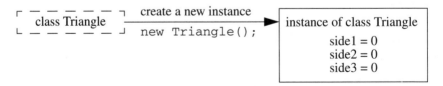

Figure 9.4 Making an instance of class Triangle.

took parameters and returned a value. Just as we defined new methods for the applet, we can define new methods for any other class as well.

Let's build on the triangle example we started in the last section. You've already seen that for a method to access variables that it defines, all it has to do is refer to the variables by name. For example, recall the findPerimeter() method given earlier that looked like this:

```
int findPerimeter() {
    int side1 = 5;
    int side2 = 12;
    int side3 = 13;

    return (side1 + side2 + side3);
}
```

This method simply referred to side1, side2, and side3 to get at the values they defined. Is there a big difference between methods accessing their own variables and objects accessing *their* own variables? Not at all! For a triangle object to access its own instance variables, all it has to do is, like the method, refer to the variables by name. For example, if triangle objects defined a method named findPerimeter(), then findPerimeter() could look like this:

```
class Triangle {
    int side1;
    int side2;
    int side3;

    int findPerimeter() {
        return (side1 + side2 + side3);
    }
}
```

As you can see, the method findPerimeter() is able to access the instance variables in the same object in which it is defined. This is important! The key point here is that findPerimeter() accesses the instance variables for its particular object. If you created two triangle objects and assigned each object its own data, invoking that object's findPerimeter() method would yield the results appropriate for that object.

For example, if you created a triangle object and gave its sides the values 6, 8, and 10, then invoking findPerimeter() for that triangle would return the value 24. If you created another triangle object and gave its sides the values 4, 4, and 4, then invoking findPerimeter() for that triangle would return the value 12.

Using Instance Variables and Methods in Other Objects

You now know how to access instance variables and invoke behavior—as long as you ever have only one object! For example, what we've shown so far works just fine for a program consisting solely of an Applet class. We can define instance variables for our applet and define new methods. These new methods can access the instance variables to set or retrieve their values, just as our methods did when the variables were defined in the methods themselves.

The true power of instance variables and instance methods is when we can work with a whole bunch of objects at once. For example, a Trigonometry applet might build up a library of triangles. It would be great to have our applet refer to these different triangles, access different triangles' data, and invoke different triangles' methods. We can't just refer to a triangle object's variables or methods by name alone from our own applet because, first of all, the computer wouldn't know we wanted the triangle's variables and methods rather than our applet's, and, second of all, the computer wouldn't know which triangle object we were referring to! If we are going to create a whole bunch of separate objects, we need a way of distinguishing triangle 1's variables from triangle 2's variables and triangle 1's methods from triangle 2's methods. In other words, if we want to ask triangle 1 for its perimeter, we want to make sure that findPerimeter() uses the values for triangle 1 and not some other triangle.

Java provides a way to do this. Java uses a dot (.) to associate a variable or a method with a given object. The best way to illustrate this is with an example.

Let's write an applet called Trig that, in its init() method, creates two triangles, assigns values to them, and then finds the perimeter for each triangle. Here's the definition for the Triangle class:

```
class Triangle {
    int side1;
    int side2;
    int side3;

    int findPerimeter() {
        return side1 + side2 + side3;
    }
}
```

Now, let's create objects out of this class and use them in our applet's init() method. Here's the top part of this method, which creates two triangle objects:

```
public class Trig extends java.applet.Applet {
    init() {
        Triangle t1;
        Triangle t2;

        t1 = new Triangle();
        t2 = new Triangle();
```

Next, we would like to set the values for t1's instance variables. We associate an instance variable to a particular object by using a dot, like this:

```
        t1.side1 = 3;
        t1.side2 = 4;
        t1.side3 = 5;
```

Now, t1's instance variables are set to 3, 4, and 5. Similarly, to assign values to t2's instance variables, we can write

```
        t2.side1 = 5;
        t2.side2 = 10;
        t2.side3 = 10;
```

At this point, the triangle referenced by t2 holds the values 5, 10, and 10 for its sides. Each instance's variable names are the same (side1, side2, and side3), but we refer to a different object when we use the dot notation. Now, t2 contains different values in its instance variables than t1. If we wanted to access t1's instance variable named side1, we could refer to it by writing t1.side1. If we wanted to refer to t2's instance variable named side3, we could refer to it by writing t2.side3.

For the last part of our Trig applet, we need to find the perimeter for each triangle by invoking each triangle's findPerimeter() method. From the preceding discussion on accessing instance variables in other objects, you can probably already guess how to invoke methods in other objects: Just connect the object with the method invocation by a dot. Here's the remainder of the code:

```
        int result1 = t1.findPerimeter();
        int result2 = t2.findPerimeter();
    }
}
```

In this example, `t1.findPerimeter()` would return the value 12 (because `t1`'s sides are equal to 3, 4, and 5), and `t2.findPerimeter()` would return the value 25 (since `t2`'s sides are equal to 5, 10, and 10). The variable `result1`, then, would be assigned 12, and `result2` would be assigned 25.

Referring to Yourself

As you saw, you don't have to connect an instance variable or an instance method with an object when you're accessing it from the same object in which these variables and methods are defined. For example, you saw how the Triangle class defined an instance method called `findPerimeter()` that just referenced its instance variables directly.

This usually works just fine, but here's a scenario that would cause the compiler to not understand what we wanted. Imagine that we define a method that initializes the triangle's sides. Perhaps we have a method definition that begins

```
void initTriangle(int side1, int side2, int side3) {
```

Are these parameter names referring to the same instance variables defined by the triangle? No. Parameter names are separate from the triangle's instance variable names. Does that mean we can write code for our `initTriangle()` method like this

```
void initTriangle(int side1, int side2, int side3) {
    side1 = side1;
    side2 = side2;
    side3 = side3;
}
```

and expect the instance variables to be assigned with the values in the parameters? No again. The compiler will think we're assigning the parameter back to its original value. If we write a method like this, the instance variables will never be assigned the values we pass to `initTriangle()`. If we could specify the object, as we did when referring to variables and methods in *other* objects, we could indicate that we wanted to assign the parameter `side1` to the instance variable `side1`, the parameter `side2` to the instance variable `side2`, and the parameter `side3` to the instance variable `side3`. In other words, you want to write code that expresses this idea:

```
(this object).side1 = side1;
(this object).side2 = side2;
(this object).side3 = side3;
```

So how do we refer to our own object? Java provides a way to do this through the use of a special variable called `this`. Java defines the variable named `this` for every instance method. You can use this variable whenever you want to. Here's how we would solve the problem just presented:

```
void initTriangle(int side1, int side2, int side3) {
    this.side1 = side1;
    this.side2 = side2;
    this.side3 = side3;
}
```

The variable named `this` is defined for you by Java. The `this` variable lets you clarify which object a variable or method belongs to. `this` is sometimes described as representing the **current object**. The current object is the one responding to a method invocation.

For example, in the example code given earlier, we created two triangle objects. The first was assigned to the variable `t1`; the second was assigned to the variable `t2`. If we invoke `t1`'s `findPerimeter()` method, then when `findPerimeter()` is executing, `this` is equal to the object represented by `t1`, and `t1` is said to be the current object, the one responding to the method invocation. Similarly, if we invoke `t2`'s `findPerimeter()` method, then when `findPerimeter()` is executing, `this` is equal to the object represented by `t2`, and `t2` is said to be the current object.

Sample Programs

We'll look at a simple program in this section and slowly extend it to illustrate instance variables and instance methods. The code here will all relate to the employee example we touched on earlier.

Employee1.µ

For our first example of instance methods and instance variables, open the subfolder `09.01 - employee 1` in the Learn Java Projects folder. Double-click the project file and compile the applet by selecting **Make** from the **Project** menu. Run the program by dropping the file `Employee1.html` onto the Metrowerks Java icon. When you do, an empty applet will appear and the Java Output window will look like the one in Figure 9.5.

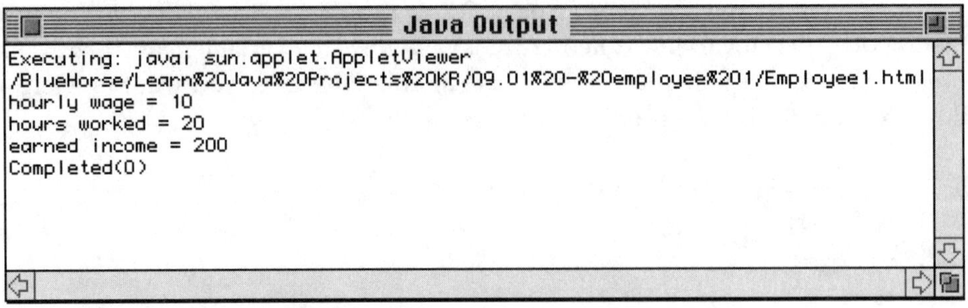

Figure 9.5 Running `Employee1.μ`

This applet displays some information in the Java Output window for a particular employee. As you can see, after all the initialization gobbledygook, this program displays three lines:

```
hourly wage = 10
hours worked = 20
earned income = 200
```

Let's see what's happening with the source code.

Stepping Through the Source Code

Open `Employee1.java` either by double-clicking this file name in the project window or by double-clicking the file icon. Once you get it open, you'll see this file defines an applet called Employee1. You might notice that the source code for this applet defines two life cycle methods—`init()` and `start()`—and one other method, called `earnedIncome()`. This applet also defines two instance variables, called `hourlyWage` and `hoursWorked`. Here's how it all works.

At the start of the applet, the applet defines two instance variables:

```
public class Employee1 extends java.applet.Applet {

    int hourlyWage;
    int hoursWorked;
```

The applet will use these variables to store and retrieve data. The applet then defines its first instance method, a custom method called `earnedIncome()`. This method does not take any parameters, but it uses the two instance variables to perform a calculation:

```
int earnedIncome() {
   return hourlyWage * hoursWorked;
}
```

Notice how this instance method can just refer to the instance variables by name. The variables belong to the object (that is, the applet object), so it's no problem accessing them from this instance method also defined for the applet object.

Next, the applet provides an `init()` method. When the applet is first initialized by the Applet Viewer, its `init()` method is invoked, and it sets the values of its instance variables. It sets `hourlyWage` to 10 and `hoursWorked` to 20:

```
public void init() {
   hourlyWage = 10;
   hoursWorked = 20;
}
```

Remember, if we don't set the instance variables, they will have the default value of 0. Again, in `init()`, we can just refer to these instance variables directly since `init()` is an instance method.

The third method, `start()`, is invoked by the Applet Viewer after `init()`. The `start()` method defines a local variable named `earnedIncome`. This method begins by displaying the values of the instance variables `hourlyWage` and `hoursWorked`:

```
public void start() {
   int earnedIncome;

   System.out.println("hourly wage = " + hourlyWage);
   System.out.println("hours worked = " + hoursWorked);
```

As you can tell from the Java Output window, `hourlyWage` and `hoursWorked` contain the values we set in the `init()` method. These values will stay with the object until we change them. Since we assigned these values to an instance variable, they are accessible from any instance method defined for the same object. As you can see, this is one way to use the same variables in different methods.

The last thing this method does is to invoke the current object's (that is, this applet's) `earnedIncome()` method. Since we want to invoke the method for this object, we can do so just by writing

```
earnedIncome = earnedIncome();
```

This statement assigns the return value of earnedIncome(), the method, to earnedIncome, the local variable. The compiler is able to distinguish between the method name and the variable name.

If we wanted to invoke a method for a different object, we would have had to prefix the method name with a variable containing the object, followed by a dot. However, earnedIncome() is defined for the same object whose code is currently executing (that is, the applet), and invoking a method in the same object can be done without the need for specifying the object.

Invoking earnedIncome() executes the method the applet defined at the top of this listing. earnedIncome() accesses the applet's instance variables hourly-Wage (which is 10) and hoursWorked (which is 20), performs the multiplication (to get 200), and returns the result. The result is then displayed in the Java Output window:

```
        System.out.println("earned income = " + earnedIncome);
    }
}
```

Throughout this listing, we used only one object, so it was straightforward to use instance variables and instance methods. The next example shows how different objects can communicate with one another by accessing their instance variables and instance methods.

Employee2.µ

For our second example, open the subfolder 09.02 - employee 2 in the Learn Java Projects folder. Open Employee2.µ. After making the project, run the program, by dropping the file Employee2.html onto the Metrowerks Java icon. Again, an empty applet will appear, but this time the Java Output window will display information for three different employees:

```
Employee 1:
hourly wage = 10
hours worked = 20
earned income = 200

Employee 2:
hourly wage = 18
hours worked = 38
earned income = 684
```

```
Employee 3:
hourly wage = 12
hours worked = 52
earned income = 624
```

The display indicates that each employee contains its own data. Now we're beginning to use objects to their full advantage! Let's step through the source code and see how we do this.

Stepping Through the Source Code

Open `Employee2.java` either by double-clicking this file name in the project window or by double-clicking the file icon. There are two class definitions in this file. The first, named Employee2, is for the applet. The second, simply called Employee, is for a class that maintains payroll information for a particular employee.

The top part of this code contains the applet. The applet defines three instance variables, which it will use to keep track of three different employees:

```
public class Employee2 extends java.applet.Applet {

    Employee e1;
    Employee e2;
    Employee e3;
```

Unlike in the previous example, this applet does not maintain the specifics of employee payroll information. Instead, the applet uses the employee objects to maintain this information. In the `init()` method, the applet creates three different employees and assigns each of the employee objects returned by the constructor to the three instance variables e1, e2, and e3. The applet then assigns values to instance variables defined for the employee objects. First, the applet sets the instance variables for the employee object assigned to e1; then, the applet sets the instance variables for the employee object assigned to e2; finally, the applet sets the instance variables for the employee object assigned to e3:

```
public void init() {
    e1 = new Employee();
    e1.hourlyWage = 10;
    e1.hoursWorked = 20;

    e2 = new Employee();
    e2.hourlyWage = 18;
    e2.hoursWorked = 38;
```

```
        e3 = new Employee();
        e3.hourlyWage = 12;
        e3.hoursWorked = 52;
    }
```

By using the variables e1, e2, and e3, the applet can reference the instance variables for specific employee objects. Notice that the applet is setting the instance variables in an object different from itself!

In the start() method, the applet displays messages indicating it is about to show the employees' payroll information. The applet then invokes the instance method displayInfo(), which is defined for the employee objects. The applet first invokes this instance method for e1, then for e2, and then for e3:

```
public void start() {
    System.out.println("");
    System.out.println("Employee 1:");
    e1.displayInfo();

    System.out.println("");
    System.out.println("Employee 2:");
    e2.displayInfo();

    System.out.println("");
    System.out.println("Employee 3:");
    e3.displayInfo();
    }
}
```

Again, by prefixing e1, e2, and e3 to the instance method, the applet can invoke an instance method for each employee object.

The Employee class defines two instance variables and two instance methods. The instance variables are hourlyWage and hoursWorked. As you saw earlier in the listing, the applet object sets these values for each of the three employee objects it creates:

```
class Employee {
    int hourlyWage;
    int hoursWorked;
```

The first instance method for the Employee class provides the calculation for earned income. This instance method can simply access the instance variables directly since the instance variables are defined in the same class as this method:

```
int earnedIncome() {
    return hourlyWage * hoursWorked;
}
```

The displayInfo() method displays the instance variables hourlyWage and hoursWorked and invokes the instance method earnedIncome():

```
void displayInfo() {
    int earnedIncome;

    System.out.println("hourly wage = " + hourlyWage);
    System.out.println("hours worked = " + hoursWorked);

    earnedIncome = earnedIncome();
    System.out.println("earned income = " + earnedIncome);
}
}
```

Since each object maintains its own data, invoking displayInfo() for e1 yields output according to the values stored in e1. Looking back, you can see that the applet stored 10 in e1's hourlyWage instance variable and 20 in e1's hoursWorked instance variable. When the applet invokes e1's displayInfo() instance method, e1 starts by displaying the values of its instance variables (10 and 20). When e1 invokes its own instance method earnedIncome(), earnedIncome() accesses the values of these same instance variables, 10 and 20, and returns 200. displayInfo() then displays this result.

The same things occur for e2 and e3. Each object responds to an instance method by using the values in its own particular instance variables. So, when the applet invokes e2's displayInfo() method, e2's data is displayed. When the applet invokes e3's displayInfo() method, e3's data is displayed.

Employee3.μ

For our third example, open the subfolder 09.03 – employee 3 in the Learn Java Projects folder. Open Example3.μ and make the project. Run the program by dropping the file Employee3.html onto the Metrowerks Java icon. Once more, an empty applet will appear. The Java Output window will look like what you saw in the previous sample. That is, it will contain employee information that looks like this:

```
Employee 1:
hourly wage = 10
hours worked = 20
earned income = 200

Employee 2:
hourly wage = 18
hours worked = 38
earned income = 684

Employee 3:
hourly wage = 12
hours worked = 52
earned income = 624
```

Let's turn to the source code and see what's up.

Stepping Through the Source Code

Open Employee3.java either by double-clicking this file name in the project window or by double-clicking the file icon. The purpose of this code is to show how this can be used to refer to an object's own instance variables. The code here is almost identical to the previous sample, except in the way the applet initializes the employees and in the method provided by the Employee class to perform this initialization.

First, the applet defines its init() method like this:

```
public void init() {
    e1 = new Employee();
    e1.initialize(10, 20);

    e2 = new Employee();
    e2.initialize(18, 38);

    e3 = new Employee();
    e3.initialize(12, 52);
}
```

The Employee class defines the `initialize()` instance method to help the applet set the instance variables in an employee object. Here's how the employee's `initialize()` method begins:

```
void initialize(int hourlyWage, int hoursWorked) {
```

Since the instance variables are also named `hourlyWage` and `hoursWorked`, we need a way to differentiate between the instance variables and the parameters. The way we do this is by using the variable named `this`:

```
    this.hourlyWage = hourlyWage;
    this.hoursWorked = hoursWorked;
}
```

Now, the compiler will know which value to assign to which variable. By using `this`, we can indicate that the values in the parameters `hourlyWage` and `hoursWorked` should be assigned to the current object's instance variables `hourlyWage` and `hoursWorked`, respectively.

Defining Class Variables and Methods

As described so far, the purpose of classes is to create objects, just as the purpose of cookie cutters is to create cookies. However, like cookie cutters, classes also exist on their own. For example, you saw that classes stamp out objects, as in Figure 9.6.

While the emphasis of Figure 9.6 is that the Employee class is used to create objects, the figure also shows that the Employee class exists in its own right. We can ask an employee object for its data or invoke an employee object's method; what happens if we try to do this kind of thing for the class?

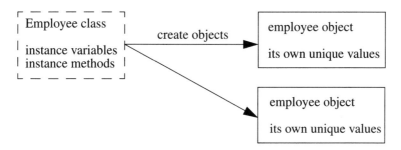

Figure 9.6 The Employee class stamping out objects but existing in its own right.

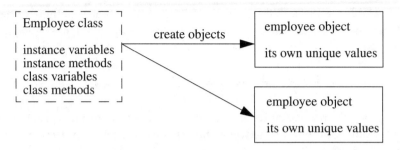

Figure 9.7 The Employee class defining class variables and class methods in addition to instance variables and instance methods.

Associating data and behavior with the class might make a lot of sense in certain situations. For example, what if we wanted to keep track of the number of employees in the company? That piece of data doesn't seem to belong to any specific employee. The number of employees seems to belong to all of the employees in general. That is, this data seems to belong with the class. For the SimpleDraw applet, the user could draw all the circles he or she desired, and each circle would have its own unique position and color. However, all circles were the same size. The radius for the circle was a property of circles in general, not of any particular circle. This value—the circle's radius—might be better kept in the Circle class itself in this case.

As you might expect, associating data and behavior with the class itself is possible to do in Java. A more complete picture of a class might be to say that while a class defines instance variables and instance methods, it also can define class variables and class methods. Figure 9.7 extends Figure 9.6 to take into account possible class variables and class methods defined in the Employee class.

Class Variables

Creating class variables and class methods is done almost identically to creating instance variables and instance methods. You write class variables and class methods the same way that you've been doing, except that you start these definitions with the keyword `static`. Remember back in Chapter 6, before you learned about methods, how you used the keyword `static` to define code that executed when a class was first loaded? Just as the keyword `static` was used to associate a chunk of code with a class, `static` can also be used to associate a variable or method with a class.

For example, here's how the Triangle class could define a class variable:

```
static int totalAngles = 180;
```

This defines an `int` variable called `totalAngles`. Since we've declared it as `static`, it belongs to the class itself. That is, `totalAngles` does not belong to any particular object, but each object can still refer to it just by using its name.

Notice that we've also initialized the variable to a value. You can do this with any type of variable, from method variables to instance variables to class variables. You can always change the value later. As mentioned previously, if you don't initialize an instance variable or class variable, Java assigns a default value to it. For `int` values, this default value is 0.

If we were to define `totalAngles` *without* the keyword `static`, each triangle object would maintain a separate value for `totalAngles` (that is, without the keyword `static`, you would have defined an instance variable). The first triangle you create could change its instance variable named `totalAngles` to 190; the second triangle could change its instance variable named `totalAngles` to 170; neither triangle's instance variable would affect the other.

By contrast, class variables are **shared variables**. That is, with a class variable, there is only one version of it, and that version is maintained with the class. All objects belonging to a particular class can access that class's `static` variables. These objects can also change the value in the variable. In other words, a `static` variable is shared among all the objects made from that class.

For example, you might imagine keeping track of the number of triangles you create in a Trig applet. Each time you create a new triangle object, you might increment a class variable defined in the Triangle class. As with instance variables, all you need to do to refer to the class variable is to use its name. For a class variable called `numTriangles`, each triangle object could increment it like this:

```
numTriangles++;
```

This is fine for accessing the class variable in an object based on the class that defined it, but how would you access the class variable from some other object—say, from the applet? The applet could not refer to `numTriangles` because `numTriangles` is undefined for the applet. We solved this same kind of problem for instance variables by prefixing the variable name that held the object to the instance variable name, placing a dot between them. Since we don't keep track of classes by using variables, how do we refer to the class variable for a particular class?

The solution is to use the class name, rather than the name of a variable that refers to an object. For example, to refer to the Triangle's class variable numTriangles, you can write

```
Triangle.numTriangles;
```

You can also use this notation if you need to distinguish between a class variable and a local variable that both share the same name. (You'll see an example of this in the upcoming sample programs.)

Class Methods

Just as you can have class variables, you can also have class methods. Class methods are good for associating behavior with a particular class.

For example, you might have defined an instance method called addAngles() that adds all the angles in a triangle, perhaps to verify that they do indeed total 180 degrees. Your method might look like this:

```
int addAngles(int angle1, int angle2, int angle3) {
    return angle1 + angle2 + angle3;
}
```

Nothing in this method, as written, relies on a particular object. Noticing this, you might decide to associate this method with the Triangle class. To do this, just prefix the word static in front of the method definition, and voilà, you have a class method:

```
static int addAngles(int angle1, int angle2, int angle3) {
    return angle1 + angle2 + angle3;
}
```

As with instance methods, an object made from the class defining the class method can invoke the method in the usual way:

```
int total = addAngles(40, 60, 80);
```

You can also prefix the class method with the class's name to invoke it from other classes or from other objects or to disambiguate it from other methods with the same name:

```
int total = Triangle.addAngles(40, 60, 80);
```

In addition to your own class instance variables and class methods, Java provides a lot of class methods and class variables for you to use. For example, Java defines the mathematical value of pi as a class variable in a class called Math. (You would access this by writing `Math.PI`.) Java defines a whole slew of colors as class variables in a class called Color. (You can access these by writing `Color.red`, `Color.blue`, and so on.) You'll learn about these and other class variables and methods in upcoming chapters.

Class Methods Versus Instance Methods

Though class methods and instance methods might seem similar at first glance, there's a crucial difference between them: Class methods are not associated with a *particular* object. Therefore, class methods are not good to use in situations where you want to access an object's data.

Similarly, the Java-supplied variable named `this` is not defined for class methods because when a class method is executing, there's no current object. The `this` variable exists only when there's an object responding to a method invocation, which is not the situation with a class method—it's the class that is responding to the method, not a particular object.

For example, the class method `addAngles()` defined in the previous section would not be able to access a particular triangle's instance variable just by naming it, such as referring to `side1` or even to `this.side1`. However, all is not lost; if the class method can get access to a variable that holds an object—say, in a variable called `t1`—then this method can still refer to `t1.side1`.

More Sample Programs

We'll illustrate how to access class variables and class methods in two more sample programs.

ClassVar.µ

For our example of using a class variable to store data with a class, open the subfolder `09.04 - variable` in the Learn Java Projects folder. Before running the applet, take a look at this definition for a class variable and an `init()` method:

```
static int test = 20;

public void init() {
   System.out.println("test = " + test);
```

```
    int test = 30;

    System.out.println("test = " + test);
    System.out.println("ClassVar.test = " + ClassVar.test);
}
```

This is the class variable and `init()` method for the applet you're about to run. What do you think each of these three `System.out.println()` statements will display in the Java Output window? You can see that the class variable starts out as 20, but what happens after we define a new local variable with the same name but set to a different value? Once you feel you've made your best guess, double-click `ClassVar.µ`, and select **Make** from the **Project** menu to compile the applet. Run the program by dropping the file `ClassVar.html` onto the Metrowerks Java icon. An empty applet will appear, and the Java Output window will contain three lines that look like this:

```
test = 20
test = 30
ClassVar.test = 20
```

How'd you do? Did you guess correctly? Let's see what causes these lines to be displayed.

Stepping Through the Source Code

Open `ClassVar.java` either by double-clicking this file name in the project window or by double-clicking the file icon. There is only one simple class definition in this file. This is for an applet named ClassVar:

```
public class ClassVar extends java.applet.Applet {
```

The first thing this applet does is define a class variable:

```
static int test = 20;
```

You can see that it's a class variable because of the keyword `static`. The applet initializes this class variable to 20.

The applet then provides an `init()` method. This method first displays the value of its instance variable, named `test`, which is what causes the first line that reads "test = 20" to appear in the Java Output window:

```
public void init() {
    System.out.println("test = " + test);
```

After this line is displayed, the method defines a *local* variable called test—the same name as the class variable! It then writes the variable test to the Java Output window. What gets displayed is the local variable, so "test = 30" appears in the Java Output window:

```
int test = 30;

System.out.println("test = " + test);
```

This brings up an interesting point. If parameters or local variables with the same name as instance variables or class variables are used in a method, it's the parameters and local variables that get preference. We can still access the class variable, however, by prefixing the class name in front of the class variable name and separating the two with a dot. In our case, we can do this by writing Class-Var.test:

```
    System.out.println("ClassVar.test = " + ClassVar.test);
    }


}
```

This time, the *class* variable appears in the Java Output window.

ClassMethod.µ

For an example of a class method, open the subfolder 09.05 – method in the Learn Java Projects folder. Open ClassMethod.µ and make the project. Run the program by dropping the file ClassMethod.html onto the Metrowerks Java icon. An empty applet will appear, and the Java Output window will contain the line

```
3 circles were created.
```

Let's see what makes this happen.

Stepping Through the Source Code

Open ClassMethod.java either by double-clicking this file name in the project window or by double-clicking the file icon. The applet starts by defining three

181

local variables in the `init()` method to hold circle objects (the Circle class is defined in this file after the Applet class) :

```
public class ClassMethod extends java.applet.Applet {

    public void init() {
        Circle c1, c2, c3;
```

The applet then creates three circle objects. Each time, it increments a class variable defined by the Circle class:

```
        c1 = new Circle();
        Circle.numCircles++;

        c2 = new Circle();
        Circle.numCircles++;

        c3 = new Circle();
        Circle.numCircles++;
```

After the three circles are created, this code invokes a class method defined by the Circle class:

```
        Circle.displayNumCircles();
    }
}
```

Notice that for the class variable `numCircles` and class method `displayNum-Circles()`, the applet has to prefix the class name onto the variable and method name since this variable and method are not defined for the applet but for a different class (that is, for class Circle).

The Circle class starts by defining `numCircles` as a class variable:

```
class Circle {

    static int numCircles;
```

The class then defines the class method called `displayNumCircles()`. This method can access the class variable named `numCircles` directly, without the need for prefixing `numCircles` with `Circle` and a dot (though that would have worked, too):

```
   static void displayNumCircles() {
      System.out.println(numCircles + " circles were created.");
   }
}
```

This class method can access the class variable by name because the class variable and the class method are both defined in the same class. Since the applet incremented the class variable numCircles three times, this line prints out "3 circles were created."

Review

So now that you've explored objects, you should have a sense of what objects are used for and how to store data and define behavior for your own objects. Variables were first discussed in Chapter 6, and now you've seen how to use them in your objects. Methods were first discussed in Chapter 7, and now you've seen how to use methods in your objects as well. You've learned about instance variables and instance methods, how to define them and use them, and about a special variable supplied by Java called this.

You've also seen that classes themselves can define data and behavior. This is a good technique to use when you have data or behavior that belongs to all of the objects of a certain class in general and does not seem to belong to any particular object. Class methods are different from instance methods, however, in that they are not associated with a particular object and so do not have easy access to a particular object's instance variables.

What's Next?

With a basic understanding of objects, it's time to look at what classes Java provides for you. You can create objects out of Java's classes and use these objects in your own programs. Java organizes its classes into packages. Chapter 10 takes you on a brief tour of these packages and shows you how you can create packages of your own.

Chapter 10 also discusses a concept central to object-oriented languages such as Java: inheritance. By using inheritance, you'll see how you can mix in your own custom data and behavior to extend the default behavior of the classes that Java provides for you. You'll also learn how you can use inheritance to organize your own classes into hierarchies.

Java's Classes and Inheritance

This chapter will delve into one of the most powerful features of object-oriented programming. This feature is inheritance, and it allows you to start with a class that is already fully functioning and create your own class by extending it, adding to its capabilities.

Since inheritance involves working with a predefined set of classes, we'll also take a better look at what classes Java supplies for you already and how you can use these classes in your own applets. In particular, we'll look at these classes with an eye toward what it means to inherit from the classes that Java provides.

What Is Inheritance?

We started programming in Chapter 5 by defining the simplest possible Applet class:

```
public class MyApplet extends java.lang.Applet {
}
```

We found that we could compile and run this applet just fine, even though it didn't appear to do much. Or did it? Actually, this applet had some behavior of its own. You could resize the applet, for example. And the applet certainly started just fine. *Something* was responding to the init() and start() methods that the Applet Viewer invoked on this applet, even if we didn't write any code ourselves to respond to these methods.

Where did this behavior come from? We didn't supply any behavior: Our class definition was empty. What happened was that our applet's default behavior came from Java's Applet class. Whenever we create our own applet, what we are really doing is starting with Java's Applet class as a base and adding to it. This idea is depicted in Figure 10.1.

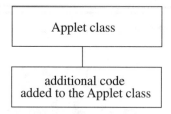

Figure 10.1   Building on the Applet class supplied by Java.

What is this combination of the Applet class and additional code? Taken together, this is a new class, an extension to the Applet class, which we've called MyApplet in the preceding code snippet. The class MyApplet can do everything that the Applet class can do, plus any additional code we write. For example, if we provide an `init()` method for MyApplet that displays "French Roast" in the Java Output window, then MyApplet behaves just like the Applet class, but it also does more: It displays "French Roast" when the applet initializes itself.

Why Is Inheritance Good?

As it turns out, Java allows you to extend just about *any* class, not just the Applet class. This means you can build your applets by extending what Java provides. The advantage of this is that you can start with something that already works. In fact, Java's classes already work great, and you can build on Java's classes to write your own.

For example, perhaps you want to keep track of a collection of data in a particular way. Well, Java already supplies a class that keeps track of a collection of data (this class is called Vector, and you'll work with vectors in Chapter 12). If you find that one of Java's classes is almost good enough for what you want, but you want it to do something more than it does by default, you can build on this class, extend it, and add your own behavior to it.

As another example, maybe you want to provide behavior that performs arithmetic with imaginary numbers, which, taken together with nonimaginary numbers, are called **complex numbers**. If you're not familiar with the idea of complex or imaginary numbers, all you need to know to understand this example is that they are extensions to the integer and fractional numbers you're already familiar with. Java provides classes that provide behavior for numbers (one of these classes is called Integer). If you want to extend the behavior for this class, you can add your extra code to the Integer class that allows you to work with complex numbers.

For a third example, perhaps you want to work with dates based on the Jewish or Chinese calendars. Java already provides a Date class. Rather than writing

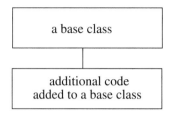

Figure 10.2 Extending a base class with your own additional code.

all your own date functionality, you can extend what Java already provides by writing your own code to work with other calendar systems.

These classes, and many more, can save you all sorts of time and effort because, if you write your own classes, you can start with a base level of behavior and then add to it. In other words, you don't have to start from scratch. This is illustrated in Figure 10.2, which makes the concept in Figure 10.1 more generic.

How Inheritance Works

As you know, classes define variables and methods for their instances. For example, let's say you have a class called Dwelling, defined like this:

```
class Dwelling {
    int squareFeet;
    void knock() {
        System.out.println("Knock, knock");
    }
}
```

This class defines an instance variable called squareFeet. If you invoke a dwelling object's knock() method, it will display "Knock, knock" in the Java Output window. We've seen examples of this kind of thing already.

Now, what happens when we want to define a class called House? Maybe our house has a boolean instance variable to indicate whether it has a fireplace or not. Do we have to start from scratch and repeat ourselves, like this:

```
class House {
    int squareFeet;
    boolean hasFirePlace;
    void knock() {
        System.out.println("Knock, knock");
    }
}
```

This seems like a waste of code to repeat this definition, and in Java it would be. Since the House class is just an extension to the Dwelling class, you can just *extend* the Dwelling class and add the additional features that make it a House class. Instead of what we just wrote, we could write our House class like this:

```
class House extends Dwelling {
    boolean hasFirePlace;
}
```

Very easy! Now house objects can do everything that dwelling objects can do, plus houses also know whether they have a fireplace or not. For example, if we have the preceding class definitions, we can write some code such as:

```
House h = new House();
h.knock();
```

and the words "Knock, knock" will appear in the Java Output window. How does this happen?

When we invoke the knock() method on the house object, Java first looks in the house object for this code. However, it doesn't find it there. So it looks in the class that was extended to make the House class—which is the Dwelling class. And there it is! The Dwelling class defines the instance method named knock(). Java executes this method, and "Knock, knock" appears in the Java Output window. Figure 10.3 illustrates this sequence of events. Notice that the method invocation gets passed up the **class hierarchy** (the structure of subclasses and superclasses) until one of the classes provides the appropriate method.

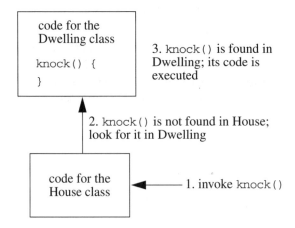

Figure 10.3 A sequence of events showing how inheritance works.

This also implies that we can access the variable `squareFeet` by using an instance of class House. We could write

```
House h = new House();
h.squareFeet = 2200;
```

The House class doesn't define `squareFeet`, of course; this instance variable is defined by Dwelling. Since House inherits everything that Dwelling has, we can set the house's `squareFeet` variable through code like that just shown.

Some Terminology

The picture that most developers envision for this relationship between classes like Dwelling and House is that Dwelling is at the top level and House is at the bottom. House is said to be a **subclass** of Dwelling, and Dwelling is a **superclass** of House. This image is shown in Figure 10.4.

House is also referred to as a **descendant** of Dwelling because it **descends from** Dwelling, and Dwelling is an **ancestor** of House. This whole process of extending classes is called **inheritance**, and thus we can say that House **inherits from** Dwelling. (As you can tell, some of this terminology comes from the idea of genetic inheritance, where children take on the characterstics of their parents.) That is, House inherits all the traits of Dwelling—all the methods and variables. House then can add some new methods and variables of its own that are completely unknown to the Dwelling class. (Notice that if we went back and added a new variable or method to the Dwelling class and House still extended Dwelling, then House would also acquire the new variable or method in Dwelling. Again, the House class does everything that Dwelling does, plus its own custom code.)

Figure 10.4 A simple diagram conveying a subclass and superclass relationship between House and Dwelling.

When to Use Inheritance

There are two great uses for inheritance that are closely related. First, you can use inheritance to extend a base set of working code to make it do a little bit more. Second, you can organize your classes into hierarchies so that similar classes can share as much code as possible.

Extending Classes

One of the most obvious examples of extending a class in Java is extending Java's Applet class. By extending this class, you can write applets that do things other than just display a blank window! Every applet around starts with the base behavior of the Applet class and builds on it to create a new, custom class. The complexity of the applet you want to create determines how much new code you need to add to Java's Applet class.

Java also defines a class called Object. This class provides some very basic behavior, such as the ability to create new objects and the ability to see whether the object is equal to another object. By extending this base Object class, you gain a core level of behavior that you'll want all of your own objects to have as well. (We'll discuss the Object class and its role in more detail later in this chapter.)

Finding Hierarchies

Sometimes, your classes might grow out of classes you've already defined. For example, perhaps you have defined a class called Square, like this:

```
class Square {
    static int diameter = 20;

    Color    color;
    int      x;
    int      y;

    void draw() {
        System.out.println("draw the square");
    }
}
```

The Square class defines a class variable called `diameter` (we could also call this variable `side`, but you'll see why we chose the name `diameter` very soon). It defines instance variables to maintain a color for the square, as well as a screen location for where the square should be drawn. The Square class defines a method for drawing the square. For now, this method just writes a message to the Java Output window. (In Chapter 11, you'll see how to actually draw a square on the screen.)

Perhaps at some time later in your application's development, you'll also find you need a Circle class, which you'll want to define like this:

```
class Circle {
    static int diameter = 20;

    Color color;
    int    x;
    int    y;

    void draw() {
        System.out.println("draw the circle");
    }
}
```

It seems like there's a lot of overlap here. Both shapes define instance variables that keep track of their current color and screen location. They also both define methods named draw(), though each shape type implements draw() differently. Is there some way we can combine these two classes into a common class and then extend that common class to implement a square and also a circle? There certainly is, and this is what inheritance is all about!

Let's create a class called Shape that groups together the common variables:

```
class Shape {
    static int diameter = 20;

    Color color;
    int x;
    int y;

}
```

Armed with this Shape class, we can now create the Square and Circle classes a little more compactly. Here's how we would create each:

```
class Square extends Shape {
    void draw() {
        System.out.println("draw the square");
    }
}

class Circle extends Shape {
    void draw() {
        System.out.println("draw the circle");
    }
}
```

Gone are the instance variables duplicated in both the Square and the Circle class definitions. Now all we have to do is extend the Shape class and implement draw(). The Square has all the methods and variables of class Shape, plus any variables and methods it defines on its own. The same goes for the Circle class. In the example here, the Square and the Circle inherit the variables color, x, and y. The Square and Circle each make themselves unique by drawing in different ways.

Creating class hierarchies is a powerful approach for developing your own software. If at some later time you need to create rectangles, ellipses, pentagons, and other shapes, you can simply extend the Shape class, and much of your work is done for you. Just as extending Java's classes can speed up your application development, extending your own classes can also speed up your application development.

Advanced Inheritance Topics

So far in this chapter, we've covered the basics of inheritance, but the power of inheritance doesn't end here. This section describes a few more features of inheritance that help you control how classes and subclasses interact with one another. For example, can you *stop* a subclass from inheriting a variable or method? Can you restrict access so that *only* subclasses can access a variable or method? The answer to both questions is yes, and this section shows you how.

Private Variables and Methods

If you define an instance variable in a class definition, and you want to ensure that only methods defined by that class can access that variable, you can define the variable using the keyword private. For example, you might define an Employee class like this:

```
class Employee {
   private String ssn;
   int employeeNumber;
}
```

This code would store the employee's Social Security number in a `private` variable, but it would make available a different employee number in a field that does not have this restriction. Now, the only methods that can access the instance variable ssn are those defined by the Employee class. For example, if we make an instance of class Employee, like this

```
Employee e = new Employee();
```

we cannot get to the variable ssn by writing e.ssn. Only the Employee class itself can do this. For example, we might write an access method for the Social Security number and put it into the Employee class. This new access method might rely on a `boolean` value that indicates whether the ssn should be made available or not:

```
class Employee {
   private String ssn;
   private boolean makeAvailable;
   int employeeNumber;

   String getSsn() {
      if (makeAvailable)
         return ssn;
      else
         return null;
   }
}
```

Now, other objects can get to the ssn via the getSsn() method, as long as the employee object does not have its makeAvailable variable set to false (of course, we would still need some way to set the value of makeAvailable, which we've declared as private here).

Suppose we created a subclass of Employee, like this:

```
class RetiredEmployee extends Employee {
   Date retirementDate;
}
```

Even instances of RetiredEmployee could not access the variable ssn. Using the keyword `private` really does make it *private* to the class defining it and stops this variable from being inherited by subclasses.

It's also possible to make a method `private`. Methods that are `private` can be invoked only by methods defined by that same class.

Protected Variables and Methods

In the example just given, suppose we thought it was OK if subclasses had access to ssn, but not other objects in general. Java provides a way to do this through the keyword `protected`. If a variable or method is `protected`, then any descendant can access it, but other objects in other parts of the class hierarchy cannot. So, our subclass of Employee called RetiredEmployee could access ssn in the Employee class and could invoke `protected` methods defined in the Employee class. Inheritance is still occurring, but access is restricted to a class's descendants.

Abstract Variables and Methods

Back in the example with the classes Shape, Square, and Circle, we defined a draw() method for the Square and Circle, but we left it out of the Shape class. Unfortunately, taking this route leads us to a problem. Consider this slightly simpler version of the classes Shape, Square, and Circle:

```java
class Shape {
    int x;
    int y;

}

class Square extends Shape {
    void draw() {
        System.out.println("draw the square");
    }
}

class Circle extends Shape {
    void draw() {
        System.out.println("draw the circle");
    }
}
```

One of the great advantages of creating a hierarchy like this is that we don't need to define different variables to hold different shape types. That is, instead of defining the variables

```
Square s;
Circle c;
```

to hold a square and a circle, depending on what we need, we can just define a variable that holds a shape

```
Shape s;
```

and use this variable with a circle object or a square object, as appropriate.

However, with our variable s defined to be a Shape instance, we run into a problem if we want to invoke the draw() method in the circle or square because the Shape class does not define draw(). For example, we can write the following statement without any problem:

```
Shape s = new Circle();
```

However, if we tried to then invoke the circle's draw() method, like this

```
s.draw();
```

the compiler would complain that draw() is not defined by the shape! We don't actually want to provide a draw() method for the shape; we just want the Shape's subclasses, Circle and Square, to implement draw(). What can we do?

What we can do is indicate in the Shape class that the subclasses will, in fact, implement this draw() method, even though it's not implemented in class Shape. The way we do this is by declaring the method, without actually providing any code for the method, and by using the keyword abstract. Our new Shape class would look like this:

```
abstract class Shape {
    int x;
    int y;

    abstract void draw();
}
```

Notice that we don't provide any behavior for draw(). What's more, we've added the abstract keyword to the class itself! The rule in Java is that if the class defines an abstract method, it can never be instantiated. That means the class itself must be abstract. Only subclasses implementing the draw() method can be instantiated.

Definition

Classes that can be instantiated are sometimes said to be **concrete**, which differentiates them from **abstract** classes, which cannot be instantiated.

So, we've solved the problem of using the variable s to hold a circle and using s to invoke the circle's draw() method. The method is indeed defined for the Shape class; it just doesn't have any behavior associated with it. Instead, the behavior is supplied by the subclasses.

Overriding Methods

Let's reconsider our example of the Dwelling and House classes, which looked like this:

```
class Dwelling {
    int squareFeet;
    void knock() {
        System.out.println("Knock, knock");
    }
}

class House extends Dwelling {
    boolean hasFirePlace;
}
```

Recall that if we created an instance of class House and invoked its knock() method, like this

```
House h = new House();
h.knock();
```

the words "Knock, knock" would appear in the Java Output window.

However, what if we wanted to provide different behavior for the house? What if we wanted to invoke the knock() method to ring the doorbell and say

"Ding dong" instead? What we would need to do is **override** the knock() method.

A subclass can override a method to change the behavior of the method. For example, here's how we could define our House class if we wanted different behavior from that of the Dwelling class:

```
class House extends Dwelling {
    boolean hasFirePlace;
    void knock() {
        System.out.println("Ding dong");
    }
}
```

Now, when you invoked the house object's knock() method, it would write "Ding dong" to the Java Output window. However, instances of Dwelling would still respond to knock() by displaying "Knock, knock."

A Special Variable for Inheritance: super

Sometimes, you want to *add to* the behavior you inherit from your superclass, not change it completely. Is there any way we can perform the Dwelling's knock() behavior in conjunction with our House's knock() behavior? You can do just such a thing by explicitly passing the method up the class hierarchy. This makes your superclass's method execute in addition to your own. For example, if we overrode knock() in the House class, the words "Ding dong" would appear in the Java Output window. If we then passed knock() to our superclass, the Dwelling's knock() method would execute, and the words "Knock, knock" would *also* appear in the Java Output window. The way we refer to our superclass is by using the word super. Here's how we could rewrite the House class to do this:

```
class House extends Dwelling {
    boolean hasFirePlace;
    void knock() {
        System.out.println("Ding dong");
        super.knock();
    }
}
```

Using the super variable to refer to our superclass is similar to using the this variable to refer to ourselves. This relationship is shown in Figure 10.5.

Figure 10.5   Using the variable `this` to represent the current object and the variable `super` to represent its superclass.

Testing Objects

We mentioned that a variable defined as holding instances of a certain class can actually hold instances of that class's subclasses as well. For example, in our example with the classes Shape, Square, and Circle, we could define a variable that could hold either a Square or Circle object by writing

```
Shape s;
```

s could now hold an instance of one of class Shape's subclasses—Circle and Square. s cannot hold an instance of class Shape only because we defined the Shape class earlier to be `abstract`, which makes it impossible to create instances of class Shape in the first place. A variable declared like this, however,

```
Circle c;
```

could hold only a circle. It would not be legal to assign c an instance of class Square.

Since it is possible for a variable like s to hold different types of objects, Java provides an operator to test the object to see what class it is or inherits from. This operator is called `instanceof` and is used in the following format:

```
object instanceof ClassName
```

where *object* is a variable containing your object and *ClassName* is the name of the class the object may or may not be an instance of. `instanceof` will return true if the object is an instance of the supplied class name. It will also return true if the object is an instance of one of its subclasses.

For example, to test whether an object is an instance of Circle, you can write

```
if (myObject instanceof Circle)
    System.out.println("myObject is an instance of Circle");
```

Since `instanceof` evaluates to true if the object is an instance of one of the class's subclasses, if `myObject` really is a circle, `instanceof` will also evaluate to true if you write

```
myObject instanceof Shape
```

Class Object

You've already seen that you can create your own hierarchies of classes, and you've read that Java provides lots of classes that you can use in your own applets. Now to combine these two ideas: Java also provides entire class hierarchies that describe its own classes. These hierarchies of preexisting classes provide a kind of scaffolding, or **framework**, on which you can build your own applets.

Java defines a class called Object, and, in Java's class framework, the role of Java's Object class is key. In fact, Java's Object class sits at the very top of Java's entire class framework. Every one of Java's classes can claim class Object as its ancestor. Figure 10.6 shows a partial class hierarchy of Java's class framework, with class Object sitting over everything.

Why is Java's class Object so important? Because it provides the minimum level of behavior that all objects in Java must provide. Whether you know it or not, you've been creating subclasses of class Object already! Of course, since you're creating subclasses of class Applet, your Applet subclasses, such as MyApplet, ultimately inherit from class Object as well, as shown in Figure 10.7.

Even a class like Circle, which we defined before like this

```
class Circle {
    Color color;
    int x;
    int y;
}
```

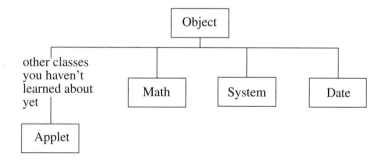

Figure 10.6   Diagram showing a simplified version of Java's class hierarchy.

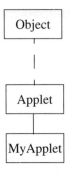

Figure 10.7 Diagram showing MyApplet as a subclass of Applet, which traces its ancestry back to class Object.

inherits from class Object! How is this possible? We didn't indicate that Circle extends class Object. Nonetheless, Java turns such class definitions into

```
class Circle extends Object{
    Color color;
    int x;
    int y;
}
```

Java does this for you because you must provide the behavior that is in class Object. Otherwise, you would never be able to create new objects, and Java would not be able to manage the objects in your computer's memory. This means that there's no escaping Java's class framework. You will always plug in somewhere. Either you will explicitly inherit from one of Java's classes, or Java will provide Object as your superclass for you.

By the Way

Since all of your own classes, as well as Java's, can trace their ancestry back to class Object, evaluating this piece of code

```
myObject instanceof Object
```

will always evaluate to true.

Now that we've looked at inheritance, and now that you have a sense that Java provides classes for you, let's look at how Java organizes its classes. Rather than just provide you with a big collection of classes, Java collects its classes into groups, called **packages**.

Packages

We've been using two of Java's packages so far, though we haven't explained this yet. Let's take a moment to understand how Java organizes its classes into packages and how we can use these packages ourselves. Then you'll see how we've been using Java's packages all along.

Java groups its many classes into six basic packages. Each package is focused on a particular feature set of Java. There's a package for developing user interfaces, there's a package for communicating over the Internet, and so on. We'll look at these different packages in this section.

Using Packages

Classes within the same package can access one another's variables and methods, as long as those variables and methods are not defined using the keywords `private` or `protected`, which changes the rules, as you've learned. You've already seen how these restrict access to variables and methods.

When you create a new applet, all of the classes that are defined as part of that applet are placed in the same default package. However, this default package is separate from Java's packages. The easiest way to use a class that is not in the same package as your own is to *import* it first. For example, if you want to use the Date class, which is in a package called util, you can import it like this:

```
import java.util.Date;
```

This line of code says that you will use a class called Date, which is located in Java's util package.

The other way to refer to a class that is not in the same package is to spell out exactly which package that class belongs to, which is what we've been doing so far with the Applet class. We've been subclassing Applet, but we can't just say

```
public class MyApplet extends Applet ...
```

unless we first import the Applet class or tell Java how to find the Applet class. So, we've been writing this instead:

```
public class MyApplet extends java.applet.Applet ...
```

This tells Java exactly which package to look in to find the Applet class—namely, the package defined by Java called applet. If we wanted to, we could instead write

```
import java.applet.Applet;
public class MyApplet extends Applet ...
```

You might have noticed that we have also been using a class called System. We've used this class extensively to write messages to the Java Output window. The reason we did not have to import System is that it belongs to a package called lang. Java's entire lang package is imported for you automatically. This package contains many classes that support Java's basic features, so Java imports all the classes in this package without your needing to ask for them.

If you want to import all the classes in a package explicitly (and you often do), you can use a wild-card notation by writing an asterisk (*). For example, there's a package called util that provides some useful utility classes. To import all of these for use by your program, you can write

```
import java.util.*;
```

Note that all of your import statements must come at the top of your source file.

Public Classes

The variables and methods in classes, and the classes themselves, are, by default, available only to other classes in the same package. If you want to make a class, variable, or method available to classes in other packages, you need to declare your class, variable, or method as public. This is why you needed to declare your Applet class as public: so that Java's classes, defined in a different package, could invoke your applet's methods. This is why the life cycle methods of init(), start(), stop(), and destroy() were declared as public. This was done so that Java could invoke these methods from the classes in its own packages.

What Classes Are in Java's Packages?

Java defines six major packages. Each package contains classes that provide a broad area of functionality. These packages are as follows:

1. The **lang** package contains classes that provide basic behavior for your applets and for Java itself. These classes include Object, which is at the root of all class hierarchies, and System, which allows you to write to the standard

output. There are many other classes in this package as well, and you'll be introduced to many of them as you progress through this book.

2. The **awt** package contains classes that help you create a user interface. This package was named awt because this is an acronym for Abstract Windowing Toolkit. The idea behind a windows toolkit is that it provides a way to create user interface components, such as buttons, text fields, and menus, and containers that organize these components. These components allow users to interact with your applet in a graphical way (that is, using the mouse, by pointing and clicking), and they allow your applet to run in a graphical environment (such as the Mac or Windows). The word *abstract* is meant to explain that the classes in this package are not specific to any particular platform. That is, if you create a button on the Mac using the classes in this package, you can create a button for Windows NT using the same classes in this package. We'll touch more on this package in the next chapter, where we'll start creating user interfaces.

3. The **io** package is used for receiving input and sending output. For example, you can use the classes in this package to read data coming in over the Internet. You can also use the classes in this package to access files on your computer's hard drive.

4. The **net** package contains some very sophisticated classes that allow you to write Internet applications with ease. For example, there are classes for dealing with Universal Resource Locators (URLs), sockets to allow communication between a client and a server over the Internet, and other Internet and networking functions.

5. The **util** package contains a bunch of miscellaneous classes that help with a variety of programming tasks. There's a class that is useful for working with dates, a class for mathematics features, such as trigonometric calculations, a class for generating random numbers, and more.

6. The **applet** package defines only the Applet class. We'll continue to explore the features of this class in upcoming chapters.

All of these packages and the classes inside them are available for you to use as you see fit. You might even want to use these classes just for the data and methods they define. For example, the Math class defines a value for pi that you might want to use at some point. This variable, named PI, is a class variable. How do you think you access it? You got it:

```
Math.PI
```

This gives you just a taste of what's available. You'll see many more examples of using Java's classes as you forge ahead.

Sample Programs

The two sample programs in this section explore overriding methods, accessing the code in an object's superclass, and using keywords to control access to variables and methods in class hierarchies.

Triangle.μ

For our first example, let's return to our friend the triangle. Open the subfolder 10.01 - triangle in Learn Java Projects. Open Triangle.μ and make the project. Run the applet by dropping Triangle.html onto the Metrowerks Java icon. A number of messages will appear in the Java Output window, as shown in Figure 10.8.

```
The triangles say:
t1 == t2? true
t1 == t3? false
The objects say:
t1 == t2? false
t1 == t3? false
```

Figure 10.8 The messages written by TriangleApplet to the Java Output window.

These messages relate to three triangles that we created in the code. At first, we checked to see whether triangle 1 was equal to triangle 2 and triangle 3 by asking the triangle itself. Next, we checked to see whether triangle 1 was equal to triangle 2 and triangle 3 by asking the triangle's superclass, the object. Notice the difference in the output. The triangles reported that triangle 1 was equal to triangle 2, while the objects reported they were different.

Let's check out the source code and see why this occurs.

Stepping Through the Source Code

The source code, located in TriangleApplet.java, defines two classes. The first is an applet; the second is a class called Triangle. Let's look at the Triangle class first.

The Triangle class starts by defining instance variables for a triangle's base and height:

```
class Triangle {
    int base;
    int height;
```

The Triangle class then overrides a method that is defined by class Object. This method is called `equals()`, and it tests to see whether the object passed in as a parameter is equal to the object responding to this method invocation. If the object passed in is equal to the triangle, this method returns true. Otherwise, this method returns false. Since `equals()` is defined as a `public` method in the Object class, we've also got to declare this method as `public` here in the Triangle class. The `equals()` method that the Triangle class defines starts by defining a variable called `t`:

```
public boolean equals(Object obj) {
    Triangle t;
```

It then tests to see whether `obj`, the parameter passed in, is an instance of class Triangle.

```
if (obj instanceof Triangle) {
```

If this parameter is a triangle, then we can go ahead and perform the special triangle test. First, in order to work with the parameter as a triangle, we have to get it into a variable that we declared as a Triangle. We had to declare it as an Object in the parameter list because that's how `equals()` is defined in class Object, and we're overriding this method. We can't change the method's signature (its name and parameters), or Java will think we're defining a new method. But now we need a Triangle. The way we get `obj` into a variable for triangles is by **casting**. (Casting is explained further in Chapter 12.) Suffice it to say that we can assign this to a variable of type Triangle by writing

```
t = (Triangle)obj;
```

Once Java recognizes this object as a triangle, we can acquire its base and height, which are instance variables of a triangle. If these are equal to the current object's base and height, then we'll consider these two objects to be equal, and we'll return true:

```
    if (t.base == base && t.height == height)
        return true;
}
```

For all other cases—that is, if the object is not an instance of class Triangle or the base and height variables were not equal—we'll indicate that these two triangles are not equal by returning false:

```
    return false;
}
```

The Triangle class also defines its own instance method called object-Equals(). The mission for this method is to see what would have happened if we had not overridden equals(), but instead had left equals() alone and let the Object class respond to this method using its own code. We can get to the Object's equals() method by using the super variable. objectEquals() returns the result of the Object's equals() method:

```
boolean objectEquals(Object obj) {
    return super.equals(obj);
}

}
```

Now, let's turn our attention to the applet and see how the applet uses this Triangle class. The applet overrides the init() method and defines three triangles. The first and second triangles are set to the same base and height; the third triangle holds a different base and height:

```
public class TriangleApplet extends java.applet.Applet {

public void init() {

    Triangle t1 = new Triangle();
    t1.base = 10;
    t1.height = 20;

    Triangle t2 = new Triangle();
    t2.base = 10;
    t2.height = 20;

    Triangle t3 = new Triangle();
    t3.base = 12;
    t3.height = 52;
```

Then, we invoke each triangle's `equals()` method. When comparing triangle 1 to triangle 2, the triangle's `equals()` method, not surprisingly, reports that these triangles are equal. Also not surprisingly, it reports that triangle 1 and triangle 3 are not equal:

```
System.out.println("The triangles say:");
System.out.println("t1 == t2? " + t1.equals(t2));
System.out.println("t1 == t3? " + t1.equals(t3));
```

The code that is in the Object class sees things differently. This code thinks that triangle 1 does not equal triangle 2, and, as far as the object is concerned, it's right. These *are* different objects. The Object's `equals()` method also reports that triangle 1 is not equal to triangle 3, as we would expect:

```
System.out.println("The objects say:");
System.out.println("t1 == t2? " + t1.objectEquals(t2));
System.out.println("t1 == t3? " + t1.objectEquals(t3));

    }


}
```

This example shows that overriding a method can change the behavior for an object. It also shows how to invoke the code for an object that is contained in the object's superclass.

Next, we'll look at some of the keywords you can use to define instance variables and instance methods, and we'll see how they affect access to these variables and methods.

AccessApplet.μ

Open `10.02 - access` in the Learn Java Projects folder. Open `AccessApplet.μ` and make the project. Drop the `AccessApplet.html` file onto the Metrowerks Java icon. The applet writes four lines to the Java Output window, as shown in Figure 10.9.

```
Circle: radius = 20
Circle: color = java.awt.Color[r=0,g=0,b=255]
Square: radius = 20
Square: color = java.awt.Color[r=255,g=255,b=255]
```

Figure 10.9 The messages written by AccessApplet to the Java Output window.

207

The applet creates an object that represents a circle and an object that represents a square. It sets the data for these objects and then prints out this data. The Java Output window shows that the radius for both shapes is 20; it then displays the colors for the shapes. The color for the circle is blue. This is indicated by the red and green components having a value of 0, while the blue component has the maximum value possible (255). The color for the square is white. This is indicated by the red, green, and blue components each having their maximum value (255). (You'll learn much more about colors in Chapter 11.)

Let's look at the source code and see how it's set up to control and limit access to data within a class hierarchy.

Stepping Through the Source Code

Open `AccessApplet.java`. There are four classes in this file: AccessApplet, Shape, Circle, and Square. Let's start with Shape, Circle, and Square.

The Shape, Circle, and Square classes are arranged in the hierarchy shown in Figure 10.10.

The Shape class maintains some information that the Circle and Square classes have in common. First, the Shape class is defined as abstract because it defines an abstract method named `draw()`. Therefore, the Shape class can never be instantiated itself. Only subclasses of the Shape class that have implemented the `draw()` method can be instantiated:

```
abstract class Shape {
```

The Shape class defines a class variable named `radius` (this variable is shared between both the Circle and the Square, which are subclasses of class Shape that we'll define next):

```
static protected final int radius = 20;
```

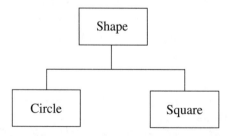

Figure 10.10 Hierarchy of the Shape, Circle, and Square classes.

Notice that this class variable is defined as `protected`. This means that the only classes that can access this variable are the Shape class itself and the subclasses of the Shape class. The applet, for example, would not be able to access this class variable. In other words, we are making this class variable "private" to this branch of the class hierarchy. (We've also defined this variable as `final`, which means it cannot be changed. You'll learn more about these variables in Chapter 13.)

The next variable is an instance variable called `color`. This variable is defined as holding an instance of class Color, which stores a color in Java. Notice that we've defined `color` to be `private`. This means that this variable can be accessed only by instance methods defined by the Shape. Not even circle or square objects, which inherit from class Shape, can access this variable:

```
private Color color;
```

Next, we've defined two `int` variables, x and y. These variables keep track of a shape's *x* and *y* locations on the screen:

```
int   x;
int   y;
```

These variables are not declared as `protected` or `private`. This means that any method in any class in the same package as the Shape can access these variables. For example, these variables can be accessed from the applet.

Next, we've defined the `abstract` method named `draw()` that the Circle and Square classes will have to implement:

```
abstract void draw();
```

Since the `color` variable is `private`, we've next provided two methods to set and get the value for `color`. The first method sets this instance variable:

```
void setColor(Color color) {
```

Now, here's the reason we made the `color` variable `private` to the Shape class. The Shape class ensures that a shape's color (for whatever reason) can never be set to black. If other objects could access the `color` variable directly, they could set this variable to any color they wanted to, including black. However, by forcing other objects to go through the `setColor()` method to set the color for this variable, the Shape class can intercept any attempt to set this color to black. `setColor()` handles

209

such an attempt by setting the color to white instead. Otherwise, it allows `color` to be set to the new color:

```
if (color == Color.black)
    this.color = Color.white;
else
    this.color = color;
}
```

The Color class defines a whole bunch of class variables that define colors for Java. These variables are common colors such as black, white, blue, red, and so on. Since they're class variables defined by the Color class, you can access these colors by writing `Color.black`, `Color.white`, `Color.blue`, `Color.red`, and so on, as we've done in the preceding code.

Since `color` is `private`, if we want other objects to be able to get at it, we also have to provide a method to retrieve the color, as well as setting it:

```
Color getColor() {
    return color;
}


}
```

The Circle and Square classes are straightforward by comparison. The Circle class, for example, starts out by indicating it is extending the definition of class Shape:

```
class Circle extends Shape {
```

Circle, then, is a subclass of class Shape; class Shape is a superclass of class Circle. (Since all classes inherit from class Object, class Object is also an ancestor of class Circle; class Circle is a descendant of class Object.)

Circle implements the `draw()` method so that it does not have to be an abstract class and can be instantiated:

```
void draw() {
```

It supplies two `println()` statements for this method. The first displays the radius for this shape (remember, this is a `protected` variable, which means subclasses can access it):

```
System.out.println("Circle: radius = " + radius);
```

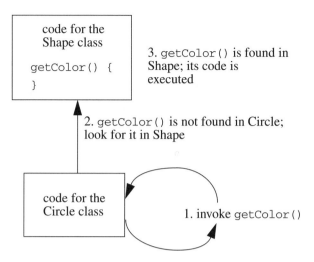

Figure 10.11 Method invocations propagating up the class hierarchy.

The next `println()` statement displays the color for the circle. It does this by accessing the color using `getColor()`. The circle object dispatches this method to itself. Not finding it there, Java will look in its superclass, which is class Shape, where it does exist. `getColor()` works as we described, returning the value of the `private` variable named `color` in the Shape class. This sequence is shown in Figure 10.11.

With the color object returned by `getColor()`, we can use a method defined for color objects called `toString()`. This method creates a string representing the color information for that color object. Putting this inside a `println()` statement makes this information appear in the Java Output window. This is the color information for red, green, and blue that we saw when we ran the applet:

```
System.out.println("Circle: color = " +
        getColor().toString());
    }
}
```

Here's the Square class, which is almost identical to the Circle class:

```
class Square extends Shape{
    void draw() {
        System.out.println("Square: radius = " + radius);
```

```
        System.out.println("Square: color = " +
            getColor().toString());
    }
}
```

Now we can look at the applet itself. First, the applet imports the Color class so that we can use it in all the classes in this file:

```
import java.awt.Color;
```

Then, we've defined an `init()` method for the applet. We start by creating instances of the Circle and Square classes:

```
public class AccessApplet extends java.applet.Applet {

    public void init() {

        Circle c = new Circle();
        Square s = new Square();
```

We then use the `setColor()` method to set the color of the circle to blue and to try to set the color for the square to black:

```
c.setColor(Color.blue);
s.setColor(Color.black);
```

However, you already know what will happen when we try to set the color to black; it will be set to white instead! This is verified by what appears later in the Java Output window.

Next, the applet sets the x and y instance variables for the circle and square. Notice how we can access these variables directly because the AccessApplet class is in the same package as the Circle and Square classes (by virtue of being defined in the same file):

```
c.x = 50;
c.y = 60;

s.x = 100;
s.y = 200;
```

And finally, invoking the `draw()` method for the circle and square makes each object display its data in the Java Output window:

```
    c.draw();
    s.draw();


  }


}
```

We'll use classes very similar to the Shape, Circle, and Square classes defined here in a number of applets coming up in the rest of this book.

Review

Inheritance allows you to extend existing classes. This allows you to start with a base level of code that already works and then add to it to write your own, custom code. Inheritance also allows you to create class hierarchies, where you can group together common code in superclasses to share code between classes.

By using special keywords, such as `private`, `protected`, `public`, and `abstract`, you can obtain a great deal of control over your class hierarchies. You can either let the default thing happen and have classes inherit all of the variables and methods defined in their superclasses, or you can control which variables are inherited and which are not.

Java defines its classes in six different packages. You must import a class defined in another package before you use its short name, and you can use only `public` classes. (All of the classes in the lang package are imported for you automatically.) Classes within the same package can freely communicate with one another. You can use a wild-card symbol (*) to import all of the classes defined in a particular package.

What's Next?

At this point, you've learned enough to begin building a graphical user interface for your applet. In the next chapter, we'll paint in the applet and display user interface components such as text fields, buttons, and checkboxes. We'll even learn how to tell when the user has interacted with them, such as when the user types in text or clicks a button. So hang on and let's have some fun!

Chapter 11

Creating a User Interface

The first ten chapters brought you up to speed on basic Java concepts. These chapters introduced you to the CodeWarrior Java development environment and stepped you through enough code that you're probably itching to make your applet *look* like something by now, by golly! Enough of these applets with empty windows! The good news is that you now know enough to start putting together a **user interface**. In this chapter, we'll create and arrange an applet's user interface. We'll display shapes, print messages, create text fields, buttons, and choice lists, and we'll start interacting with the user by responding to mouse clicks and keyboard entry.

There are two ways that your applet can present a face to the world:

1. Your applet can draw, paint pictures, and display messages. Users generally cannot interact with drawn pictures and messages—they're just for display purposes.

2. Your applet can display user interface elements, such as buttons, text fields, and choice lists. Users interact with these elements by clicking them, typing text into them, and selecting choices they present. These elements allow users to work with your applet and control what it does.

Generally, you will use a combination of these two techniques when you make your applet appear the way you want it to. For example, the SimpleDraw applet you worked with earlier is a prime example of using both of these techniques in one applet. SimpleDraw provides two choice lists to allow the user to select a shape type and a color. Then, this applet paints a shape on the screen when the user clicks the applet. SimpleDraw uses user interface elements *and* drawing techniques when presenting its face to the world.

This chapter will explain how to go about arranging your applet's display using both drawing techniques and user interface elements. We'll start with drawing and then move on to creating and arranging interactive user interface elements.

Drawing

Java provides a number of ways for you to draw in your applet. You can draw lines, dots, circles, and squares. You can display images. You can draw in different colors. You can even display text in your applet by drawing it. When you display text, you can also control the way the text looks by choosing its font and color.

The idea of "drawing" text might sound strange, but think of it as painting the text with a brush. The difference between drawing text and using a user interface element, such as a text field, to display text is that when you draw text, the user cannot edit the text. By contrast, when you use a text field to display text, the user can edit the text (unless you set the property of the text field to read-only). This section will show you how to draw text; the next section will explain how to create and display text fields to allow the user to enter text.

Drawing is centered around the `paint()` method. So, let's start by looking at `paint()`.

The `paint()` Method

Every time your applet needs to be redrawn, Java will invoke your applet's `paint()` method. You can provide a `paint()` method or not provide one, as you desire. Up until now, we did not provide one. And what was the result? We had an empty applet! Our applet did not provide any behavior when it was asked to paint itself, so it presented an empty, gray window instead.

When does Java try to invoke your applet's `paint()` method? This will occur whenever the user does something that makes your applet's display obsolete. For example, if the user resizes your applet, your applet's display will no longer be current, and Java will invoke your applet's `paint()` method. If the user is displaying another window on top of your applet and then closes that window, Java will recognize that your applet must redisplay itself. Again, Java will invoke your applet's `paint()` method.

What happens if the program itself does something that makes the applet's current display obsolete? For example, what if the applet changes the color of a circle it's displaying every 10 seconds? If the applet wants to repaint itself, it can ask for its `paint()` method to be invoked. The applet does this by invoking its own `repaint()` method. Java then knows to invoke the applet's `paint()` method.

You should never invoke your own `paint()` method directly because Java keeps track of which parts of your applet have been recently refreshed and which parts are "dirty." If you invoke `paint()` directly, you circumvent Java's efforts to keep track of this information. However, if you invoke `repaint()`, Java can then keep tabs on what's going on, so this is definitely the safer method to invoke.

Here's the definition for an empty `paint()` method:

```
public void paint(Graphics g) {
}
```

This method is declared as `public` and does not return a value, just like the life cycle methods. However, unlike the life cycle methods, `paint()` takes one parameter. This is an object that is created for you by Java. This object is an instance of the Graphics class.

Let's take a look at what the Graphics class is all about and how you can use the graphics object to perform drawing operations.

The Graphics Class

When Java invokes your `paint()` method, it passes you an instance of class Graphics. The simple way to understand the Graphics class is to think of it as defining many methods for drawing. A graphics object can draw all sorts of shapes and lines, and it can display text as well, but this ignores the question of where your drawing *goes*. If you use a graphics object to draw a blue diamond, for example, where is this blue diamond drawn? The whole truth is that a graphics object is more than just a collection of methods that draw on the screen. Every graphics object is also tied to a particular user interface object. When you draw by invoking a graphics object's method, the particular graphics object you use determines where your drawing shows up. If you use a graphics object tied to your applet, your drawing ends up in your applet. If you use a graphics object tied to a button, your drawing shows up in the button.

When you supply a `paint()` method for a user interface object, Java hands you a graphics object tied to the object for which you've defined your `paint()` method. So, for your applet's `paint()` method, the graphics object is tied to your applet. If you create your own subclass of Button called MyButton and you supply a `paint()` method for MyButton, the graphics object passed to you in MyButton's `paint()` method will be tied to the particular button that is being painted.

As we mentioned, graphics objects allow you to draw shapes such as rectangles and ovals, lines such as straight lines and arcs, images, and even text. The methods you'll use the most when drawing with a graphics object are:

- `fillOval()`, which draws a solid oval (you can draw a circle by setting the width and height of the oval to the same value).

- `fillRect()`, which draws a solid rectangle (as with the oval, you can draw a square by setting the width and height of the rectangle to the same value).

- `drawLine()`, which draws a line between two points.

- `drawArc()`, which draws an arc within a rectangle, given an initial angle (0 is at the three o'clock position) and an ending angle (positive angles make the arc draw in a counterclockwise rotation).

- `drawImage()`, which draws the image you pass to it.

- `drawString()`, which displays the text you pass to it.

You can also use a graphics object to find out about the current state of graphics information. For example, here are two useful methods for setting useful graphics information:

- `setColor()`, which sets the color to use when drawing.

- `setFont()`, which sets the font to use when displaying text.

There are many more instance methods defined by the Graphics class. You can check out the documentation for the classes for a complete list. You can also look in Chapter 15 for information on how to look up information using the HTML files documenting Java's packages.

Warning

In general, you should never try to create your own graphics object. Instead, use the one that Java provides for you in the `paint()` method. Another way to get a graphics object is to ask Java for the one that is tied to a particular user interface component. You can do this by invoking the component's `getGraphics()` method, which will return a graphics object. If the component is not currently displayed on the screen, `getGraphics()` returns null.

Color

Java provides a class called Color. This class makes it unlikely that you'll ever create any color objects yourself, although it's easy enough to do so. The beauty of Java's Color class is that it defines a number of class variables that already contain predefined color objects. These include most common colors, such as blue, red, yellow, green, orange, black, white, and gray. These class variables are named after the colors they encode, so to get a color object that represents red, for example, you can simply refer to `Color.red`. To get a color that is set for blue, you can use `Color.blue`.

To create your own color, you need to supply the Color's constructor with the red, green, and blue components of your color. Each of these three color components ranges on a scale of 0 (no trace of this color is in the overall color) to 255 (use this color at full intensity).

You would need a color chart to figure out all the many colors you can create by ranging the red, green, and blue components between 0 and 255, but here's a sense of what's happening. You can think of each of these colors (red, green, and blue) as a spotlight. If none of them is on, you have darkness (black). If all of them are on, the total light appears white. If only one spotlight is on, the light appears to be that color (red, green, or blue). If different spotlights are on with different intensities, you can create every other color there is. (Your television and computer monitor use this exact same technique to create colors, by the way.) Here are some examples.

If you had the blue component set to 255 and the red and green components set to 0, the resulting color would be blue. If you had the red and green components set to 255 and the blue component set to 0, the resulting color would be yellow (really). To get black, you would set all three components to 0. To get white, you would set all components to 255. To get gray, you would set all components midway between 0 and 255, or to 127.

Here's an example of creating a new color object that produces orange, which results from a combination of red and green in different intensities and no blue component:

```
Color myOrange = new Color(255, 200, 0);
```

As we said, you'll usually just use a color object that has been created for you and is maintained by the Color class. You'll use a color object when you draw. For example, to set the current drawing color, you use a method provided by the graphics object called `setColor()`. To set the current drawing color to pink, for example, you could write `setColor(Color.pink)`. Then, any lines, shapes, or text you drew using that graphics object would show up in pink.

Fonts

When you want to use the graphics object to draw text, you'll sometimes be concerned about what font your text appears in. You can use the getFont() and set-Font() methods provided by the graphics object to get and set the current font, and you'll use a font object, much as you use a color object, to specify a particular font.

Java does not predefine a bunch of fonts, as it does with colors. However, it's very easy to create a particular font object. All you need to do is specify the name of the font, its style, and its point size when you invoke the constructor for the Font class.

These are pretty easy parameters as far as the font name and point size are concerned. The style is a little trickier, and we'll get to that in a moment. You can refer to a font name using a string, as in "Helvetica," "Courier," "Times Roman," and so on. Typical point sizes are 10, 12, 14, and 18. The styles are provided by class variables defined by the Font class. Here are the ones you'll use most often (it's clear what style each class variable represents):

- Font.PLAIN
- Font.BOLD
- Font.ITALIC

For simple styles—for example, for a font that is italic or bold or plain—you use the appropriate constant on its own. Here's an example of creating a font that is an italic Helvetica in size 14:

```
Font f = new Font("Helvetica", Font.ITALIC, 14);
```

In case you're wondering,

the font looks like this.

If you want to combine italic and bold, you use the logical OR operator that we touched on in a tech block in Chapter 6. This combines the values represented by Font.ITALIC and Font.BOLD and produces a value that Java recognizes as meaning *both*. So, to make the preceding font italic and bold, we would write

```
Font f = new Font("Helvetica", Font.ITALIC | Font.BOLD, 14);
```

In this case,

the font looks like this.

Java's User Interface Elements

Java provides a whole bunch of classes that define user interface elements. The way that you use these classes is by creating instances of them and then arranging them inside your applet. This chapter will go about showing you how to do this. Keep in mind that Java's user interface elements work in any operating environment—Windows NT/95, Solaris, the Mac, and wherever else Java exists. Of course, we'll use the Mac to develop our own user interfaces, but the same code we develop on the Mac to present a user interface will work anywhere.

Some User Interface Components You Can Use

Java provides classes that implement all of the standard user interface elements you've come to expect from modern software applications. These include:

- Text fields, which allow the user to enter text using the keyboard.

- Choice lists, which present a pop-up list of choices for the user to select from.

- Buttons, which perform some action when the user clicks them.

- Checkboxes, which allow the user to choose an option (if assigned to a checkbox group, only one checkbox will be selected at a time).

- Labels, which display some text for titles and information (but which the user cannot edit).

Figure 11.1 shows an example of an applet that displays a choice (currently displaying "Apple"), a text field (currently blank), a button (that says "Click me"), a label (that says "I am a label"), and three checkboxes (Yes, No, and Maybe) in a checkbox group. (You can find the source code for this applet in the Learn Java Projects folder under 11.01 - components.)

Figure 11.2 shows how you can interact with these components, displaying new choices to select from, entering text into the text field, and selecting a new checkbox (you can also click the button, but you can't interact with the label). Here, the user has clicked the choice list and is currently holding down the mouse button. This makes the choices in the choice list visible, allowing the user to slide the mouse cursor to the appropriate choice to select it. The user has also typed some text into the text field and has selected a new checkbox. Selecting the new

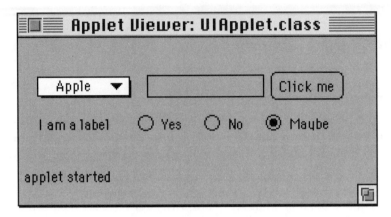

Figure 11.1 An applet that displays several user interface elements.

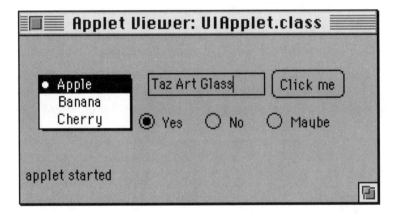

Figure 11.2 Interacting with the user interface elements.

checkbox has unselected the previously selected checkbox, which was Maybe. This occurred because these three checkboxes are part of the same group. If they did not belong to the same group, they would behave independently, and more than one checkbox could be selected at the same time.

Java provides some other user interface components that we won't go into here. These include menus, scroll bars, and text areas, among others. Check out Appendix G for information on where to find examples of these other components.

There is also another set of classes that allows you to arrange these components in relation to one another and to group together related components. We'll examine some of these classes, called *layout managers* and *containers*, later in this chapter. For now, let's take a look at each one of the user interface components displayed in the applet in Figure 11.1 to understand how we can go about creating them.

Creating New Elements

It's fairly straightforward to create user interface components like the ones in the applet in Figure 11.1. All you have to do is perform the following three steps:

1. Create a new instance of the appropriate component class.

2. Initialize the component so that it contains the choices you want.

3. Add the component to your applet's display.

When you create a user interface, you most likely want to create it once, when your applet begins, and never again. This means that, most of the time, you will create your user interface in your applet's `init()` method. That's what we've done for the applet in Figure 11.1. Let's look at each of the five components we displayed in our simple applet one at a time.

Buttons

One of the button's constructors takes a string, which allows you to name the button when you create it. For example, one way you can create a button titled "Click me," like we did in the applet just shown, is to write

```
Button myButton = new Button("Click me");
```

Labels

Labels are created similarly to buttons. You can provide a string for the label when you create it. The difference between buttons and labels is that you can interact with a button by clicking it; labels are for display only:

```
Label myLabel = new Label("I am a label");
```

Text Fields

To create an instance of class TextField, you can use one of a few different constructors. One of these specifies what text the text field should contain initially. (The purpose of text fields is for users to type their own text into these fields.) When you create a text field, you can also specify the width of the text field by indicating its number of columns. This is a rough indication of how many characters the field can contain.

For example, to create a text field that initially contains the character 0 (zero) and can hold 8 characters (approximately), you can write

```
TextField tf = new TextField("0", 8);
```

Choices

Choices provide a selection list for the user to pick one of a few different strings. Creating the choice itself is easy enough:

```
Choice c = new Choice();
```

To fill up the choice with the strings the user can select, you can use the choice's addItem() method, like this:

```
c.addItem("First Choice");
c.addItem("Second Choice");
```

and so on, for however many choices you have.

Checkboxes

To create a checkbox, you can use one of two common constructors. The first creates a checkbox that is not related to any other checkbox:

```
Checkbox c = new Checkbox("first choice");
```

This would create a new checkbox that was initially unselected. (You can always select it from your own code by invoking its setState() method and passing it true or false.)

If you created another checkbox, like this,

```
Checkbox c2 = new Checkbox("second choice");
```

and displayed both checkboxes, the user would be able to turn them on or off (select them and unselect them) independently of each other. If you wanted them to be tied together so that only one of these checkboxes could be selected at one time, you could create an **exclusive-choice** checkbox. (Exclusive choice checkboxes are often called Radio Buttons.)

The way you do that is by creating an instance of class CheckboxGroup and assigning the mutually exclusive checkboxes to the same checkbox group. You assign the checkbox group when you create the checkbox, and you also indicate whether the checkbox should be on or off (by also passing the constructor the value `true` or `false`). For example, you can write

```
CheckboxGroup group = new CheckboxGroup();
Checkbox c1 = new Checkbox("first choice", group, true);
Checkbox c2 = new Checkbox("second choice", group, false);
```

This would create two checkboxes, and the checkbox group would make sure that only one of these was selected at a time. At first, the checkbox in `c1` would be on, and the checkbox in `c2` would be off (notice the `true` and `false` values passed to the constructor that indicate this).

Making the Components Appear

To make a user interface component part of the applet's display, you can invoke the applet's `add()` method and pass it the component you want to add to the display. (We'll look at what's going on with the `add()` method in just a moment.) Listing 11.1 shows the `init()` method for the applet we displayed in Figure 11.1. Later in this chapter, we'll show you how to detect when the user has interacted with these components.

Listing 11.1 Creating user interface components.

```
import java.awt.*;

public class UIApplet extends java.applet.Applet {

    Button          button;
    Choice          choice;
    TextField       textField;

    /** Create a user interface. */
    public void init() {

        Checkbox        checkbox;
        CheckboxGroup   checkboxGroup;
        Label           label;
```

```
// create a choice list
choice = new Choice();
choice.addItem("Apple");
choice.addItem("Banana");
choice.addItem("Cherry");
add(choice);

// create a text field
textField = new TextField(10); // 10 columns wide
add(textField);

// create a button
button = new Button("Click me");
add(button);

// create a label
label = new Label("I am a label");
add(label);

// create 3 exclusive-choice checkboxes
checkboxGroup = new CheckboxGroup();

checkbox = new Checkbox("Yes", checkboxGroup, false);
add(checkbox);
checkbox = new Checkbox("No", checkboxGroup, false);
add(checkbox);
checkbox = new Checkbox("Maybe", checkboxGroup, true);
add(checkbox);

    }
}
```

Arranging User Interface Elements

So far, we've created components just fine, and we've even added them to our applet's display so that they appeared on the screen. We used the add() method to make them appear, but we haven't investigated what the add() method is doing; we just trusted this method to arrange our user interface components for us and to make sure they were displayed. It's time to look at what's really going on here and what you can do to influence the arrangement of your user interface elements.

Placing Components in Containers

Your components can't just be displayed on their own, independently of the rest of your user interface. Instead, they need to be contained in something. What you need to do is place your components into a subclass of Java's Container class. This idea is shown in Figure 11.3.

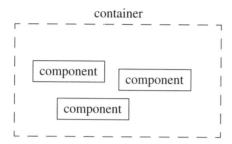

Figure 11.3 Component objects placed within an instance of class Container or a subclass of class Container.

As it happens, the Applet class itself is a subclass of class Container! This means that your Applet class can contain user interface components. Very convenient! This is what happened when we invoked the add() method for the applet in the example in the previous section: The component we passed along as a parameter for add() was added to the applet; the applet became the component's container. This idea is shown in Figure 11.4.

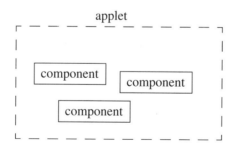

Figure 11.4 Component objects contained within the applet since it is an instance of a subclass of class Container.

Arranging Elements with Layouts

One thing we haven't covered yet is how these components know where they should appear within a container. When you use add() to add a user interface component to a container, where does the component go? That is, how does the container know how to position the component? Does the container position objects left to right? Top to bottom? Do all the components end up on top of one another in the middle of the container?

The answer is that it depends. What it depends on is the **layout manager** assigned to the container in which you're placing the components. Java defines five different types of layout managers, and each one does something a little bit differently. We'll list the five here, discuss two of them in more detail, and then use these two in the sample programs at the end of this chapter.

The layout managers supplied by Java are

- FlowLayout, which arranges components left to right until it must move to the next line to fit a new component into the display. At the end, each line will be centered.

- GridLayout, which arranges components in a rectangular grid the size that you specify.

- BorderLayout, which arranges components on either the left, right, top, bottom, or center. BorderLayout uses directions to indicate where to place a component. These directions are "East" for left, "West" for right, "North" for top, and "South" for bottom. "Center" places the component in the center of the container.

- CardLayout, which presents different screen arrangements (or cards, as in cards in a deck) to the user.

- GridBagLayout, which allows you to create sophisticated arrangements of objects on the screen. These arrangements are gridlike, but almost more in the sense of a game of Tetris than in a strict grid because user interface components can take up more than one grid.

Let's look at the first two types of layout managers in this list in more detail.

FlowLayout

FlowLayout is perhaps the easiest layout manager to use. This is the default layout manager for applets. FlowLayout starts placing components at the top left of your container (if you're adding components to your applet, then FlowLayout

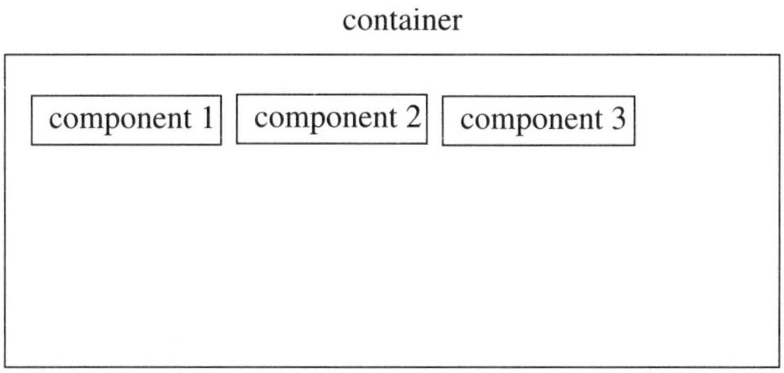

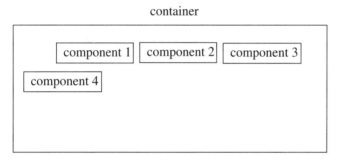

Figure 11.5 First row of components arranged by FlowLayout in a container left to right, starting along the top.

container

Figure 11.6 New component added to the second row by FlowLayout, at which point everything on the first row is centered.

starts at the top left of your applet). As you add more components to this container, FlowLayout will continue adding components along the top, moving left to right. This layout is shown in Figure 11.5.

When the next component to be added no longer fits on the current row, FlowLayout begins a new row. It then centers everything on the first row. This layout is shown in Figure 11.6.

New components are now added to the second row, moving left to right. New components will be added on this second row until they no longer fit on the second row, at which time FlowLayout begins a third row. Again, everything on the second row is centered. When the container is finally displayed, all of the rows are centered. Figure 11.7. shows what the final display would look like for three rows of objects.

In the applet we created that displayed the choice, text field, button, label, and three checkboxes, these components were added to the applet using the applet's default layout manager—FlowLayout. If you resize the applet, FlowLayout will

container

component 1	component 2	component 3

component 4	component 5

component 6

Figure 11.7   A container with three rows of components that used FlowLayout to arrange them.

rearrange the components according to the rules we just covered. For example, Figure 11.8 shows what the applet would look like if we decreased the width and increased its height.

The reason that FlowLayout is easy to use is that you don't really have to worry about it. You just keep adding your components to the container, and Flow-Layout takes care of arranging them.

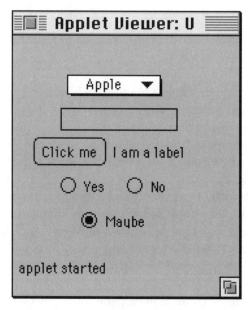

Figure 11.8   The resized applet of Figure 11.1 with its components rearranged by FlowLayout.

GridLayout

GridLayout can help you arrange your user interface elements in a precise grid. When you create GridLayout, you can indicate the number of rows and columns you want the grid to have. Here's an example of creating a grid layout object that would arrange objects in a grid that is 5 rows by 3 columns:

```
GridLayout layout = new GridLayout(5, 3);
```

To attach GridLayout to the container, you need to invoke that container's `setLayout()` method and pass this method the new layout manager. (You would have to use the `setLayout()` method for any new layout manager you assign to a container. For an applet, its default layout manager is FlowLayout, so we didn't have to create our own.) For example, here's how you can assign a new grid layout object in a variable called `layout` to the applet inside the applet's `init()` method:

```
setLayout(layout);
```

When you add new components to a container using GridLayout, the components are arranged row by row, starting in row 1, column 1, then row 1, column 2, and so on, through the number of columns. Then, GridLayout starts in the next row at column 1, and so on, until all of the columns and rows are filled. This layout progression is shown in Figure 11.9.

The sample programs provide examples of using FlowLayout (which is the default for applets) and GridLayout (which we'll create especially to arrange a user interface in a precise grid within an applet).

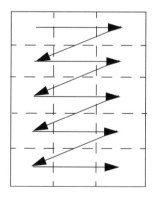

Figure 11.9   GridLayout progressing left to right, row by row so that all the components end up occupying one cell in the grid.

Building User Interface Hierarchies

Applets make great containers. For the applets in this book, we'll always use an applet as our container. However, one of the flexible things about containers is that containers can contain *other* containers. This allows you to build up fairly complex user interfaces. This section will touch on how you can go about doing this and what classes Java provides to help you.

While you can often just use a layout manager to arrange your components in your applet, sometimes your user interface will be too complex to arrange inside only one container. For example, imagine the front panel of a stereo. If stereo designers just added controls to the stereo as they thought of them, the front panel of the stereo might be a confusing jumble of options—something like what's shown in Figure 11.10.

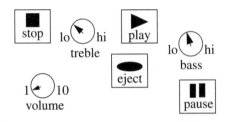

Figure 11.10 A confusing arrangement of controls on a stereo.

There are many controls here, but if you group them together, they're not so confusing. You might group together dials for the volume, treble, and bass. You might group together buttons to control your compact disc player. Each of the different sets of controls might be organized into separate collections, as shown in Figure 11.11.

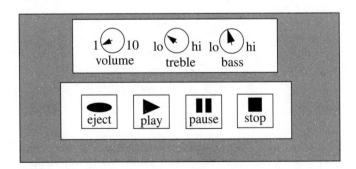

Figure 11.11 An organized arrangement of controls on a stereo.

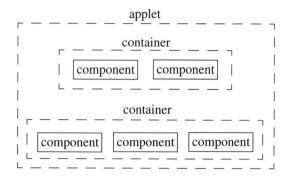

Figure 11.12 An organized arrangement of user interface components.

User interface controls in your applet are not much different from the controls on a stereo. If you have a complex arrangement of items, you might decide to create containers to hold each group of items and then add the different containers to your applet, as shown in Figure 11.12. One way to do this, for example, is to use GridLayout to arrange your containers within your applet in a grid that is 2 rows by 1 column.

To help you arrange items, Java provides some additional subclasses of class Container (in addition to the Applet class). These include

- Frames, which can display a title and a menu bar.
- Panels, which act as generic containers.

Check out Appendix G for where to look for more examples of using these containers in your own applets.

Events

Remember, in Chapter 4, when you played around with the SimpleDraw applet? In SimpleDraw, you clicked on the applet, and a new square or circle appeared, drawn in the color that you selected from a choice list. Every time you clicked the mouse on the applet, you generated an **event**. In Java, an event represents some action taken by the user. Every time the user interacts with your applet, the user generates an event. For example, if the user clicks the mouse, this generates an event. If the user types in characters, this generates an event. Java tells your program about events generated by the user, and that allows your program to take the appropriate action to react to the user.

How Java Informs You of Events

How do these events reach you? If the user is constantly clicking and creating new shapes, how do you hear about it? Thinking over what you've learned about how Java works, you might be able to figure it out. For example, when your applet needs to know about a new phase in life that it's entering, the appropriate life cycle method is invoked. Similarly, when your applet needs to know about a new event, the appropriate event method is invoked.

How Events Are Propagated

Java starts by informing the particular component that the user interacted with that an event occurred. Figure 11.13 shows a possible arrangement of objects on the screen and which component is initially told about the event.

If the button handles this event, then that's the end of the event. If the button does not handle the event, Java sees whether some other object wants it. The object that Java informs next is the user interface container in which the button is placed. In Figure 11.13, we've placed the button inside a panel. So, next, Java informs the panel of the event that happened to the button. This is shown in Figure 11.14.

If the panel handles this event, then that's the end of the event. If the panel does not handle the event, the event goes to the panel's container, which in the diagrammed example is the applet. This is shown in Figure 11.15.

At this point, either the applet handles the event or it doesn't. There's nowhere else for the event to go if the applet does not handle the event here. The event will just "disappear" if no one ever handles it.

One useful consequence of this event propagation is that you don't have to go around subclassing every user interface component there is and writing your own methods to make it do what you want. Instead, you can subclass a container that groups together many other objects, or you can simply use your applet that

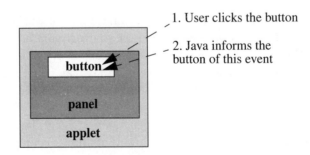

Figure 11.13 First step in event propagation: Java informs the component (that the user interacted with) that there was an event.

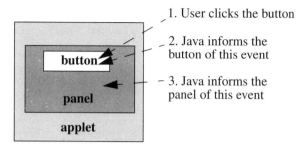

Figure 11.14 Next step in event propagation: If the button does not handle the event, Java tells its container—in this case, a panel—about the event that happened to the button.

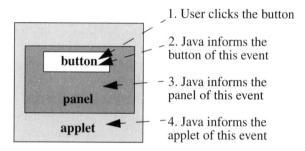

Figure 11.15 Final step in event propagation: If the panel does not handle the event, Java tells its container—in this case, the applet—about the event that happened to the button.

contains everything and supply a method that will react to an event that occurs to one of the components contained within your container or applet. Your method can detect where the event occurred and to what component and can take the appropriate action based on what the user clicked or entered with the keyboard. You'll see examples of this in the sample programs coming up.

Event Methods

There are a variety of event methods that are invoked for different situations—in particular, for mouse clicks, mouse movements, and keystrokes. These are the methods you're likely to deal with the most, and we'll get to these in a moment. Before we look at them, however, you need to know about a method called `handleEvent()`.

The method `handleEvent()` is a method that is always invoked for every type of event. This method takes an object that is created by Java. This object encodes the information for the event and is an instance of class (drum roll, please...) Event! The event object you receive identifies the user interface component in which the event occurred as well as what type of event actually occurred. The two instance variables that you might deal with when using an event object are

- `target`, which contains the user interface component that the user interacted with to trigger this event.

- `id`, which contains an identifier for this event.

The `id` variable can be one of a few different values, and Java supplies a whole bunch of these as class variables in the Event class. So, for example, you can check to see whether the event's `id` is equal to `Event.MOUSE_DOWN` (that is, if the user clicked the mouse) or `Event.SCROLL_PAGE_UP` (which will be the case if the user scrolled up by a page) or `Event.KEY_ACTION` (if the user pressed a key on the keyboard). There are many more values for the wide variety of events that can occur; these are documented with the Event class.

If you choose to supply a `handleEvent()` method, you can use the event object that is passed to you as a parameter to identify what the user did and take the appropriate action. However, `handleEvent()` is not necessarily the most convenient method to override because `handleEvent()` is invoked for every little thing that happens. If all you're interested in is mouse clicks, it would be great to override a method that deals only with mouse clicks. In fact, Java makes this possible. The default behavior for `handleEvent()` is to invoke other methods, depending on the type of event the user generated. These other methods (and their parameters) are

- `mouseEnter (Event e, int x, int y)`, which indicates if the mouse enters the boundaries of a component.

- `mouseExit (Event e, int x, int y)`, which indicates if the mouse leaves the boundaries of a component.

- `mouseMove (Event e, int x, int y)`, which is invoked every time the mouse moves across the screen.

- `mouseDrag (Event e, int x, int y)`, which is invoked when the mouse moves across the screen while the mouse button is being held down.

- `mouseUp (Event e, int x, int y)`, which signals that the mouse button has been released.

- mouseDown (Event e, int x, int y), which indicates that the mouse button has been pressed.

- keyDown (Event e, int key), which is invoked whenever the user types in a new character using the keyboard (the parameter key indicates which key the user typed).

- action(Event e, Object obj), which is invoked for every action that occurs, such as a mouse click or the user pressing enter (but not for every event, such as the user typing a keyboard character).

The x and y parameters indicate where the user clicked if the event was generated using the mouse. So, if all you care about are mouse clicks, you might decide not to override handleEvent() and filter the events that rush in like a tidal wave, but instead pan in the stream of special events, looking for the event in which you're interested. In other words, if you're interested in mouse clicks, you have two choices:

1. You can override handleEvent() and check every event object's id variable for a match to Event.MOUSE_UP.

2. You can override mouseUp().

The same event object is passed along to the special event methods, so you can still check the target of the event to make sure the event occurred in a component that you want to handle.

Earlier in this chapter, we arranged a user interface containing a choice list, a text field, a button, a label, and three checkboxes. All we've shown so far is the init() method that created these components. Now, let's look at what we might do if we wanted to detect which components the user selected.

We can do this by overriding the action() method for our applet. Since we saved the text field, button, and choice objects in instance variables, we can compare these directly to the event's target variable to see whether one of these is the component the user interacted with. Since we did not save the individual checkboxes (though we could have done so easily enough), we will check instead to see whether the target object is in fact an instance of a checkbox. Here's the code:

```
public boolean action(Event e, Object arg) {

    if (e.target == textField)
        System.out.println("User entered text into the text field");

    else if (e.target == button)
        System.out.println("User clicked the button");
```

```
    else if (e.target == choice)
        System.out.println("User selected a new choice");

    else if (e.target instanceof Checkbox)
        System.out.println("User clicked a checkbox");

    else
        System.out.println("Unrecognized event");

    return super.action(e, arg);

}
```

At the end, we call the superclass's implementation of `action()` and return what the superclass feels is appropriate for this action. We'll look at other examples of handling events in the sample programs.

One last thing. All of the event methods return a `boolean` value. This return value lets Java know whether the method handled the event or not. If you do handle the event yourself, you should return true. That stops the event from propagating up to the next container. If you don't handle the event, you should return false so that Java can see whether any other object in the hierarchy of containers above the event's original target is interested in what the user did. You can also invoke your superclass's method and return the same value that your superclass returns.

Sample Programs

We'll look at a few different sample programs in this section, starting simply at first before building up more sophisticated user interfaces. We'll start with an applet that displays a message inside the applet itself.

PaintHello.μ

Open `11.02 - paint hello` in the Learn Java Projects folder. Double-click the project file `PaintHello.μ` to open it, then make the project by selecting **Make** form the **Project** menu. Drop the file `PaintHello.html` onto the Metrowerks Java icon. When the applet appears, it will actually do something within the applet window itself! You won't have to look to the Java Output window to see the results of running this applet. What it does is display a greeting inside the applet. Figure 11.16 shows what the applet looks like.

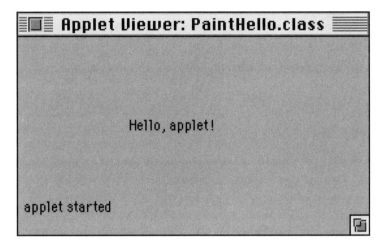

Figure 11.16 The PaintHello applet displaying a greeting message inside the applet itself.

A friendly little applet, isn't it? Let's look at the source code.

Stepping Through the Source Code

Open `PaintHello.java`. You'll see there are only a few lines to this applet. The applet doesn't override any applet life cycle methods, but it does define what happens when the applet paints itself.

This file starts by importing the Graphics class, which is in Java's awt library:

```
import java.awt.Graphics;
```

We need this class because an instance of this class is passed to the `paint()` method as a parameter. We'll use an instance method defined by Graphics to write "Hello, applet!" to the applet's display.

The applet is defined in the usual way, by extending Java's Applet class:

```
public class PaintHello extends java.applet.Applet {
```

We then provide the behavior for the `paint()` method. This method is invoked for you by Java whenever your applet's display needs to be refreshed. Java passes an instance of the Graphics class to `paint()`:

```
public void paint(Graphics g) {
```

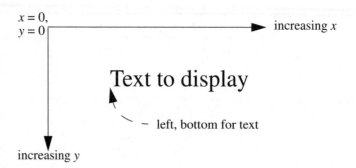

Figure 11.17 Positioning text using the horizontal and vertical positions in drawString().

We use an instance method defined by the Graphics class to display the text in the applet. This method, drawString(), takes three parameters. The first is the string to display; the second is the horizontal position (moving from the left edge of the applet the specified number of pixels) to start writing the text; the third is the vertical position (moving from the top edge of the applet the specified number of pixels) to place the text. The horizontal and vertical positions indicate the bottom left of the text, as shown in Figure 11.17.

Here's the code we'll use in PaintHello:

```
        g.drawString("Hello, applet!", 80, 50);
    }


}
```

That's all there is to it! drawString() "draws" the string into the applet. For our next example, we'll look at how to paint a shape into the applet.

SimpleDraw.µ, Version 1

Open 11.03 - paint circle in the Learn Java Projects folder. Open Simple-Draw.µ, and select **Make** from the **Project** menu. Run this applet as you're used to, by dropping the file SimpleDraw.html onto the Metrowerks Java icon. When the applet runs, you'll see a red circle appear inside the applet. Figure 11.18 shows what this looks like (in gray-scale, of course, though the circle really is red on the screen).

That's all there is here. This applet is almost as simple as the applet that painted the string "Hello, applet!" in the previous example. Let's take a look at the source code.

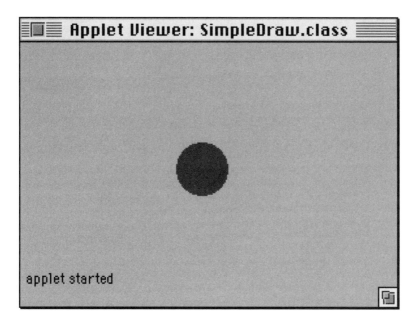

Figure 11.18 Our first version of SimpleDraw showing a red circle painted in the center of the applet.

Stepping Through the Source Code

Open SimpleDraw.java. This is your first exposure to the source code for the SimpleDraw applet you played with in Chapter 4. Over this chapter and the next, we'll build up this applet until it has all the functionality you saw in Chapter 4.

Like the PaintHello applet, this applet also only overrides the paint() method. This applet needs two statements to display the red circle. First, it must set the current drawing color to red; then, it must draw the circle.

This file starts by importing the Applet class and the classes in the awt package:

```
import java.applet.Applet;
import java.awt.*;
```

We actually need only two classes in the awt package—Color and Graphics—but it's common to make the entire awt package available to an applet, so we'll start adopting this technique for many of the sample applications.

Then, we define the Applet subclass, which we'll call SimpleDraw:

```
public class SimpleDraw extends Applet {
```

Now, to override the paint() method. You already know how to do this:

```
public void paint(Graphics g) {
```

The paint() method will do two things. First, it will set the current drawing color. We'll use an instance method defined for graphics objects called set-Color() to do this. We'll supply one of Java's predefined colors that it makes available as a class variable in the Color class. This color will be red, and it's kept in the class variable named red that is in the Color class:

```
g.setColor(Color.red);
```

And finally, we'll draw the circle. Java defines a method for graphics objects called fillOval(). This method takes four parameters. The first two are the top left and top right of the oval; the second two are the width and height of the oval, as shown in Figure 11.19. The pattern for fillOval() is:

```
fillOval(left, right, width, height);
```

Here's the code we'll use in SimpleDraw:

```
        g.fillOval(115, 55, 40, 40);
    }


}
```

By using the same value for the width and height of the oval, we've drawn a circle. The placement of the circle (at left = 115 and top = 55) was chosen to center

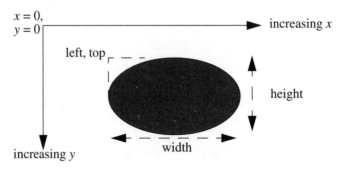

Figure 11.19 Drawing an oval using the four paremeters in fillOval().

the circle based on the dimensions of the applet supplied in the HTML file and also taking into account the diameter of the circle.

SimpleDraw.μ, Version 2

Now it's time to react to user input events, such as mouse clicks. Enough of these passive applets! In this version, we'll move the painted circle to wherever the user clicks.

Open `11.04 - circle at click` in Learn Java Projects. Open `SimpleDraw.μ` and make the project. Drop `SimpleDraw.html` onto the Metrowerks Java icon. Now, start clicking away on the applet. The red circle doesn't just stay in one place, as it did in the previous applet. This time, it hops over to draw where you clicked! Figure 11.20 shows where the circle appears when you click near the top right of the applet.

This version of SimpleDraw might seem very similar to the previous one, but we've changed things around quite a bit. Let's look at what's new.

Stepping Through the Source Code

Open `SimpleDraw.java`. There are two classes defined here: the applet and a class called Circle. The applet defines three methods. Each of these methods overrides a

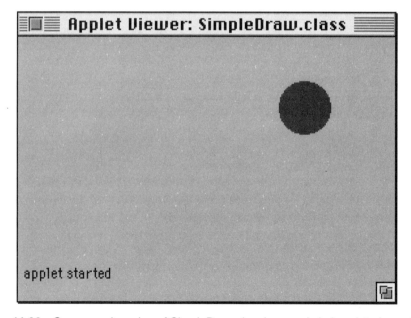

Figure 11.20   Our second version of SimpleDraw showing a red circle painted near the top right of the applet (or wherever the user clicks).

243

method defined by the Applet class itself. The first method, init(), creates a circle to start with. The method mouseUp() detects where the user has clicked. The method paint() redraws the circle. For the Circle class, we defined two methods. The first draws the circle; the second initializes new circles.

The file starts by importing the Applet class as well as the classes in the awt package:

```
import java.applet.Applet;
import java.awt.*;
```

Again, we need the Graphics and Color classes. We also need a class called Event that is defined in awt.

The SimpleDraw applet defines an instance variable to keep track of the current circle:

```
public class SimpleDraw extends Applet {

    Circle   c;
```

In the init() method, we create a circle, assign it to the applet's instance variable named c, and initialize the circle's position to 50, 50 (that is, 50 pixels from the left and 50 pixels from the top of the applet). We have written the Circle class so that when the circle redraws, it will offset itself so that 50, 50 becomes the center of the circle, rather than the top left. To initialize the circle's position, we use an instance method supplied by the circle called initialize() (we'll look at initialize() in a moment):

```
public void init() {
    c = new Circle();
    c.initialize(50, 50);
}
```

Whenever the user clicks the applet with the mouse, Java will invoke a number of applet methods to tell the applet that an event occurred. One of these methods is mouseUp(), and we can override this method to find out where the user clicked since this information is passed in as parameters. We'll create a new circle, just as in init(). This time, however, we won't hard-code the circle's position to 50, 50. We'll use the x and y values of the mouse click to determine this position:

```
public boolean mouseUp(Event e, int x, int y) {
    c = new Circle();
    c.initialize(x, y);
```

Now that we've defined a new circle, we have to tell the applet to redraw itself. We can do this by invoking repaint():

```
repaint();
```

Since mouseUp() returns a boolean value, we have to return true or false. The return value indicates whether this event has been handled or not, and indeed we have handled it. So, we can return true:

```
        return true;
    }
```

The paint() method asks the circle to redraw itself. We pass the graphics object to the circle to help it get the job done:

```
    public void paint(Graphics g) {
        c.draw(g);
    }
}
```

The next step is to look at the Circle class. From the applet, we can see the Circle class defines two instance methods: initialize() and draw(). Let's take a look.

The Circle class starts out by defining three instance variables. These will be used to keep track of the circle's color and center:

```
class Circle {
    Color color;
    int x;
    int y;
```

The draw() method is very similar to what you saw in the previous version of SimpleDraw in that applet's paint() method. draw() is our own custom method. It takes one parameter, the graphics object provided to the applet by Java, and uses this graphics object to set the current color and draw the circle. Notice that we offset the circle by half the circle's diameter (that is, by its radius) so that the x and y values become the center of the circle, rather than the top left of the circle:

```
    void draw(Graphics g) {
        g.setColor(this.color);
        g.fillOval(this.x - 20, this.y - 20, 40, 40);
    }
```

The `initialize()` method sets the instance variables for the circle. The circle's color is always set to red, and the *x* and *y* values are set to the position of the user's mouse click (which is passed in to the `initialize()` method as the x and y parameters):

```
void initialize(int x, int y) {
   color = Color.red;
   this.x = x;
   this.y = y;
}


}
```

SimpleDraw.μ, Version 3

So far, the SimpleDraw applet is doing a lot—namely, it's painting and responding to user input events. Now, let's put in a couple of user interface components to really start to give the user some control over the proceedings.

Open `11.05 - simple draw` in Learn Java Projects. Open `SimpleDraw.μ` and make the project. Drop `SimpleDraw.html` onto the Metrowerks Java icon. You'll notice the applet that appears now has two choice lists. The first provides the shape choices of "Circle" and "Square." The second offers the color choices of "Red," "Green," and "Blue."

At first, the applet works just as in the previous version. The default shape is circle, and the default color is red. The applet displays a red circle wherever the user clicks. This is shown in Figure 11.21.

However, in this version, the user is not limited to red circles. By using the choice lists, the user can choose to draw a green circle, or a blue square, or any combination of shape and color. Drawing a blue square is shown in Figure 11.22.

Let's look at the source code.

Stepping Through the Source Code

Let's look at the classes that define the shapes first and then backtrack to the applet. The Circle and Square classes are organized similarly to the hierarchy we developed in the sample programs section in Chapter 10. You might recall that we created an abstract Shape class to act as the superclass to a Circle and a Square class. We'll do the same thing here.

The Shape class defines common variables to the Circle and Square classes. These include the shape's radius, color, and *x* and *y* positions. Since the radius will not change, it can be declared to be a class variable that is `final`:

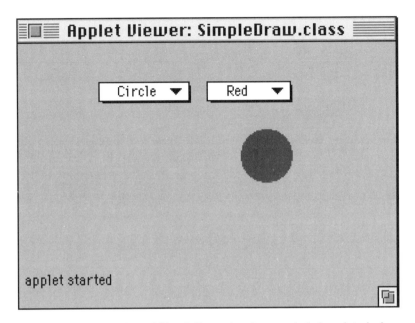

Figure 11.21 Our third version of SimpleDraw showing a red circle painted wherever the user clicks.

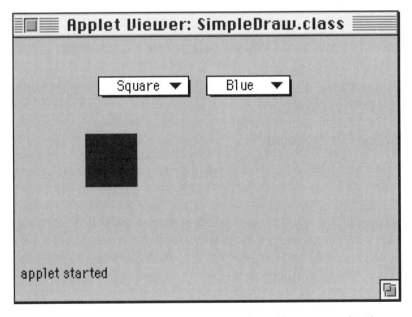

Figure 11.22 Our third version of SimpleDraw showing a blue square after the user clicks in the applet to draw this shape.

```
abstract class Shape {
    static public final int shapeRadius = 20;

    Color color;
    int   x;
    int   y;
```

The Shape class also defines an abstract method called draw(). This means that the subclasses of Shape—Circle and Square—will have to implement this method. By defining this method here, we enable the draw() method to be invoked using variables declared as instances of class Shape, which we'll want to do in the applet:

```
    abstract void draw(Graphics g);
}
```

Declaring this abstract method meant we had to declare the class as abstract as well. This prevents us from instantiating the Shape class directly; instead, we'll end up instantiating its subclasses, Circle and Square.

The definitions for the Circle and Square classes can be fairly simple, and you've seen similar code already. These classes define only one method, a new method called draw(). The Circle and Square classes set the current color to what they've stored in their instance variables, and then draw the appropriate shape, centered at the *x* and *y* positions in their instance variables:

```
class Circle extends Shape {
    void draw(Graphics g) {
        g.setColor(this.color);
        g.fillOval(this.x - shapeRadius, this.y - shapeRadius,
shapeRadius * 2, shapeRadius * 2);
    }
}

class Square extends Shape{
    void draw(Graphics g) {
        g.setColor(this.color);
        g.fillRect(this.x - shapeRadius, this.y - shapeRadius,
shapeRadius * 2, shapeRadius * 2);
    }
}
```

The file itself starts out in the usual way, by importing the Applet class and awt classes:

```
import java.applet.Applet;
import java.awt.*;
```

As before, the applet overrides three methods: `init()`, `paint()`, and `mouseUp()`, and we'll look at each of these methods in turn.

The applet starts by declaring three instance variables. The first enables the applet to keep track of the current shape that the user has drawn; the next two keep track of the choice components that contain the shape and color choices (we'll create these choices in the `init()` method):

```
public class SimpleDraw extends Applet {
    Shape    currentShape = null;
    Choice   shapeChoice;
    Choice   colorChoice;
```

The variable `currentShape` is set to `null` initially. This lets the `paint()` method know later on not to try to draw a shape until the user has actually defined one.

User interface components are often created in the `init()` method. We'll use this approach to create the choices for the shape and color. Creating choice components is fairly straightforward. There is a simple, three-step process:

1. Create a new choice object.

2. Use the method `addItem()` to add a string to the choice representing one of the choices.

3. Add the choice object to the container where it will appear (in this case, the container is the applet).

Here's the `init()` method and the code to create the choices:

```
public void init() {

    shapeChoice = new Choice();
    shapeChoice.addItem("Circle");
    shapeChoice.addItem("Square");
    add(shapeChoice);
```

```
colorChoice = new Choice();
colorChoice.addItem("Red");
colorChoice.addItem("Green");
colorChoice.addItem("Blue");
add(colorChoice);
}
```

The default layout manager for the applet is FlowLayout. This is fine for what we want. With the applet sized as it is according to the width in the HTML file, the two choices fit easily in the first row along the top of the applet.

The paint() method doesn't do any drawing itself but delegates that task to the shape. If there is a current shape (that is, if the instance variable currentShape is not equal to null), then the paint() method invokes that shape's draw() method. We'll pass the draw() method the graphics object so that it can set the current color and draw the appropriate shape (a circle or square, depending on the object):

```
public void paint(Graphics g) {
    if (currentShape != null)
        currentShape.draw(g);
}
```

All that remains is to handle user input events. Again, all we have to do is override mouseUp(). Here's our approach. When Java tells us the user has just clicked the mouse, we'll find out the current choice in the shape and color choice components. Then, we'll find out the color to use, create the appropriate shape, and initialize the new shape. Here we go:

```
public boolean mouseUp(Event e, int x, int y) {
    Color  color;
    String shapeString = shapeChoice.getSelectedItem();
    String colorString = colorChoice.getSelectedItem();
```

We'll use the variable color to hold the color in which to draw the new shape. By using the method getSelectedItem(), we've retrieved the string representing the user's current choices as displayed in each of the choice components.

Now, let's determine the color in which to draw this new shape. We need to obtain the appropriate color object based on the string we retrieved from the choice object. What we need to do is test each string, see whether it is one of the three colors, and, when we've identified the color represented in the string, assign the variable color to the matching color.

```
if (colorString.equals("Red"))
    color = Color.red;
else if (colorString.equals("Green"))
    color = Color.green;
else
    color = Color.blue;
```

Notice at the end we just assume the color is blue since it wasn't red or green.

Then, we do a similar thing with the shape. If the string in the shape choice is "Circle," we create a new circle. Otherwise, the string must be "Square," so we create a new square:

```
if (shapeString.equals("Circle"))
    currentShape = new Circle();
else
    currentShape = new Square();
```

Notice that we're creating a Circle or Square instance and assigning it to an instance variable defined to hold a Shape. Since circles and squares are subclasses of shapes, this is perfectly legal. If we did not use inheritance to create a common shape superclass, we would need to have duplicate variables and code to handle the two different class types. With one superclass, we can combine the variable and code into one.

Next, we initialize the values for the new shape (its color as we just determined, and the location of the mouse click as passed into this method):

```
currentShape.color = color;
currentShape.x = x;
currentShape.y = y;
```

All that's left to do is issue a `repaint()` and return true, indicating we handled this event:

```
repaint();

return true;
    }


}
```

That's all we'll do with SimpleDraw for now. In the next chapter, you'll learn how to keep track of all of the shapes the user created—that is, each shape made with each click—and you'll redraw all these shapes each time the applet repaints.

Payroll.μ

The next applet, Payroll, shows how you can work with keyboard input. We'll create three text fields and respond to events generated by these text fields. We won't do anything with the text the user entered until the next chapter, when you'll learn more about working with data. We'll just start the Payroll applet here, arranging the user interface and recognizing when the user has pressed enter in a text field.

Open 11.06 – payroll in Learn Java Projects. Open Payroll.μ, make the project. Drop Payroll.html onto the Metrowerks Java icon. The Payroll applet will appear. Its user interface consists of 2 columns and 4 rows. The first column on the left contains labels that identify what each row is about. The first three rows in the second column contain text fields that allow the user to type in integers using the keyboard. There is a label in the fourth row of the second column that is blank for now but will eventually be used to display the employee's earned income. This arrangement is shown in Figure 11.23.

To enter text into one of these text fields, click the text field, enter a number, and press enter. Figure 11.24 shows what the applet looks like when the user has entered some data into it.

At the moment, all this applet does is detect the event generated by pressing enter. When the applet detects this event, it writes a message to the Java Output window indicating it has identified which text field the user entered text into. Figure 11.25 shows a sequence of such messages.

In the next chapter, you'll turn this applet into a fully functional database. Let's work our way there by checking out the source code for how these components are arranged.

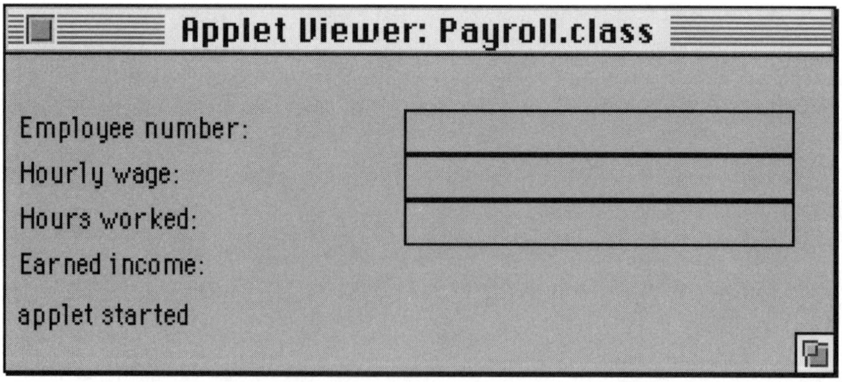

Figure 11.23 The Payroll applet with its display arranged in a grid of 2 columns and 4 rows.

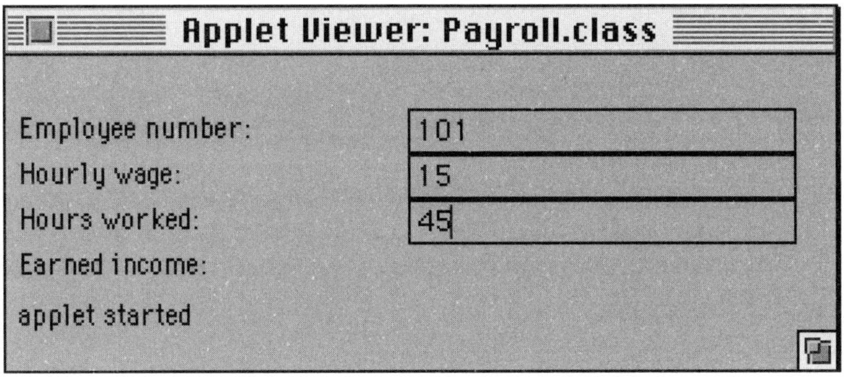

```
╔═════════════════════════════════════════════╗
║ ▓□ ═══ ═══  Applet Viewer: Payroll.class ═══ ║
╠═════════════════════════════════════════════╣
║                                             ║
║   Employee number:      ┌─────────────────┐ ║
║                         │ 101             │ ║
║   Hourly wage:          ├─────────────────┤ ║
║                         │ 15              │ ║
║   Hours worked:         ├─────────────────┤ ║
║                         │ 45|             │ ║
║   Earned income:        └─────────────────┘ ║
║                                             ║
║   applet started                            ║
║                                        ┌──┐ ║
║                                        │ ▣│ ║
╚════════════════════════════════════════└──┘═╝
```

Figure 11.24 The Payroll applet after the user enters some data.

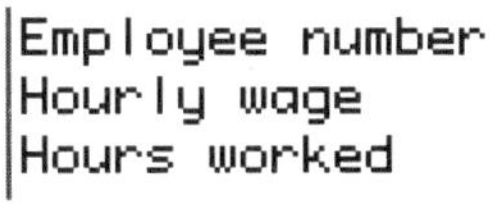

```
Employee number
Hourly wage
Hours worked
```

Figure 11.25 The messages displayed in the Java Output window when the user presses enter in each of the fields in succession.

Stepping Through the Source Code

The applet begins by importing the Applet class and the awt package, as usual:

```
import java.applet.Applet;
import java.awt.*;
```

The applet defines four instance variables to identify each of the components in the second column. These components include the three text fields and the label that we'll use later:

```
public class EmployeeApplet extends Applet {
    TextField   textFieldEmployee;
    TextField   textFieldWage;
    TextField   textFieldHours;
    Label       labelEarned;
```

We create the user interface in the init() method. Since we want an arrangement of 4 rows and 2 columns, we set the layout manager for the applet to be an instance of class GridLayout. We initialize this instance so that it is set to 4 rows, 2 columns:

```
public void init() {

    // Arrange the user interface in a grid.
    setLayout(new GridLayout(4,2)); // 4 rows, 2 columns
```

Now, we begin adding components to the applet. The layout manager will ensure that the components are arranged row by row, first filling in column 1, then column 2, then column 1 for the next row, then column 2, and so on. For each row, we'll create a label to identify the row. We'll put this label in the first column. Then, we'll create a new text field, set to be 20 columns wide, and we'll add this text field to the applet. (The value of 20 columns wide is fairly arbitrary, but this should be large enough to hold our values for the employee number, salary, and hours worked.) GridLayout will complete the row by putting the text field into the second column before moving to the next row:

```
    // 1st row
    add(new Label("Employee number:"));
    textFieldEmployee = new TextField(20); // 20 columns wide
    add(textFieldEmployee);

    // 2nd row
    add(new Label("Hourly wage:"));
    textFieldWage = new TextField(20); // 20 columns wide
    add(textFieldWage);

    // 3rd row
    add(new Label("Hours worked:"));
    textFieldHours = new TextField(20); // 20 columns wide
    add(textFieldHours);
```

The fourth row is a little different in that we place a blank label at the end:

```
    // 4th row
    add(new Label("Earned income:"));
    labelEarned = new Label();
    add(labelEarned);
}
```

To detect input events, we'll override the method called `action()`. As with `mouseUp()`, this method returns a `boolean` value, indicating whether or not it handled the event. It takes two parameters. The first is an object representing the input event; the second is an object representing the action that is occurring, which we won't use in this method.

Here's what we'll do. We'll use the instance variable named `target` in the event object to identify whether the input event we're handling occurred in one of the three text fields. Since we saved the text field objects in the applet's instance variables, this is easy to check. If one of these text fields does match up with the target of the input event, we'll write a simple message to the Java Output window to indicate we have identified the text field in which the user pressed enter:

```
public boolean action(Event e, Object arg) {

    if (e.target == textFieldEmployee) {

        System.out.println("Employee number");

    } else if (e.target == textFieldWage) {

        System.out.println("Hourly wage");

    } else if (e.target == textFieldHours) {

        System.out.println("Hours worked");

    }
```

To determine what value to return (true or false), we'll pass this method up to our superclass and let the default behavior take over:

```
    return super.action(e, arg);
    }

}
```

Though we haven't done so yet, we intend to make use of an object that maintains information for each employee. Each employee object will maintain the employee's number, hourly wage, and hours worked. Each employee will also be able to calculate its own earned income. Here's how we'll define the Employee class to handle these chores:

```
class Employee {
    int idNumber;
    int hourlyWage;
    int hoursWorked;

    int earnedIncome() {
        return hourlyWage * hoursWorked;
    }
}
```

Once you learn how to work with data in Chapter 12, we'll be able to make this applet really come alive.

Review

This chapter showed you how to put together a user interface. You've seen how to paint on the screen using a graphics object. You've learned what components Java makes available to you and how to use some of the more common components to interact with the user. You've also learned how to arrange these components into containers and how layout managers arrange your components inside containers.

Moreover, you've learned that your applet itself is a container, which allows you to add new components directly to your applet. The applet uses FlowLayout as its default layout manager, though you can also change this default to another type of layout manager if you want to.

Finally, you've learned about events, which are generated when the user interacts with your applet. By detecting when the user moves the mouse or clicks a button, you can execute your own code to make things happen. For example, you can detect when the user clicks the mouse to create a new shape at the location of that mouse click.

What's Next?

We're beginning to reach the limit of what we can do based on the data types considered so far. We need better ways of working with data, organizing data, and keeping track of the objects we create. That's what the next chapter is all about. Once you work through Chapter 12, we'll be able to complete the SimpleDraw and Payroll applets we started here.

Chapter 12

Working with Data

You already learned about variables in Chapter 6, and you've been working with data since then in your methods and objects. You've learned about `int` variables, which hold integers, and `boolean` variables, which hold true/false values. This chapter will provide more details about integers and Booleans. It will also discuss other types of data, such as floating-point numbers and characters. You'll learn how you can turn the characters that users type with the keyboard, which are represented in Java as string objects, into numbers that you can store using an `int` variable. This is an important type of conversion to be able to perform because variables that expect to hold `int` values cannot hold string objects. Performing this type of conversion also means being able to respond to error conditions, which you'll also learn how to do here.

In addition, this chapter will introduce a number of classes supplied by Java that you can use to help manage the data in your applets. These classes, Vector and Hashtable, will enable us to finish the SimpleDraw and Payroll applets we started in Chapter 11.

To kick off this chapter, let's start with the types of data you've already seen and discuss more details about storing integers.

Integer Data

In addition to the data type `int`, which you will use most often to store integers, there are three other data types that also store integers. The difference between these different data types is the size of the number that they can maintain and, correspondingly, the amount of memory in the computer they need to store their data. The larger the number, the more memory they need in the computer.

Data Type `byte`

`byte` data types are integers that can range in value from –128 to 127. `byte` values take up the least amount of room in the computer (they require only 1 byte, as you might have guessed).

When dealing with only a few integer variables in your entire program, it's not that important to worry about whether a particular variable takes up 1 byte of memory or a little bit more—but let's say you're General Motors and you're using the applet we discussed earlier to maintain payroll for your employees. If you need to keep track of an integer value for each employee that will always fall within the range of byte values (–128 to 127), it might save you a great deal of memory to use bytes instead of ints for your hundreds of thousands of employees.

Detail

> A single byte represents a very small amount of memory in modern computers. For example, it's likely that the hard drive on your Mac holds many millions of bytes, perhaps 500 million or more (each meg of storage represents approximately 1 million bytes).

byte variables are declared by using the keyword byte, like this:

```
byte myByte;
```

You can use byte variables just like the int variables you're already familiar with, assigning values to them, using them in formulas, and so on:

```
myByte = 5;
myByte *= 2;
System.out.println("The value of myByte is " + myByte);
```

This code snippet will display "The value of myByte is 10" in the Java Output window.

Data Type short

short data types take up twice the memory of byte values, though this is still not very much in terms of your computer's memory. To use a short value, just declare it using short as its data type:

```
short myShort;
```

Data Type long

long values take up a whopping 8 bytes in your computer (which still is not that much, relatively speaking, but it's the largest integer size there is in Java). long values are great for storing extremely large positive and negative integers, but you should use them only when it's possible you'll be dealing with such a huge number. (An `int` value can be as large as 2,147,483,647 and as small as –2,147,483,648, and this usually works out just fine.)

Definition

If you want to know how big and how small your numbers can be for a `long`, try running the following program:

```java
public class MinMax extends java.applet.Applet {
    public void init() {
        System.out.println("max long is " + Long.MAX_VALUE);
        System.out.println("min long is " + Long.MIN_VALUE);
    }
}
```

This code uses a Java class called Long that provides behavior for `long` data types. This applet displays the largest and smallest values that a `long` value can contain.

To use a `long` value, just declare your variable as a `long`:

```java
long myLong;
```

Data Type `int`

Where do `int` values fit in? Variables declared as `int` take up 4 bytes. You'll almost always use `int` values in your own programs. These offer a great combination of holding large positive and negative numbers, as well as requiring half the memory of `long` values.

Floating-Point Data

Calculations involving integer values take place much faster in a computer than floating-point calculations. However, while integer values often get the job done, sometimes you'll reach the limit of what an integer can offer. For example, we've already seen some code snippets that would cause our data to be inaccurate if we used integers. One such calculation involved finding the area for a triangle. Earlier, we defined a Triangle class like this:

```java
class Triangle {
    int base;
```

```
    int height;
    int area() {
        return (base * height) / 2;
    }
}
```

If a triangle's base was 5 and its height was 3, the `area()` method would return 7. Clearly, this is not correct! The triangle's area is 7.5. What we need is a way to represent fractional values as well as integral values. What we need are floating-point numbers.

By the Way

The term *floating-point* refers to the way numbers requiring a decimal point can maintain a varying degree of accuracy in the computer. For example, if you divide 10 by 3, a floating-point number can be 3.3, 3.33, 3.333, and so on, up to the level of accuracy desired and depending on the amount of storage allocated to that floating-point number. In other words, the decimal point "floats." Floating-point numbers are different from fixed-point numbers (which Java does not define). Fixed-point numbers always maintain the same level of accuracy (for example, two places after the decimal point). Floating-point numbers, which do not have this constraint of a fixed level of accuracy, are therefore much more powerful and flexible.

There are two types of floating-point numbers in Java. As with integral numbers, floating-point numbers offer a trade-off between the size of a number they can maintain and the amount of memory required to store that number.

Types `float` and `double`

The type of floating-point number you may end up using the most is `float`. `float` values take up 4 bytes of storage, just like `int` values. However, they can store incredibly large numbers. Up to a certain point, these numbers are extremely accurate. However, for very large numbers, `float` values trade off accuracy to keep up with how big the number actually is.

For example, most numbers you'll deal with, such as 7.5 in our triangle example, or a value like 1/8, which is .125, are handled with complete accuracy. Numbers that range into the number of seconds that have elapsed since the big bang, however, are less precise, though they are accurate as far as the order of magnitude is concerned. For example, at 15 billion years and 5 seconds (to be exact), the number of seconds since the beginning of the big bang is 473,040,000,000,000,005. How would Java handle such a number? If you run this program,

```
public class BigBang extends java.applet.Applet {
    public void init() {
        float f = (float)473040000000000005.0;
        System.out.println("elapsed seconds are " + f);
    }
}
```

the Java Output window will contain the message

```
elapsed seconds are 4.73040e+17
```

which is scientific notation for 4.73040 times 10 raised to the 17th power. Or put another way, it is 47,304 followed by 13 zeros. This is pretty accurate—but what happened to the 5 at the end? Java had to drop off the 5 in order to maintain the order of magnitude of the number. If you would like more information, check out Dave Mark's *Learn C on the Macintosh*, from Addison-Wesley.

double values take up 8 bytes, and double variables can store much larger values than even a float. Decimal numbers are double values by default. For example, if you have a number that you've written as 3.14, Java assumes this number is a double value.

Conversions

Floating-point numbers are represented differently in the computer than integer numbers. With this in mind, what do you think would happen if you tried to execute a code snippet like the following?

```
int myInt;
float myFloat = 5;

myInt = myFloat;
```

This code seems reasonable enough, but the Java compiler would complain about it! This code is requesting that data stored in a variable that can maintain very large and potentially fractional numbers (float) be assigned to a variable that stores smaller and integral numbers (int). The compiler will have none of this foolishness!

There is a way to assure the compiler that everything is all right, that it should go ahead and make the assignment, even if it results in a loss in accuracy. This is done by **casting**. To cast between data types, you need to write the data type that you'd like the value to become, in parentheses, in front of the value itself. For example, to perform the preceding conversion from float to int, you can write

```
myInt = (int)myFloat;
```

This code tells the compiler to go ahead and make the conversion from a `float` value to an `int`, even if the number loses accuracy by dropping a fractional value.

You can also cast objects in addition to data types. Here's a quick example (you'll see lots of examples of this throughout this book, including some more later in this chapter):

```
double areaOfACircle(Shape s) {
    if (s instanceof Circle) {
        Circle c = (Circle)s;   // cast a shape to a circle
        return c.radius * c.radius * Math.PI;
    } else
        return 0;
}
```

This code first checks to see whether a shape that has been passed to it as a parameter is in fact a circle. If it is, this shape object is cast to become a circle. We can then use this object just as we would use a circle, by accessing instance variables and invoking methods. (This example also uses a class supplied by Java called Math to obtain the value for pi.) The reason we must cast the object in question to a circle is that we defined Shape as being abstract, and we must work with an instance of a concrete class.

Division by Zero

Integer numbers and floating-point numbers behave very differently at times. One such example is when dividing by zero. Generally, dividing by zero is not something you would want to do on purpose. Arithmetically, performing an operation such as "10 divided by 0" is not defined. The result of such a division is taken to be infinity.

With integral values, if you perform a division by zero, Java will generate an error when your program executes. This error will have the likely consequence of displaying a nasty-looking error message and halting your program in midstride. This is definitely *not* what you want to have happen! When performing division with integers that might result in a division by zero, you should check first that this will not occur, as with code that looks like this:

```
if (divisor > 0)
    ratio = dividend/divisor;
```

This code assumes, of course, that `divisor`, `dividend`, and `ratio` are all declared as `int` values and that `divisor` and `dividend` have been initialized before this code executes.

With floating-point values, however, dividing by zero will not cause Java to generate an error. Instead, Java supplies a meaning to division by zero for floating-point values: The result in Java for such a division is infinity. If you want to, you can just go ahead and perform division with floating-point numbers:

```
ratio = dividend/divisor;
```

If `divisor` is equal to 0, `ratio` will be positive infinity if `dividend` is positive and negative infinity if `dividend` is negative. Java defines special variables called `Float.POSITIVE_INFINITY` and `Float.NEGATIVE_INFINITY` that represent these values.

Boolean Data

We covered `boolean` data (true/false values) in the previous chapters. There are just a couple of details to recap here.

You cannot convert between a number, such as an `int` or a `float`, and a `boolean` value. This is important to know, especially if you have tried your hand at programming in some other language such as C. In C, for example, you can assign numbers to `boolean` values. If the number is 0, the `boolean` value will be false. If the number is anything other than 0, the `boolean` value will be true. In Java, this kind of thing just isn't possible. Instead, if you want to use a number to determine whether a `boolean` variable should contain the value true or false, you have to use the number in an expression that evaluates to true or false, such as

```
boolean isZero = (myInt == 0);
```

In this example, the expression `myInt == 0` is evaluated first. This yields a result that is true or false, depending on the value of `myInt`. If `myInt` is equal to 0, this expression will evaluate to true, and `isZero` will be true. If `myInt` is anything other than 0, such as 1, this expression will evaluate to false, and `isZero` will be false.

Also, if you declare a `boolean` variable but do not assign a value to it, its default value will be false.

Character Data

There's a special data type that you can use to store characters such as *a*, *b*, or $. This data type is needed because characters, clearly, are not numbers. The way you define a character variable is by using the keyword char, like this:

```
char myChar;
```

You can assign values using single quotes (unlike double quotes, which are used with strings). For example, to assign the character *x* to myChar, you could write

```
myChar = 'x';
```

Normally, you'll use string objects to store text, but sometimes it's more convenient to use char variables. For example, each time the user presses a key on the keyboard, Java generates an input event. This event supplies your applet with the character that the user typed by passing your applet a variable declared as char.

An example of when you might use a char in your own program is when storing a selection of choices. Let's say you're keeping track of the size of a pizza ordered over the Web. You want to know whether the individual ordered a small, medium, or large. Rather than keeping track of "magic numbers" in an int variable, where you might use 1 to represent small, 2 to represent medium, and 3 to represent large, you could instead define a char variable and use 'S' for small, 'M' for medium, and 'L' for large. Now, just glancing at the data stored in this variable makes it clear what the user has ordered.

In case you're curious, in Java, char variables take up 2 bytes. This is the required amount of memory necessary to work with the wide range of international characters, ranging from the Greek alphabet to Japanese kanji characters.

Objects

As you know, variables can refer to objects in addition to maintaining values such as integers and floating-point numbers. You've already seen examples of variables that refer to objects. All you have to do to declare a variable that refers to an object is to use the class name as the data type, such as

```
Triangle t1;
```

or

```
Employee  jpFinch; // from How to Succeed in Business...
```

The first example would be able to maintain an object that was an instance of class Triangle (or an instance of a subclass of class Triangle). The second example would be able to maintain an object that was an instance of class Employee (or an instance of a subclass of class Employee).

There is one more thing to say at this point about variables that refer to objects. You know that the default value for a number is 0, but what about the default value for an object? If you have a variable for an object that does not actually refer to an object yet, it is set to the value null. This allows you to do things like test to see whether a variable is initialized to an object or not. For example, say you have a triangle applet containing a method that searches for a particular triangle. This method might be called searchForTriangle() and might be defined to return a triangle object, like this:

```
Triangle searchForTriangle() {
   // Code to search for a triangle goes here.
}
```

What happens if searchForTriangle() doesn't find the triangle it's searching for? One option in this situation is for searchForTriangle() to return null. This method would do so with a statement that was written like this:

```
return null;
```

The code that invoked this method might be prepared for a possible null value and could be written as follows:

```
triangle myTriangle; //initialized to null by default

myTriangle = searchForTriangle(); //assigned some value
if (myTriangle != null) {
   // We found the triangle. Do something here.
}
```

This code shows that after searching for the triangle, we only execute the code that uses myTriangle if myTriangle has been assigned to the triangle we were searching for.

Strings

We've been working with strings since we first started writing programs in this book. Everything written between double quotes is a string in Java, and Java even supplies a class whose instances manage the text inside strings. Java's class is called, naturally enough, String, and it is defined in the lang package.

By encoding text in the String class, you can manipulate and work with text very easily. The String class supplies a number of methods for manipulating and searching for text within a string and for comparing different strings to one another.

Creating Strings

Creating a string is easy to do in Java. We've already seen examples of this in Chapter 9 when we illustrated how to pass parameters to constructors. Here's the standard way to create a new string:

```
String belushi = new String("cheeseburger, cheeseburger, cheeseburger");
```

Here, the string named belushi would maintain the data for the characters supplied in double quotes.

Warning

> Strings are read-only! This means that if you do not supply text for a string when you create it, the string will never have any text because you can't *write* to it. You can only read the text it contained when it was first created. Therefore, you'll almost always supply text when you create a new string. If you want to change a string after you've created it, you should use an instance of class StringBuffer instead of String. The StringBuffer class is described later in this chapter.

`System.out.println()` Explained

Now, you've reached a point in your studies of Java where you know enough to understand one of the first Java statements you learned in this book:

```
System.out.println("Hello, world!");
```

We left it as more or less a mystery as to how this statement got its message to the Java Output window (that is, to the standard output). Let's clear up this little mystery and explain this line of code once and for all.

The primary thing you're doing in this line of code is invoking an instance method named `println()`. This method takes one parameter, a string. Whenever you write quoted text, Java creates a string object for you. So, defining a method like this

```
public void println(String s) {
    // print code goes here
}
```

and invoking `println()` like this

```
println("Hello, world!");
```

creates an object of class String with the text "Hello, world!" and assigns this new string to the parameter s in the `println()` method.

The `println()` method is defined for instances of the class PrintStream (which is defined in Java's io package). This method displays text in the standard output, which CodeWarrior maps to the window called Java Output. Since `println()` is an instance method, you have to be able to get access to an instance of this class to invoke this method. Rather than Java forcing you to create such an instance, Java's System class, defined in the lang package, defines such an object as one of its class variables. The name of the class variable in the System class that refers to an instance of class PrintStream is called `out`.

Now, let's put all the pieces together. To get to a predefined instance of class PrintStream, you can write `System.out`. The variable `System.out`, then, refers to an object (an instance of class PrintStream). To invoke the instance method called `println()` that is defined for instances of class PrintStream, you write `System.out.println()`. To pass a string as a parameter, you can put the text in quotes so that Java will create an instance of class String and assign it to the string parameter in the method you're invoking. There you have it: `System.out.println("Hello, world!");` in all its glory!

Formatting Strings

You've already learned that you can combine numbers with strings, as in

```
int scoreMets = 4;
int scorePirates = 3;

if (scoreMets > scorePirates)
    String s = new String("The Mets beat the Pirates " +
            scoreMets + " to " + scorePirates);
```

```
else
    String s = new String("The Pirates beat the Mets " +
            scorePirates + " to " + scoreMets);
```

You can also use special characters to format what the string displays. For example, how do you think you can write a quote (") in a string? If you tried to create a string like this,

```
String s = new String("Adam said, "Madam, I'm Adam"");
```

the Java compiler would complain about a syntax error because it would have thought that the string actually read "Adam said, " and that everything starting at and to the right of the letter *M* was a mistake. In order to tell Java to make the quote part of the string, you can use a backslash (\) in front of the quote, like this:

```
String s = new String("Adam said, \"Madam, I'm Adam\"");
```

There are also some formatting commands you can put into your strings using a combination of a backslash and a letter. Here are two that you might find the most useful.

To make Java start displaying text on the next line, we can use \n (the *n* stands for "new line"). For example, we can write out the colors of the rainbow as we did earlier, but this time we can use just one println() statement instead of seven by using \n, like this:

```
System.out.println(
    "red\norange\nyellow\ngreen\nblue\nindigo\nviolet");
```

StringBuffers

If you want to be able to modify a string, you should use an instance of class StringBuffer. String instances are read-only; StringBuffer instances are read/write. You can create a new StringBuffer object just as you do for String objects:

```
StringBuffer sb = new StringBuffer("I like Paris ");
```

To add text to the end of sb, you can use the method append(), as in

```
sb.append("in the springtime.");
```

StringBuffer is not a replacement for String. That is, StringBuffer objects are not the same as String objects, because they have the ability to write to them. This is important because most methods use strings as parameters. If you have defined a StringBuffer, you have to convert the StringBuffer object to a String object before you can use it where a string is expected. The way you do this is to use the method toString(), like this:

```
String s = sb.toString();
```

Then, you can use the variable s wherever you need to use a string.

The Integer and Floating-Point Classes

In Java, the data types fall into two categories. There are the simple data types, which are the integers, floating-point numbers, Boolean values, and character data (not strings) that we covered in the first part of this chapter. Then there are the objects, which is everything else. You'll almost always use the simple data types of int and float when you want to use numbers. With variables declared as int and float, you can use all the arithmetic operators to perform calculations, compare values, and control the flow through your code.

Sometimes, however, you want your numbers to have some behavior. The most common example is converting a number to a string object—that is, being able to invoke a method for the number that would cause it to return a string object representing its value. Another example is being able to tell what the largest and smallest value is that a number can hold.

To do things like this, Java supplies classes that maintain a number and provide behavior for that number. When you make an instance of one of these classes, you provide the number that this object will maintain. These objects are just like all of Java's other objects—you can't use them in calculations or for comparisons, as you can do with regular numbers, but they do provide methods to help you do things.

These classes are called Integer, Long, Float, and Double. Objects created from these classes are great for maintaining a value and providing methods to manipulate that value. For example, you can create a new instance of class Integer by writing

```
Integer number = new Integer(10);
```

If you wanted a string representing the value in this Integer instance (say, to display the value inside a text field), you could use the instance method toString(), like this:

```
String s = number.toString();
```

Now, s would contain the text "10".

These classes also define some very useful class variables and class methods. For example, they define class variables that hold the maximum and minimum values that these data types can store. (These variables are called MAX_VALUE and MIN_VALUE.) These classes also provide methods that we'll use in the next section to convert a string into an instance of an Integer, a Long, a Float, or a Double.

Handling Exceptions

The subject of handling exceptions is a topic that belongs more strictly in a discussion of flow control. However, you'll use exception handling most frequently when working with data, so we've included this discussion where it flows most naturally with what you've learned so far.

Let's say you want to convert a string into a floating-point number. Fortunately, Java provides a class that does this, and it's easy to use. You can find the value of a string named s that represents a floating-point number by writing

```
float f = Float.valueOf(s).floatValue;
```

This code works fine as long as the string says something like "100.51" or "–.003" or is some other valid floating-point number, but what do you think Java does if the conversion runs into trouble? For example, what happens if the string contains "100A" or "1.2.3"? These are not valid floating-point numbers, and Float.valueOf() would not be able to perform the conversion.

In situations like this, the designers of Java had an interesting problem to solve. They could have displayed a message to the standard output when something like this occurred (in CodeWarrior, that would have made a message appear in the Java Output window). Float.valueOf() returns a value—in particular, an object representing a Float instance—so what value should this method return if there's an error? This method could have returned null, but then what would happen when the code hit null.floatValue()? The code would have fallen apart at the seams!

The solution for a Java method encountering this kind of problem lies in *not* handling the error at all, and instead just reporting that an error occurred. That is, the method doesn't display an error message or return null or any other value that might indicate an error. What the method does do is to tell the method invoking it that something went awry. It does this by **throwing an exception**.

Throwing an Exception

The terminology "throwing an exception" is very visual, and it is a good image. If something goes wrong deep in the bowels of Java's own methods, Java creates an object based on a class called Exception (or on one of Exception's subclasses, some of which we'll mention soon) and throws this object back to the code that invoked it. This is depicted in Figure 12.1.

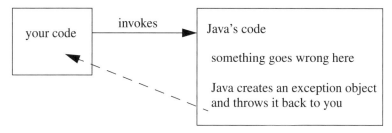

Figure 12.1 Throwing an exception.

Catching an Exception

So what do you think you have to do when Java throws you an exception? Right! You have to **catch** it. There's a keyword called `catch` that you can use for just this purpose. Here's the way it works:

1. First, you try to execute some code that might cause an exception to be thrown.

2. Then, you use the `catch` keyword to catch any exceptions that Java actually throws. If Java doesn't throw an exception, then everything's fine, and you can continue along as normal. If Java does throw an exception, you need to execute special code. This is the code that follows the `catch` keyword.

   Here's an outline of what this looks like in Java code:

```
try {

    // do something here that might throw an exception

} catch (Exception e) {

    // do something appropriate for the error that occurred

}
```

For example, when performing the conversion from a string to a `float` value, the `try` block would contain code that performs the conversion and might cause the exception to be thrown:

```
String s = new String("1.23");
float f;

try {
    f = Float.valueOf(s).floatValue();
    System.out.println("f is " + f);
} catch (Exception e) {
    f = (float)0.0;
}

System.out.println("We're past the try-catch statements");
```

Here, we try to execute the conversion code. If everything goes fine with the conversion, f would be assigned the `float` value, and the very next line of code to execute would write the line "f is 1.23" to the Java Output window. Following that, the very next line of code to execute would write "We're past the try-catch statements" to the Java Output window.

However, if Java found that s did not contain a valid floating-point number, it would throw an exception. In that case, the statement that wrote the value of f to the Java Output window *would never execute*. Instead, Java would throw an exception, and our `catch` statement would execute next. This would assign the object that Java threw to the variable e, and we would set f to 0.0. The next line of code to execute after setting f to 0.0 would write "We're past the try-catch statement" to the Java Output window.

It's helpful in learning about `try-catch` statements to compare them to if-else statements. How does the `try-catch` just shown compare with the following code?

```
if (noError()) {
    f = Float.valueOf(s).floatValue();
    System.out.println("f is " + f);
} else {
    Exception e = errorType();
    f = (float)0.0;
}
```

Is this the same as the `try-catch`? Not quite. This code says that if the method `noError()` returns true, then execute the `if` block. Otherwise, execute the `else` block. This is very different from the `try-catch` statements, but in very subtle ways. First, the `try` keyword is not an `if`. There is no expression that is evaluated to see whether we should execute the code in the `try` block. We just start executing it. We keep on executing the statements, line by line, and if there are no errors, we branch around the `catch` block (which is just like branching around the `else` block in the preceding code). However, if, in the course of executing the statements in the `try` block, there is an error, we jump immediately to the `catch` block. In the preceding code, we assigned to the variable e the type of error that occurred, and this is similar to the `catch` block, where the error that occurred is assigned to an object with the name e (though you can name this variable anything you want to, such as x, `exception`, or `error`—not just e).

Types of Exceptions

Java defines lots of subclasses of the Exception class. The purpose of these different types of exceptions is to be able to identify exactly what went wrong. For example, if you try to use a string that is supposed to contain a number but contains something that is not a number, Java doesn't just throw an instance of class Exception; it throws an instance of a subclass of class Exception called NumberFormatException.

Here's another example. If you try to create a new object but there is no more memory in the computer, Java will throw an instance of OutOfMemoryError. Java defines many, many types of exceptions. Since they all descend from class Exception, you can always just catch an instance of class Exception, and you'll be fine. You can also use the specific exception type in the `catch` block, as in

```
catch (OutOfMemoryError error) {
    // error-handling code
}
```

The reason for supplying these different exception subclasses is to be able to distinguish between exceptions. Chapter 13 shows you how to do that.

Knowing When You Need to Handle an Exception

The documentation files for Java's classes let you know when you need to handle an exception. Chapter 15 describes how to read the HTML documentation for Java's class files. You might have looked at these files already. If not, here's a sneak preview.

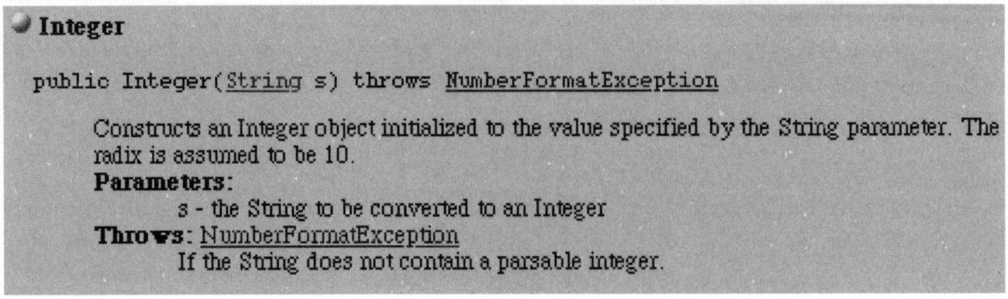

> **Integer**
>
> public Integer(<u>String</u> s) throws <u>NumberFormatException</u>
>
> > Constructs an Integer object initialized to the value specified by the String parameter. The radix is assumed to be 10.
> > **Parameters**:
> > > s - the String to be converted to an Integer
> > **Throws**: <u>NumberFormatException</u>
> > > If the String does not contain a parsable integer.

Figure 12.2   The documentation for one of the Integer class's constructors.

All of Java's classes are defined using HTML files that you can look at in a Web browser. Figure 12.2 shows what the documentation looks like for one of the Integer class's constructors.

This constructor takes a string object and indicates that it will throw an exception if it cannot create an Integer object based on the string supplied to it. For example, what would happen if you tried to create a number like this?

```
Integer number = new Integer("Doo wop doo wop");
```

The Integer class would not be able to make heads or tails of this. Rather than creating any old number, it throws an exception. The documentation indicates it throws an exception called NumberFormatException.

If a method or constructor indicates that it might throw an exception, you must be prepared to catch it. (If you forget to use a `try-catch` block with a method that might throw an exception, you'll know about it because the compiler will warn you and won't let you compile the code.) So, the real way to create a new Integer instance based on a string would be to write

```
try {

    Integer number = new Integer("Doo wop doo wop");

} catch (NumberFormatException x) {

    System.out.println("Guaranteed to execute in this case!");

}
```

Always check the documentation to see whether you need to handle an exception, especially if the compiler tells you that you do!

Arrays

Using individual variables to keep track of data works fine—usually. For example, for the triangle example, using an `int` variable to keep track of the base and an `int` variable to keep track of the height works perfectly fine. As another example, if an Applet class created a triangle object, it could keep track of the triangle by using a variable declared like this:

```
Triangle t1;
```

This is fine for one triangle, but what happens if the applet needs to keep track of three triangles? This still isn't so bad; the applet can declare three variables:

```
Triangle t1, t2, t3;
```

You might begin to see where this could lead to problems. What if the applet needs to create 100 triangles? Or 1000 triangles? Does the program need to declare 1000 variables, from `t1` up to `t1000`?

There is an easier approach, and that approach involves using an array.

What Are Arrays?

Arrays are collections of variables of the same type. When you declare an array, you indicate to the compiler that you want to work with a whole set of variables, all of the same type. For the triangle example, you can declare an array that holds 1000 triangles. As another example, if you needed to keep track of 254 integers, you could declare an array that holds 254 integers. Then, if you wanted to access a particular triangle or a particular integer, you would access one of the **elements** of that array.

When you declare a variable to hold one integer, you tell the compiler to set aside enough memory to hold that one integer. When you declare a variable to hold an array of a certain number of integers, you tell the compiler to set aside enough memory to hold all of those integers, one right after the other. Figure 12.3 provides a high-level picture of what happens in your computer's memory when you declare one integer and when you declare an array of integers.

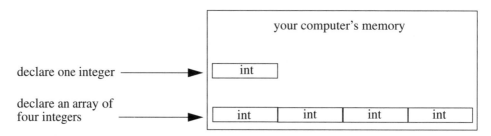

declare one integer

declare an array of
four integers

Figure 12.3   Declaring one integer and an array of four integers.

Declaring an Array

When you declare an array, you define a variable that will represent that array. The way that you indicate you want to declare an array of values, instead of a single value, is to use square brackets. For example, to declare a variable that will hold an array of integers, you write code like this:

```
int[]  myIntArray;
```

Style

There's another notation that programmers often use for declaring arrays, and that is to put the square brackets after the variable name, rather than after the data type. For example, it's perfectly legal to declare an array called `myIntArray` that will hold an array of integers like this:

```
int  myIntArray[];
```

Programmers coming from other languages, where this is the only way to declare an array, often prefer this syntax since this is what they're used to. However, this has a subtle disadvantage over the first method. The disadvantage is that the data type is not truly reflecting the type of variable you are declaring. For example, here are two variable declarations:

```
int  temp;
int  results[];
```

You can't tell what kind of variables `temp` and `results` are just by looking at the data type. You have to look at the variable itself, not at its data type, and see whether the variable contains a set of square brackets at the end. In this book, we'll use the approach of putting square brackets on the data type itself. In other words, our variable declarations will look like this:

```
int    temp;
int[] results;
```

After you've defined the variable that will be used to reference the array, you still need to indicate how large the array should be—that is, how many elements the array will contain. The way that you do this is by using the same new operator you've used before to create other objects. This time, however, instead of using parentheses to indicate the parameter list, you use square brackets and indicate how large to make the array. For example, here's how you would create an array of four integers:

```
int[] myIntArray = new int[4];
```

This code sets aside enough room in the computer to hold four int values. You'll use the variable myIntArray to access these four ints (as you'll see in a moment).

This kind of thing works for any type of data whatsoever, including objects. For example, to declare an array of 1000 triangle objects, you could write

```
Triangle[] theTriangleLibrary = new Triangle[1000];
```

One other thing that can be very useful in declaring an array is that the size of the array can be provided in a variable. For example, instead of writing the preceding statement, you could write the following (as long as numTriangles is declared as an integer):

```
Triangle[] theTriangleLibrary = new Triangle[numTriangles];
```

You might do this kind of thing, for example, if you need to calculate how large to make your array because you don't know how large your array will be at compile time. (For example, this might occur if you're reacting to choices made by the user.)

Accessing Elements in an Array

Once you have set aside enough memory for your array, you can put elements into the array and retrieve elements from the array. You access elements in the array by indicating which element number you want, using notation like this:

```
int oneInt = myIntArray[2];
```

This code accesses the integer stored as element number 2 in an array of ints declared as myIntArray. You can also put values into an array using notation such as this:

```
myIntArray[2] = 421;
```

Arrays can sometimes be tricky because of the way that elements in the array are numbered. If you want the first element in an array, you do not start at element 1. Instead, you start at element 0! Here's an example. What do you think this chunk of code does?

```
int[] myIntArray = new myIntArray[4];

for (int i = 0; i < 3; i++)
    myIntArray[i] = i;
```

The first statement declares a variable that will hold an array of integers. It then **allocates** (sets aside) the memory in the computer by using the new operator and specifies how many ints this array will hold (in this case, this array will hold four ints).

The next statement sets up a loop from 0 to 3. The loop contains a single statement. In that statement, we access an element in the array and assign a value to it. The first time through the loop, i will be 0. We access element 0 and assign it the value of i (which is 0). The second time through the loop, i will be 1. We access element 1 and assign it the value of 1. The third time, we assign element 2 the value of 2. The fourth time, we assign element 3 the value of 3.

This chunk of code has accessed all the elements in the array—elements 0, 1, 2, and 3—and assigned each element the value corresponding to its position in the array. Note that there is no element 4! Figure 12.4 shows what the array of ints looks like in memory after the ints have been initialized by the loop we just went through.

Figure 12.4 An array holding four integers initialized to values corresponding to their position in the array.

Warning

Starting with element 0 as the first element often confuses programmers new to arrays—and for good reason! It's only natural for a person to think of the first element as starting in position 1. However, this is not the way that computers think. For a computer, the first position is 0.

This is most often an issue when you're accessing the last element in an array. For example, it's quite natural for you to think of the last element in an array 1000 elements long as being number 1000. However, with arrays, this is not the case! Since arrays start at 0, the last element in an array 1000 elements long is at position 999. If you try to access an element beyond the end of the array (say, element 1000 in an array 1000 elements long), you will cause Java to generate an error. In particular, Java will—you guessed it—throw an exception.

Determining the Size of an Array

To help you keep out of trouble by inadvertently accessing an element beyond the length of an array, Java provides a way for you to test how big an array actually is. The way you find the length of an array named `myIntArray`, for example, is to refer to `myIntArray.length`. This represents the number of elements that the array can hold. For example, what do you think the `System.out.println()` statement will display in the Java Output window in the following block of code?

```
int[] myIntArray = new int[52];

System.out.println("myIntArray is " + myIntArray.length +
    "elements long.");
```

In this case, the message "myIntArray is 52 elements long" will appear in the Java Output window. To recap: An array of `int`s 52 elements long starts at element 0, ends at element 51, and can hold a total of 52 `int`s.

These are all examples of **one-dimensional** arrays. One-dimensional arrays are good for holding data where you want a list of things, such as a list of the distances you jog each day over the course of a month (which might be a floating-point array that is 31 elements long) or the list of test scores from each pupil in a class (which might be an integer array whose length is equal to the number of students in the class).

Sometimes, a one-dimensional array is not powerful enough to do the job. For example, how would you maintain the squares on a checkerboard with a one-dimensional array? Perhaps you are maintaining whether a square contains a red checker, contains a black checker, or is empty: three values. Perhaps you want to store a 1 for a red checker, a 2 for a black checker, and a 0 if the square is empty (we'll ignore kings for now). You would need 8 arrays of integers 8 elements long.

Working with all these arrays can be a little awkward. What would come in handy right now would be an **array of arrays**—and, fortunately, you can do this in Java. You can define an array of arrays for a checkerboard like this:

```
int[][] checkerBoard;
```

Notice the double set of brackets? This means we want a two-dimensional array. What about a three-dimensional array for a game of 3-D Tic-Tac-Toe? You would define it like this:

```
int[][][] ticTacToe;
```

To allocate the memory for our checkerboard (a grid of squares 8 by 8), you can write

```
checkerBoard = new int[8][8];
```

As with all uninitialized `int` values, each element in the checkerboard starts out set to 0. To access the first row, second column, you can write `checkerBoard[0][1]`. To access the very last square in the eighth row, eighth column, you can write `checkerBoard[7][7]`.

Warning

Be careful not to try to access an element in an array that has not yet been allocated. For example, even though you might have defined a variable that will hold an array, like this,

```
int[][][] ticTacToe;
```

don't start accessing elements in the array until you've allocated it (by writing `new int[3][3][3]`). If you try to access an element in an array that has not yet been allocated, Java will throw an exception.

Vectors

Arrays are great for maintaining a collection of items when you know how many items you'll need before you allocate the array. For example, if you need to determine the population of the United States and you happen to know the population for each state, you can declare an array of integers, allocate it to 50 elements, and store each state's population in each element. Then, you can loop through the array and add each entry in the array to your running total:

```
int population;
int[] state = new int[50];

// set each entry in the array to the population of a state
.
.
.

// then find the total population
for (int i = 0; i < 50; i++)
   population += state[i];
```

This is a fine technique for a fixed number of items, but what happens when you need to maintain a collection of items where the number of items changes over time? For example, for the SimpleDraw applet, the user is continually creating new shapes. We need a way to keep track of these shapes without locking ourselves into a predetermined maximum number of shapes. Java provides a class that allows us to work with a list of objects whose number changes over time. This class is called Vector, and it is defined in Java's util package.

Objects created based on Java's Vector class can keep on growing in number as more items are added to the vector. This is like an array without limits—except that you'll still generate an error if you try to access an element number beyond the bounds of what the vector contains. You can construct a vector object just like any other object:

```
Vector v = new Vector();
```

Then, you can use instance methods defined by the Vector class to access elements in the vector. Here are four methods you might use most often with vectors:

1. To add a new object to the end of the vector, use the method addElement(). This method takes one parameter: the object to add to the end of the vector.

2. To retrieve an object from the vector at a specific location within the vector, use `elementAt()`. This method takes one parameter: the index of the element to retrieve. This method returns the object at that location.

3. To change an object in the vector at a specific location within the vector, use `setElementAt()`. This method takes two parameters: The first is the object to place into the vector; the second is the entry in which to place it.

4. There's also a useful method that allows you to tell how many objects a vector contains. This method is called `size()`.

Here's an example of how the SimpleDraw applet uses a vector to keep track of all the circles created by the user. First, the applet creates a vector object in `init()`:

```
Vector circlesToDraw = new Vector();
```

At first, the vector is empty and doesn't contain anything; the method `circlesToDraw.size()` would return 0.

When the user creates a new circle, we could add this new circle object (referenced, for example, by a variable named `circle`) to the end of the vector like this:

```
circlesToDraw.addElement(circle);
```

And finally, when it is time to draw all of the circles, the applet could loop through the vector by accessing each element in order. One important piece of information you need to know about retrieving objects from a vector is that you must cast the object returned by `elementAt()` to the type of object stored there. For example, you could retrieve circles (created from a class called Circle) like this:

```
Circle circle;
int numCircles = shapesToDraw.size();

for (int i = 0; i < numCircles; i++)
   circle = (Circle)shapesToDraw.elementAt(i);
```

Notice the last line of this code snippet. `shapesToDraw.elementAt(i)` returns the object at position `i` in the vector. The object returned is declared in the `elementAt()` method to be of type Object. This means, to use the returned object as a circle, you have to cast it to a circle and assign it to a variable defined to reference a Circle instance. This is what we do in this code snippet. The sample code coming up contains more examples of this.

Hash Tables

Vectors work great when all you want is to step through the elements in the list of objects sequentially. For example, SimpleDraw has no need to access the fourth shape (and only the fourth shape) that the user created, or the first one, or the last one. All that SimpleDraw has to do is to add a new shape to the list and step through the entire list in the applet's `paint()` method. (You'll do this yourself in the sample programs in this chapter.)

This is not the case for all your programs. For example, the Payroll applet we started earlier would very likely have a need to access one, and only one, employee. That is, if we wanted the employee with an employee number of 987-12-3456, it would be great just to look up the employee by this number and have it hop out of the collection, without the need for looking through each item in the collection ourselves. We could create an array that was 987,123,456 elements long (at a minimum), and keep track of all of the employees by storing them in their corresponding location in the array. While this would work, such an array would require a large amount of storage, and would not be very practical. To do this more efficiently, Java provides a class called Hashtable. Like Vector, Hashtable is also defined in Java's util package.

The Hashtable Class

Hash tables are actually very simple to use considering the power they provide. Here's the idea. Using a hash table is like using a good filing system in a file cabinet. When you put away a file, you put it in its proper place in the file cabinet, stored in the right drawer and in the right folder, so that when you return at some future time to retrieve the file, you know where it is. You don't have to look through every file in order, starting with the first drawer—you can go directly to the drawer and folder where you put it simply by remembering some unique, identifying aspect of the thing you filed.

Using a hash table, you can file an object and retrieve it later by going directly to it. When you file an object, you need to specify two things. The first is the object you wish to file. Simple enough. The second is a key that you can use to find the object again later.

An index can be anything that makes the object unique. It could be a Social Security number in the case of an employee. It might be the employee's e-mail address. For a collection of baseball cards, it might be the card number on the back of the card. Whatever you use as a key doesn't matter, as long as it's unique (and as long as you'll be able to remember what the key is that you can retrieve your object at a later date!).

To create a hash table, you can write the following:

```
Hashtable db = new Hashtable();
```

The variable name db in this example stands for "database." To place and retrieve data from the hash table, let's look at two methods that hash tables define just for this purpose.

get() and put()

Putting an object into a hash table is easy. All you have to do is use the hash table object's put() method and specify two parameters: the key you'll use to identify the object and the object you want to put away. For example, for an instance of class Employee defined like this,

```
class Employee {
    String name;
    String ssn;
}
```

you might store an employee object named e in the hash table like this:

```
db.put(e.ssn, e);
```

Notice that we use the key as the first parameter, and the object itself as the second. Notice also that the key is an object! If you want to use a number as a key, you first have to find a way to convert the number to an object. The sample programs show you how to do this.

Now, to retrieve an object, you use the hash table's get() method and supply the key. The get() method returns an object, which you have to cast to the proper *type* of object (just as you did with vectors). So, to access an employee with the Social Security number represented by the string ssn, you could write

```
Employee e = (Employee)db.get(ssn);
```

Pretty easy! You can fill up the hash table and retrieve values as if there were no tomorrow.

Sample Programs

We'll start the sample programs by looking at floating-point numbers and arrays. Then, we'll get back to the applets we started in Chapter 11, finishing Simple-Draw and Payroll by using vectors and hash tables.

FloatingPt.µ

Open `12.01 - floating pt` in the Learn Java Projects folder, make the project in the ususal way, and drop the file `FloatingPt.html` onto the Metrowerks Java icon. You'll see the following two lines appear in the Java Output window:

```
area of t1 is 67.5
area of t2 is 23.4451
```

This applet calculates the areas for two triangles. Notice the decimal points! How did we finally achieve this kind of precision? We used floating-point numbers! Let's take a look at the source code.

Stepping Through the Source Code

Open `FloatingPt.java`. You'll see two classes here: an applet and a Triangle class. The Triangle class looks like what we've seen before, except this time it defines its data using the floating-point data type `double`, rather than the integer data type `int`:

```java
class Triangle {
   double base;
   double height;

   double area() {
      return base * height / 2.0;
   }
}
```

Now, the applet can interact with this Triangle class in a way very similar to what we've already seen. Here's what the applet does in its `init()` method. First, it defines a couple of triangles. The first triangle takes the values 9 and 15 for its base and height. (We can assign an integer value to a floating-point value without casting it since floating-point values are more accurate than integers.) The second triangle has the value 14.232 for the base and 3.2947 for the height:

```
public class FloatingPt extends java.applet.Applet {

    public void init() {

        Triangle t1 = new Triangle();
        t1.base    = 9;
        t1.height = 15;

        Triangle t2 = new Triangle();
        t2.base    = 14.232;
        t2.height = 3.2947;
```

Then, all we do is print out the area for each triangle. The triangle performs the floating-point calculation, and we display the results in the Java Output window:

```
        System.out.println("area of t1 is " + t1.area());
        System.out.println("area of t2 is " + t2.area());


    }


}
```

So, now you know how to work with two different kinds of numbers: integer and floating-point. As you can see, floating-point values are as easy to work with as integer values; simply declare a data type as `float` or `double` and away you go. Just remember these two rules:

1. When written out, floating-point numbers, such as 4.0, 3.14, or –100.0292, have the data type of `double`.

2. If you assign a floating-point number to an integer, remember to cast it so that the compiler won't complain. (If the floating-point number contained a fractional value, that value would be dropped when assigned to an integer.)

ArrayApplet.µ

Open `12.02 - arrays` in the Learn Java Projects folder, double-click `Array-Applet.µ`, make the project, and drop the file `ArrayApplet.html` onto the Metrowerks Java icon. This applet displays fortunes and advice. There are five fortunes, chosen for display at random. A new fortune is displayed every time you resize the applet. A sample session is shown in Figures 12.5 and 12.6.

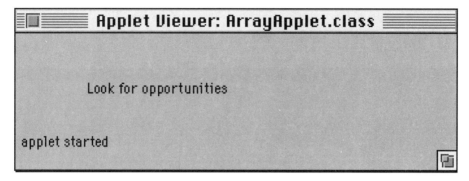

Figure 12.5   A fortune displayed by ArrayApplet.

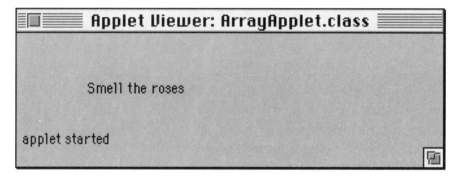

Figure 12.6   Another fortune displayed by resizing the applet.

Let's take a look at the source code to get a feel for working with arrays.

Stepping Through the Source Code

This applet illustrates how to create and work with an array. It also uses three other classes you'll sometimes take advantage of in your own programs: the Date class (in the util package), the Random class (also in the util package), and the Math class (in the lang package). The only class this applet creates is the Applet subclass called ArrayApplet.

At the top of this file, before we define our new class, we need to import three of Java's classes used by this applet that are not part of the lang package (remember, the classes in the lang package are imported for us automatically). These are the Graphics class, which we'll need in order to override the `paint()` method; the Random class, which we'll use to randomly select a fortune; and the Date class, which we'll use to seed the random number, initializing it to a value so that the

287

applet is unlikely to repeat the same sequence of fortunes the next time you run
the applet:

```
import java.awt.Graphics;
import java.util.Random;
import java.util.Date;
```

The applet defines three instance variables. The first, numStrings, is used to
keep track of the number of fortunes in our array of strings. The second, paint-
Strings, defines the string array, but it does not yet allocate it. The third, r, will be
used to hold an instance of a class called Random, which we'll use to generate
random numbers:

```
public class ArrayApplet extends java.applet.Applet {
    int       numStrings = 5;
    String[] paintStrings;
    Random    r;
```

In the init() method, we'll create an instance of the Random class. We could
create this instance with an empty parameter list, with code like r = new Ran-
dom(), but, instead, we'll supply a long value to seed the random number. Supplying a seed value makes it likely that we'll get a different sequence of numbers
every time we run the applet. To seed this number, we need a fairly random number to start with! Here's how we'll proceed. We'll find the number of milliseconds
that have elapsed between 1970 and the current date and time. Since this value
will change every time we run the applet (that is, the number of elapsed milliseconds keeps on increasing from second to second), we can use this as our random
number seed. Java provides a way to get these milliseconds. Given the current
date and time as maintained by an instance of class Date, there's a method called
getTime() that returns the number of milliseconds since 1970. To create a new
date object with today's date and time, all you have to do is create a new date
without supplying any parameters. This is shown in the following code:

```
    public void init() {
        Date d = new Date();
        r = new Random(d.getTime());
```

Now we have a random number object assigned to our instance variable r.
We'll use this random number object in our paint() method to choose a fortune
at random.

Our next step is to allocate the array of strings that will hold our fortunes and to initialize this array. We'll create a new string array set to hold five strings. Then, we'll create a new string for each element in the array:

```
paintStrings = new String[numStrings];
paintStrings[0]  = new String("Look for opportunities");
paintStrings[1]  = new String("Take chances");
paintStrings[2]  = new String("Beware of tricks");
paintStrings[3]  = new String("Take the day off");
paintStrings[4]  = new String("Smell the roses");
}
```

Everything's initialized. All that remains is to display a random fortune when the applet repaints. We can do this in three lines of code by overriding the `paint()` method.

First, we'll use the random number object to generate a random number. There's a method called `nextInt()` defined by random numbers that returns a random integer over the range of all integers, both positive and negative. By dividing this number by the number or strings we have and taking the remainder, we can whittle this number down to the range of −4 to 4. This operation is called **modulo**, as in "nextInt() modulo 5," and it is written using the % character:

```
public void paint(Graphics g) {

    int index = r.nextInt() % numStrings;
```

We're going to use the variable `index` as an index into the array. However, we can't use a negative number as an index! The only valid indexes range from 0 to 1 minus the number of elements in the array (in this case, from 0 to 4). So, we need to take the absolute value of `index` to turn a possible negative value into a positive value. The Math class defines a class method called `abs()` that provides this behavior:

```
index = Math.abs(index);
```

Now `index` ranges from 0 to 4. We want to use `index` to select a string in the string array. We do this by writing `paintStrings[index]`. We can use the `drawString()` method supplied by the graphics object to make this new string appear inside the applet:

```
        g.drawString(paintStrings[index], 50, 25);


    }
}
```

Now, every time the applet repaints, such as when it's resized, it will contain a new fortune, randomly selected from its array of strings.

SimpleDraw.μ, Final Version

Open 12.03 - SimpleDraw in the Learn Java Projects folder. Open SimpleDraw.μ and make the project. Run the applet by dropping SimpleDraw.html onto the Metrowerks Java icon. At long last, we've recreated the applet you first saw in Chapter 4! Figure 12.7 shows what the applet looks like when you create a number of different shapes in different colors.

In the previous chapter, we got as far as drawing a shape according to the user's preference (shape type and color). However, we were only able to draw the most recent shape; we did not keep a list of all the shapes the user had created with each click of the mouse. Here, we remember each shape and redraw each shape in the applet's paint() method. Let's see how we are able to keep track of all these shapes.

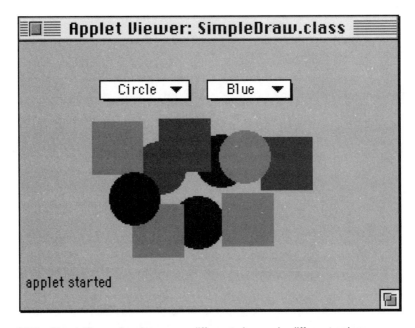

Figure 12.7 SimpleDraw showing many different shapes in different colors.

By the way, it's not quite accurate to say this is the final version! You'll see three more versions of this applet in the upcoming chapters. First, you'll see a version where you can pass parameters to this applet from your HTML file; second, you'll see a version of this applet that runs separately from a Web browser or Applet Viewer; and third, you'll see a version that illustrates the basics of multi-threading. All of these versions await you in Chapters 13, 14, and 15.

Stepping Through the Source Code

Open `SimpleDraw.java`. You might notice that this code looks almost identical to what you saw in the previous version in Chapter 11. It's very similar, but there's one crucial difference: the use of the Vector class. We'll point out the differences here.

First, in addition to importing the Applet class and the classes in the awt package, we also import the classes in the util package. This package defines the Vector class that we'll use to keep track of the shapes drawn by the user:

```
import java.applet.Applet;
import java.util.*;
import java.awt.*;
```

The SimpleDraw class starts by defining an instance variable that will hold the vector; it also defines the choice objects that you saw before:

```
public class SimpleDraw extends Applet {
    Vector    drawnShapes;
    Choice    shapeChoice;
    Choice    colorChoice;
```

The `init()` method is next. It starts by creating a new instance of the Vector class:

```
    /** Create the GUI. */
    public void init() {
        drawnShapes = new Vector();
```

The `init()` method then moves on to create the choice objects for selecting the shape to draw and the color in which to draw it. This is the same code you already saw; we'll mark its place here with a comment:

```
        // Create the two choice objects and add them to the applet

    }
```

After the `init()` method, we've defined the `mouseUp()` method. This method starts by creating a new shape just as it did before. Again, we'll put in a placeholder for this code by using a comment:

```
public boolean mouseUp(Event e, int x, int y) {

    Shape s; // This shape will be either a circle or a square.

    // Create the shape just like before
```

The previous version of SimpleDraw assigned the new shape to an instance variable maintained by the applet. This time, we don't keep track of individual shapes in the applet itself; we keep track only of the collection of shapes in the vector. So, here, we add the new shape to the vector and then invoke `repaint()`, as we did before:

```
    drawnShapes.addElement(s);

    repaint();

    return true;
}
```

We also return true to indicate we handled this event.

The final method that has changed is the `paint()` method. This time, instead of repainting the single shape maintained by the applet, we repaint every shape in the vector. This means we have to perform these steps:

1. Determine how many shapes are in the vector.

2. Access each shape, one at a time, and redraw that shape.

Here's how we do that. First, `paint()` defines two variables: s will hold the shape we access from the vector, and numShapes will hold the number of shapes in the vector:

```
public void paint(Graphics g) {
    Shape s;
    int numShapes;
```

We'll determine the number of shapes in the vector by using an instance method supplied by the vector, called `size()`:

```
      numShapes = drawnShapes.size();
```

Then, we'll loop through the number of shapes in the vector, accessing each one in turn:

```
      for (int i = 0; i < numShapes; i++) {

         s = (Shape)drawnShapes.elementAt(i);
```

Notice that we need to cast the object returned by `elementAt()` to the proper class type. `elementAt()` is defined as returning an object of class Object; we know this object will be a shape object, and we want to assign it to a variable that holds a shape. To do this, we must cast the returned object to be of type Shape. (Be aware that this code works only because we are dealing with objects that really are shapes; you can't just go around casting any old object into a shape or some other class type that it is not. However, you'll use this technique a lot in situations like this.)

At the end of this method, we redraw the shape by invoking its `draw()` method:

```
         s.draw(g);
      }
   }


}
```

The Shape, Circle, and Square classes are identical to what you saw before; we won't repeat them here.

Notice that using an array to keep track of the shapes would not have worked as well as using a vector. With an array, we would constantly have to worry about adding a new shape to the array beyond the bounds of the array. If we ever maxed out the array, we would have to allocate a new array a little bit larger than the one we were using, move all the elements from the old array to the new array, and then add our new shape to the new array. The vector object handles all these details for us. This is another good example of Java supplying a class that makes our programming task easier.

`Payroll.µ`, Final Version

Open `12.04 - Payroll` in the Learn Java Projects folder. Open `Payroll.µ` and make the project. Drop the file `Payroll.html` onto the Metrowerks Java icon to run the applet.

This applet is fully functional and allows you to enter new employees into a database and retrieve previously entered information for employees. (Of course, a commercial payroll applet would have better lookup methods, offer confirmation of changes, provide some security, allow for data other than integers, and so on. While all these features would be great, the point of this applet is to show how to develop a user interface that accepts keyboard entry, illustrate how to keep track of data using a hash table, and provide an example of handling an exception.)

To enter a new employee into the Payroll applet or to search for an existing employee, click in the text field for the employee number, enter a number, and press enter. If information for that employee exists in the payroll applet, that information is displayed in the text fields. Otherwise, the payroll information will be all zeros.

To enter new values or change the values for the employee's hourly wage and hours worked, click in the appropriate text field, enter a new number, and press enter. When there is data for both the hourly wage and hours worked, the applet will display the employee's earned income.

Figure 12.8 shows the payroll information for employee number 1. The user typed 1 into the text field for the employee number and pressed enter. The user then typed in the hourly wage and hours worked and pressed enter for each text field. Once all the data was entered, the applet totaled that employee's earned income. All this data was saved in the employee object and made part of the database.

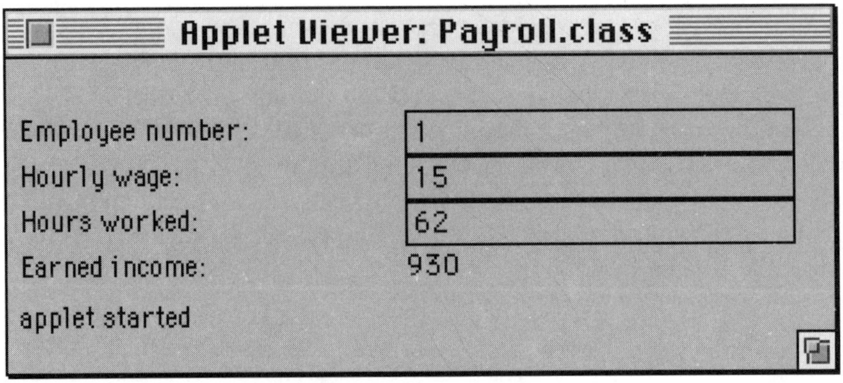

Figure 12.8 The payroll information for employee number 1.

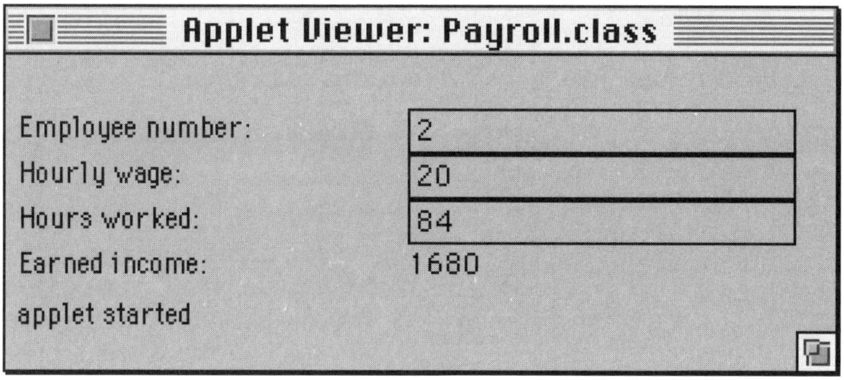

Figure 12.9   The payroll information for employee number 2.

Figure 12.9 shows the payroll information for employee number 2. Here, the applet saved all of employee number 2's information into the database. Now there are two employees in the database. If the user now typed a 1 into the employee number field and pressed enter, the applet would look up the payroll data for employee number 1 and redisplay that information in its text fields.

Stepping Through the Source Code

Open `Payroll.java` to see what's changed from the previous version. Here's the concept of what we're going to do. We're going to create new employee objects based on the information the user enters into the text fields. We're going to use an instance of class Hashtable to keep track of the employee objects. By using a hash table, we'll be able to retrieve any employee object, as long as we have the employee number. We'll use the employee number for each employee as the employee's key. When the user types a new number into the employee number text field, we'll take the characters the user typed and turn them into a number and then use that number as the key to look up that employee object in the hash table. If the employee is found, we'll display the employee's payroll information in the other text fields. If the employee is not found, we'll create a new employee object using this number and add it to the hash table.

We'll start looking at the code by examining three utility methods. The first is `intFromTextField()`, an instance method defined as part of the applet. This method's purpose in life is to take the characters a user enters into a text field and convert them into an `int` data type. This method takes a text field as a parameter and returns an `int`:

```
int intFromTextField(TextField tf) {
```

It starts off defining two variables. The string s will be used to hold the character data in the text field; value will be used to hold the int we'll return:

```
String  s;
int     value;
```

This method starts by retrieving the characters in the text field passed to this method. The method getText() returns a string object that has the characters the user typed:

```
s = tf.getText();
```

To convert this into an int, we'll use a class method defined by Integer called parseInt(). This method takes a string and returns an int. Since this method might throw an exception, we have to use a try-catch block so that we're prepared to catch the exception. We'll try to perform the conversion in the try block; we'll catch any exceptions thrown in the catch block:

```
try {
    value = Integer.parseInt(s);
} catch (Exception e) {
    value = 0;
    setCurrent(null);
}
```

If the conversion to an int did not work and Java threw an exception, we set value to 0 and set the current employee to null. (You'll look at the method set-Current() in a moment. The purpose of the setCurrent() method is to save the current employee object in an instance variable named current. This instance variable is maintained by the applet. setCurrent() also redisplays the information in the text fields so that it's appropriate to the current employee.) Finally, we return the value, and the method ends:

```
    return value;
}
```

Next, let's look at a method called findEmployee(). This is also an instance method defined as part of the applet. This method takes an int as a parameter and returns an instance of class Employee:

```
Employee findEmployee(int number) {
```

This method consists of a single statement, but there's a lot going on in this statement. This method returns an employee object that it finds in the hash table. To get the employee object, this statement uses the `get()` method, supplied by the hash table. The instance variable we use in this applet to keep track of the hash table is called `db` (for "database"). To invoke `get()`, then, we can say `db.get()`. The `get()` method takes a key, and hash table keys must be objects. To obtain an appropriate object based on the employee number, we can create an instance of class Integer to represent this number. We can do this by writing `new Integer(number)`. The full statement looks like this:

```
    return (Employee)db.get(new Integer(number));
}
```

Notice that, as with the vector, `get()` returns an object of class Object. This means that if we want to work with an instance of class Employee, we need to cast it to Employee. We can safely do this because all the objects in the hash table are instances of class Employee; if they were instances of some other class, we could not do this.

One more thing. If there is no employee object that uses the key we've indicated, then `get()` will return null, and that's what `findEmployee()` will return as well.

For our third utility method, take a look at `addNew()`. This instance method creates a new employee object given an employee number and adds this employee to the database. This method takes the employee number as a parameter and returns the newly created employee object:

```
Employee addNew(int number) {
```

After creating the new employee object, this code initializes the employee number and sets the other instance variables to 0:

```
    Employee e = new Employee();
    e.idNumber = number;
    e.hourlyWage = 0;
    e.hoursWorked = 0;
```

It then uses the hash table's `put()` method to put the new employee object into the hash table. The `put()` method requires a key as its first parameter. Again, we'll create an Integer instance out of the employee number. The second parameter for put() is the employee object to add:

```
db.put(new Integer(number), e);
```

At the end of this method, we again use the method setCurrent() to set the current employee maintained by the current variable and to display this new employee's information in the text fields. Then, we return the new employee object:

```
setCurrent(e);

return e;
}
```

With an understanding of these methods and the approach taken by this applet, let's look at the rest of the applet.

The file begins by importing the Applet class and the awt and util packages (we need the util package for the hash table):

```
import java.applet.Applet;
import java.awt.*;
import java.util.*;
```

As with the previous version of Payroll, we define instance variables to hold the text fields. We also define an instance variable to hold the hash table:

```
public class Payroll extends Applet {
    Hashtable   db;
    TextField   textFieldEmployee;
    TextField   textFieldWage;
    TextField   textFieldHours;
    Label       labelEarned;
```

In addition, we also define an instance variable to hold the current employee:

```
Employee    current;
```

The init() method creates a new hash table. The rest of the init() method creates the same labels and text fields in a grid layout you saw before. We'll mark its place with a comment:

```
public void init() {

    // Create the employee database.
    db = new Hashtable();

    // Create the labels and text fields.
```

Before we leave the `init()` method, we also invoke `setCurrent()` and indicate that we're not currently looking at any employee object—since there aren't any yet to look at:

```
    setCurrent(null);
}
```

The method `action()` handles the events generated by this applet. The previous version showed how we could tell when the user typed into a text field and pressed return. In this version, we'll access the data in the text fields and use them to initialize the employee objects.

The `action()` method starts off by defining variables to hold an employee object and the employee number:

```
public boolean action(Event e, Object arg) {
    Employee employee;
    int      number;
```

One of the parameters passed to this method is an event object, which contains the information that indicates what generated this event. Just as with the previous version, we test to see what text field the user has typed text into. The event's `target` instance variable holds this text field. The first possibility is the employee number text field:

```
    if (e.target == textFieldEmployee) {
```

If the text field is the one used for the employee number, we use the method `intFromTextField()`, which we've already seen, to retrieve the employee number. Then, we use the method `findEmployee()`, which we've also seen, to retrieve the employee with this number from the hash table:

```
        number = intFromTextField(textFieldEmployee);
        employee = findEmployee(number);
```

If an employee with this number could not be found in the hash table, `em-ployee` will be equal to `null`. If this is the case, then we want to create a new employee using this number. We use the method `addNew()`, which we also covered earlier:

```
if (employee == null)
    employee = addNew(number);
```

Now, we invoke `setCurrent()` with this new employee to set the `current` variable and display this employee's payroll information:

```
setCurrent(employee);
}
```

If the event's target is the hourly wage field, then we want to set the current employee object's hourly wage to the value the user entered into this field. We can use the method `intFromTextField()` to retrieve this `int` from the characters in this field:

```
else if (e.target == textFieldWage) {

    if (current != null) {
        current.hourlyWage = intFromTextField(textFieldWage);
```

We also want to update the display for the earned income. If the user has just changed the value for the hourly wage, we can reflect that change in the earned income display immediately. The method `recalcEarned()` performs this simple recalculation and displays the new value in the appropriate label in the applet:

```
recalcEarned();
}
```

We want to do the identical kind of thing with the hourly wage text field. That is, we want to retrieve the value the user entered into the text field, assign it to the appropriate instance variable for the current employee, and recalculate the value for the earned income:

```
} else if (e.target == textFieldHours) {

    if (current != null) {
        current.hoursWorked =intFromTextField(textFieldHours);
```

```
            recalcEarned();
        }
    }
```

When we exit this `action()` method, we'll return whatever the superclass thinks is appropriate (true or false):

```
    return super.action(e, arg);
}
```

Let's take a quick look at the two methods we haven't seen yet for this applet: `setCurrent()` and `recalcEarned()`. `setCurrent()` starts by assigning the new employee object to the applet's instance variable named `current`:

```
void setCurrent(Employee e) {
    current = e;
```

If there is not a current object (that is, if it is equal to `null`), then set the text fields to contain 0:

```
    if (e == null) {
        textFieldEmployee.setText("0");
        textFieldWage.setText("0");
        textFieldHours.setText("0");
    }
```

Otherwise, if there is an employee object, convert the `int` data maintained by this employee into a string and display this text in the text field:

```
  else{
    textFieldWage.setText(Integer.toString(current.hourlyWage));
    textFieldHours.setText(Integer.toString(current.hoursWorked));
}
```

At the end, recalculate the earned income to reflect any new data:

```
    recalcEarned();
```

```
}
```

recalcEarned() asks the current employee object to calculate its own earned income (hourly wage times hours worked). If there is no current employee, then we set the earned income to be 0. The last line sets the label in the applet that displays the earned income:

```
void recalcEarned() {
    int earned;

    if (current != null)
        earned = current.earnedIncome();
    else
        earned = 0;

    labelEarned.setText(Integer.toString(earned));
}


}
```

The Employee class is identical to what you saw before, so we won't repeat it here.

This applet illustrates a lot of functionality. It shows you how to arrange a user interface, how to acquire data from the user, how to convert between int data types and objects (such as Integers and Strings), and how to store and retrieve data in a hash table. You are likely to do many of these things when writing your own Java applets.

Review

This chapter rounded out your knowledge of how to work with data in Java. Working with data involves integer and Boolean data as well as floating-point values, characters, and objects that maintain data such as strings and instances of class Integer. You also learned about exceptions, so you'll know what to do if you encounter any error conditions that might arise when working with your data.

To keep track of collections of data, you can use arrays. Java also defines two useful classes called Vector and Hashtable. Vectors contain a simple list of objects; hash tables allow you to find objects based on a key.

What's Next?

Chapter 13 snoops around some advanced areas of Java programming, including how to pass values to your applet from your HTML file, how to define more than one method with the same name, and how to throw exceptions (that is, in addition to catching them, which you learned about here).

In Chapter 14, we'll cover how to make your Java programs run separately from a Web browser, and we'll close in Chapter 15 by pointing out areas you can explore further to learn even more about Java.

Advanced Topics

This chapter will highlight some advanced features you can take advantage of in your own applications. Even if you don't use these features right away, they're useful to know about because you're likely to run across them when you look over other Java programs generally available on the Web. The advanced features of Java discussed here include applet parameters, method overloading, constructors, constants, and throwing exceptions.

Applet Parameters

So far, all of the HTML files that have incorporated our applets have been very simple. These HTML files used the `<applet>` tag to specify the name of the applet to run as well as the initial height and width of the applet's window. With only these parameters, our applets had to be self-contained. That is, the HTML file that launched the applet did not change anything about the applet, other than its initial size.

However, it is possible to embed values, or parameters, in your HTML file that the applet can access. The way you do this is to place the parameters within tags named `<param>` right between the `<applet>` and `</applet>` tags.

For example, if you wanted to supply a parameter named "minimumwage" to the Payroll applet to make sure you don't initialize any employees to an illegal value, you could write something like this:

```
<applet code="Payroll.class" width=270 height=150>
<param name=minimumwage value="4.25">
</applet>
```

Now, when Congress passes a new minimum wage law or when a business in another country wants to use the Payroll applet, users of this applet can set this value according to the new conditions.

To retrieve this value in an applet, you use an applet instance method defined by Java called `getParameter()`. This method takes a string with the name of the parameter to access. `getParameter()` returns a string representing the value of this parameter. Here's a snippet:

```
String wageString = getParameter("minimumwage");
```

In this example, `wageString` is now "4.25." If we want a `float` number, we have to convert this string to a number before we can use it like a number. For example, we can write

```
float wageFloat;

try {
   float wageFloat = Float.getValue(wageString).toFloat;
} catch (Exception e) {
   wageFloat = 4.25; // default
}
```

The sample programs at the end of this chapter contain an example of how to customize your applet by passing values to it from your HTML file.

Method Overloading

So far, all of our methods have used unique names. This might seem to be a requirement for methods—that each one have its own, unique name—but this is not precisely true. The *real* requirement is that each method belonging to the same class have a unique **signature**. What do we mean by a signature? A signature consists of a method's name and parameter types. This means that two methods in the same class can be named identically—as long as either the number of parameters or, if two methods with the same name have the same number of parameters, the *types* of parameters are different. Here are some examples that illustrate this rule.

Let's start with a simple method called `addTheseNumbers()`, defined like this:

```
int addTheseNumbers(int num1, int num2) {
   return num1 + num2;
}
```

This method would work fine as long as there were only two numbers to add. However, what if we sometimes wanted to add two numbers and other times wanted to add three numbers? It would be nice not to have to worry about different method names, but to always invoke a method called `addTheseNumbers()`, regardless of how many numbers we had to add.

One way to solve this problem is by writing two methods, *both* called add-TheseNumbers(). The first method would define two parameters; the second would define three parameters. Here's how these two method definitions might look:

```
int addTheseNumbers(int num1, int num2) {
    return num1 + num2;
}

int addTheseNumbers(int num1, int num2, int num3) {
    return num1 + num2 + num3;
}
```

What happens when we write a line of code that looks like the following?

```
int sum = addTheseNumbers(10, 20);
```

In this case, Java is smart enough to invoke the first method named addTheseNumbers() since that method defines two parameters.

What happens with the following line of code?

```
int sum = addTheseNumbers(10, 20, 15);
```

You guessed it—Java invokes the second method, matching the three values here to the method that declares three int parameters.

As before, the parameters in your method invocations must match up with one of your method definitions. If Java cannot find a method that matches an invocation, you'll either receive a compiler error or a runtime error (depending on the class you're compiling and the class defining the method).

In addition to defining a different number of parameters for two methods with the same name, it's also perfectly legal to define a second method with the same name and the same number of parameters—as long as at least one of those parameters is of a different type than in the first method. For example, here's another method with the same name:

```
double addTheseNumbers(double num1, double num2) {
    return num1 + num2;
}
```

Now, if you invoke addTheseNumbers() like this,

```
int i = addTheseNumbers(10, 15);
```

the method for `int` values will execute, and it will return the `int` value 25. If you invoke `addTheseNumbers()` like this,

```
double d = addTheseNumbers(10.3, 14.6);
```

the method for double values will execute, and it will return the double value of 24.9.

Even with the same number of parameters, Java is smart enough to figure out which method is the appropriate one to invoke. Notice that in all of these examples, the return value does not play a role in determining what method to invoke! Only the method name, the number of parameters, and the types of parameters are used to distinguish between methods.

Constructors

When you create a new object from a class, Java allocates the appropriate amount of memory in the computer to hold your new object. Then, Java invokes any constructors that are defined for your new object. Your constructor can do whatever it wants to do. The most common task for a constructor is initializing instance variables, and this is what you'll do most often if you define your own constructor.

Constructors are defined somewhat similarly to methods, except they don't take any keywords or define a return value. For example, here's a class called Employee that defines a constructor:

```
class Employee {
    int ssn;
    int hourlyWage;
    int hoursWorked;

    // Define a constructor.
    Employee() {
        hourlyWage = 10;
    }

    // Define an instance method.
    int earnedIncome() {
        return hourlyWage * hoursWorked;
    }
}
```

This class is similar to what we worked with before when we defined an Employee class, but this time we have defined a constructor for the class. The constructor initializes a new employee's hourly wage to 10. Perhaps after a few months, the employee will get a raise, but new hires start out with 10 as their base wage. What this means, then, is that when you create an instance of an Employee class like this,

```
Employee e = new Employee();
```

`e.hourlyWage` will start out equal to 10, and `e.hoursWorked` will start out equal to 0 (remember, Java sets your `int` variables to 0 if you don't initialize them yourself).

You can also pass parameters to constructors. You'll find that Java defines lots of constructors that take parameters for its classes. For example, if we wanted to set the employee's number when we created it, we might write a constructor like this:

```
Employee (int ssn) {
   this.ssn = ssn;
   hourlyWage = 10;
}
```

Now we can create a new employee like this:

```
Employee e = new Employee(401);
```

We might write this code for the 401st person to join the company. Even if this were the only constructor we defined, we could still create an employee object without passing a value for the `ssn` parameter value to the constructor. That is, we could still create an employee like this:

```
Employee e = new Employee();
```

We can do this because Java always defines a default constructor for you, and this default constructor does not take any parameters. With the default constructor, all of your object's instance variables will be set to their default values, but at least Java saves you the trouble of needing to create a constructor if you only want the default behavior.

By the Way

> You don't have to invoke your superclass's constructor. Java will do this for you automatically.

Constants

Variables are great for keeping track of data that changes over time. Sometimes, however, you'll want to keep track of data that won't change, *ever*, while your program is running.

We saw an example of this kind of thing already in SimpleDraw. The user was able to tell the applet what shape to draw and what color to draw it in, but the user was unable to set the size of the shape—the size of the shape was always constant. Appropriately enough, programming languages refer to these types of data as **constants**. In other words, a variable that has a value, but cannot be changed, is called a constant.

You can define a constant in Java by using the keyword `final`, meaning the value can never be changed. For example, SimpleDraw can define a constant to represent the radius of a circle like this:

```
final int radius = 20; // circles are 20 pixels in radius
```

Often, constants are placed in the class. This allows any part of your code to easily access the constant. So, you could also define `radius` like this:

```
static final int radius = 20; // circles are 20 pixels in radius
```

By the Way

> Why use a constant? Why not just use the value 20 wherever the program needed to know the radius of a circle? There are three reasons for using a constant. First, a well-named constant documents what the number is used for. Second, using constants can speed up Java's execution. And third, if the value ever changes, all you need to do is change the number in one place.

Throwing Exceptions

You've learned the basics about handling exceptions, but, like packages, exceptions are available for *you* to use as well. That is, they're not just something you have to catch; your code can also throw its own exceptions. All you have to do is create your own Exception subclass or use one of Java's. If you hit an error condition in your own code, you can write

```
throw new MyException();
```

and your code exits, tossing the exception object to the code that invoked your method. Your method must declare that it might throw an exception if you use a throw keyword. For example, you might write

```
void myMethod() throws MyException {
    if (errorCondition())
        throw new MyException();
}
```

This code also assumes you've defined your own subclass of Exception, called MyException:

```
class MyException extends Exception {
}
```

There's also a nifty keyword called finally that allows you to execute a block of code, no matter what happened. For example, you can write

```
try {
    // try something here
} catch (Exception e) {
    // catch an exception here
} finally {
    // execute this code no matter what happened in the above try
    // and catch blocks
}
```

Remember how we talked about different types of exceptions in the previous chapter? By catching a particular type of exception, you can choose to do different things, depending on the exception that occurred. You can catch more than one type of exception by presenting a few different catch blocks, like this:

```
try {
    // try something here
} catch (ExceptionSubclass1 e) {
    // catch an exception of type ExceptionSubclass1 here
} catch (ExceptionSubclass2 {
    // catch an exception of type ExceptionSubclass2 here
```

```
} catch (Exception e) {
   // catch any other type of exception here
}
```

You can also "handle" an exception by rethrowing it. For example, you can write

```
try {
   // try something here
} catch (Exception e) {
   throw e;
}
```

If you do this, you must declare your method as indicating it throws an exception. Also, be aware that if no one else handles the exception, your program (or more technically, the thread that is currently executing) will come to a halt. Barry Boone's *Java Essentials for C and C++ Programmers*, from Addison-Wesley, has many more examples of why, when, and how to create and use your own exceptions.

Sample Programs

We'll look at three different programs in this section. The first shows you how to pass values to your applet from your HTML file. The second shows you how to initialize objects by rolling your own constructor. The third program provides an example of throwing your own custom exception.

SimpleDraw.µ

Open the file SimpleDraw.µ in the subfolder 13.01 - applet params in the Learn Java Projects folder. Make the project, then run this applet by dropping the HTML file SimpleDraw.html onto the Metrowerks Java icon. An applet similar to the SimpleDraw applet will appear—except that you'll notice the colors are different than before (Figure 13.1). Once you're done playing around with these new shape colors, quit the Applet Viewer and take a look at the source code.

Stepping Through the Source Code

The original SimpleDraw applet hard-coded the colors that were used to display the shapes. These colors were built into the applet's init() method and were set to red, green, and blue. In the version here, rather than forcing red, green, and blue to be the colors, we have instead structured the applet so that every person placing the applet in a Web page can choose which colors the applet will use.

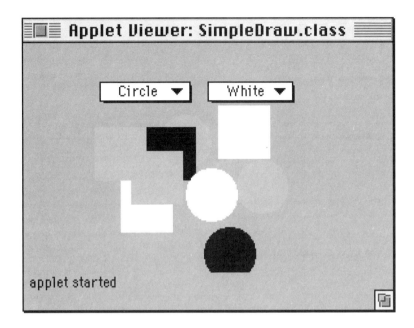

Figure 13.1 Shapes that are white, black, and pink.

What's wrong with pink, cyan, and orange? You have a problem with that? With applet parameters, this is no problem at all because you can change them just by changing the HTML file.

Double-click SimpleDraw.html to see how this file is set up. This file will appear as in Figure 13.2.

This file names each parameter so that the applet can find it later. Here, we're supplying three colors. We've called these colors color1, color2, and color3. We use the name keyword to define the parameter's name. Immediately following the name, we use the value keyword to supply a value for this parameter:

```
<applet code="SimpleDraw.class" codebase= "SimpleDraw" width=270 height=150>
<param name=color1 value="White">
<param name=color2 value="Black">
<param name=color3 value="Pink">
</applet>
```

The values are defined inside quotes in case the values contain spaces in their text.

The next step is to access these values in your applet. Originally, we defined a new choice object and added the choices to it by writing

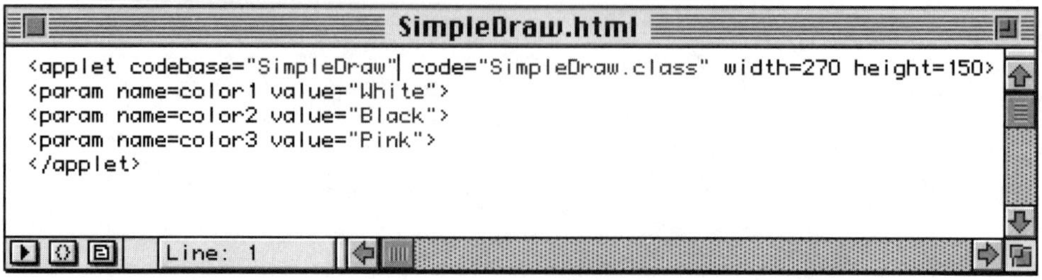

```
╔═════════════════════ SimpleDraw.html ═════════════════════╗
║ <applet codebase="SimpleDraw"| code="SimpleDraw.class" width=270 height=150>
║ <param name=color1 value="White">
║ <param name=color2 value="Black">
║ <param name=color3 value="Pink">
║ </applet>
║
╟ [▶][{}][B]   Line: 1     [◁][▥]                              [⇨][▣]
```

Figure 13.2 The `SimpleDraw.html` file, which supplies custom colors to the applet.

```
colorChoice = new Choice();
colorChoice.addItem("Red");
colorChoice.addItem("Green");
colorChoice.addItem("Blue");
```

Now, however, we want to get the parameter given its name. To do this, we use the method `getParameter()`. This method takes a string with the name of the parameter to access. `getParameter()` returns a string, which is exactly what we want for the `addItem()` method for choices. Here's how we would get the value for the color parameters embedded in the HTML file:

```
colorChoice = new Choice();
colorChoice.addItem(getParameter("color1"));
colorChoice.addItem(getParameter("color2"));
colorChoice.addItem(getParameter("color3"));
```

`getParameter("color1")` would retrieve the value "White," given the HTML file we supplied. Similarly, `getParameter("color2")` would retrieve the value "Black," and `getParameter("color3")` would retrieve the value "Pink."

With all these color possibilities, we need more choices in our color selection code. We can expand the choices of red, green, and blue to look more like this:

```
if (colorString.equals("Red"))
    s.color = Color.red;
else if (colorString.equals("Green"))
    s.color = Color.green;
else if (colorString.equals("Black"))
    s.color = Color.black;
else if (colorString.equals("Blue"))
    s.color = Color.blue;
```

```
    else if (colorString.equals("Pink"))
        s.color = Color.pink;
    else if (colorString.equals("Cyan"))
        s.color = Color.cyan;
    else if (colorString.equals("Orange"))
        s.color = Color.orange;
    else
        s.color = Color.white;   // default color
```

Red, green, pink, and the other colors are a few of the color choices predefined in the Color class. You can look at the documentation for the Color class supplied in the Java APIs (application programming interfaces) to see a complete list of colors that are provided by Java. As we covered in Chapter 11, you can always create your own custom colors as well.

You might want to play around with this applet and HTML file, changing the colors to get a feel for how this all works. (It's even more fun with colors like cyan and orange, but the screenshots for this book required colors that would be somewhat distinct in gray-scale.)

Constructor.μ

Go to the subfolder 13.02 – constructor in the Learn Java Projects folder. Open Constructor.μ and make the project. Run the applet by dropping Constructor.html onto the Metrowerks Java icon. This applet will write the following three messages to the Java Output window:

```
This circle's radius is 10
This circle's radius is 20
This circle's radius is 20
```

Each of the three circles created in this applet is created with a different constructor. Let's take a look at the source code.

Stepping Through the Source Code

Open Constructor.java to view the source code. There are two classes defined in this file: Constructor, which is an applet, and Circle. The top part of the Circle class defines one instance variable and one class variable, set to a default radius:

```
class Circle {
    static int defaultRadius = 10;
    int radius;
```

Then, the class defines three constructors. The first constructor overrides the default constructor, which does not take any parameters. The code for this constructor simply assigns the circle's radius to be the value of the default radius:

```
Circle() {
    radius = defaultRadius;
}
```

The second constructor takes a radius as a parameter and uses this value to set the radius for this circle:

```
Circle(int radius) {
    this.radius = radius;
}
```

The third constructor takes a circle object as a parameter and uses this object to set the radius to the same value in this object:

```
Circle(Circle referenceCircle) {
    this.radius = referenceCircle.radius;
}
```

We can write three constructors, all with the same name, because of method overloading. The first constructor is distinguished from the second and third because of the different number of parameters (zero and one). The second and third constructors can be distinguished by the different parameter types (int and Circle).

The Circle class also defines an instance method that displays the radius for the current circle:

```
void displayInfo() {
    System.out.println("This circle's radius is " + radius);
}
}
```

Going back up to the top of the code, the Constructor applet defines an init() method. The init() method defines three variables, one to hold each circle it will create:

```
public class Constructor extends Applet {
    public void init() {
        Circle c1, c2, c3;
```

The init() method then creates three circles, each time using a different constructor defined in the Circle class. The first time, init() does not supply any parameters, so the circle will take on the default radius (the value 10). The second time, init() supplies a radius, so the circle will take on that radius value (the value 20). The third time, init() passes the second circle as a reference circle, so the third circle will have the same radius value as the second circle (that is, it will be 20):

```
c1 = new Circle();
c2 = new Circle(20);
c3 = new Circle(c2);
```

Then, each of the circle's information is printed, resulting in the display to the Java Output window:

```
    c1.displayInfo();
    c2.displayInfo();
    c3.displayInfo();
  }
}
```

ExceptionApplet.µ

For our last example, go to the subfolder 13.03 - exception in the Learn Java Projects folder. Open ExceptionApplet.µ, make the project, and run the applet by dropping ExceptionApplet.html onto the Metrowerks Java icon. Here are the messages this applet will write to the Java Output window:

```
Exception with radius -20
This circle's radius is 10
This circle's radius is 20
This circle's radius is 10
This circle's radius is 20
```

This applet is very similar to the one we just saw that defined three constructors for the Circle class. This time, we created four circles, and creating one of these circles caused an exception to be thrown! Let's take a look at the source code.

Stepping Through the Source Code

Open `ExceptionApplet.java`. At the very bottom of this file, we've defined our own Exception subclass, called ImaginaryCircleException. We've simply created an empty class; the class's name is enough to identify what exception this defines:

```
class ImaginaryCircleException extends Exception {
}
```

The Circle's class definition is the same as before, except we've changed the constructor that takes the `int` parameter for the circle's radius. This time, instead of writing

```
Circle (int radius) {
    this.radius = radius;
}
```

we're a little more careful about the circle we're creating! Instead of creating a circle with any old radius, we first verify that the radius is in fact not a negative number. If it is, someone is attempting to create an imaginary circle. If that is the case, we want to throw an exception so that the code creating this circle can handle this problem in a way it finds appropriate. The circle constructor does not presume to know what the code creating the circle wants to do when it tries to create an illegal circle. All the circle constructor does is notify the code that this kind of circle can't exist. Here's the new constructor:

```
Circle(int radius) throws ImaginaryCircleException {

    if (radius < 0)
        throw new ImaginaryCircleException();
    else
        this.radius = radius;

}
```

As you can see, the constructor must indicate that it might throw an exception. It does this by using the `throws` keyword, followed by the type of exception it might throw. The code creates and throws an instance of ImaginaryCircleException if the radius is negative. Otherwise, all is fine, and the circle takes on the radius value supplied to it.

The ExceptionApplet code progresses in a way similar to what you saw earlier. Its init() method starts out defining variables to hold the new circle objects it will create. It then creates a circle using the default constructor, which hasn't changed from before:

```
public class ExceptionApplet extends Applet {
   public void init() {
      Circle c1, c2, c3, c4;

      c1 = new Circle();
```

Next, the init() method tries to create two circles using the new circle constructor. First, it tries to set the circle's radius to 20. In order to use the new constructor, which might throw an exception, the call to this constructor must be wrapped in a try block. The try is followed by a catch:

```
      try {

         c2 = new Circle(20);

      } catch (ImaginaryCircleException e) {

         System.out.println("Exception with radius 20");
         c2 = new Circle();

      }
```

If the constructor throws an exception of type ImaginaryCircleException, the catch block will be able to handle this situation. It will display a message to the Java Output window indicating what went wrong, and it will then create a default circle. As it happens, everything goes fine with creating a circle of radius 20; the constructor never throws the exception since the radius value supplied is not negative.

However, the init() method then tries to create a circle with a radius of –20. Trying to do *that* triggers the circle's constructor to throw an exception. You can see the exception message appear in the Java Output window, and the third circle has a radius of 10, which is what's created by the default constructor:

```
      try {

         c3 = new Circle(-20);
```

319

```
        } catch (ImaginaryCircleException e) {

            System.out.println("Exception with radius -20");
            c3 = new Circle();

        }
```

The rest of the `init()` method is similar to what was there before: A new circle is created using the third constructor, and then the information for each circle is displayed:

```
        c4 = new Circle(c2);

        c1.displayInfo();
        c2.displayInfo();
        c3.displayInfo();
        c4.displayInfo();
    }
}
```

As this example shows, you don't just have to respond to Java's exceptions; you can also use exceptions to signal and handle error conditions that arise in your own code.

Review

This chapter brought you up to speed on some advanced topics and concepts in Java that you are likely to use as you develop ever more sophisticated programs. This includes how to customize your applets by supplying values for your applet as part of a Web page, how to write methods with the same name but that take a different set of parameters, how to get into the act of initializing your objects by creating your own custom constructors, and how to throw your own exceptions. There are a few more features of the language that we'll touch on in Chapter 15, where we'll also suggest places for learning more about Java.

What's Next?

You've almost reached the end of your complete tour of the Java language. Before you take a peek at the remaining language topics in Chapter 15, you should familiarize yourself with how to create Java applications that run apart from a Web browser. That is the subject of Chapter 14, coming up next.

Chapter 14

Stand-Alone Applications

So far, all of the programs in this book have been applets. That is, the Java programs we developed were all meant to run either in a Web browser or in CodeWarrior's Applet Viewer. This is not the only way you can write and run a Java program. There is no requirement that Java programs run only as part of the Web—only that the computer on which a Java program is running has a Java interpreter. When you run a Java application that is not meant to be run as part of the Web, it is said that the program runs **stand-alone** (that is, apart from a Web browser).

In fact, you can do just about everything (and, in some cases, a little bit more) in an environment that is *not* connected to the Web that you can do in an applet that *is* part of the Web. For example, some security restrictions are lifted when running separately from the Web—such as gaining access to the local file system—because the browser does not need to guard the gate, as it were. There's nothing coming in over the wild and woolly Internet that might be dangerous to your computer. Everything is running locally on your machine, the programs exist on your hard drive, and you are in complete control of what's happening.

You can't just launch an applet stand-alone, however, without making some minor adjustments to your program so that it can run without a browser. This chapter will show you how to make these changes and how to plan out a stand-alone application.

What Is a Stand-Alone Application?

A Review of the Java Virtual Machine

Stand-alone applications run just like any other application you might be used to from the Mac. You don't need a modem, an Internet access provider, a Web browser, MacTCP, and so on. All you need is a Java interpreter to act as the Java

Virtual Machine (JVM). Remember, your Java programs are compiled into a machine language that does not run on any *particular* chip. Instead, the machine language produced by a Java compiler is tailored to a virtual machine—the JVM. The Java interpreter implements the JVM in software and acts as a translator between your compiled Java code and your Mac. Different Java interpreters translate between your program and other environments on which you want to run your Java program. The JVM is called Metrowerks Java in the CodeWarrior environment. This is depicted in Figure 14.1.

A Review of the Applet Viewer

With a Web browser, the Java interpreter is built into the browser itself. In the CodeWarrior environment the Applet Viewer acts as a stand-in for the browser. The Applet Viewer uses the Java interpreter that is in Metrowerks Java. Even though you're not running in a Web browser, the Applet Viewer still carries on the applet life cycle dialog with the applet. That is, the Applet Viewer tells the applet when to initialize, start, stop, and destroy itself. This is shown in Figure 14.2.

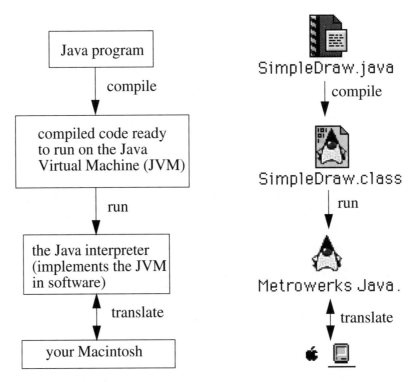

Figure 14.1 Compiling, running, and translating a Java program on your Mac.

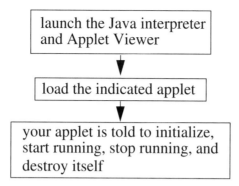

Figure 14.2 Schematic showing how the Applet Viewer carries on the life cycle dialog with your applet.

Executing a Class

When you write a stand-alone application, you don't need to extend the Applet class. In fact, you can execute any class at all. When you run a stand-alone application, you don't use the Applet Viewer because you do not have an applet. Therefore, your application never receives the applet life cycle method invocations. So how does your application know what to do and when to do it? You have to know what to do and when to do it *yourself!* The only thing the Java interpreter tells your program to do is to start running. (We'll get into how the Java interpreter does this in just a moment.) You must do the rest. This is depicted in Figure 14.3.

So how does the Java interpreter tell your class to start? The Java interpreter invokes your class's `main()` method.

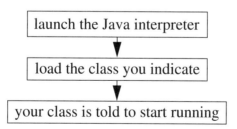

Figure 14.3 Schematic showing how the Java runtime environment loads your class and tells it to start running.

The `main()` Method

You must include a `main()` method for a class if you want to execute that class as a stand-alone application. This is different from the life cycle methods for applets, where you could choose not to implement a particular life cycle method if you didn't want to (in fact, you could ignore *all* the life cycle methods and the applet would still run). However, if you do not have a `main()` method for a class that you want to execute, the Java interpreter will halt your program. (Only the class that you run needs to have a `main()` method; any other classes that it uses do not need to have a `main()` method.) This is depicted in Figure 14.4.

The declaration of the `main()` method is not nearly as simple as the `init()` or `start()` methods for an applet—but then, since it's the only method that is invoked by the interpreter, it has more responsibilities.

First of all, your `main()` method must belong to the class. Why? Because when you run a class, the Java interpreter does not automatically create an instance of your class, as the browser and Applet Viewer do with your applet. You can create any objects yourself that you want to, but the interpreter does not try to guess that this is what you want to do. In fact, stand-alone applications never have to create objects if they don't want to! (We'll take a look at an example of this in a moment.) As you'll recall, to declare a method as belonging to a class, you use the keyword `static`.

Second, your `main()` method must be able to accept data as part of launching the program. This data can be any length at all. The data that can be passed to your `main()` method is a list of words—in particular, a list of String objects. You

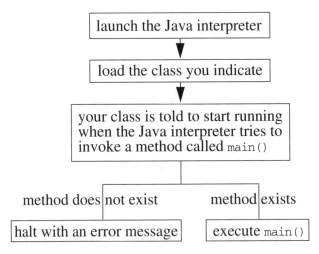

Figure 14.4 What happens when the Java interpreter tries to start a stand-alone application at a method called `main()`.

already know how to work with a list of strings: You make an array of them. As you learned in Chapter 12, the way you declare an array is by using square brackets. The way that you declare an array of String objects, then, is by writing `String[]`. Your `main()` method must accept an array of String objects as a parameter.

The two other keywords required by your `main()` method include `public`, which allows `main()` to be invoked from anywhere, and `void`, which indicates that `main()` does not return a value. Here, then, is the `main()` method's declaration:

```
public static void main(String[] args) {
}
```

Why the name `main()`? Where does this come from? The name `main()` is a holdover from the C language. In C, all programs begin at a block of code named `main()`. The keywords and parameters are different, but the name remains the same.

Hello, Java!

So now you know enough to write a complete stand-alone application. Let's write a stand-alone application that writes the words "Hello, Java!" to the Java Output window. How do you think you should go about doing this?

First, you need to declare a class. This class does not need to be `public`, though it often is declared as `public`. It does not need to extend a class other than Object, though it sometimes does. The class can define the one class method it needs, `main()`. `main()` can then do anything it wants to do, such as writing to the Java Output window. Here's the code for a simple stand-alone program:

```
public class WriteHello {
    public static void main(String[] args) {
        System.out.println("Hello, Java!");
    }
}
```

As you can see, this program ignores the parameter we've called `args`. If the user executed this application and supplied any data, that data would be ignored. Notice also that we don't create an object at all! There's only one method here, named `main()`, that belongs to the class. We run the class, the class executes its behavior, and then that's it! The `main()` method comes to an end, and so does the

```
┌────────────────────────────────────────────────────┐
│ ▣▤  ▤▤▤▤▤▤  HelloJaua.μ  ▤▤▤▤▤  ▣▤ │
├────────────────────────────────────────────────────┤
│ ☑ File                    Code    Data ✹ │
├────────────────────────────────────────────────────┤
│ ▽ ✹  Group 1                0       0    ▼  ⇧ │
│   ✹    HelloJaua.java       0       0    ▶   │
│   ✹    classes.zip          0       0    ▶   │
│                                               │
│                                            ⇩ │
├────────────────────────────────────────────────────┤
│   2 file(s)                 0       0       ▣ │
└────────────────────────────────────────────────────┘
```

Figure 14.5   The HelloJava.μ project window.

program. There's no applet window sitting around. There's no other user interface. This program just writes its message to the Java Output window and halts.

Let's look at the HelloJava program in CodeWarrior and see what happens when it runs. Go to the subfolder named 14.01 - hello, java in the Learn Java Projects folder and open the project file HelloJava.μ. The project window will appear as in Figure 14.5.

Notice that this project window, unlike the project windows for applets, contains only one section, not two. The section missing here is for HTML files. We're not intending to run this Java program as part of the Web, so we don't need any HTML files.

When you compile this source file by selecting **Make** from the **Project** menu, CodeWarrior will generate a file named HelloJava.out (Figure 14.6).

The file HelloJava.out is a double-clickable icon that will launch the Java interpreter and run your program. Go ahead and double-click this file now to see

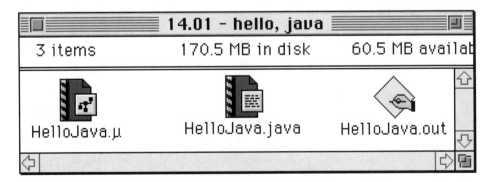

Figure 14.6   The subfolder 14.01 - hello, java after compiling the application.

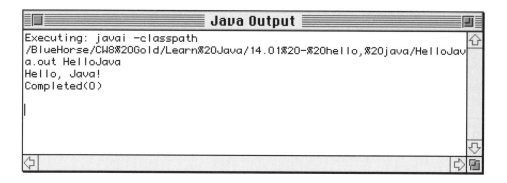

Figure 14.7   "Hello, Java!" in the Java Output window.

your program run. The result will be that the words "Hello, Java!" will appear in the Java Output window, as in Figure 14.7.

In addition to the Java Output window, you can also displays a window called "javai." To do this, select **File**, **New**, **javai** from the Metrowerks Java menu options at the top of the screen. This window can be used to interact with the Java interpreter and your stand-alone applications. Figure 14.8 shows what this window looks like when it first appears.

Here's an example of how you can use this window. If you would like to run HelloJava again, type "HelloJava" into this window (Figure 14.9) and click the **Execute** button. The words "Hello, Java!" will appear again in the Java Output window.

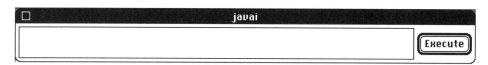

Figure 14.8   The javai window when it first appears.

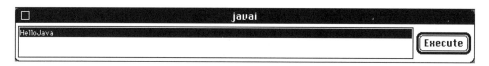

Figure 14.9   Typing "HelloJava" into the javai window to run the application once you're already in the Java interpreter.

Warning

> If you make a change to your applet and then recompile it, you'll need to quit Metrowerks Java and relaunch your application to see the changes come into effect. Otherwise, Metrowerks Java will keep on running the class that it loaded originally.

You can also use the javai window to pass parameters to your application when you execute it. The next section will explain how this is done.

By the Way

> When working with CodeWarrior, you must indicate whether you would like to create an applet or a stand-alone application when you first create your project file. There are also preferences you can set that indicate what kind of files the CodeWarrior compiler will generate. That's how we got the double-clickable file to be created for the stand-alone application. For stand-alone applications, you expect it to behave like any other Mac application, and so we want to generate a double-clickable icon.
>
> That's also how we generated the compiled class files in their own folder for applets. For applets, you need compiled class files so that your applet can be downloaded over the Web.
>
> All of the project files in this book have already been created for you, so you don't have to worry about this. For more information on creating new projects in the full version of CodeWarrior (that is, not the Lite version) and in setting the preferences for a project, check out the documentation that comes with CodeWarrior.

Differences Between Applications and Applets

For the most part, everything you've learned in this book concerning applets is the same for applications. This includes defining classes, creating and using objects, writing and invoking methods, defining and using variables, implementing flow control, using inheritance, creating constructors, and handling exceptions—to name just a few of the features of Java that carry over from applets to applications. It's still Java, after all, and the language is the same. However, there are a few subtle differences between applications and applets. This section will point out some of the more important ones.

The Command Line

Applets are somewhat sheltered from the operating environment because they run in a browser; applications are executed directly in the operating environment itself. For example, stand-alone applications are meant to run in an operating environment such as your Macintosh. They can also run in Windows 95, Solaris, OS/2, and wherever else there's a Java interpreter.

In graphical environments, such as the Mac, stand-alone applications can be created to run when the user double-clicks an icon, as you saw with the HelloJava application. However, in environments that also allow for command line input, where the user types commands from the keyboard rather than using the mouse, applications can also be launched by using typed commands.

CodeWarrior provides a way into this capability by displaying the window titled "javai." This is a window that allows you to execute commands by typing them in and clicking the **Execute** button. For example, you've already seen how to execute your application class by typing its name. You can also pass parameters to your application by using the command line. To do that, you can type the parameters you want to pass to your class's main() method after the name of the class you want to execute. We set up main()'s parameter as an array of String objects. This is exactly how the parameters you supply are passed to main(): as String objects in the string array.

Here's an example. Remember our NextPrime applet back in Chapter 8? That applet found the next prime number after an initial starting point. Here is the start of that applet:

```
public class NextPrime extends java.applet.Applet {
    public void init() {

        int     startingPoint, candidate, last, i;
        boolean isPrime;

        startingPoint = 19;
```

How would we rewrite this code so that it is a stand-alone application and so that it accepts its value for startingPoint as a command line parameter? We would start by writing the following:

```
public class NextPrime {
    public static void main(String[] args) {

        int     startingPoint, candidate, last, i;
        boolean isPrime;
```

329

Now, what should we set startingPoint equal to? The whole intent here is to avoid hard-coding the value for startingPoint and instead use the first parameter passed to NextPrime. The first parameter passed to NextPrime will be the first string in the string array. From our discussion of arrays, you know how to access this: The first value will be in the variable args, and you can get at it by writing args[0].

The sample programs section in this chapter shows you how to make the changes to NextPrime to get this all to work.

The Top-Level Frame

The HelloJava application simply displayed some text in the Java Output window. It did not allow the user to interact with the application. To do this, you have to create a user interface. You've already developed user interfaces in Chapter 11, and everything you learned there applies to creating a user interface for a stand-alone application. However, there is one important difference between applets and applications when it comes to user interfaces, and that is where your user interface is displayed.

For applets, this is not really an issue. An applet displays its user interface inside a Web browser (or inside the Applet Viewer). This is shown in Figure 14.10.

However, an application has no such place to display its user interface. This means that the application must create its own place to display its user interface. How do we go about doing this? To gain insight into this question, let's think through how your user interface is displayed in a Web browser. The Web browser automatically created your applet instance for you. All you had to do was to create the user interface objects that went inside it. For stand-alone applications, no one is creating this place to put your user interface objects. You have to do so yourself.

Java supplies a class called Frame that you can use as a place to put your user interface. Frames contain other user interface objects, which is exactly what you want. What you can do, then, is create your own instance of class Frame, arrange

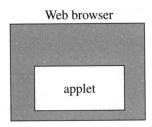

Web browser

applet

Figure 14.10   An applet's user interface displayed inside a Web browser.

Frame you create

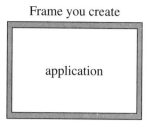

application

Figure 14.11   Your application's user interface displayed inside a frame your application created itself.

your user interface objects inside your Frame object, and display the frame. This is shown in Figure 14.11.

Here are the steps you might follow when creating your own frame in which to contain your user interface (this assumes that you are still defining an Applet subclass but want to run this applet as a stand-alone application. This technique is easily transferable to other types of classes as well):

1. In your applet's `main()` method, create a new instance of the applet. When running your applet in a browser, the browser (or Applet Viewer) creates a new instance of your Applet class for you. If you're running stand-alone, you have to do this yourself.

2. Invoke your new applet instance's `init()` method. Again, the browser normally does this for you; you must initialize your own applet if you are running stand-alone.

3. Create an instance of class Frame to contain your applet. In a browser, your applet is contained within the browser itself. As a stand-alone application, you have to supply your own container for your applet and then add your applet to the frame.

4. Resize the frame. The HTML file sets the size for the applet; without an HTML file, you still must set the size in your code.

5. Finally, make the frame display itself on the screen.

We'll take a look at an example of all this in the next section.

Sample Programs

In this section, we'll take two programs that we've seen before—NextPrime and SimpleDraw—and turn both of these applets into stand-alone applications.

331

NextPrime.µ

Open the subfolder `14.02 - next prime` in the Learn Java Projects folder. Open `NextPrime.µ` and select **Make** from the **Project** menu. This time, instead of dropping the HTML file onto the Metrowerks Java icon, double-click the file named `NextPrime.out`. This will run the stand-alone application.

The Java Output window will appear. Display the javai window by selecting **File**, **New**, **javai** from the Metrowerks Java menu options at the top of the screen. At first, nothing will seem to have happened. That's because the application is set up to halt gracefully if no data is supplied for it. So, let's run it again, this time supplying it with data. In the javai window, type `NextPrime 19`, and click **Execute**. A message will appear in the Java Output window indicating that the next prime is 23. Change the 19 in the javai window to 153 (so that it reads `NextPrime 153`), and click **Execute** again. A second message will appear in the Java Output window indicating that the next prime is 157. This is shown in Figure 14.12.

This version of NextPrime is set up to take its starting point as a command line parameter, allowing you to easily rerun the application to find a different prime number. Let's check the source code to see how we do this.

Stepping Through the Source Code

Open `NextPrime.java`. First of all, you'll notice that this class no longer inherits from Applet. In fact, it doesn't inherit from any other class (other than Object). We've also removed the `init()` method. In its place, we've defined a `main()` method:

```
public class NextPrime {
    public static void main(String[] args) {
```

We then define the same variables as before:

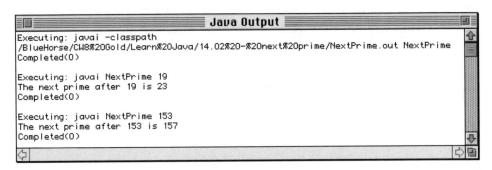

Figure 14.12   NextPrime, when run as a stand-alone application.

```
int      startingPoint, candidate, last, i;
boolean isPrime;
```

This time, however, instead of setting `startingPoint` to 19, we attempt to retrieve it from the command line parameters. Before grabbing this value, we might want to check to make sure the user actually supplied a command line parameter in the first place! Otherwise, imagine that the user did not supply a command line parameter. In that case, the array would be empty—it would have a length of 0. If we tried to access a value in the array's first position, we would be looking beyond the end of the array, which would cause Java to throw an exception called ArrayIndexOutOfBoundsException, which would cause our program to come to a halt with an error message. So, before accessing the `args` array, we might want to check to make sure the array does in fact contain one element. If it doesn't, we can return right away, which would cause the program to halt without an error message. Here's how we could write this:

```
if (args.length == 1) {
    // try accessing the first command line parameter
} else
    return;
```

If `args.length` does equal 1, then there is a command line parameter. Each command line parameter is a string object. This means, if we want to assign the first command line parameter, which is a string, to `startingPoint`, which is an `int`, we must first convert the string to an `int`. One way to do that is to create a new instance of class Integer based on the value in the string and then use the integer's instance method `toInt()` to return an `int` data type. Since the constructor for the Integer instance might throw an exception if the string does not contain a valid integer, you have to be prepared to catch the exception (if you want to prevent your program from halting with an error message). Here's the code:

```
try {

    Integer integer = new Integer(args[0]);
    startingPoint = integer.intValue();

} catch (Exception e) {

    return;

}
```

Alternatively, you could also use `Integer.parseInt()` as we saw in an example in Chapter 12. The rest of NextPrime is the same as what you saw before.

SimpleDraw.µ

Displaying a user interface in a stand-alone application requires providing a frame for the user interface. We can write an applet just as usual, but instead of relying on the browser to tell us what to do, our `main()` method can do this work itself.

Run the SimpleDraw application that is in the subfolder 14.03 - stand alone in the Learn Java Projects folder. First open `SimpleDraw.µ` and select **Make** from the **Project** menu. You can run this by double-clicking the file `Simple-Draw.out`.

You can interact with SimpleDraw just as you're used to. Create new shapes by clicking in the applet; change the type of shape and color to draw in by using the choice lists. Notice that there is no Applet Viewer. This application is truly running separately from the Applet Viewer. Let's check out the source code.

Stepping Through the Source Code

Open `SimpleDraw.java`. The only thing that has changed since you saw this program last is the addition of a `main()` method. We're still creating an applet; we still have an `init()` method; and so on. Let's take a look at this `main()` method and see what it does.

First, `main()` creates a new instance of the applet. Remember, `main()` is a class method. When `main()` starts executing, there is no instance at all; all that exists is the class itself:

```
public static void main(String[] args) {

    SimpleDraw sd = new SimpleDraw();
```

Since there is no Web browser or Applet Viewer invoking the new instances `init()` method for us, we have to do this ourselves:

```
    sd.init();
```

Since a Web browser or an Applet Viewer is not supplying a place to display our applet, we have to create our own place. We can create an instance of Java's class Frame to contain our applet. One of the constructors of class Frame allows us to supply a title for this window; we'll use that constructor here:

```
    Frame f = new Frame("SimpleDraw");
```

Frames use a type of layout manager called BorderLayout. As mentioned in Chapter 11, BorderLayout arranges its user interface components according to directions: North, South, East, West, and Center. We'll put our applet smack-dab in the center:

```
f.add("Center", sd);
```

For applets, the HTML file supplies the default size in its `width` and `height` keywords. For stand-alone applications, we have to supply this size ourselves:

```
f.resize(200,100);
```

The last thing to do is display the frame, which makes our applet appear as well since it is contained within the frame:

```
f.show();
}
```

As mentioned, the rest of the program is the same. This `main()` routine does everything the Applet Viewer did, and so our application can run stand-alone.

Review

This chapter outlined how to create applications in Java that do not rely on Web browsers. You've seen how you must define a `main()` routine for stand-alone applications. In fact, you can execute any class at all—as long as it has a `main()` routine.

`main()` is a class method. If you want to interact with instances of your class (for example, if you want to invoke instance methods), you must create an instance of your class and use that for invoking methods. To display a user interface, you have to take over the responsibilities of a Web browser in `main()` by supplying a place to display the applet, adding your applet to this place, sizing the window that will appear, and then displaying the window (and so displaying your applet inside it).

What's Next?

At this point, you've learned the basics of Java and explored its more advanced topics. The next chapter highlights some concepts that are important to Java and offers some insights into how you can continue your pursuit of Java excellence.

Chapter 15

Where Do You Go from Here?

Congratulations! By learning Java, you've begun to travel the road to great Web sites, fun programming, and a rewarding career as a Java programmer. Now that you've started your journey, we're not just going to drop you off in the middle of nowhere! This chapter will provide a link to the rest of the great, wide world of Java. In particular, you'll learn about a number of advanced concepts concerning Java and where you can go to find out more information about them.

You've come a long way since Chapter 1. You started your journey learning about a Java development environment called CodeWarrior and then waded through the concepts of Web programming and how to solve problems in Java using classes, objects, and methods. You developed very simple applets at first, but then, as you learned about variables, methods, and the applet life cycle, you were able to customize your applets to do things. Once you learned about objects and Java's classes, you were able to put together user interfaces that allowed users to interact with your applets. By learning about different ways of working with data, you were able to complete these applets. Finally, you learned a few advanced topics and then took a look at what you needed to do to create applets that ran stand-alone, apart from a Web browser.

What more is there? There are lots of details, and this chapter will show you where to look to dig down deeper. Having gained a strong footing in the language, you should feel confident about exploring any of these areas and learning many of the details that are not quite appropriate for a beginning book on Java. Some of the topics presented here might fill up entire books on their own, so we can't go into much more detail other than to point out that they exist and offer some links to where you can learn more about them. Here's the path you should take for further exploration:

- Learn about interfaces.
- Define your own packages.

- Learn about threads.

- Learn how Java works on the inside.

- Read the HTML files that describe Java's packages.

- Explore Java's packages.

- Study other resources.

- Experiment with a multithreading applet.

Appendix G also offers a path to your continuing education by listing additional resources where you can find out more about Java as the language develops and finds uses all over the Web. You might also want to attempt to create your own programs that implement the features mentioned here. One of the best ways to learn the language is to experiment. Try them out, play around with them, and push them to their limits to learn what these features are all about.

Learn about Interfaces

Interfaces define a set of behavior for classes to implement. The idea behind an interface is that different classes might share the same characteristics, even if these classes are not part of the same class hierarchy.

For example, you might have a class hierarchy for a Navy application that describes a whole bunch of jets, destroyers, aircraft carriers, tug boats, and so on. Some of the more modern of these aircraft and ships might be nuclear powered; the rest, diesel powered. How can you give different classes of crafts the roles and responsibilities of a nuclear-powered craft without building it right into a class? You can create an interface. Figure 15.1 provides an idea of how an interface can be sprinkled into your class hierarchy.

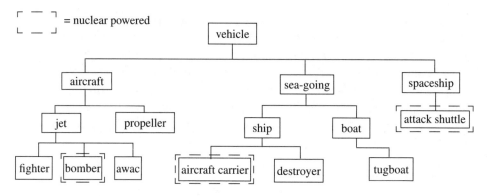

Figure 15.1 Example of how an interface can be sprinkled into a class hierarchy.

This class hierarchy has the characteristic of "nuclear powered" sprinkled into different parts of the hierarchy. Only those classes that have this characteristic are nuclear powered; the rest of the classes are normal. Those vehicles that are nuclear powered must implement the specific behavior of what being nuclear powered means for them.

An interface is somewhat similar to a class, except that it can be shared among different classes. Interfaces only define method names, parameters, and return values; they do not provide any behavior. The specific behavior for a method defined in an interface is left up to the class that implements that interface. Interfaces can define variables, but these variables must be constants.

Java provides a number of interfaces, and you'll run across these as you continue programming in Java. For example, one of the most common interfaces defined by Java is called Runnable. This interface defines a method called run() but does not supply any code for run(). Instead, if your class implements the Runnable interface, your class must supply a method for run() that tells run() what to do.

The way you declare a class as implementing an interface is to use the `implements` keyword. For example, to indicate that your applet implements the Runnable interface, you can declare your applet like this:

```
public class MyApplet extends Applet implements Runnable {

    // your applet code goes here

    public void run() {
        // your code for run() goes here
    }
}
```

This particular interface (that is, Runnable) is used with multithreading, as touched on later in this chapter. For more information concerning interfaces, check out *Java Essentials for C and C++ Programmers*, written by Barry Boone and published by Addison-Wesley.

Define Your Own Packages

All of Java's classes come in packages, and you can do the same thing with your own classes—that is, you can group your classes into packages as well. This can help you share classes among different applets that you write, just as Java's classes are shared among applets.

What Are Packages?

Packages are Java's way of grouping together related classes. The advantage of packages over a bunch of individual classes is that packages are easy to share among applications. If you have a collection of classes you would like to share between two or more applications, it's very useful to place all of these classes into a package and then simply share the package.

For example, you might have two applications that could make use of the Square and the Rectangle classes discussed in this chapter. One of these applications might be used for drawing, and the other might be used in an application that teaches geometry to students. Figure 15.2 shows how each application might be organized without packages.

Rather than duplicating the classes between the applications, you could split out the classes for the square and rectangle (as well as any other shape classes you've defined), place these classes into a package called "shapes," and then share this package between the two applications. This would allow you to use the same classes in both applications, without duplicating any work, in a way that's very easy to manage. Figure 15.3 shows this organization.

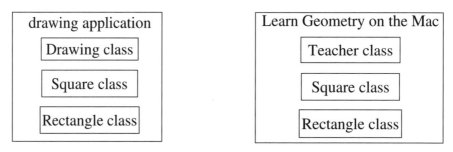

Figure 15.2   Duplicating classes for different applications.

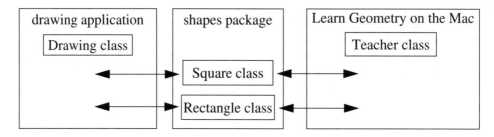

Figure 15.3   Sharing classes between applications.

Creating Packages

To indicate that the classes in a particular file belong to a particular package, you must use the `package` keyword. For example, the following line at the top of a file indicates that all of the classes in that file should belong to the package shapes:

```
package shapes;
```

When you want to use a class in another package, you must import it, just as you import Java's classes, by writing

```
import shapes.*;
```

Learn about Threads

All of the programs in this book work by asking the computer to do one thing at a time. This is how most programs in other languages work, and you can write many great Java programs like this. Java contains an advanced feature, however, that makes it easy to ask the computer to do *two or more* things at the same time, and this makes Java much different from other languages (Figure 15.4). This section will introduce you to this concept and to Java's capabilities. We won't go into too much code here, but, by the time you finish this section, you'll at least understand what Java means by **multithreading**.

Knowing When to Do More Than One Thing at a Time?

Many programs are perfectly content to do one thing at a time. The SimpleDraw applet is happy enough responding to user input and displaying squares and circles. The Triangle applet is content to calculate the area of the triangle when the user clicks the "area" button.

What would happen if we changed SimpleDraw to be called SimpleDraw-Blink? Perhaps such an applet would "blink" the squares and circles in the applet.

Figure 15.4 Multithreading in Java: asking the computer to do more than one thing at a time.

For example, you click in the applet, and a red square appears. Every second, it changes to yellow for a quarter of a second and then redraws itself in red. You click again, and a blue circle appears. Every second, it changes to yellow for a quarter of a second and then redraws itself in blue. Soon, your applet is filled up with blinking shapes, all blinking to yellow at different times.

Other than becoming hypnotized by such an applet, we would run into some trouble if we wanted all the shapes to start blinking independently of one another. If the applet managed each shape's blink, we would have to enter some kind of loop, draw each shape in yellow, then loop back, redraw the shape in its original color, and so on, forever—and still we would probably end up with them all blinking in unison, which is not what we want. In addition to this, when would we respond to user input if all we did was draw and redraw these shapes? Would we be using system resources correctly?

Difficult questions indeed, and a problem tailor-made for **threads**.

What Is a Thread?

A thread is like a miniprogram in that it maintains its own **thread of execution** or **thread of control**. Your program can use as many threads as it wants to; each thread will do its own thing, independently of the others. For example, you could have a thread that controls how to draw each shape. Each thread would decide when to blink each shape. You could create a thread and assign it to the first red square you create; you could create a second thread and assign it to the blue circle you create next. Each time a new shape is created, you create a new thread for it as well.

In this scenario, we've assigned each shape its own miniprogram, and each program executes independently of the other and at the same time. SimpleDraw *itself* does not have to go around blinking each shape; the threads and shapes working together make this happen. This is depicted in Figure 15.5.

Creating and Starting a Thread

Java supplies a class called Thread. One way to work with threads is to create your own subclass of the Thread class. By creating your own subclass, you can provide behavior for the thread that will make it do what you want.

All you have to do to create a new thread is to create an instance of your thread subclass. To start a thread going, you need to give it a little nudge. You tell it to start by invoking its start() method.

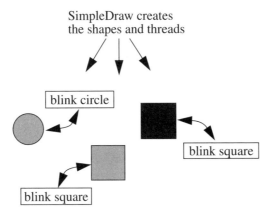

Figure 15.5 Example of how threads and shapes work together to make shapes blink.

Telling a Thread What to Do

How does a thread know what to do? You have to tell it! You can tell your thread, for example, to redraw a particular shape. You can tell your thread to perform some animation. You can tell your thread to access a Web page while the user is busy interacting with the application. Remember, threads are miniprograms—they can do whatever you tell them to do.

The way you tell a thread what to do is by supplying a method called `run()`. Once you start your thread by invoking its `start()` method, Java will invoke its `run()` method for you, as shown in Figure 15.6.

You can also create a thread without subclassing it and indicate to Java that you want another class, such as your applet, to provide a `run()` method for the thread. You would then implement a `run()` method in your applet to provide the behavior for the thread and declare your applet as implementing the Runnable interface.

Once the `run()` method begins, it will continue to execute until one of two things happens:

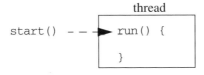

Figure 15.6 Starting a thread, which invokes the thread's `run()` method.

1. Java reaches the end of the code in the thread's run() method. If run() exits, your thread will no longer be doing anything. Many times, threads enter an infinite loop so that they run forever (that is, until the thread is destroyed, usually because the user quit the applet). This is one of the few times when you want to write an infinite loop.

2. Someone puts your thread to sleep. Who might do this to your thread? Any object can put a thread to sleep—including the thread itself! If your thread goes to sleep, you can always wake it up again, and it will continue along its merry way. There are a few different methods to make your thread sleep and a few corresponding methods to make your thread wake up.

One way to make a thread go to sleep is for the thread to invoke its own sleep() method, which waits the indicated number of milliseconds before re-awakening. The sample program in this chapter uses this technique. For other techniques for putting a thread to sleep and reawakening a thread, check out the different methods associated with class Thread in the Java API (application programming interface) documentation.

Synchronizing Threads

Traditionally, with other languages, threads can be a nightmare. Having all these threads running around doing things is a little like having dozens of ants running around, each one doing its own task. How do you control all these little critters? How do you stop one ant (or thread) from doing something that another one is doing at the same time?

This is a difficult problem in other languages because other languages were not developed with the idea of threads in mind. In Java, however, this idea is built right into the language. Java supplies two keywords (the primary one being the keyword synchronized) that ask Java to take on the responsibility of making sure that threads don't step on one another's toes. If you ever see a method declared as synchronized, this means the author of the code wanted to make sure that only one thread could invoke that method at a time. If another thread comes along and also wants to invoke that method, it must wait patiently until the first thread is done and the method exits.

Detail

> To be complete about this, there's also a keyword, called volatile, that is rarely used. This keyword ensures that if a thread changes a variable that another thread is using, that other thread will see the change.

The Thread Life Cycle

There's also a thread life cycle, which applies to the Thread class; in particular, threads can start and stop. Very often, you will put your thread's life cycle in sync with your applet's life cycle: When your applet starts, you should start your applet's threads; when your applet stops, you should stop your applet's threads.

There are some good explanations of multithreading on the Web at JavaSoft's site, as well as applets you can run at this site to see examples of multithreading in action. Also, Barry Boone's *Java Essentials for C and C++ Programmers*, from Addison-Wesley, describes multithreading, including the `synchronized` and `volatile` keywords, in much more detail.

Learn How Java Works on the Inside

Garbage Collection

The applets in this book all created a number of objects. We kept track of almost all of these, from shapes to employees. Sometimes, however, you'll create objects only temporarily, and then you won't have need or use for them again. As we mentioned earlier, objects take up memory in your computer. If you create an object and then don't use it again, does the object continue to sit in memory, using up space unnecessarily?

Not in Java. Java provides a mechanism called **garbage collection**. When your program can no longer access a particular object, Java has ways of finding out. If it discovers an object that you won't be using any more (because you no longer can access it from your program), it frees up the memory used by that object.

It's not strictly necessary to know about garbage collection to use Java, but it does enhance your understanding of what's happening behind the scenes. Check out the specifications for the Java Virtual Machine and the documentation for the Object class for more information concerning what Java's garbage collection is all about.

The Java Virtual Machine

You know what the Java Virtual Machine (JVM) *does*; one advanced area of study is learning how the JVM *works*. For example, the JVM does not allow any code to execute that contains a virus. How does it know? What do the machine language instructions for the JVM look like? What can you learn about Java by knowing these details?

The answers to these and many more questions can be found in the specifications for the Java Virtual Machine. If you really want to try to figure out what's going on behind the scenes, you might want to gain an overview of the JVM.

Explore Java's Packages

You've now seen just about all there is to know about the Java language. Java is much more than a language, however. Java comes with lots and lots of predefined classes for you to use in your own programs. We've already seen many of these, from String to Applet to Vector to Math. This section provides an overview of some of the classes you might want to investigate first as you continue learning about what Java has to offer. For more information on the classes mentioned here, check out the HTML files containing the Java package information.

Understanding the HTML Files

First, let's look at the structure of the HTML files that contain Java's class documentation. These files can be found on your CD; you can use a Web browser to view them. (Check with your development environment for more information about what's available on the CD.) You can also go to the JavaSoft Web site containing the most up-to-date documentation (see Appendix G).

The documentation files are arranged in a hierarchy. The first level is a listing of all of Java's packages that are available for you to use in your own Java programs. This is shown in Figure 15.7

By clicking on one of these hypertext links (say, java.lang, for example), you'll go to a listing of the classes that are found within this package. The lang package contains lots of classes that are at the heart of Java. The beginning of the listing of classes in the lang package is shown in Figure 15.8.

The top part of this listing presents the interfaces that are defined in this package. The interfaces are followed by the classes. To learn more about an interface or a class, click on it to view a page describing all the variables and methods for that class.

The top part of the class's detailed information shows where this class fits into Java's class hierarchy. For example, clicking on Integer displays the information shown in Figure 15.9.

If you'd like to navigate to an ancestor class, simply click it. For example, you can click java.lang.Number or java.lang.Object in the display shown in Figure 15.9 to go to information about the Number or Object class.

Beneath this hierarchy information, you'll find the complete definition for the class, as well as documentation concerning what this class is all about. (You can see from this HTML file that the Integer class is defined as final, which means it cannot be subclassed.)

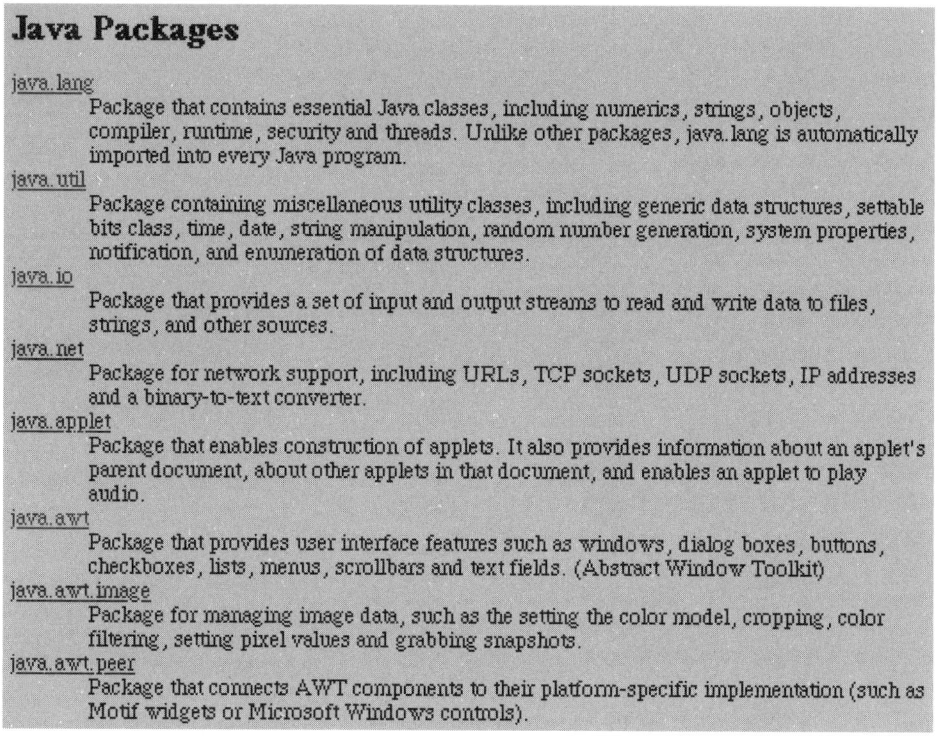

Java Packages

java.lang
> Package that contains essential Java classes, including numerics, strings, objects, compiler, runtime, security and threads. Unlike other packages, java.lang is automatically imported into every Java program.

java.util
> Package containing miscellaneous utility classes, including generic data structures, settable bits class, time, date, string manipulation, random number generation, system properties, notification, and enumeration of data structures.

java.io
> Package that provides a set of input and output streams to read and write data to files, strings, and other sources.

java.net
> Package for network support, including URLs, TCP sockets, UDP sockets, IP addresses and a binary-to-text converter.

java.applet
> Package that enables construction of applets. It also provides information about an applet's parent document, about other applets in that document, and enables an applet to play audio.

java.awt
> Package that provides user interface features such as windows, dialog boxes, buttons, checkboxes, lists, menus, scrollbars and text fields. (Abstract Window Toolkit)

java.awt.image
> Package for managing image data, such as the setting the color model, cropping, color filtering, setting pixel values and grabbing snapshots.

java.awt.peer
> Package that connects AWT components to their platform-specific implementation (such as Motif widgets or Microsoft Windows controls).

Figure 15.7 The index of Java's packages as found at the JavaSoft Web site.

The next part of the HTML file is divided into two broad sections. The first section provides indexes for the variables, constructors, and methods. Each entry in this first section jumps to the appropriate spot in the second section, where you'll find the detailed information for a variable, constructor, or method. For example, Figure 15.10 shows the Variable Index for the Integer class.

If you click one of these hyperlinked variable names, you'll jump to the part of this same HTML document that defines these variables. This is shown in Figure 15.11.

You can tell by looking at the definitions for the variables named MIN_VALUE and MAX_VALUE that they cannot be changed—that is, they are constants by virtue of being defined as final. Since they are also defined as static, they are class variables, and you can access these variables by writing Integer.MIN_VALUE and Integer.MAX_VALUE. (The values for these constants are given as hexadecimal values in the documentation. In base 10, these values are 2,147,483,647 and –2,147,483,648.)

After the Variable Index comes the Constructor Index. The Constructor Index lists the constructors defined by the class. And finally, following the Constructor

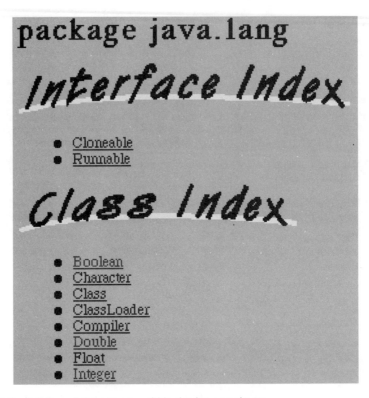

Figure 15.8   A listing of the classes within the lang package.

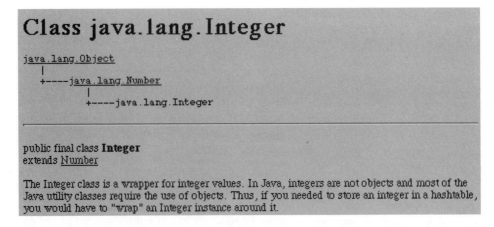

Figure 15.9   The definition for the Integer class, including a simple diagram of where the Integer class fits into Java's class hierarchy.

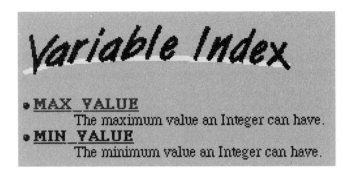

Figure 15.10   The Variable Index for the Integer class.

Index is the Method Index. As with all of the HTML documentation, click any link to find out more about a variable, constructor, method, or parameter. Figure 15.12 shows an example of what a typical method definition looks like. This definition shows the method declaration, including all its keywords and parameters. The details for the method indicate the meaning of the parameters and return values and indicate which method it is overriding, if any.

Another convenient aspect to the documentation is an alphabetical index. If you need to find a particular method and are not sure what class to go to, you can use this index to look up variables and method names alphabetically. You can access the index by clicking on Index at the top right of the documentation (Figure 15.13).

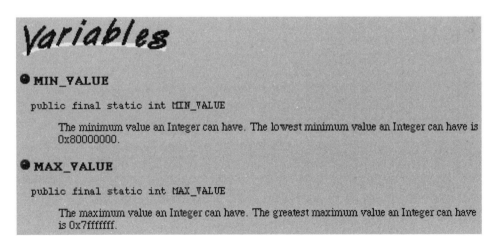

Figure 15.11   The definitions for the variables MIN_VALUE and MAX_VALUE.

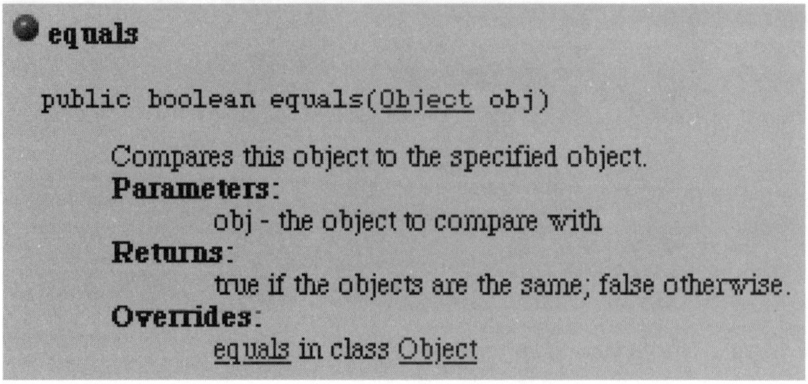

```
  ● equals

    public boolean equals(Object obj)

            Compares this object to the specified object.
            Parameters:
                    obj - the object to compare with
            Returns:
                    true if the objects are the same; false otherwise.
            Overrides:
                    equals in class Object
```

Figure 15.12   The `equals()` instance method for the Integer class.

That brings you to a large document listing everything in alphabetical order. The top part of this index is shown in Figure 15.14. Simply click on a variable or method name to jump right to its definition.

By the Way

The original Sun JDK (Java Developer's Kit) had a feature that automatically produced nicely formatted HTML files containing documentation for your source code. When the tool that generated these HTML files read your source files, they sought out comments that started with /** and added these to the HTML documentation files. For example, you could write

```
/** Shapes provide a common ancestor for the circle and
square. */
abstract class Shape {
    // definition for the Shape class here
}
```

and these comments would be added to the HTML file automatically generated for you that contained your class's documentation.

It's likely that other development environments will implement this documentation tool as well. Check the documentation with your development environment for details.

```
  Index
```

Figure 15.13   Clicking the `Index` link to access an alphabetical index for the documentation.

350

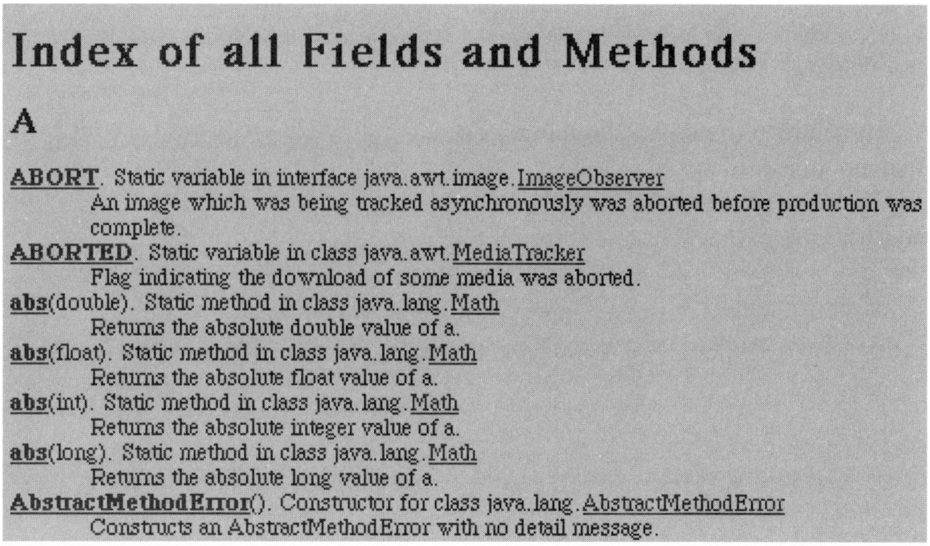

Index of all Fields and Methods

A

ABORT. Static variable in interface java.awt.image.ImageObserver
    An image which was being tracked asynchronously was aborted before production was complete.
ABORTED. Static variable in class java.awt.MediaTracker
    Flag indicating the download of some media was aborted.
abs(double). Static method in class java.lang.Math
    Returns the absolute double value of a.
abs(float). Static method in class java.lang.Math
    Returns the absolute float value of a.
abs(int). Static method in class java.lang.Math
    Returns the absolute integer value of a.
abs(long). Static method in class java.lang.Math
    Returns the absolute long value of a.
AbstractMethodError(). Constructor for class java.lang.AbstractMethodError
    Constructs an AbstractMethodError with no detail message.

Figure 15.14   The top part of the Index of all Fields (that is, variables) and Methods.

Spend some time looking around these class documentation files. They'll provide many insights into how Java is put together, and you'll learn about lots of classes you can use in your own applets. The next few sections provide an introduction to what you'll find in these packages.

The awt Package

With the awt (or "abstract windows toolkit") package, you can create very sophisticated graphical user interfaces that run on any platform. The classes and methods in this package will allow your applet to interact with the user and will make your applet sparkle.

You've already created some user interfaces in this book, and what you've learned has taken you far. You can also generate much more complex user interfaces with Java than you've created up to this point. And, as more graphical development environments emerge, you'll be able to create user interfaces simply by arranging objects on the screen. Soon, you may not even realize what classes you're using, and creating an interface will be a matter of "drawing." Nonetheless, it's always helpful to know what you're doing; working with Java's awt classes directly can be very educational when learning what makes Java tick.

Some of Java's classes that will help you develop more complex user interfaces include

- Panels, which contain other user interface elements inside them.

- Frames, which are top-level windows with a title.

- Dialogs, which are windows that take input from the user.

These are all types of Containers. The Container class defines user interface elements that contain other user interface elements. In addition to all the other user interface classes we've already covered (such as TextFields, Labels, and Buttons), the awt package also defines

- Scrollbars, which allow the user to scroll the contents of a window.

- TextAreas, which display multiple lines of text and can be used to display or edit text.

- Menus, which are choices in MenuBars.

- Canvases, which you can subclass to create your own custom components.

These are all types of Components. The Component class defines things with which the user can interact. The JavaSoft Web site has a number of examples of applets that create user interfaces. You'll also find some examples on the CD that comes with CodeWarrior.

The net Package

The net (or "network") package contains classes for communicating over networks, including the Internet and the Web. You can use all sorts of great networking classes by using the net package, including

- URLs, which encapsulate Universal (also sometimes called Uniform) Resource Locators and allow you to get a file or open a connection to the URL simply by creating this object and specifying an Internet address.

- Sockets, which handle low-level connections between a computer and a network.

- ContentHandlers, which construct an object based on data read over the Internet.

The io Package

The io (or "input/output") package contains classes that support reading and writing data to files. These classes include

- Files, which represent a file stored in a computer.

- InputStreams, which help you to read incoming data.

- OutputStreams, which help you to write outgoing data.

The lang Package

The lang (or "language") package defines many classes that are at the core of Java. Many of these classes support keywords that are part of the language itself. For example, Exceptions are used with the `try`, `catch`, and `throw` keywords. Threads are used with the `synchronized` and `volatile` keywords. Objects are used with the `new` operator. Some of the key classes in this package include

- Exceptions, which are used to signal and handle error conditions arising when your code executes.

- Integers, Longs, Floats, and Doubles, which provide behavior for their corresponding data types.

- Objects, which support all base-level object capabilities, such as the ability to create and destroy objects.

- Strings, which maintain character data and provide methods for searching and manipulating the text they contain.

- Systems, which allow access to the functionality of the operating environment.

Study Other Resources

Other than the HTML files, what else is there? Where to start? There are so many educational resources out there, especially on the Web. There are news groups, mailing lists, corporate Web sites from Java licensees, "official" Java Web sites from JavaSoft (Sun's spin-off company now responsible for the Java language), homegrown Web sites by Java fans, and many other sites that use Java without calling attention to the fact that they *are* using Java—their Java applets are just part of the Web page.

There are magazines devoted to Java. Some of these are Web based; some are available at your newsstand.

There are also many good books available, and you'll find, as you probably have already, that you have lots to choose from on the bookstore shelves. You're now ready for an intermediate book (or perhaps even an advanced book, if you've gone through the exercises in the appendixes), so definitely pick up a reference to the Java language if you plan to continue on.

All of these resources, and more, are listed in Appendix G.

Sample Program

Even though we just scratched the surface of multithreading, we've included a sample program that implements the SimpleDraw applet so that each shape actually does blink, just as we described in this chapter.

SimpleDrawBlink.µ

Open the subfolder 15.01 - threads in the Learn Java Projects folder. Open SimpleDraw.µ and select **Make** from the **Project** menu. Run the applet by dropping the SimpleDraw.html file onto the Metrowerks Java icon.

Interact with the SimpleDraw applet in the usual way. You'll soon notice that all the shapes start blinking—and generally not at the same time! When you're done playing with this applet, quit the Applet Viewer. Let's take a look at the source code.

Stepping Through the Source Code

Open SimpleDraw.java. Here are the changes we've made from the version you've come to know and love.

1. We renamed the vector object from drawnShapes to threads. Instead of keeping track of the shapes, we'll create threads and keep track of them instead. Each thread, in turn, will keep track of and control its own shape:

   ```
   threads = new Vector();
   ```

2. We created a new class, a subclass of Thread called BlinkThread. Here's how we defined this subclass (the run() method is coming up):

```
class BlinkThread extends Thread {
    static Graphics g;
    Shape s;

    BlinkThread(Shape s) {
        this.s = s;
    }

    public void run() {
        // we'll supply the code in just a moment
    }
}
```

3. In `init()`, we find the graphics object that is used by the applet. We'll keep track of this object in a class variable in BlinkThread:

```
BlinkThread.g = getGraphics();
```

4. We removed the `paint()` method from the applet. Now, each thread invokes a shape's draw method itself when it finds the shape should be redrawn. You'll see this in the `run()` method for the thread.

5. When the user clicks the mouse, the applet creates a new instance of Blink-Thread and assigns it the shape just created. It does this by supplying the shape as a parameter to a custom constructor we've created for this Blink-Thread class. The applet then starts the thread by invoking its `start()` method and adds the new thread to the Vector instance.

```
t = new BlinkThread(s);
t.start();
threads.addElement(t);
```

6. The applet supplies `start()`, `stop()`, and `destroy()` methods. When the browser stops or starts the applet, the applet suspends or resumes each thread, as appropriate. The applet also stops each thread for good when the applet itself goes away:

```
/** Resume all the threads when the applet starts. */
public void start() {
    BlinkThread t;
    int          numThreads

    numThreads = threads.size();
    for (int i = 0; i < numThreads; i++) {

        t = (BlinkThread)threads.elementAt(i);
        t.resume();
    }
}

/** Suspend all the threads when the applet stops. */
public void stop() {
    BlinkThread t;
    int          numThreads;

    numThreads = threads.size();
    for (int i = 0; i < numThreads; i++) {
```

```
            t = (BlinkThread)threads.elementAt(i);
            t.suspend();
        }
    }

    /** Stop all the threads when the applet goes away. */
    public void destroy() {
        BlinkThread t;
        int         numThreads;

        numThreads = threads.size();
        for (int i = 0; i < numThreads; i++) {

            t = (BlinkThread)threads.elementAt(i);
            t.stop();
        }
    }
}
```

7. Each shape defines an additional draw method that draws the shape in yellow, called `drawBlink()`. For example, here's the `drawBlink()` method for the circle (the square's `drawBlink()` method is similar):

```
void drawBlink(Graphics g) {
    g.setColor(Color.yellow);
    g.fillOval(this.x - shapeRadius, this.y - shapeRadius,
        shapeRadius * 2, shapeRadius * 2);
}
```

8. And finally, here's the moment you've been waiting for: the `run()` method for the BlinkThread instances. This method loops forever. It draws the shape in yellow and then goes to sleep for a quarter of a second (250 milliseconds). When it wakes up, it draws the shape in the shape's defined color and then goes to sleep for a full second (1000 milliseconds). This sequence, repeating endlessly, makes it appear that the shape is blinking:

```
public void run() {

    // don't ever exit the thread
    while(true) {

        try {
            s.drawBlink(g);
            sleep(250);
```

```
        s.draw(g);
        sleep(1000);

    } catch (Exception e) {
    }


}
```

Each time the user clicks the mouse, the applet creates a new shape and a new thread, assigning the new shape to the new thread. Each thread, then, keeps track of one shape object. Since threads are all running at the same time, independently of the other, each thread's `run()` method is executing simultaneously with all the other threads. Each thread is telling the shape for which it's responsible to draw in yellow and then to draw in its original color. This makes it appear that each shape is marching to the beat of its own drummer—which is exactly what each shape is doing, blinking in time with the beat of its own thread.

You can investigate this applet and the source code further to get a sense of what's going on. Try altering the times each thread goes to sleep. Try writing messages to the Java Output window in a thread's `run()` method.

Threads are a complex topic, and they're used frequently in Java applets. Now that you've been introduced to them, you can start to find your way around what they're all about by reading over the available documentation and by studying other applets on the Web that also use threads.

Review

This chapter provided some ideas of where you can go next to learn more about Java. There are a few additional features of the language and many, many classes provided by Java that you can use in your own applications. Also, be sure to check out Appendix G, with its listing of books and Web resources that point the way to even more information on Java.

What's Next?

Your next step is to become a Java master. You started this book as a white belt, but you've come a long way. At this moment, you're somewhere in the middle of your studies toward gaining a black belt. (You're already a force to be reckoned with.)

As you continue to learn more about Java and improve your skills, remember to have fun and develop some exciting applets and applications. We hereby graduate you into the community of Java programmers! Good luck in all your future Java endeavors.

Glossary

abstract class: An abstract class cannot be instantiated. See also **concrete class**.

allocate: To allocate a variable means to set aside enough memory to contain the type of data that this variable will refer to.

ancestor: An ancestor is a class from which another class inherits.

applet: An applet is a Java application that is meant to run over the World Wide Web in a Web browser.

array: An array is a collection, or list, of data, all of the same type, that is allocated in one contiguous block of memory.

assignment operator: The assignment operator, which is an equal sign (=), tells the computer to compute the value to the right of the = and to assign that value to the variable on the left of the =.

binary operator: A binary operator takes two variables. Examples of binary operators are +, *, and /.

bitwise operator: A bitwise operator combines two values by working with their individual bits.

block: A block of code combines any number of statements into a single superstatement. A block is delimited by a pair of curly braces ({ }).

Boolean expression: A Boolean expression evaluates to either true or false.

Boolean value: A Boolean value can be either true or false; there are no other possibilities.

bytecodes: Bytecodes refer to the compiled class instructions, which are the machine language instructions contained in the compiled class files (the files that end in `.class`). Bytecodes are ready to run on the Java Virtual Machine.

case-sensitive language: A case-sensitive language differentiates between uppercase and lowercase letters.

casting: Casting data types means making one type of data become a different type of data (for example, you might cast a floating-point number into an integer).

catch an exception: To catch an exception means to handle an error condition. See also **throw an exception**.

character-mode user interface: A character-mode user interface relies only on text to interact with the user. See also **graphical user interface**.

class: A class is a template or cookie cutter for instantiating objects of the same type. A class defines behavior and data for objects (as well as for the class itself). Classes can inherit the behavior and variables of other classes, which allows them to be arranged in hierarchies.

class variable or **method:** A class variable or method is a variable or method belonging to a class. See also **instance variable** or **method**.

comparative operator: A comparative operator is an operator that compares two expressions and evaluates to either true or false.

compile: To compile a program means to convert source code into machine language.

compiled class file: A compiled class file contains the definition for a class that is ready to run.

compiled language: A compiled language is a programming language whose references to variables, memory, method invocations, and the flow through the program are determined at compile time (as opposed to runtime).

compiler: A compiler converts an application's source code into machine language.

complex numbers: Complex numbers are defined by combining real numbers (such as integers) with imaginary numbers.

component: A component is a user interface object that the user interacts with directly (such as a button or a text field). See also **container**.

concrete class: A concrete class can be instantiated. See also **abstract class**.

constant: A constant is a variable whose value never changes.

constructor: A constructor is a special method that initializes an object.

container: A container is a user interface object that groups together components and other containers. See also **component**.

counter: A counter is a variable used to keep track of the current iteration in a loop.

current object: The object responding to a method invocation is known as the current object. (Java automatically sets the variable named `this` to the current object.)

data type: Variables in Java must be declared as representing a certain data type, which includes numbers such as integers or floating-point values, characters, Boolean values, or objects.

debugging: Debugging is the process of finding and fixing "bugs," or problems, in a program.

decrement: To decrement means to subtract 1 from the value of a number.

descendant: A class is said to be a descendant of another class when it inherits from that class.

development cycle: The development cycle consists of the steps that programmers follow when developing a software application.

event: Java signals that an event has occurred every time the user interacts with your applet's user interface.

exception: An exception is Java's way of reporting errors.

execute: To execute a program means to run it on a computer.

expression: An expression is any snippet of code that has a value.

floating-point numbers: Floating-point numbers are numbers containing fractional values, such as numbers like 3.14159, 2.5, and .0001. (Floating-point data types in Java can hold integer numbers as well.)

flow control: Flow control defines the order in which the statements in your program are executed. Controlling your program's flow means determining when to branch around code, under which conditions to execute code, and when to perform loops.

fractional numbers: See **floating-point numbers**.

framework: A framework consists of classes that you use to build your application.

garbage collection: Garbage collection is Java's way of reclaiming memory that your program has allocated at some point during its execution but which your program no longer needs.

graphical user interface (GUI): A GUI is a user interface that takes advantage of graphical elements, such as windows, buttons, checkboxes, and text fields. GUIs take advantage of the mouse and are different from character-mode user interfaces, which rely solely on text characters.

Hypertext Markup Language (HTML): HTML is a standard that defines formatting commands for laying out documents.

i/o: This is an abbreviation for input/output. Input refers to ways to get information into the computer, such as through the keyboard or mouse. Output refers to ways for the program to get information back to the user, such as displaying information using a monitor or printer.

increment: To increment means to add 1 to the value of a number.

infinite loop: An infinite loop is a loop that never terminates and instead repeats a sequence of statements forever.

inheritance: Classes can be set up in relationships whereby subclasses build on and extend their superclasses and inherit all of the variables and methods in their superclasses.

initialization: Initialization refers to any code that affects a loop but occurs before the loop is entered.

instance: See **object**.

instance variable or **method:** An instance variable or method belongs to an object (as opposed to a class). See also **class variable** or **method**.

instantiate: To instantiate an object means to create an instance (an object) based on a class.

integers: Integers are whole numbers like –37, 0, and 22. Variables declared in Java as integers cannot hold floating-point or fractional values.

interface: An interface is like a class, except that it only defines a set of behavior for classes to implement. Interfaces can also define class constants.

interpreted language: An interpreted language is a programming language whose references to variables, memory, method invocations, and the flow through the program are determined at runtime (as opposed to compile time).

invoke: To invoke a method means to execute its instructions.

Java: This object-oriented programming language is especially appropriate to use for developing applications for the Internet and the World Wide Web.

Java-enabled Web browsers: These Web browsers are capable of running software applications written in Java.

Java interpreter: A Java interpreter implements the Java Virtual Machine. There is a different Java interpreter for each hardware/software environment, which allows the same Java program you write to be run in these different environments without modification.

Java Virtual Machine (JVM): The JVM is a theoretical machine, at the time of this writing only implemented in software, that all Java programs are compiled to run on.

label: A label identifies a line of code.

layout manager: A layout manager is an object that controls how a container arranges its user interface components.

literals: Literals are values not stored in a variable, such the number 123 or the character *a*.

load a class: When Metrowerks Java first reads a compiled class file, it loads the class into the interpreter.

local variable: A local variable is accessible only to the method in which it is defined.

logical operator: A logical operator is an operator that evaluates to either true or false.

loop: To loop means to repeat a sequence of statements (usually for a set number of times). See also **initialization, modification,** and **termination**.

machine language: Machine language is the set of symbolic instruction codes that tell a computer what to do. Machine language is written using only 1s and 0s. See also **compiler**.

method: A method is a chunk of code that defines behavior for an object or a class.

method signature: A method signature is defined by a method's name and parameter types.

modification: When used in conjunction with a loop, modification refers to any code that changes the value of the loop's expression.

multithreading: Multithreading is the ability to run multiple threads at once (that is, to do more than one thing at the same time). See also **thread**.

nested loop: A nested loop is a loop defined inside of another loop.

numeric expression: A numeric expression is an expression that evaluates to a number.

object: An object is a specific instance of a class. Objects maintain data and provide access to behavior. All objects that belong to the same class store the same types of data and have access to the same types of behavior. Each object maintains data that makes it unique from other objects.

operator: An operator is a special character (or set of characters) representing a specific computer operation.

override a method: To override a method involves changing the default behavior for a method that a class inherits from one of its ancestors.

parameter: A parameter is a local variable that is initialized as part of invoking a method.

porting: Porting is the process of getting source code created with a specific environment in mind to run in a different environment.

postfix notation: Writing in postfix notation means placing the operator to the right of a variable or an expression. (Only certain operators are appropriate to use with postfix notation.)

prefix notation: Writing in prefix notation means placing the operator to the left of a variable or an expression. (Only certain operators are appropriate to use with prefix notation.)

program: A program consists of the code that implements an application or applet.

project: In CodeWarrior, a project is a way to organize the different files that make up an application or applet.

project file: In CodeWarrior, a project file contains information about the files used to build a Java application or applet.

project window: In CodeWarrior, a project window displays information about the files used to build a Java application or applet.

return control: To return control means to exit one method and resume program execution in the invoking method.

scope: A variable's scope defines where in the program you have access to the variable.

shared variables: Shared variables are class variables. They are shared in the sense that if one object changes the value of a class variable, a different object will see the new value in that class variable as well.

signature: See **method signature**.

source code: Your source code is a set of instructions that determines what your application or applet will do and when it will do it.

source file: A source file contains source code for an application or applet.

stand-alone applications: Java applications that do not run as part of the World Wide Web or in a Web browser are said to be stand-alone applications (as opposed to applets).

standard input: Standard input is a place where new input from the user first arrives to the program. This concept comes from a time when the user only communicated with a computer using a keyboard (and not also with a mouse). Hence, standard input almost always refers to the keyboard.

standard output: Standard output is the place where information displayed by the program appears. This concept comes from a time when the computer almost always displayed characters on the screen (without graphics). In a graphical environment such as the Mac, Java environments often supply a place for standard output. In CodeWarrior, this place is the Java Output window.

statement: A statement is a line of Java code that actually *does* something. All statements (simple and compound) in Java end in a semicolon (;).

static initializer: When your class loads, Java looks to see whether the class has defined a static initializer. If it has, then this code is executed.

string: You use a string to store text in Java.

subclass: A subclass is the immediate descendant of a particular class, a class that directly inherits from that class.

superclass: A superclass is the immediate ancestor of a particular class, a class from which a class directly inherits.

syntax: A language's syntax involves the rules for writing in that language.

syntax error: A syntax error occurs when your program does not follow the rules of the language (such as by leaving off a semicolon accidentally or forgetting to use curly braces where they should appear).

termination: When used in conjunction with a loop, termination refers to any condition that causes the loop to end.

thread: A thread of control, or thread of execution, defines a specific sequence of tasks that a program should perform. Many programs need only one thread to do their thing, but some programs need to do more than one thing at the same time; these programs need multiple threads. See also **multithreading**.

throw an exception: To throw an exception means to signal an error in Java. See also **catch an exception**.

type: See **data type**.

unary operator: A unary operator takes only one variable.

user interface (UI): A user interface defines the "look and feel" of your application, which includes the way in which the user interacts with your application.

variable: A variable is a container for your program's data. Variables refer to specific locations in memory where a program can store numbers, characters, true/false values, or any other type of data.

whole numbers: See **integers**.

zip files: A zip file is a computer standard for combining files so that they take up less room on the computer's hard drive. Sun Microsystems picked this standard as an easy way to organize and manage many different compiled class files.

Source Code Listings

02.01 - hello, world _____

```
/* -----------------------------------------------------------
This displays "Hello, world!" when it repaints.

Java's classes: Applet    (applet)
                Graphics  (awt)      used for drawing

Custom classes: HelloWorld

------------------------------------------------------------ */
public class HelloWorld extends java.applet.Applet {

   public void paint(java.awt.Graphics g) {
      g.drawString("Hello, world!", 100 , 25);
   }

}
```

04.01 - simple draw _____

See 12.03 - SimpleDraw.

05.02 - static init _____

```
/* -----------------------------------------------------------
This applet displays a message when it loads.

Java's classes: Applet    (applet)
                System    (lang)
```

Custom classes: StaticInit

```
----------------------------------------------------------- */
public class StaticInit extends java.applet.Applet {

   static {
      System.out.println("I like Java in the springtime");
   }

}
```

06.01 - operator

```
/* -------------------------------------------------------------
This applet performs some arithmetic operations when it loads.

Java's classes: Applet      (applet)
                System      (lang)

Custom classes: Operator

----------------------------------------------------------- */
public class Operator extends java.applet.Applet {

   static {

      int myInt;

            myInt = 3 * 2;
            System.out.println("myInt ---> " + myInt);

            myInt += 1;
            System.out.println("myInt ---> " + myInt);

            myInt -= 5;
            System.out.println("myInt ---> " + myInt);

            myInt *= 10;
            System.out.println("myInt ---> " + myInt);
```

```
        myInt /= 4;
        System.out.println("myInt ---> " + myInt);

        myInt /= 2;
        System.out.println("myInt ---> " + myInt);

    }

}
```

06.02 - postfix

```
/* -------------------------------------------------------------
This applet illustrates prefix and postfix notation.

Java's classes: Applet      (applet)
                System      (lang)

Custom classes: Postfix

-------------------------------------------------------------- */
public class Postfix extends java.applet.Applet {

    static {

        int             myInt;

        myInt = 5;

        System.out.println("myInt ---> " + myInt++);

        System.out.println("myInt ---> " + ++myInt);

    }
}
```

07.01 - life cycle

```
/* -----------------------------------------------------------
This applet displays a message at each phase in its life cycle.
```

```
Java's classes: Applet      (applet)
                System      (lang)

Custom classes: LifeCycle

------------------------------------------------------------ */

public class LifeCycle extends java.applet.Applet {

   public void init() {
      System.out.println("init()");
   }

   public void start() {
      System.out.println("start()");
   }

   public void stop() {
      System.out.println("stop()");
   }

   public void destroy() {
      System.out.println("destroy()");
   }

}
```

07.02 - init

```
/* -----------------------------------------------------------
This applet invokes methods when it initializes.

Java's classes: Applet      (applet)
                System      (lang)

Custom classes: InitMethod

------------------------------------------------------------ */
public class InitMethod extends java.applet.Applet {
```

```java
    public void init() {
        System.out.println("init()");
        setUpGUI();
    }

    void setUpGUI() {
        System.out.println("setUpGUI()");
        makeWindow1();
        makeWindow2();
    }

    void makeWindow1() {
        System.out.println("makeWindow1()");
    }

    void makeWindow2() {
        System.out.println("makeWindow2()");
    }
}
```

07.03 - average

```java
/* ------------------------------------------------------------
This applet finds the average for three sets of numbers.

Java's classes: Applet     (applet)
                System     (lang)

Custom classes: Average

------------------------------------------------------------ */
public class Average extends java.applet.Applet {

    public void start() {

        int average;

        average = findAverage(10, 20, 30);
        System.out.println(average);
```

```
        average = findAverage(-400, 182, 213);
        System.out.println(average);

        average = findAverage(9901, 20201, 41);
        System.out.println(average);

    }

    int findAverage(int num1, int num2, int num3) {
        return (num1 + num2 + num3)/3;
    }

}
```

08.01 - truth tester

```
/* --------------------------------------------------------------
This applet illustrates if-else statements.

Java's classes: Applet      (applet)
                System      (lang)

Custom classes: TruthTester

----------------------------------------------------------- */

public class TruthTester extends java.applet.Applet {
    public void init() {

        boolean  hasCar, hasTimeToGiveRide;
        boolean  nothingElseOn, newEpisode, itsARerun;

        hasCar = true;
        hasTimeToGiveRide = true;

        if (hasCar && hasTimeToGiveRide)
            System.out.println("Hop in - I'll give you a ride!");
        else
            System.out.println(
                "I've either got no car, no time, or both!");
```

```
        nothingElseOn = true;
        newEpisode = true;

        if (newEpisode || nothingElseOn)
            System.out.println("Let's watch Star Trek!");
        else
            System.out.println(
                "Something else is on or I've seen this one.");

        nothingElseOn = true;
        itsARerun = true;

        if (nothingElseOn || (!itsARerun))
            System.out.println("Let's watch Star Trek!");
        else
            System.out.println(
                "Something else is on or I've seen this one.");
    }
}
```

08.02 - loop tester

```
/* --------------------------------------------------------------
This applet performs a few loops.

Java's classes: Applet      (applet)
                System      (lang)

Custom classes: LoopTester

------------------------------------------------------------ */
public class LoopTester extends java.applet.Applet {
    public void init() {

        int i;

        i = 0;
        while (i++ < 4)
            System.out.println("while: i=" + i);
```

```
        System.out.println("After while loop, i=" + i);
        System.out.println(" ");

        for ( i = 0; i < 4; i++ )
            System.out.println("first for: i=" + i);

        System.out.println("After first for loop, i=" + i);
        System.out.println(" ");

        for ( i = 1; i <= 4; i++ )
            System.out.println("second for: i=" + i);

        System.out.println("After second for loop, i=" + i);

    }
}
```

08.03 - is odd

```
/* ------------------------------------------------------------
This applet illustrates simple flow control.

Java's classes: Applet      (applet)
                System      (lang)

Custom classes: IsOdd

------------------------------------------------------------ */
public class IsOdd extends java.applet.Applet {
    public void init() {

        int   i;

        for ( i = 1; i <= 20; i++ ) {
            System.out.print( "The number " + i + " is ");

            if ( (i % 2) == 0 )
                System.out.print( "even" );
            else
                System.out.print( "odd" );
```

```
            if ( (i % 3) == 0 )
                System.out.print( " and is a multiple of 3" );

            System.out.println("");

        }
    }
}
```

08.04 - next prime

```
/* -------------------------------------------------------------
This applet finds the next prime number after a starting point.

Java's classes: Applet     (applet)
                System     (lang)
                Math       (lang)


Custom classes: NextPrime

--------------------------------------------------------- */


public class NextPrime extends java.applet.Applet {
    public void init() {

        int     startingPoint, candidate, last, i;
        boolean isPrime;

        startingPoint = 19;

        if ( startingPoint < 2 ) {
            candidate = 2;
          } else if ( startingPoint == 2 ) {
            candidate = 3;
          } else {

            candidate = startingPoint;
              if (candidate % 2 == 0) /* Test only odd numbers */
                candidate--;
```

```
                    do {

                        isPrime = true;    /* Assume glorious success */
                        candidate += 2;    /* Bump to the next number */
                        last = (int)Math.sqrt( candidate );
                                /* We'll check to see if candidate */
                                /* has any factors, from 2 to last */

                        /* Loop through odd numbers only */
                        for ( i = 3; (i <= last) && isPrime; i += 2 ) {
                            if ( (candidate % i) == 0 )
                                isPrime = false;
                        }
                    } while ( ! isPrime );
                }

            System.out.println(
                "The next prime after " +
                startingPoint + " is " + candidate);


        }
    }
```

08.05 - next prime 2

```
/* -------------------------------------------------------------
This applet finds the prime numbers from 1 to 100.

Java's classes: Applet     (applet)
                System     (lang)
                Math       (lang)


Custom classes: NextPrime2

--------------------------------------------------------------- */


public class NextPrime2 extends java.applet.Applet {
    public void init() {

        int    candidate, i, last;
```

```
      boolean isPrime;

      System.out.println( "Primes from 1 to 100: 2, " );

      for ( candidate = 3; candidate <= 100; candidate += 2 ){

         isPrime = true;
         last = (int)Math.sqrt( candidate );

         for ( i = 3; (i <= last) && isPrime; i += 2 ) {

            if ( (candidate % i) == 0 )
               isPrime = false;

         }

         if ( isPrime )
            System.out.println( candidate );

      }
   }
}
```

08.06 - next prime 3

```
/* ------------------------------------------------------------
This applet finds the primes between 1 and 100.

Java's classes: Applet     (applet)
                System     (lang)

Custom classes: IsOdd

------------------------------------------------------------ */

public class NextPrime3 extends java.applet.Applet {
   public void init() {

      int     primeIndex, candidate, i, last;
      boolean isPrime;
```

```
        System.out.println( "Prime #1 is 2." );

        candidate = 3;
        primeIndex = 2;

        while ( primeIndex <= 100 ) {

            isPrime = true;
            last = (int)Math.sqrt( candidate );

            for ( i = 3; (i <= last) && isPrime; i += 2 ) {
                if ( (candidate % i) == 0 )
                    isPrime = false;
            }

            if ( isPrime ) {
                System.out.println("Prime " + primeIndex +
                        " is " + candidate );
                primeIndex++;
            }

            candidate += 2;
        }
    }
}
```

09.01 - employee 1

```
/* -----------------------------------------------------------
This applet illustrates using instance variables and instance
methods.

Java's classes: Applet     (applet)
                System     (lang)

Custom classes: Employee1

------------------------------------------------------------ */
public class Employee1 extends java.applet.Applet {

    int hourlyWage;
```

```
    int hoursWorked;

    int earnedIncome() {
        return hourlyWage * hoursWorked;
    }

    public void init() {
        hourlyWage = 10;
        hoursWorked = 20;
    }

    public void start() {
        int earnedIncome;

        System.out.println("hourly wage = " + hourlyWage);
        System.out.println("hours worked = " + hoursWorked);

        earnedIncome = earnedIncome();
        System.out.println("earned income = " + earnedIncome);
    }
}
```

09.02 - employee 2

```
/* -------------------------------------------------------------
This applet illustrates working with instance variables
and instance methods in different objects.

Java's classes: Applet    (applet)
                System    (lang)

Custom classes: Employee2
                Employee


----------------------------------------------------------- */
public class Employee2 extends java.applet.Applet {

    Employee e1;
    Employee e2;
    Employee e3;
```

```
public void init() {
    e1 = new Employee();
    e1.hourlyWage = 10;
    e1.hoursWorked = 20;

    e2 = new Employee();
    e2.hourlyWage = 18;
    e2.hoursWorked = 38;

    e3 = new Employee();
    e3.hourlyWage = 12;
    e3.hoursWorked = 52;
}

public void start() {
    System.out.println("");
    System.out.println("Employee 1:");
    e1.displayInfo();

    System.out.println("");
    System.out.println("Employee 2:");
    e2.displayInfo();

    System.out.println("");
    System.out.println("Employee 3:");
    e3.displayInfo();
}
}

class Employee {
    int hourlyWage;
    int hoursWorked;

    int earnedIncome() {
        return hourlyWage * hoursWorked;
    }

    void displayInfo() {
        int earnedIncome;
```

```
    System.out.println("hourly wage = " + hourlyWage);
    System.out.println("hours worked = " + hoursWorked);

    earnedIncome = earnedIncome();
    System.out.println("earned income = " + earnedIncome);
    }
}
```

09.03 - employee 3

```
/* ------------------------------------------------------------
This applet shows when you might want to use the variable "this".

Java's classes: Applet      (applet)
                System      (lang)

Custom classes: Employee3
                Employee


------------------------------------------------------------ */
public class Employee3 extends java.applet.Applet {

    Employee e1;
    Employee e2;
    Employee e3;

    public void init() {
        e1 = new Employee();
        e1.initialize(10, 20);

        e2 = new Employee();
        e2.initialize(18, 38);

        e3 = new Employee();
        e3.initialize(12, 52);
    }

    public void start() {
        System.out.println("");
        System.out.println("Employee 1:");
        e1.displayInfo();
```

```
            System.out.println("");
            System.out.println("Employee 2:");
            e2.displayInfo();

            System.out.println("");
            System.out.println("Employee 3:");
            e3.displayInfo();
        }
}


class Employee {
    int hourlyWage;
    int hoursWorked;

    int earnedIncome() {
        return hourlyWage * hoursWorked;
    }

    void displayInfo() {
        int earnedIncome;

        System.out.println("hourly wage = " + hourlyWage);
        System.out.println("hours worked = " + hoursWorked);

        earnedIncome = earnedIncome();
        System.out.println("earned income = " + earnedIncome);
    }

    void initialize(int hourlyWage, int hoursWorked) {
        this.hourlyWage = hourlyWage;
        this.hoursWorked = hoursWorked;
    }

}
```

09.04 - variable _____

```
/* ------------------------------------------------------------
This applet shows a simple example of accessing a class variable.
```

```
Java's classes: Applet     (applet)
                System     (lang)


Custom classes: ClassVar

------------------------------------------------------------ */
public class ClassVar extends java.applet.Applet {

    static int test = 20;

    public void init() {
        System.out.println("test = " + test);

        int test = 30;

        System.out.println("test = " + test);

        System.out.println("ClassVar.test = " + ClassVar.test);
    }

}
```

09.05 - method _____

```
/* ------------------------------------------------------------
This applet shows an example of accessing a class variable and
a class method.

Java's classes: Applet     (applet)
                System     (lang)


Custom classes: ClassMethod
                Circle

------------------------------------------------------------ */
public class ClassMethod extends java.applet.Applet {

        public void init() {
            Circle c1, c2, c3;
```

```
                          c1 = new Circle();
                          Circle.numCircles++;

                          c2 = new Circle();
                          Circle.numCircles++;

                          c3 = new Circle();
                          Circle.numCircles++;

                          Circle.displayNumCircles();
                      }
     }

class Circle {

             static int numCircles;

             static void displayNumCircles() {
                 System.out.println(numCircles +
             " circles were created.");
             }
     }
```

10.01 - triangle

```
/* -----------------------------------------------------------
This applet shows how overriding a method can change its
behavior. It also shows how to invoke the behavior that's defined
in the superclass for an object.

Java's classes: Applet      (applet)
                System      (lang)

Custom classes: TriangleApplet
                Triangle

------------------------------------------------------------ */


public class TriangleApplet extends java.applet.Applet {
```

```
    public void init() {

        Triangle t1 = new Triangle();
        t1.base = 10;
        t1.height = 20;

        Triangle t2 = new Triangle();
        t2.base = 10;
        t2.height = 20;

        Triangle t3 = new Triangle();
        t3.base = 12;
        t3.height = 52;

        System.out.println("The triangles say:");
        System.out.println("t1 == t2? " + t1.equals(t2));
        System.out.println("t1 == t3? " + t1.equals(t3));

        System.out.println("The objects say:");
        System.out.println("t1 == t2? " + t1.objectEquals(t2));
        System.out.println("t1 == t3? " + t1.objectEquals(t3));

    }

}


class Triangle {
    int base;
    int height;

    public boolean equals(Object obj) {
        Triangle t;

        if (obj instanceof Triangle) {

            t = (Triangle)obj;
            if (t.base == base && t.height == height)
                return true;
        }
```

```
            return false;
        }

    boolean objectEquals(Object obj) {
        return super.equals(obj);
        }


    }
```

10.02 - access

```
/* ------------------------------------------------------------
This applet uses a small class hierarchy to illustrate how to
define abstract classes, superclasses, subclasses, and private
and protected variables.

Java's classes: Applet     (applet)
                System     (lang)
                Color      (awt)

Custom classes: AccessApplet
                Shape
                Circle
                Square


------------------------------------------------------------ */
import java.awt.Color;

public class AccessApplet extends java.applet.Applet {

    public void init() {

        Circle c = new Circle();
        Square s = new Square();

        c.setColor(Color.blue);
        s.setColor(Color.black);

        c.x = 50;
        c.y = 60;
```

```
        s.x = 100;
        s.y = 200;

        c.draw();
        s.draw();

    }

}

/** Shapes provide common characteristics for the circle and
square. */

abstract class Shape {
    static protected final int radius = 20;

    private Color color;
    int    x;
    int    y;

    abstract void draw();

    void setColor(Color color) {
        if (color == Color.black)
            this.color = Color.white;
        else
            this.color = color;
    }

    Color getColor() {
        return color;
    }

}

/** Draws and maintains circle information. */
class Circle extends Shape {
    void draw() {
        System.out.println("Circle: radius = " + radius);
```

```
           System.out.println("Circle: color = " +
               getColor().toString());
       }
   }


   /** Draws and maintains square information. */
   class Square extends Shape{
       void draw() {
           System.out.println("Square: radius = " + radius);
           System.out.println("Square: color = " +
               getColor().toString());
       }
   }
```

11.01 - components

```
   /* ------------------------------------------------------------
   This applet creates a few different user interface components
   and detects when the user interacted with them.

   Java's classes: Applet          (applet)
                   System          (lang)
                   Button          (awt)
                   Choice          (awt)
                   TextField       (awt)
                   Checkbox        (awt)
                   CheckboxGroup   (awt)
                   Label           (awt)
                   Event           (awt)


   Custom classes: UIApplet


   ------------------------------------------------------------ */
   import java.awt.*;

   public class UIApplet extends java.applet.Applet {

       Button          button;
       Choice          choice;
       TextField       textField;
```

```
/** Create a user interface. */
public void init() {

    Checkbox        checkbox;
    CheckboxGroup   checkboxGroup;
    Label           label;

    // create a choice list
    choice = new Choice();
    choice.addItem("Apple");
    choice.addItem("Banana");
    choice.addItem("Cherry");
    add(choice);

    // create a text field
    textField = new TextField(10); // 10 columns wide
    add(textField);

    // create a button
    button = new Button("Click me");
    add(button);

    // create a label
    label = new Label("I am a label");
    add(label);

    // create 3 exclusive-choice checkboxes
    checkboxGroup = new CheckboxGroup();

    checkbox = new Checkbox("Yes", checkboxGroup, false);
    add(checkbox);
    checkbox = new Checkbox("No", checkboxGroup, false);
    add(checkbox);
    checkbox = new Checkbox("Maybe", checkboxGroup, true);
    add(checkbox);

}

/** Respond to user input events. */
public boolean action(Event e, Object arg) {
```

```
            if (e.target == textField)
                System.out.println(
                    "User entered text into the text field");

            else if (e.target == button)
                System.out.println("User clicked the button");

            else if (e.target == choice)
                System.out.println("User selected a new choice");

            else if (e.target instanceof Checkbox)
                System.out.println("User clicked a checkbox");

            else
                System.out.println("Unrecognized event");

            return super.action(e, arg);

    }

}
```

11.02 - paint hello

```
/* ------------------------------------------------------------
This applet displays a friendly greeting.

Java's classes: Applet    (applet)
                Graphics  (awt)

Custom classes: PaintHello

------------------------------------------------------------ */
import java.awt.Graphics;

public class PaintHello extends java.applet.Applet {

    public void paint(Graphics g) {
        g.drawString("Hello, applet!", 80, 50);
    }

}
```

11.03 - paint circle

```
/* ------------------------------------------------------------
This applet paints a red circle.

Java's classes: Applet      (applet)
                Graphics    (awt)      used for drawing
                Color       (awt)      defines colors


Custom classes: SimpleDraw


------------------------------------------------------------ */


import java.applet.Applet;
import java.awt.*;

public class SimpleDraw extends Applet {

   /** Draw a red circle when the applet paints itself. */
   public void paint(Graphics g) {
      g.setColor(Color.red);
      g.fillOval(115, 55, 40, 40);
   }

}
```

11.04 - circle at click

```
/* ------------------------------------------------------------
This applet paints a red circle wherever you click.

Java's classes: Applet      (applet)
                Event       (awt)      user-generated action
                Graphics    (awt)      used for drawing
                Color       (awt)      defines colors


Custom classes: SimpleDraw
                Circle                 defines and draws circles


------------------------------------------------------------ */
```

```java
import java.applet.Applet;
import java.awt.*;

public class SimpleDraw extends Applet {

    Circle   c;

    /** Create a circle to start with. */
    public void init() {
        c = new Circle();
        c.initialize(50, 50);
    }

    /** Create a new red circle when the user clicks the mouse. */
    public boolean mouseUp(Event e, int x, int y) {
        c = new Circle();
        c.initialize(x, y);

        repaint();

        return true;
    }

    /** Repaint the newest circle. */
    public void paint(Graphics g) {
        c.draw(g);
    }
}

/** Maintain circle information and provide drawing capabilities. */

class Circle {
    Color color;
    int x;
    int y;

    /** Draw a circle that is 20 pixels in radius. */
    void draw(Graphics g) {
        g.setColor(this.color);
        g.fillOval(this.x - 20, this.y - 20, 40, 40);
    }
```

```
   /** Initialize a red circle at the given pixel location. */
   void initialize(int x, int y) {
      color = Color.red;
      this.x = x;
      this.y = y;
   }

}
```

11.05 - simple draw

```
/* -------------------------------------------------------------

This applet paints a circle or square of the color you've chosen
wherever you click.

Java's classes: Applet     (applet)
                Event      (awt)       user-generated action
                Graphics   (awt)       used for drawing
                Color      (awt)       defines colors
                Choice     (awt)       shape and color selection
choices

Custom classes: SimpleDraw
                Circle                 defines and draws circles
                Square                 defines and draws squares

------------------------------------------------------------ */

import java.applet.Applet;
import java.awt.*;

public class SimpleDraw extends Applet {
   Shape   currentShape = null;
   Choice  shapeChoice;
   Choice  colorChoice;

   /** Create the GUI. */
   public void init() {
```

```
        shapeChoice = new Choice();
        shapeChoice.addItem("Circle");
        shapeChoice.addItem("Square");
        add(shapeChoice);

        colorChoice = new Choice();
        colorChoice.addItem("Red");
        colorChoice.addItem("Green");
        colorChoice.addItem("Blue");
        add(colorChoice);
    }

    /** Draw the current shape. */
    public void paint(Graphics g) {
        if (currentShape != null)
            currentShape.draw(g);
    }

    /** Create a new shape. */
    public boolean mouseUp(Event e, int x, int y) {
        Color  color;
        String shapeString = shapeChoice.getSelectedItem();
        String colorString = colorChoice.getSelectedItem();

        if (colorString.equals("Red"))
            color = Color.red;
        else if (colorString.equals("Green"))
            color = Color.green;
        else
            color = Color.blue;

        // Create a new shape of the appropriate type.
        // Without inheritance, we have to write duplicate
        // code for each of the shape types.

        if (shapeString.equals("Circle"))
            currentShape = new Circle();
        else
            currentShape = new Square();

        currentShape.color = color;
```

```java
        currentShape.x = x;
        currentShape.y = y;

        repaint();

        return true;
    }

}

/** Shapes provide common characteristics for the circle and
square. */

abstract class Shape {
    static public final int shapeRadius = 20;

    Color color;
    int    x;
    int    y;

    abstract void draw(Graphics g);
}

/** Draws and maintains circle information. */
class Circle extends Shape {
    void draw(Graphics g) {
        g.setColor(this.color);
        g.fillOval(this.x - shapeRadius, this.y - shapeRadius,
            shapeRadius * 2, shapeRadius * 2);
    }
}

/** Draws and maintains square information. */
class Square extends Shape{
    void draw(Graphics g) {
        g.setColor(this.color);
        g.fillRect(this.x - shapeRadius, this.y - shapeRadius,
            shapeRadius * 2, shapeRadius * 2);
    }
}
```

11.06 - payroll

```
/* ----------------------------------------------------------
   This illustrates the beginning of an applet to keep track
   of employees in a database. This version defines an
   Employee class but only adds the text fields to the applet
   for use once more of the applet is developed.

   Java's classes: Applet      (applet)
                   TextField   (awt) for entering new employee data
                   Label       (awt) read-only text
                   GridLayout (awt) aligns by columns and rows

   Custom classes: Payroll
                   Employee          payroll information

   ---------------------------------------------------------- */
import java.applet.Applet;
import java.awt.*;

public class Payroll extends Applet {
    TextField   textFieldEmployee;
    TextField   textFieldWage;
    TextField   textFieldHours;
    Label       labelEarned;

    /* Create user interface needed by this applet. */
    public void init() {

        // Arrange the user interface in a grid.
        setLayout(new GridLayout(4,2)); // 4 rows, 2 columns

        // 1st row
        add(new Label("Employee number:"));
        textFieldEmployee = new TextField(20); // 20 columns wide
        add(textFieldEmployee);
```

```java
        // 2nd row
        add(new Label("Hourly wage:"));
        textFieldWage = new TextField(20); // 20 columns wide
        add(textFieldWage);

        // 3rd row
        add(new Label("Hours worked:"));
        textFieldHours = new TextField(20); // 20 columns wide
        add(textFieldHours);

        // 4th row
        add(new Label("Earned income:"));
        labelEarned = new Label();
        add(labelEarned);
    }

    /** Detect keyboard entry. */
    public boolean action(Event e, Object arg) {

        if (e.target == textFieldEmployee) {

            System.out.println("Employee number");

        } else if (e.target == textFieldWage) {

            System.out.println("Hourly wage");

        } else if (e.target == textFieldHours) {

            System.out.println("Hours worked");

        }

        return super.action(e, arg);
    }


}

/** Maintain payroll information for an employee. */
class Employee {
```

```
    int idNumber;
    int hourlyWage;
    int hoursWorked;

    int earnedIncome() {
        return hourlyWage * hoursWorked;
    }
}
```

12.01 - floating pt

```
/* ------------------------------------------------------------
This applet uses floating-point numbers as instance variables.

Java's classes: Applet     (applet)
                System     (lang)


Custom classes: FloatingPt
                Triangle


------------------------------------------------------------ */

public class FloatingPt extends java.applet.Applet {

    public void init() {

        Triangle t1 = new Triangle();
        t1.base   = 9;
        t1.height = 15;

        Triangle t2 = new Triangle();
        t2.base   = 14.232;
        t2.height = 3.2947;

        System.out.println("area of t1 is " + t1.area());
        System.out.println("area of t2 is " + t2.area());


    }


}
```

```
class Triangle {
    double base;
    double height;

    double area() {
        return base * height / 2.0;
    }
}
```

12.02 - arrays

```
/* ------------------------------------------------------------
This applet displays your fortune whenever you resize the applet.

Java's classes: Applet     (applet)
                Graphics   (awt)      used for drawing
                Math       (lang)     to find the absolute value
                Date       (util)     gets the current date
                Random     (util)     finds a random number


Custom classes: ArrayApplet

------------------------------------------------------------ */
import java.awt.Graphics;
import java.util.Date;
import java.util.Random;

public class ArrayApplet extends java.applet.Applet {
    int      numStrings = 5;
    String[] paintStrings;
    Random   r;

    public void init() {
        Date d = new Date();          // today's date
        r = new Random(d.getTime()); // milliseconds since 1970

        paintStrings = new String[numStrings];
        paintStrings[0]  = new String("Look for opportunities");
        paintStrings[1]  = new String("Take chances");
        paintStrings[2]  = new String("Beware of tricks");
```

```
        paintStrings[3]   = new String("Take the day off");
        paintStrings[4]   = new String("Smell the roses");
    }


    public void paint(Graphics g) {

        int index = r.nextInt() % numStrings;
        index = Math.abs(index);
        g.drawString(paintStrings[index], 50, 25);


    }
}
```

12.03 - SimpleDraw

```
/* ------------------------------------------------------------
This applet paints a circle or square of the color you've chosen
wherever you click. This applet keeps a list of the shapes you've
drawn
and paints all the shapes in the list when it repaints.

Java's classes: Applet     (applet)
                Event      (awt)     user-generated action
                Graphics   (awt)     used for drawing
                Color      (awt)     defines colors
                Choice     (awt)     shape and color selection
choices
                Vector     (util)    list of shapes

Custom classes: SimpleDraw
                Circle   defines and draws circles
                Square   defines and draws squares
                Shape    a common ancestor for circles and squares


------------------------------------------------------------- */

import java.applet.Applet;
import java.util.*;
import java.awt.*;
```

```java
public class SimpleDraw extends Applet {
   Vector   drawnShapes;
   Choice   shapeChoice;
   Choice   colorChoice;

   /** Create the GUI. */
   public void init() {
      drawnShapes = new Vector();

      shapeChoice = new Choice();
      shapeChoice.addItem("Circle");
      shapeChoice.addItem("Square");
      add(shapeChoice);

      colorChoice = new Choice();
      colorChoice.addItem("Red");
      colorChoice.addItem("Green");
      colorChoice.addItem("Blue");
      add(colorChoice);
   }

   /** Create a new shape. */
   public boolean mouseUp(Event e, int x, int y) {

      Shape s;   // This shape will be either a circle or a square.

      String shapeString = shapeChoice.getSelectedItem();
      String colorString = colorChoice.getSelectedItem();

      if (shapeString.equals("Circle"))
         s = new Circle();
      else
         s = new Square();

      if (colorString.equals("Red"))
         s.color = Color.red;
      else if (colorString.equals("Green"))
         s.color = Color.green;
      else
         s.color = Color.blue;
```

```
            s.x = x;
            s.y = y;

            drawnShapes.addElement(s);

            repaint();

            return true;
        }

        /** Draw all the shapes. */
        public void paint(Graphics g) {
            Shape s;
            int numShapes;

            numShapes = drawnShapes.size();
            for (int i = 0; i < numShapes; i++) {

                s = (Shape)drawnShapes.elementAt(i);

                // When the shape draws, circles and squares each
                // invoke their own draw method, depending on
                // which shape this is.
                s.draw(g);
            }
        }

    }

    /** Shapes provide common characteristics for the circle and
    square. */
    abstract class Shape {
        static public final int shapeRadius = 20;

        Color color;
        int x;
        int y;

        abstract void draw(Graphics g);
    }
```

```
/** Draws and maintains circle information. */
class Circle extends Shape {
   void draw(Graphics g) {
      g.setColor(this.color);
      g.fillOval(this.x - shapeRadius, this.y - shapeRadius,
         shapeRadius * 2, shapeRadius * 2);
   }
}

/** Draws and maintains square information. */
class Square extends Shape{
   void draw(Graphics g) {
      g.setColor(this.color);
      g.fillRect(this.x - shapeRadius, this.y - shapeRadius,
         shapeRadius * 2, shapeRadius * 2);
   }
}
```

12.04 - Payroll

```
/* ---------------------------------------------------------
   This illustrates a few standard classes and basic applet
behavior. Enter an employee number for an employee into a text
field. If this employee exists, the applet will find the employee
and display the employee's payroll information. Otherwise, the
applet will create a new employee and add the employee to the
database.

   Java's classes: Applet     (applet)
                   TextField  (awt)     to enter new employee data
                   Label      (awt)     read-only text
                   GridLayout (awt)     aligns by columns and rows
                   Event      (awt)     user-generated action
                   Hashtable  (util)    database
                   String     (lang)    text
                   Integer    (lang)    number

   Custom classes: Payroll
                   Employee             payroll information

   --------------------------------------------------------- */
```

```java
import java.applet.Applet;
import java.awt.*;
import java.util.*;

public class Payroll extends Applet {
    Hashtable   db;
    TextField   textFieldEmployee;
    TextField   textFieldWage;
    TextField   textFieldHours;
    Label       labelEarned;
    Employee    current;

    /* Create user interface needed by this applet. */
    public void init() {

        // Create the employee database.
        db = new Hashtable();

        // Arrange the user interface in a grid.
        setLayout(new GridLayout(4,2)); // 4 rows, 2 columns

        // 1st row.
        add(new Label("Employee number:"));
        textFieldEmployee = new TextField(20); // 20 columns wide
        add(textFieldEmployee);

        // 2nd row.
        add(new Label("Hourly wage:"));
        textFieldWage = new TextField(20); // 20 columns wide
        add(textFieldWage);

        // 3rd row.
        add(new Label("Hours worked:"));
        textFieldHours = new TextField(20); // 20 columns wide
        add(textFieldHours);

        // 4th row.
        add(new Label("Earned income:"));
        labelEarned = new Label();
        add(labelEarned);
```

```
            setCurrent(null);
        }


    /** Handle events that propagate to the applet. This will
include new text field data. */

    public boolean action(Event e, Object arg) {
        Employee employee;
        int    number;

        // Create/retrieve the employee.
        if (e.target == textFieldEmployee) {

            number = intFromTextField(textFieldEmployee);
            employee = findEmployee(number);

            // Create a new employee if not already there.
            if (employee == null)
                employee = addNew(number);

            // Display this employee's payroll information.
            setCurrent(employee);

            // Set the hourly wage for the current employee.
        } else if (e.target == textFieldWage) {

            if (current != null) {
                current.hourlyWage = intFromTextField(textFieldWage);
                recalcEarned();
            }

            // Set the number of hours worked for the current employee.
        } else if (e.target == textFieldHours) {

            if (current != null) {
                current.hoursWorked =
                    intFromTextField(textFieldHours);
                recalcEarned();
            }
        }
```

```
            return super.action(e, arg);
        }

    /** This is a utility routine to retrieve an integer from a
text field. */

        int intFromTextField(TextField tf) {
            String   s;
            int      value;

            s = tf.getText();
            try {
                value = Integer.parseInt(s);
            } catch (Exception e) {
                value = 0;
                setCurrent(null);
            }

            return value;
        }

    /** Do a database lookup using the employee's number as the
key. */

        Employee findEmployee(int number) {
            return (Employee)db.get(new Integer(number));
        }

    /** Set the text fields to display the correct information for
the current employee. */

        void setCurrent(Employee e) {
            current = e;

            // If there isn't a current employee, initialize the fields.
            if (e == null) {
                textFieldEmployee.setText("0");
                textFieldWage.setText("0");
                textFieldHours.setText("0");
```

```
      } else {
         textFieldWage.setText(
             Integer.toString(current.hourlyWage));

         textFieldHours.setText(
             Integer.toString(current.hoursWorked));
      }

      recalcEarned();

   }


   /** Create a new employee and add it to the database */
   Employee addNew(int number) {
      Employee e = new Employee();
      e.idNumber = number;
      e.hourlyWage = 0;
      e.hoursWorked = 0;

      db.put(new Integer(number), e);   // Add to the database

      setCurrent(e);

      return e;
   }


   /** Recalculate the text to display in the "Earned income:"
label. */

   void recalcEarned() {
      int earned;

      if (current != null)
         earned = current.earnedIncome();
      else
         earned = 0;

      labelEarned.setText(Integer.toString(earned));
   }


}
```

```
/** Maintain payroll information for an employee. */
class Employee {
    int idNumber;
    int hourlyWage;
    int hoursWorked;

    int earnedIncome() {
        return hourlyWage * hoursWorked;
    }
}
```

13.01 - applet params

```
/* -------------------------------------------------------------
This applet paints a circle or square of the color you've chosen
wherever you click. This applet keeps a list of the shapes you've
drawn and paints all the shapes in the list when it repaints. It
allows the HTML file to supply a list of colors for the shapes.

Java's classes: Applet     (applet)
                Event      (awt)     user-generated action
                Graphics   (awt)     used for drawing
                Color      (awt)     defines colors
                Choice     (awt)     shape and color choices
                Vector     (util)    list of shapes

Custom classes: SimpleDraw
                Circle defines and draws circles
                Square defines and draws squares
                Shape  a common ancestor for circles and squares

------------------------------------------------------------ */

import java.applet.Applet;
import java.util.*;
import java.awt.*;

public class SimpleDraw extends Applet {
    Vector   drawnShapes;
    Choice   shapeChoice;
    Choice   colorChoice;
```

```
/** Create the GUI. */
public void init() {
    drawnShapes = new Vector();

    shapeChoice = new Choice();
    shapeChoice.addItem("Circle");
    shapeChoice.addItem("Square");

    add(shapeChoice);

    colorChoice = new Choice();
    colorChoice.addItem(getParameter("color1"));
    colorChoice.addItem(getParameter("color2"));
    colorChoice.addItem(getParameter("color3")); t

    add(colorChoice);
}

/** Draw all the shapes. */
public void paint(Graphics g) {
    Shape s;
    int numShapes;

    numShapes = drawnShapes.size();
    for (int i = 0; i < numShapes; i++) {

        s = (Shape)drawnShapes.elementAt(i);

        // When the shape draws, circles and squares each
        // invoke their own draw method, depending on
        // which shape this is.
        s.draw(g);
    }
}

/** Create a new shape. */
public boolean mouseUp(Event e, int x, int y) {

    Shape s;  // This shape will be either a circle or a square.

    String shapeString = shapeChoice.getSelectedItem();
    String colorString = colorChoice.getSelectedItem();
```

```
        if (shapeString.equals("Circle"))
            s = new Circle();
        else
            s = new Square();

        if (colorString.equals("Red"))
            s.color = Color.red;
        else if (colorString.equals("Green"))
            s.color = Color.green;
        else if (colorString.equals("Black"))
            s.color = Color.black;
        else if (colorString.equals("Blue"))
            s.color = Color.blue;
        else if (colorString.equals("Pink"))
            s.color = Color.pink;
        else if (colorString.equals("Cyan"))
            s.color = Color.cyan;
        else if (colorString.equals("Orange"))
            s.color = Color.orange;
        else
            s.color = Color.white;   // default color

        s.x = x;
        s.y = y;

        drawnShapes.addElement(s);

        repaint();

        return true;
    }

}

/** Shapes provide common characteristics for the circle and
square. */
abstract class Shape {
    static public final int shapeRadius = 20;

    Color color;
```

```
   int x;
   int y;

   abstract void draw(Graphics g);
}

/** Draws and maintains circle information. */
class Circle extends Shape {
   void draw(Graphics g) {
      g.setColor(this.color);
      g.fillOval(this.x - shapeRadius, this.y - shapeRadius,
         shapeRadius * 2, shapeRadius * 2);
   }
}

/** Draws and maintains square information. */
class Square extends Shape{
   void draw(Graphics g) {
      g.setColor(this.color);
      g.fillRect(this.x - shapeRadius, this.y - shapeRadius,
         shapeRadius * 2, shapeRadius * 2);
   }
}
```

13.02 - constructor _____

```
/* -----------------------------------------------------------
This applet creates circles using different constructors.

Java's classes: Applet     (applet)
                System     (lang)

Custom classes: Constructor
                Circle

----------------------------------------------------------- */

import java.applet.Applet;

public class Constructor extends Applet {
```

```java
        public void init() {
            Circle c1, c2, c3;

            c1 = new Circle();
            c2 = new Circle(20);
            c3 = new Circle(c2);

            c1.displayInfo();
            c2.displayInfo();
            c3.displayInfo();
        }
    }

class Circle {
    static int defaultRadius = 10;
    int radius;

    Circle() {
        radius = defaultRadius;
    }

    Circle(int radius) {
        this.radius = radius;
    }

    Circle(Circle referenceCircle) {
        this.radius = referenceCircle.radius;
    }

    void displayInfo() {
        System.out.println("This circle's radius is " + radius);
    }
}
```

13.03 - exception

```
/* ------------------------------------------------------------
This applet creates circles using different constructors. One
of these constructors throws an exception.
```

```
Java's classes: Applet    (applet)
                System    (lang)
                Exception (lang)

Custom classes: Constructor
                Circle
                ImaginaryCircleException


------------------------------------------------------------- */

import java.applet.Applet;

public class ExceptionApplet extends Applet {
   public void init() {
      Circle c1, c2, c3, c4;

      c1 = new Circle();

      try {
         c2 = new Circle(20);
      } catch (ImaginaryCircleException e) {
         System.out.println("Exception with radius 20");
         c2 = new Circle();
      }

      try {
         c3 = new Circle(-20);
      } catch (ImaginaryCircleException e) {
         System.out.println("Exception with radius -20");
         c3 = new Circle();
      }

      c4 = new Circle(c2);

      c1.displayInfo();
      c2.displayInfo();
      c3.displayInfo();
      c4.displayInfo();
   }
}
```

```java
class Circle {
   static int defaultRadius = 10;
   int radius;

   Circle() {
      radius = defaultRadius;
   }

   Circle(int radius) throws ImaginaryCircleException {
      if (radius < 0)
         throw new ImaginaryCircleException();
      else
         this.radius = radius;
   }

   Circle(Circle referenceCircle) {
      this.radius = referenceCircle.radius;
   }

   void displayInfo() {
      System.out.println("This circle's radius is " + radius);
   }
}

class ImaginaryCircleException extends Exception {
}
```

14.01 - hello, java

```
/* ------------------------------------------------------------
This stand-alone application writes the words "Hello, Java!" to
the standard output.

Java's classes: System    (lang)
                String    (lang)

Custom classes: HelloJava (inherits from Object)

------------------------------------------------------------ */
```

```
public class HelloJava {
   public static void main(String[] args) {
      System.out.println("Hello, Java!");
   }
}
```

14.02 - next prime

```
/* -----------------------------------------------------------
This stand-alone application finds the next prime after the
integer passed to it as a command line parameter.

Java's classes: Applet    (applet)
                Exception (lang)
                String    (lang)
                Integer   (lang)
                Math      (lang)     to find the square root


Custom classes: NextPrime

------------------------------------------------------------- */

public class NextPrime {
   public static void main(String[] args) {

   int     startingPoint, candidate, last, i;
   boolean isPrime;

   if (args.length == 1) {
      try {
         Integer integer = new Integer(args[0]);
         startingPoint = integer.intValue();
      } catch (Exception e) {
         return;
      }
   } else
      return;

      if ( startingPoint < 2 ) {
         candidate = 2;
```

```
        } else if ( startingPoint == 2 ) {
          candidate = 3;
        } else {

          candidate = startingPoint;
          if (candidate % 2 == 0)    /* Test only odd numbers */
            candidate--;
          do {

            isPrime = true;   /* Assume glorious success */
            candidate += 2;   /* Bump to the next number to test */
            last = (int)Math.sqrt( candidate );
                /* We'll check to see if candidate */
                /* has any factors, from 2 to last */

            /* Loop through odd numbers only */
            for ( i = 3; (i <= last) && isPrime; i += 2 ) {
              if ( (candidate % i) == 0 )
                isPrime = false;
            }
          } while ( ! isPrime );
      }

      System.out.println( "The next prime after " +
        startingPoint + " is " + candidate);

    }
}
```

14.03 - stand alone _____

```
/* -------------------------------------------------------------
This stand-alone application paints a circle or square of the
color you've chosen wherever you click. This application keeps a
list of the shapes you've drawn and paints all the shapes in the
list when it repaints.

Java's classes: Applet    (applet)
                Event     (awt)       user-generated action
                Graphics  (awt)       used for drawing
```

```
                Color     (awt)      defines colors
                Choice    (awt)      shape and color selection
choices
                Vector    (util)     list of shapes

Custom classes: SimpleDraw
                Circle  defines and draws circles
                Square  defines and draws squares
                Shape   a common ancestor for circles and squares

------------------------------------------------------------- */

import java.applet.Applet;
import java.util.*;
import java.awt.*;

public class SimpleDraw extends Applet {
    Vector   drawnShapes;
    Choice   shapeChoice;
    Choice   colorChoice;

    /** Be able to run as a stand-alone application. */
    public static void main(String[] args) {

        // create a new instance of this applet
        SimpleDraw sd = new SimpleDraw();

        // initialize the applet
        sd.init();

        // create a frame to hold this applet
        Frame f = new Frame("SimpleDraw");

        // put the applet into the frame
        f.add("Center", sd);

        // give the frame a default size
        f.resize(200,100);

        // make the frame appear
        f.show();
    }
```

```java
/** Create the GUI. */
public void init() {
    drawnShapes = new Vector();

    shapeChoice = new Choice();
    shapeChoice.addItem("Circle");
    shapeChoice.addItem("Square");
    add(shapeChoice);

    colorChoice = new Choice();
    colorChoice.addItem("Red");
    colorChoice.addItem("Green");
    colorChoice.addItem("Blue");
    add(colorChoice);
}

/** Repaint all the shapes. */
public void paint(Graphics g) {
    Shape s;
    int numShapes;

    numShapes = drawnShapes.size();
    for (int i = 0; i < numShapes; i++) {

        s = (Shape)drawnShapes.elementAt(i);

        // When the shape draws, circles and squares each
        // invoke their own draw method, depending on
        // which shape this is.
        s.draw(g);
    }
}

/** Create a new shape. */
public boolean mouseUp(Event e, int x, int y) {

    Shape s;   // This shape will be either a circle or a square.

    String shapeString = shapeChoice.getSelectedItem();
    String colorString = colorChoice.getSelectedItem();
```

```java
        if (shapeString.equals("Circle"))
            s = new Circle();
        else
            s = new Square();

        if (colorString.equals("Red"))
            s.color = Color.red;
        else if (colorString.equals("Green"))
            s.color = Color.green;
        else
            s.color = Color.blue;

        s.x = x;
        s.y = y;

        drawnShapes.addElement(s);

        repaint();

        return true;
    }

}

/** Shapes provide common characteristics for the circle and
square. */
abstract class Shape {
    static public final int shapeRadius = 20;

    Color color;
    int x;
    int y;

    abstract void draw(Graphics g);
}

/** Draws and maintains circle information. */
class Circle extends Shape {
    void draw(Graphics g) {
        g.setColor(this.color);
```

```
            g.fillOval(this.x - shapeRadius, this.y - shapeRadius,
                shapeRadius * 2, shapeRadius * 2);
        }
    }

    /** Draws and maintains square information. */
    class Square extends Shape{
        void draw(Graphics g) {
            g.setColor(this.color);
            g.fillRect(this.x - shapeRadius, this.y - shapeRadius,
                shapeRadius * 2, shapeRadius * 2);
        }
    }
```

15.01 - threads

```
/* ------------------------------------------------------------
This applet paints a circle or square of the color you've chosen
wherever you click. Every second, it blinks the shape to yellow.
All shapes blink independently of each other.

This applet keeps a list of the shapes you've drawn
and paints all the shapes in the list when it repaints.

Java's classes: Applet      (applet)
                Event       (awt)      user-generated action
                Graphics    (awt)      used for drawing
                Color       (awt)      defines colors
                Choice      (awt)      shape and color selection
choices
                Vector      (util)     list of shapes
                Thread      (lang)

Custom classes: SimpleDraw
                Circle   defines and draws circles
                Square   defines and draws squares
                Shape    a common ancestor for circles and squares
                BlinkThread   controls drawing for a shape

------------------------------------------------------------ */
```

```java
import java.applet.Applet;
import java.util.*;
import java.awt.*;

public class SimpleDraw extends Applet {
    Vector   threads;
    Choice   shapeChoice;
    Choice   colorChoice;

    /** Create the GUI. */
    public void init() {
        threads = new Vector();

        shapeChoice = new Choice();
        shapeChoice.addItem("Circle");
        shapeChoice.addItem("Square");
        add(shapeChoice);

        colorChoice = new Choice();
        colorChoice.addItem("Red");
        colorChoice.addItem("Green");
        colorChoice.addItem("Blue");
        add(colorChoice);

        BlinkThread.g = getGraphics(); // Get the graphics object
    }

    /** Create a new shape. */
    public boolean mouseUp(Event e, int x, int y) {

        BlinkThread t;
        Shape s;   // This shape will be either a circle or a square.

        String shapeString = shapeChoice.getSelectedItem();
        String colorString = colorChoice.getSelectedItem();

        if (shapeString.equals("Circle"))
            s = new Circle();
        else
            s = new Square();
```

```
        if (colorString.equals("Red"))
            s.color = Color.red;
        else if (colorString.equals("Green"))
            s.color = Color.green;
        else
            s.color = Color.blue;

        s.x = x;
        s.y = y;

        t = new BlinkThread(s);
        t.start();
        threads.addElement(t);

        return true;
    }


    /** Resume all the threads when the applet starts. */
    public void start() {
        BlinkThread t;
        int         numThreads;

        numThreads = threads.size();
        for (int i = 0; i < numThreads; i++) {

            t = (BlinkThread)threads.elementAt(i);
            t.resume();
        }
    }

    /** Suspend all the threads when the applet stops. */
    public void stop() {
        BlinkThread t;
        int         numThreads;

        numThreads = threads.size();
        for (int i = 0; i < numThreads; i++) {

            t = (BlinkThread)threads.elementAt(i);
```

```
            t.suspend();
        }
    }

    /** Stop all the threads when the applet goes away. */
    public void destroy() {
        BlinkThread t;
        int         numThreads;

        numThreads = threads.size();
        for (int i = 0; i < numThreads; i++) {

            t = (BlinkThread)threads.elementAt(i);
            t.stop();
        }
    }
}

/** Shapes provide common characteristics for the circle and
square. */
abstract class Shape {
    static public final int shapeRadius = 20;

    Color color;
    int x;
    int y;

    abstract void draw(Graphics g);
    abstract void drawBlink(Graphics g);
}

/** Draws and maintains circle information. */
class Circle extends Shape {
    void drawBlink(Graphics g) {
        g.setColor(Color.yellow);
        g.fillOval(this.x - shapeRadius, this.y - shapeRadius,
            shapeRadius * 2, shapeRadius * 2);
    }

    void draw(Graphics g) {
        g.setColor(this.color);
```

```
            g.fillOval(this.x - shapeRadius, this.y - shapeRadius,
                shapeRadius * 2, shapeRadius * 2);
        }
    }

    /** Draws and maintains square information. */
    class Square extends Shape{
        void drawBlink(Graphics g) {
            g.setColor(Color.yellow);
            g.fillRect(this.x - shapeRadius, this.y - shapeRadius,
                shapeRadius * 2, shapeRadius * 2);
        }

        void draw(Graphics g) {
            g.setColor(this.color);
            g.fillRect(this.x - shapeRadius, this.y - shapeRadius,
                shapeRadius * 2, shapeRadius * 2);
        }
    }

    /** Thread to control when to blink a shape. */
    class BlinkThread extends Thread {
        static Graphics g;
        Shape s;

        BlinkThread(Shape s) {
            this.s = s;
        }

        public void run() {

            // don't ever exit the thread
            while(true) {

                try {
                    s.drawBlink(g);
                    sleep(250);   // Go to sleep for a 1/4 of a second
```

```
        s.draw(g);
        sleep(1000); // Go to sleep for 1 second

    } catch (Exception e) {
    }


    }
  }
}
```

Java Syntax Summary

The if Statement

syntax:

```
if (expression)
    statement
```

example:

```
if (numEmployees > 20)
    buyNewBuilding();
```

alternate syntax:

```
if (expression)
    statement
else
    statement
```

example:

```
if (temperature < 60)
    wearAJacket();
else
    buyASweater();
```

The while Statement

syntax:

```
while (expression)
    statement
```

example:

```
while (fireTooLow())
    addAnotherLog();
```

The for Statement

syntax:

```
for (expression1; expression2; expression3)
    statement
```

example:

```
int[] myArray = new myArray[100];
int   i;

for (i = 0; i < 100; i++)
    myArray[i] = i;
```

The do Statement

syntax:

```
do
    statement
while (expression)
```

example:

```
do
    invokeThisMethod();
while (keepGoing());
```

The switch Statement

syntax:

```
switch (expression){
    case constant:
        statements
```

```
    case constant:
        statements
    default:
        statements
}
```

example:

```
switch (disneyNumber) {
    case 7:
        System.out.println("dwarves");
        break;
    case 101:
        System.out.println("dalmations");
        break;
    default:
        System.out.println("not used yet");
}
```

The break Statement _____

syntax:

```
break;
```

example:

```
int i = 1;

while (i <= 9) {
    playAnInning(i);

    if (itsRaining())
        break;

    i++;
}
```

The return Statement

syntax:

```
return;
```

example:

```
if (allDone())
    return;
```

syntax:

```
return expression;
```

example:

```
int addThese (int num1, int num2)
    return num1 + num2;
```

The new Operator

syntax:

```
new ClassName();
```

example:

```
Button b = new Button();
```

The instanceof Operator

syntax:

```
variable instanceof ClassName
```

example:

```
if (myObject instanceof Button)
    System.out.println("this is a button");
```

The throw Statement

syntax:

```
throw exception;
```

example:

```
if (seriousProblem())
    throw new Exception();
```

The try, catch, and finally Statements

syntax without finally:

```
try
    statement
catch (ExceptionName variable) {
    statement
```

example:

```
try {
    doSomethingDangerous();
} catch (Exception e) {
    handleTheException()
}
```

syntax with finally:

```
try
    statement
catch (ExceptionName variable) {
    statement
finally
    statement
```

example:

```
try {
    doSomethingDangerous();
} catch (Exception e) {
    handleTheException()
} finally {
    alwaysDoThis();
}
```

About
CodeWarrior Gold

You've spent a lot of time with CodeWarrior as you've made your way through the pages of this book. We hope you have enjoyed the experience. However, you have just skimmed the surface of the power and potential available to you in CodeWarrior.

This appendix is all about what you can do in CodeWarrior, not about how to do it. In this appendix, we take a closer look at this industry-leading development environment and at some of the amazing things you can do with CodeWarrior. The documentation and tutorials you get when you buy CodeWarrior will teach you how to use the tools quickly and effectively.

It is important to note that this appendix describes the full commercial version of CodeWarrior called *CodeWarrior Gold*, not the Lite version that comes with this book. CodeWarrior Gold includes many more features, tools, and toys.

What Is CodeWarrior?

As you've seen throughout this book, CodeWarrior is an integrated development environment—the CodeWarrior IDE—that consists of a project window, editor, browser, compilers, and linkers. In addition, a source-level debugger lets you check your code. There are other IDE-type environments out there. What makes CodeWarrior so special?

The true beauty of the CodeWarrior IDE is that CodeWarrior is host, language, and target independent. What does this mean?

- The host is the machine running the CodeWarrior IDE. Currently, you can run CodeWarrior under the Mac OS or Be OS. CodeWarrior will be available for Windows in the near future, if it is not already.

- The language is the programming language you use. You can use CodeWarrior to write programs in assembly language, Pascal, Object Pascal, C, C++, or Java. You pick the language you want to use.

- The target is the platform on which your code will finally run. Among the targets you can choose are the 68K and PowerPC Macs, any Win32 operating system such as Windows NT or Windows 95 running on the Intel x86 chip, the Java Virtual Machine, the Be OS, and the Magic OS.

This mix-and-match flexibility means that you can use a single environment—CodeWarrior—to create code for a variety of platforms using your language of choice while working on your favorite computer.

There are two limitations to keep in mind. First, CodeWarrior does not include compilers for all targets for every language. However, the CodeWarrior compiler and linker interface is publicly available to compiler developers who wish to create plug-in tools that work with CodeWarrior. Such third-party tools may be available for free as part of CodeWarrior Gold, or they can be purchased from the manufacturer.

Second, CodeWarrior does not automatically convert your code so that it runs properly on the target operating system or chip. If you want to write code for a Windows program, you must still understand the Windows operating system and write the code accordingly. CodeWarrior does not automatically convert your Mac code into Windows code, or vice versa.

Nevertheless, having a single environment for all your development needs is a great benefit. Metrowerks is continuously developing compilers and other tools for new targets. With CodeWarrior's public compiler interface, so are third parties.

The end result of CodeWarrior's unique modular design is a tool of unbelievable flexibility and power unmatched by any development environment anywhere in the world. You choose your favorite host, your preferred language, your desired target.

Projects

CodeWarrior is a project-based IDE. To write a program using CodeWarrior, you first need to create a project to track the source files, project preferences, and object code. The project is your central control panel that brings all the pieces together.

With all of the possible targets, this could be very complicated. However, CodeWarrior provides you with premade default projects (stationery). When you create a new project, a pop-up menu lets you choose from a list of stationery projects. There are stationery projects available for every target. CodeWarrior has stationery for making ANSI console applications, Mac OS applications, Java applications, Windows applications, and so on.

The project window is the central command center for a CodeWarrior project. A new project built from stationery may contain temporary "placeholder" source files, real source files from a framework like PowerPlant, and all the necessary code libraries.

Source code files are like those you've been using in this book. They are text files with code to be compiled. Resource files are a Macintosh-standard way of storing data, such as icons, strings, and alert boxes.

Source code file names typically end with some kind of extension such as `.c`, `.p`, `.cp`, `.java`, and so forth. The naming extension tells CodeWarrior which compiler to use to compile the source code. You control the mapping between file name extensions and compilers in the Preferences panel.

Libraries are precompiled code that your code can call. For example, `printf()` is a function in the ANSI C library that you can call from your code. You can't see the source code for a library because it has already been compiled.

Each target requires its own libraries. The stationery project files eliminate most of the complication. CodeWarrior also comes with a "targeting guide" for each target, such as the Mac OS, Win32, and so forth. The targeting guides tell you about the libraries that come with CodeWarrior and which are appropriate for your projects.

You can add any number of source, resource, and library files to your project. You can even use the project window to organize files that contain notes, progress reports, documentation, or other information related to a project but not compiled. You can open and view these ancillary files directly from the project window.

When you compile, CodeWarrior parses the code in each source file, locates any related headers, and generates object code appropriate for the desired target. The object code is stored in the project. The project window keeps track of which files need to be recompiled when you make changes, including any interdependencies. If you change a file, the project manager marks it for update and marks all dependent files as well. Next time you compile, only those files marked for update are recompiled.

When you **Make** a program, the linker connects the object code into the final product—be it application, code resource, plug-in tool, system extension, or other program. The linkers are very smart and "dead-strip" any code that isn't actually used. This keeps the final product as lean as possible. Metrowerks compilers and linkers are among the fastest in the industry. They generate fast, stable, reliable code and give you full control over the level of optimization you want to impose on the final result.

Editing

The *CodeWarrior IDE User's Guide* explains all the features of the CodeWarrior source code editor. Here are a few highlights.

You can work on as many as 32 source code files simultaneously. You can easily open any included file, jump to any function in the file, go to any line number, split the editor window to view different parts of the file simultaneously, and so on. There are all kinds of powerful code navigation features.

The CodeWarrior editor is aware of source code control systems and will preserve the integrity of controlled files. It supports colorized syntax and keywords, so you can easily see comments, keywords, function calls, and so forth.

The editor can convert between Mac OS, DOS, and Unix line endings. You don't have to worry about the format. And, the editor handles large amounts of text—up to several megabytes.

CodeWarrior features a search-and-replace mechanism. You can search and replace text in a single file or any arbitrary group of files. You can even save sets of files for easy reference in the future. The `Batch` option lets you see the results of your search in a list if you wish.

Compiling, Linking, and Running

Compiling is as easy as making a menu selection or typing a key command. The CodeWarrior compilers list all errors, so you can fix them before going on. You can even edit code directly in the error message window. When you choose **Make** (or **Run**) from the **Project** menu, CodeWarrior compiles any uncompiled source files and then locates and links in the libraries and builds the final program.

After the final code is built, you can then use that code in whatever way is appropriate. If it is a plug-in of some type, you can hook it up with the appropriate host and give it a test. You can even run some kinds of code (such as applications) directly from the project window!

Using the stationery when you create a new project automatically includes all the correct libraries required for a typical project. If you use other libraries, you must add them yourself.

If your code calls a library routine that is not included in any of the libraries in your project, you'll see an error message that this function or symbol is undefined. You must then locate the library that contains the desired code and add it to your project. CodeWarrior includes a Find Library utility you use in conjunction with the Find window to locate the library that defines the symbol or routine you want to use.

Debugging

CodeWarrior includes a debugger for every target and language. You build debugger information directly in the project when you compile and link your code. Depending on the type of code, you may be able to launch the debugger directly from the project. If not, you can launch the debugger separately. The *CodeWarrior Debugger Manual* and the various targeting guides tell you how. You can use the debugger to control program execution in a variety of ways. You can step into a function, over a function, out of a function; you can stop, run, resume, or kill a program. You can also set breakpoints, conditional breakpoints, and watchpoints. You can control the debugging process using the keyboard, menu commands, or a floating toolbar.

The Metrowerks debugger is essentially identical for every language and target. Some languages and targets have unique characteristics, so certain debugger features aren't always available. However, the debugger interface is the same for every language and target. You'll feel right at home no matter what kind of code you're writing.

The debugger displays variables in many useful formats, including strings and structures. It supports expression evaluation, provides hex dumps of various memory locations, and displays processor registers. You can switch instantly between source code and assembly language. You can debug multiple threads (in threaded environments). The debugger even debugs code resources and dynamically linked (shared) libraries.

CodeWarrior and ANSI C/C++ Programming

CodeWarrior comes with the Metrowerks Standard Libraries (MSL). These are the platform-independent, ANSI-standard libraries for C and C++. You can use these libraries in any code you write. CodeWarrior comes with a porting guide to help you convert code designed for other environments and operating systems into CodeWarrior projects.

The *C, C++, and Assembly Language Manual* describes the way that the compiler and linker implement the ANSI C and C++ standards. The ANSI standards leave many definitions "compiler dependent." This manual explains how CodeWarrior treats these options.

CodeWarrior comes with other manuals that describe the standard libraries and how to use them. The *C Library Reference* document describes the ANSI C library. It describes each call and its parameters and return value, plus provides general information on usage. This document also covers the Metrowerks SIOUX console library and the Unix functions that allow CodeWarrior programs to use standard Unix calls. The *C++ Library Reference* does the same for the C++ standard library.

Frameworks

Application frameworks help object-oriented programmers write applications quickly and efficiently. CodeWarrior comes with, not one or two, but three complete, world-renowned frameworks in source code format. For the Mac OS, you get Metrowerks' own PowerPlant. For Windows, you get the Microsoft Foundation Classes (MFC). For Java, you get Sun's Java API.

Not only do you get the frameworks, Metrowerks provides you with powerful learning tools to help you get up to speed. *The PowerPlant Book*, Microsoft's own help files for MFC, and Sun's Java API documentation all come with CodeWarrior.

For PowerPlant development, you also get Constructor, the Metrowerks visual interface builder for rapid application development.

Other Great Tools

Professional developers know that there is more to creating great software than writing code. CodeWarrior comes with a complete set of tools to analyze memory usage, to create and edit resources, to profile code at runtime with microsecond accuracy, to create a visual interface interactively, and much, much more.

What You Get with CodeWarrior Gold

CodeWarrior Gold comes with

- CodeWarrior IDE with project manager, editor, browser
- Source-level debugger
- Compilers and linkers for several languages
- Support for Mac OS, Win32, Java Virtual Machine, Magic OS, Be OS targets
- MPW shell and Metrowerks compiler and linker tools for 68K and PowerPC Macs
- Profiling and memory-tracking tools
- PowerPlant application framework
- Constructor visual interface builder
- MFC application framework
- Java API framework
- Metrowerks Standard Libraries

- SIOUX input/output console library (for command line programs)
- Macintosh Toolbox libraries
- Thousands of pages of helpful documentation
- Megabytes of tutorial and example code
- Helpful source code and libraries
- Demos of various programmer tools
- Two *free* updates when you register

CodeWarrior Updates

When you register your purchase of CodeWarrior Gold, Metrowerks will send you two additional update CDs within the first year. After that, you can purchase the next update at a reduced rate. You also get free responsive technical support by phone or e-mail.

Contact Information

CodeWarrior is available in various packages. For example, Metrowerks sells an academic version of CodeWarrior at a greatly reduced price to students and other individuals associated with educational institutions. Metrowerks' Discover Programming series of products also includes CodeWarrior with various compilers and linkers depending upon the CD.

For information on the latest developments, prices, and other Metrowerks products, contact sales@metrowrks.com or visit their Web site at http://www.metrowerks.com.

To order, contact your local software store, university computer store, or Metrowerks Mail Order at

- voice: (800) 377-5416
- fax: (512) 873-4901

By mail, you can find Metrowerks Corporation at Suite 310, 2201 Donley Drive, Austin, TX 78758.

By telephone, you can reach Metrowerks at:

- voice: (512) 873-4700
- fax: (512) 873-4900

Exercises

Chapter 5: The Development Cycle

1. Open the project `SimplestApplet.µ`. Double-click `SimplestApplet.java`, erase anything else that's there, and type in the following program:

```
public class SyntaxApplet extends java.applet.Applet {
    static {
        System.out.println("static initializer");
    }
}
```

Select **Make** from the **Project** menu and then run this applet in the way you learned about, by dropping the HTML file named `SimplestApplet.html` onto the Metrowerks Java icon.

Once you've verified that this applet works and that it displays the words "static initializer" in the Java Output window, make the following changes to experiment with syntax errors. For each of these three examples, make the suggested change and try to remake the project. Describe the syntax error messages that result.

a. Change the line

```
static {
```

to say

```
static (
```

b. Change things back. Now change the line

```
public class SyntaxApplet extends java.applet.Applet {
```

to say

```
public class SyntaxApplet java.applet.Applet {
```

c. Change things back. Now change the line:

```
System.out.println("static initializer");
```

to say

```
System.out.println(static initializer);
```

Chapter 6: Variables and Operators

1. Find the error in each of the following code fragments:

    a. `System.out.println(Hello, world);`

    b. `int  myInt myOtherInt;`

    c. `myInt =+ 3;`

    d. `myInt + 3 = myInt;`

2. Compute the value of `myInt` after each code fragment is executed:

    a.
```
myInt = 5;
myInt *= (3 + 4) * 2;
```

    b.
```
myInt = 2;
myInt *= ( (3 * 4) / 2) - 9;
```

    c.
```
myInt = 2;
myInt /= 5;
myInt--;
```

    d.
```
myInt = 25;
myInt /= 3 * 2;
```

    e.
```
myInt = 5;
System.out.println("myInt = " + myInt = 2);
```

    f.
```
myInt = 1;
myInt /= 10;
```

Chapter 7: Introduction to Methods

1. What is wrong with each of the following methods?

a.
```
void myMethod {
    return 3;
}
```

b.
```
void anotherMethod(int num1) {
    return num1 * 2;
}
```

c.
```
int addThese(int num1, int num2) {
    int sum = num1 + num2;
}
```

2. What is the result of executing myMethod() in the following example?

```
void myMethod() {
    int i = 3;
    System.out.println("result = " + anotherMethod(i));
}

int anotherMethod(int number) {
    return number * number;
}
```

3. Write an applet that, in its init() method, invokes another method that writes your name to the Java Output window.

Chapter 8: Controlling Your Program's Flow

1. What is wrong with each of the following code fragments?

a.
```
if i
    i++;
```

b.
```
for (i = 0; i < 20; i++)
    i--;
```

c.
```
while ( )
    i++;
```

d.
```
do (i++)
    until (i == 20);
```

```
e. switch (i) {
       case firstChoice:
       case secondChoice:
           System.out.println("first or second choice");
           break;
       default:
           System.out.println("other choice");
   }
```

```
f. if (i < 20)
       if (i == 20)
           System.out.println("never...");
```

```
g. while (done = true)
       done = !done;
```

```
h. for (i = 0; i < 20; i*2)
       System.out.println("modification...");
```

2. What is the output from each of the following code fragments?

```
a. for (i = 4; i > 0; i--)
       System.out.println(i);
```

```
b. while (true)
       System.out.println("hello");
```

```
c. int i;
   do {
       System.out.println(i++);
   } while (i < 5);
```

```
d. int i = 5;
   int j = 10;
   if (i < j && j > 10)
       System.out.println("first option");
   else
       System.out.println("second option");
```

```
e. int i = 5;
   int j = 10;
   if (i < j || j > 10)
       System.out.println("first option");
   else
       System.out.println("second option");
```

3. Modify `nextPrime.java` to compute the prime numbers from 1 to 100.

4. Modify `nextPrime.java` to compute the first 100 prime numbers.

Chapter 9: Objects

1. Given a class defined like this,

```
class Elephant {
    static int population;
    int     age;

    int tuskLength() {
        return age * 2;
    }

    int pop() {
        return population;
    }
}
```

and given code that creates two elephants, like this,

```
Elephant e1 = new Elephant();
e1.age = 3;
e2.age = 5;
```

what do you expect the output to be for each of the following two code snippets?

   a. `System.out.println(e1.tuskLength());`
      `System.out.println(e2.tuskLength());`

   b. `Elephant.population = 3000;`
      `System.out.println(e1.pop());`
      `Elephant.population = 4000;`
      `System.out.println(e2.pop());`

2. What is wrong with each of the following class definitions?

   a. `class {`
       `int length;`
       `int width;`
    `}`

b.
```
class Car {
    int speed();
}
```

c.
```
class Boat {
    int length;
    void init(int length) {
        length = length;
    }
}
```

d.
```
class Flower {
    int petals;
    static int numPetals() {
        return petals;
    }
}
```

3. Write an applet that uses a class called Student. The Student class should define a method that can determine whether a student has passed (with a score of 60 and above) or failed (with a score below 60). Each student object will keep track of a test score. The applet should create four students, assign different student objects the test scores 94, 72, 52, and 90, and write out whether each one has passed or failed.

Chapter 10: Java's Classes and Inheritance

1. Given two classes defined like this:

```
class Plant {
    boolean isAlive;
    boolean beautiful() {
        return isAlive;
    }
}

class Flower extends Plant {
    int numPetals;
    boolean beautiful() {
        if (numPetals > 4 && isAlive)
            return true;
        else
            return false;
    }
}
```

These definitions say, basically, that if a plant is alive it's beautiful, but if we're dealing with a flower, we have a little more restrictive definition of beautiful. Now let's create three flowers:

```
Flower f1 = new Flower();
f1.isAlive = true;
f1.numPetals = 4;

Flower f2 = new Flower();
f2.isAlive = true;
f2.numPetals = 5;

Flower f3 = new Flower();
f3.isAlive = false;
f2.numPetals = 100;
```

What are the results of each of the following code snippets?

    a. `System.out.println(f1.beautiful());`

    b. `System.out.println(f2.beautiful());`

    c. `System.out.println(f3.beautiful());`

2. What if the flower did not provide its own `beautiful()` method? What do you think the results would be for `f1`, `f2`, and `f3` if we used the plant's `beautiful()` method instead of the flower's?

3. If `isAlive` was turned into a `private` variable, how could you rewrite the flower's `beautiful()` method so that it would still work?

4. Imagine making `isAlive` `protected` instead of `private`.

    a. Would the flower's `beautiful()` method need to be changed at all to determine whether it was alive?

    b. Could a class defined like this,

```
class FlowerPot {
    int diameter;
}
```

    determine whether a flower it contained was alive or not by directly accessing `isAlive`?

EXERCISES

5. What is wrong with each of the following class definitions?

a.
```
class Computer {
    int processorSpeed();
}
```

b.
```
class Tree {
    abstract String genus();
}
```

c.
```
abstract class Bird {
    abstract int flightSpeed();
}

class Seagull extends Bird {
}
```

d.
```
class Animal {
    private int numLives;
}

class Cat extends Animal;
    Cat() {
        numLives = 9;
    }
```

Chapter 11: Creating a User Interface

1. Given an empty `paint()` method to build upon defined like this,

```
public void paint(Graphics g) {
}
```

how would you

a. Draw a solid, green circle that has its top left edge 30 pixels from the left, 30 pixels from the top, and that is 20 pixels in diameter?

b. Display the text "Who's zooming who?" with its bottom, left edge 40 pixels from the left and 20 pixels from the top?

2. Create an applet that displays two mutually exclusive checkboxes labeled "male" and "female." If you are using CodeWarrior Lite, modify the empty Java source file located in the folder `05.01 - empty applet`.

448

3. Adapt the program you developed in question 2 and write a message to the Java Output window that identifies which checkbox the user selected whenever the user clicks one of the checkboxes.

4. Create an applet that contains a single button. Each time you click the button, alternate between drawing a red and a blue square that has its left edge located 10 pixels from the left, 10 pixels from the top, and that is 40 pixels on each side.

Chapter 12: Working with Data

1. What is wrong with each of the following code snippets?

a.
```
double myDouble = 50.1;
int    myInt    = myDouble;
```

b.
```
int numStudents;
int totalScores = 891;
int average = totalScores/numStudents;
```

c.
```
String schoolMascot = new String();
int numStudents = 409;
schoolMascot = "tiger";
```

d.
```
int myIntArray = new myIntArray[10];
```

e.
```
try {
    Integer number = new Integer(4);
}

if (number != null)
   System.out.println("we have a number");
```

f.
```
try {
    doAConversion();
} catch {
   handleException();
}
```

g.
```
boolean[] toggles = new boolean[3];
for (int i = 0; i <= 3; i++)
    toggles[i] = true;
```

h.
```
int[] myIntArray;
System.out.println(myIntArray.length);
```

2. What do you expect the output to be for each of the following lines of code?

a.
```
try {
    Integer number = new Integer('1');
    System.out.println("created a new Integer instance");
} catch (Exception e) {
    System.out.println("trouble in River City");
}
```

b.
```
float myFloat = (float)50.75;
int   myInt   = (int) myFloat;
System.out.println(myInt);
```

c.
```
int[] myIntArray = new myIntArray[3];
for (int i = 0; i < 3; i++)
    myIntArray[i] = i;
System.out.println(myIntArray.length);
System.out.println(myIntArray[2]);
```

3. Change the program contained in NextPrime3.java, located in the subfolder 08.06 – next prime 3. Instead of writing out the prime number as soon as it is found, save the prime number in the next unused element in an array of 100 integers. At the very end of the init() method, loop through the array and write out each entry.

Chapter 13: Advanced Topics

1. What is wrong with each of the following class definitions?

a.
```
class Rocket {
    int liftoff(int speed, boolean successful) {
        return 0;
    }
    double liftoff(int velocity, boolean reachOrbit) {
        return 0.0;
    }
}
```

b.
```
class Mountain {
    int height;
    int Mountain(int height) {
        this.height = height;
        return height;
    }
}
```

c. class Sun {
```
    final Color color = Color.yellow;
    int age;
    int setAge(int years) {
        age = years;
        if (years > 10000000)
            color = Color.orange;
    }
}
```

d. class Trouble {
```
    void rightHere() {
        throws new Exception();
    }
}
```

2. What do you expect the output to be for the following code snippet?

```
try {
    Integer myInteger = new Integer("$");
} catch (Exception x) {
    System.out.println("error");
} finally {
    System.out.println("clean up");
}
```

3. Write an applet that creates the number of checkboxes indicated by a parameter in the HTML file that launches the applet and adds these checkboxes to its user interface. You can leave off the names of the checkboxes if you'd like. You can use the empty Java source file located in 05.01 – empty project.

Solutions
to the Exercises

Chapter 6: Variables and Operators

1. a. There should be quotes around the words to be displayed, as in

```
System.out.println("Hello, world");
```

b. There should be a comma separating variables declared on the same line, as in

```
int  myInt, myOtherInt;
```

c. To add 3 to a number, use the operator += like this

```
myInt += 3;
```

d. The left side of the equation must be a variable, not an expression, as in

```
myInt = myInt + 3;
```

2. a. 120

b. −6

c. −1

d. 4

e. "myInt = 2" will appear in the Java Output window.

f. 0

Chapter 7: Introduction to Methods

1. a. A method declared as void cannot return a value. To return a value such as an int, declare the method using int instead of void, like this:

```
int myMethod {
    return 3;
}
```

b. Again, the method must be declared as an int to return an int:

```
int anotherMethod(int num1) {
    return num1 * 2;
}
```

c. A method declared as returning a value must return a value:

```
int addThese(int num1, int num2) {
    int sum = num1 + num2;
    return sum;
}
```

2. "result = 9" will appear in the Java Output window.

3.
```
public class WriteNameApplet extends java.applet.Applet {
    public void init() {
        writeYourName();
    }
    void writeYourName() {
        System.out.println("Henry Higgens");
    }
}
```

Chapter 8: Controlling Your Program's Flow

1. a. Parentheses are needed around the expression in the if test, and the expression must yield a Boolean result, as in

```
if (i != 0)
    i++;
```

b. Since we decrement i by 1 in the body of the for loop, and since we increment i by 1 in the modification of the loop counter, this will result in an infinite loop!

c. We need some expression in the parentheses for a `while` loop; these parentheses cannot be empty.

d. The syntax is not `do-until` but `do-while`. This might be updated to read

```
do (i++)
    while (i < 20);
```

e. `case` statements require constants and will not take variables. If `firstChoice` was equal to 1 and `secondChoice` was equal to 2, this could be rewritten as

```
switch (i) {
    case 1:
    case 2:
        System.out.println("first or second choice");
        break;
    default:
        System.out.println("other choice");
}
```

f. Since the first `if` test passes only if i is less than 20, the second `if` test will never execute, and hence the line that reads "never..." will never appear in the Java Output window.

g. Since the result of the assignment operator is the value that was assigned, the expression `done = true` results in the value of `true`. This means the `while` loop will never end, and we'll be caught in an infinite loop.

h. The loop counter, i, is never actually modified. If the intent was to multiply i by 2, the loop should have been written

```
for (i = 0; i < 20; i *= 2)
    System.out.println("modification...");
```

2. a. 4
3
2
1

b. `hello`
`hello`
`hello`

The word "hello" will be written to the Java Output window forever.

c. 0
1
2
3
4

d. `second option`

e. `first option`

3. The solution can be found in the subfolder `08.05 – next prime 2`.

4. The solution can be found in the subfolder `08.06 – next prime 3`.

Chapter 9: Objects

1. a. 6
10

b. 3000
4000

2. a. You must supply the name of the class when defining a class. You could fix this snippet by writing

```
class MyClass {
    int length;
    int width;
}
```

b. You must supply a method body when defining a method (the part between the curly braces). It is possible to define a method without a body (see Chapter 10). To fix this snippet, you could simply provide an empty body (though it must return an `int`, as indicated in the method declaration):

```
class Car {
    int speed() {
        return 0;
    }
}
```

c. The intent of this `init()` method seems to be to set the instance variable, but parameters and local variables take precedence over instance and class variables. Therefore, the instance variable would never be set, and the parameter would be set back to itself! This snippet needs to prefix the instance variable with the special variable named `this`:

```
class Boat {
    int length;
    void init(int length) {
        this.length = length;
    }
}
```

d. The variable `petals` is defined as an instance variable, but the method named `numPetals()` is defined as a class (that is, a `static`) method. Methods defined as `static` cannot access an instance variable without referencing a particular object. If `numPetals()` was an instance method, then this would be legal:

```
class Flower {
    int petals;
    int numPetals() {
        return petals;
    }
}
```

3. a.

```
public class ScoreApplet extends java.applet.Applet {
    public void init() {
        Student s1 = new Student();
        s1.score = 94;
        Student s2 = new Student();
        s2.score = 72;
        Student s3 = new Student();
        s3.score = 52;
        Student s4 = new Student();
        s4.score = 90;

        System.out.println("s1 passed? " + s1.passed());
        System.out.println("s2 passed? " + s2.passed());
        System.out.println("s3 passed? " + s3.passed());
        System.out.println("s4 passed? " + s4.passed());
```

```
        }
    }

    class Student {
        int score;
        boolean passed() {
            if (score >=60)
                return true;
            else
                return false;
        }
    }
```

Chapter 10: Java's Classes and Inheritance

1. a. false

   b. true

   c. false

2.   The results would be true, true, and false for f1, f2, and f3, respectively.

3.   First of all, to set the value for isAlive, you could write a method in the Plant class that took a boolean value and set this value, as in

```
void setIsAlive(boolean newValue) {
    isAlive = newValue;
}
```

Then, when creating the flowers, instead of setting isAlive directly, you could invoke its setIsAlive() method, as in

```
f1.setIsAlive(true);
```

and so on. Instead of accessing isAlive directly, methods in the Flower class could invoke their superclass's beautiful() method, which would return the value of the private isAlive variable.

4. a. If isAlive was defined as protected, the flower's beautiful() method need not be changed.

b. Other classes that were not descendants of Plant, such as FlowerPot, could not access isAlive.

5. a. There is no body defined for the method processorSpeed(). In this case, the method and the class must both be declared as abstract:

```
abstract class Computer {
    abstract int processorSpeed();
}
```

b. If a class contains an abstract method, the class itself must also be declared as abstract:

```
abstract class Tree {
    abstract String genus();
}
```

c. Descendants of an abstract class must define the abstract methods or they must be declared abstract themselves, as in

```
abstract class Bird {
    abstract int flightSpeed();
}
```

```
abstract class Seagull extends Bird {
}
```

d. Subclasses cannot access their superclass's private variables. To allow this, the variable must be made protected. (Or, you can use the default access restrictions, which are defined by not using any keywords. This allows all methods defined in the same package to access that variable.)

```
class Animal {
    protected int numLives;
}
```

```
class Cat extends Animal;
    Cat() {
        numLives = 9;
    }
```

Chapter 11: Creating a User Interface

1. a. `g.setColor(Color.green);`
`g.fillOval(30, 30, 20, 20);`

b. `g.drawString("Who's zooming who?", 40, 20);`

2.
```
public class CheckboxApplet extends java.applet.Applet {
    public void init() {
        checkboxGroup = new CheckboxGroup();

        checkbox = new Checkbox("male", checkboxGroup, false);
        add(checkbox);
        checkbox = new Checkbox("female", checkboxGroup, false);
        add(checkbox);
    }
}
```

3. One way to do this is to keep track of the two checkboxes and identify which object the user selected in the `action()` method for your applet, like this:

```
public class CheckboxApplet extends java.applet.Applet {
    Checkbox male, female;

    public void init() {
        checkboxGroup = new CheckboxGroup();

        male = new Checkbox("male", checkboxGroup, false);
        add(male);
        female = new Checkbox("female", checkboxGroup, false);
        add(female);
    }

    public boolean action(Event e, Object arg) {
        if (e.target == male)
            System.out.println("male");
        else if (e.target == female)
            System.out.println("female");

        return super.action(e, arg);
    }
}
```

```
4.    import java.applet.Applet;
      import java.awt.*;

      public class TestApplet extends Applet {
         Button   toggle;
         Color    color = Color.blue;

         public void init() {
            toggle = new Button("toggle");
            add(toggle);
         }

         public boolean action (Event e, Object arg) {

            if (e.target == toggle) {
               if (color == Color.red)
                  color = Color.blue;
               else
                  color = Color.red;
             }

            repaint();
            return true;
         }

         public void paint(Graphics g) {
           g.setColor(color);
           g.fillOval(10, 10, 40, 40);
         }

      }
```

Chapter 12: Working with Data

1. a. You cannot assign a double to an int without casting:

```
double myDouble = 50.1;
int    myInt    = (int)myDouble;
```

b. Dividing by zero with `int` values is not legal. (The variable `numStudents` will contain the value zero because it has not yet been assigned a different value.)

c. A string cannot be assigned a value after it is created. Instead, set the string's value at the time it is created. (To work with strings that you can write to as well as read from, use instances of StringBuffer instead.)

```
String schoolMascot = new String("tiger");
int numStudents = 409;
```

d. Make sure all arrays are declared with brackets after the data type, like this:

```
int[] myIntArray = new myIntArray[10];
```

(Alternatively, arrays can be declared by placing the square brackets after the variable name.)

e. A `try` block should have a matching `catch` block immediately following it.

f. The `catch` block needs to declare a variable that will be assigned the exception object:

```
try {
    doAConversion();
} catch (Exception exception) {
    handleException();
}
```

g. The only legal elements in an array declared to be 3 in length are the elements 0, 1, and 2. Therefore, the loop must end before it gets to 3:

```
boolean[] toggles = new boolean[3];
for (int i = 0; i < 3; i++)
    toggles[i] = true;
```

h. You cannot access the length of an array before it is created using the `new` operator.

2. a. Since the *character* 1 is being passed to the Integer constructor (because of the single quotes rather than double quotes surrounding the 1), Java will throw an exception. The output will be simply

```
trouble in River City
```

b. The floating-point value will be truncated, and the value 50 will appear in the Java Output window.

c. The two lines in the Java Output window will be:

3
2

3.   One possible version of the new program is:

```
public class NextPrime3 extends java.applet.Applet {
    public void init() {

        int     primeIndex, candidate, i, last;
        boolean isPrime;
        int[]   primeNumbers = new int[100];

        primeNumbers[0] = 2;

        candidate = 3;
        primeIndex = 1;

        while ( primeIndex < 100 ) {

            isPrime = true;
            last = (int)Math.sqrt( candidate );

            for ( i = 3; (i <= last) && isPrime; i += 2 ) {
                if ( (candidate % i) == 0 )
                    isPrime = false;
            }

            if ( isPrime ) {
                primeNumbers[primeIndex] = candidate;
                primeIndex++;
            }

            candidate += 2;
        }
```

```
        for (i = 0; i < 100; i++) {
            System.out.println("Prime #" + (i+1) +
                    " is " + primeNumbers[i] );
        }


    }
}
```

Chapter 13: Advanced Topics

1. a. Methods with the same name must have unique signatures. Signatures include the method name and the data types of its parameters (not the return values).

b. Constructors cannot return a value, such as `int`. (They don't even return `void`.) Here's how the Mountain class could be rewritten:

```
class Mountain {
    int height;
    Mountain(int height) {
        this.height = height;
    }
}
```

c. Constants (that is, variables declared as `final`) cannot be changed. To be able to change a variable, leave off the `final` keyword:

```
class Sun {
    Color color = Color.yellow;
    int age;
    int setAge(int years) {
        age = years;
        if (years > 10000000)
            color = Color.orange;
    }
}
```

d. Methods that throw an exception must include the `throws` keyword, followed by the type of exception they throw, in the method declaration, like this:

```
class Trouble throws Exception {
```

```
   void rightHere() {
       throws new Exception();
   }
}
```

2. The following two lines will appear in the Java Output window:

```
error
clean up
```

3.
```
import java.awt.Checkbox;

public class CheckboxApplet extends java.applet.Applet {
    public void init() {
        int      num;
        Checkbox checkbox;
        String   s = getParameter("checks");

        try {
            num = Integer.parseInt(s);
        } catch (Exception e) {
            num = 0; // default
        }

        for (int i = 0; i < num; i++) {
            checkbox = new Checkbox();
            add(checkbox);
        }
    }
}
```

Here's a possible HTML file for this code:

```
<applet codebase="Checkbox" code="CheckboxApplet.class" width=250
height=100>
<param name=checks value="25">
</applet>
```

465

Additional Resources

This section provides a number of links to additional resources for learning more about Java.

Web Resources

Sites Supporting This Book

There are two places where you can go on the Web to learn more about *Learn Java on the Macintosh*. The first site is maintained by Metrowerks and can be found at

```
http://www.metrowerks.com/products/discover/java/
```

The second site is maintained by Addison-Wesley and can be found by starting at the Addison-Wesley home page, located at

```
http://www.aw.com/devpress/
```

You'll find *Learn Java on the Macintosh* at

```
http://www.aw.com/devpress/19157.html
```

Documentation

JavaSoft, Sun Microsystem's spin-off company that develops and supports Java, has posted lots of great documentation on their site. For the latest API (application programming interface) documentation, look under

```
http://java.sun.com/JDK-1.0/api/packages.html
```

For a directory of other documentation sources maintained by JavaSoft, check out

```
http://java.sun.com/java.sun.com/doc/programmer.html
```

The documentation at this site includes the Java Language Specifications, the Java Virtual Machine, and additional introductory material to learn more about Java programming.

Java Applets on the Web

There are many examples of great Java applets on the Web, and more are being added everyday. Lots of these samples include the source code. You can find many of these at the Gamelan site, located at:

```
http://www.gamelan.com/noframe/Gamelan.programming.html
```

Internet Resources

Among the best Internet resources are the newsgroups. In particular, you should check out

```
comp.lang.java
```

for lively discussions on programming in Java and the latest directions in Java software.

There are also ftp sites where you can download the latest software samples and documentation. Start at

```
http://java.sun.com/java.sun.com/devcorner.html
```

and follow the links to the latest and greatest that JavaSoft has to offer.

For one of the best sites to find useful Mac and Internet related utilities (such as Apple's Thread Manager), check out the Website at

```
http://wwwhost.ots.utexas.edu/mac/index-by-product.html
```

Books

Java Essentials for C and C++ Programmers, by Barry Boone

This book, published by Addison-Wesley, will help you find out more about Java's advanced features, such as exceptions, multitasking, interfaces, and constructors. Though this book is written for programmers, once you are up to speed on Java programming, this book is a great resource for learning about these advanced topics.

Learn C on the Macintosh, by Dave Mark

Java is very similar to C in some fundamental ways. This book, published by Addison-Wesley, can help you learn the basics of variables, operators, data types, and flow control. Most of the information in *Learn C on the Macintosh* that is relevant to Java is included in the chapters of *Learn Java on the Macintosh*. However, if you want to learn more about a language that is a predecessor to Java, Dave's book is a great place to start.

ERKS AUTHORIZED REPRESENTATIVE HAS BEEN ADVISED OF THE POSSIBILITY OF SUCH DAMAGES. SOME JURISDICTIONS DO NOT ALLOW THE LIMITATION OR EXCLUSION OF LIABILITY FOR INCIDENTAL OR CONSEQUENTIAL DAMAGES SO THE ABOVE LIMITATION OR EXCLUSION MAY NOT APPLY TO YOU.

In no event shall Metrowerks' total liability to you for all damages, losses, and causes of action (whether in contract, tort [including negligence] or otherwise) exceed that portion of the amount paid by you which is fairly attributable to the Software and fonts.

10. Controlling Law and Severability. This License shall be governed by and construed in accordance with the laws of the United States and the State of California, as applied to agreements entered into and to be performed entirely within California between California residents. If for any reason a court of competent jurisdiction finds any provision of this License, or portion thereof, to be unenforceable, that provision of the License shall be enforced to the maximum extent permissible so as to effect the intent of the parties, and the remainder of this License shall continue in full force and effect.

11. Complete Agreement. This License constitutes the entire agreement between the parties with respect to the use of the Software, the related documentation, and fonts, and supersedes all prior or contemporaneous understandings or agreements, written or oral, regarding such subject matter. No amendment to or modification of this License will be binding unless in writing and signed by a duly authorized representative of Metrowerks.

Should you have any questions or comments concerning this license, please do not hesitate to write to Metrowerks Corp., 2201 Donley Drive Suite 310, Austin TX 78758, USA. attn: Warranty Information.

Appendix A: Software Redistribution Information for CodeWarrior SDK

The following list describes the Software and Materials that licensees hereunder may incorporate into their own programs and distribute (in object code form only), solely with their own programs, pursuant to the terms of this Software License in the event the Software and Materials listed hereunder are distributed by Metrowerks to the licensee as part of the current CodeWarrior CD-ROM.

Metrowerks Software and Materials

• The PowerPlant Library and sample code. Licensees cannot distribute the source code or any derivations thereof to the PowerPlant Library and Sample code without express written permission from an authorized officer of Metrowerks Inc.

Apple Computer Software and Materials

Object-code derivations of sample code and final versions of the following files:

• AppleScript runtime files (AppleScriptÅ, Inline Filter, AppleScriptLib, ObjectSupportLib, Beep, Choose Application, Choose File, Current Date, Display Dialog, File Commands, Load Script, New File, Numerics, Read/Write Commands, Run Script, Scripting Components, Store Script, String Commands, Time to GMT, English Dialect).

52.227-19(c)(2) of the FAR or, in the case of NASA, in Clause 18-52.227-86(d) of the NASA Supplement to the FAR.

7. Limited Warranty on Media. Metrowerks warrants the diskettes and/or compact disc on which the Software and fonts are recorded to be free from defects in materials and workmanship under normal use for a period of ninety (90) days from the date of purchase as evidenced by a copy of the receipt. Metrowerks' entire liability and your exclusive remedy will be replacement of the diskettes and/or compact disc not meeting Metrowerks' limited warranty and which is returned to Metrowerks with a copy of the receipt. Metrowerks will have no responsibility to replace a disk/disc damaged by accident, abuse, or misapplication. ANY IMPLIED WARRANTIES ON THE DISKETTES AND/OR COMPACT DISC, INCLUDING THE IMPLIED WARRANTIES OF MERCHANTABILITY AND FITNESS FOR A PARTICULAR PURPOSE, ARE LIMITED IN DURATION TO NINETY (90) DAYS FROM THE DATE OF DELIVERY. THIS WARRANTY GIVES YOU SPECIFIC LEGAL RIGHTS, AND YOU MAY ALSO HAVE OTHER RIGHTS WHICH VARY BY JURISDICTION.

8. Disclaimer of Warranty on Metrowerks Software. You expressly acknowledge and agree that use of the Software and fonts is at your sole risk. Except as is stated above, the Software, related documentation, and fonts are provided "AS IS" and without warranty of any kind and Metrowerks and Metrowerks' Licensor(s) (for the purposes of provisions 7 and 8, Metrowerks and Metrowerks' Licensor(s) shall be collectively referred to as "Metrowerks") EXPRESSLY DISCLAIM ALL OTHER WARRANTIES, EXPRESS OR IMPLIED, INCLUDING, BUT NOT LIMITED TO, THE IMPLIED WARRANTIES OF MERCHANTABILITY AND FITNESS FOR A PARTICULAR PURPOSE. METROWERKS DOES NOT WARRANT THAT THE FUNCTIONS CONTAINED IN THE SOFTWARE WILL MEET YOUR REQUIREMENTS, OR THAT THE OPERATION OF THE SOFTWARE WILL BE UNINTERRUPTED OR ERROR-FREE, OR THAT DEFECTS IN THE SOFTWARE AND THE FONTS WILL BE CORRECTED. FURTHERMORE, METROWERKS DOES NOT WARRANT OR MAKE ANY REPRESENTATIONS REGARDING THE USE OR THE RESULTS OF THE USE OF THE SOFTWARE AND FONTS OR RELATED DOCUMENTATION IN TERMS OF THEIR CORRECTNESS, ACCURACY, RELIABILITY, OR OTHERWISE. NO ORAL OR WRITTEN INFORMATION OR ADVICE GIVEN BY METROWERKS OR AN AUTHORIZED REPRESENTATIVE SHALL CREATE A WARRANTY OR IN ANY WAY INCREASE THE SCOPE OF THIS WARRANTY. SHOULD THE SOFTWARE PROVE DEFECTIVE, YOU (AND NOT METROWERKS OR AN METROWERKS AUTHORIZED REPRESENTATIVE) ASSUME THE ENTIRE COST OF ALL NECESSARY SERVICING, REPAIR, OR CORRECTION. SOME JURISDICTIONS DO NOT ALLOW THE EXCLUSION OF IMPLIED WARRANTIES, SO THE ABOVE EXCLUSION MAY NOT APPLY TO YOU.

9. Limitation of Liability. UNDER NO CIRCUMSTANCES. INCLUDING NEGLIGENCE, SHALL METROWERKS BE LIABLE FOR ANY INCIDENTAL, SPECIAL, OR CONSEQUENTIAL DAMAGES THAT RESULT FROM THE USE OR INABILITY TO USE THE SOFTWARE OR RELATED DOCUMENTATION, EVEN IF METROWERKS OR A METROW-

2. Restrictions. The Software contains copyrighted material, trade secrets, and other proprietary material. In order to protect them, and except as permitted by applicable legislation, you may not decompile, reverse engineer, disassemble, or otherwise reduce the Software to a human-perceivable form. You may not modify, network, rent, lease, loan, distribute or create derivative works based upon the Software in whole or in part. You may not electronically transmit the Software from one computer to another or over a network. If the Software was licensed to you for academic use, you may not use the Software for commercial product development. You may use the Software to develop freeware or shareware.

3. Software Redistribution. Appendix A hereunder contains specific information concerning software redistribution of different binaries licensed to you under this software license agreement.

In all cases of software redistribution and in order to protect Metrowerks and Metrowerks' Licensors intellectual property rights in the Software and Materials herein, you must reproduce on each copy a copyright notice that clearly states "Copyright © by Metrowerks and it's Licensors," and distribute such Software and Materials pursuant to a valid agreement that is at least as protective of Metrowerks and Metrowerks' Licensors rights in the Software and Materials as this License.

4. Termination. This License is effective until terminated. You may terminate this License at any time by destroying the Software, related documentation and fonts, and all copies thereof. This License will terminate immediately without notice from Metrowerks if you fail to comply with any provision of this License. Upon termination you must destroy the Software, related documentation and fonts, and all copies thereof.

5. Export Law Assurances. You agree and certify that neither the Software nor any other technical data received from Metrowerks, nor the direct product thereof, will be exported outside the United States except as authorized and as permitted by the laws and regulations of the United States. If the Software has been rightfully obtained by you outside of the United States, you agree that you will not re-export the Software nor any other technical data received from Metrowerks, nor the direct product thereof, except as permitted by the laws and regulations of the United States and the laws and regulations of the jurisdiction in which you obtained the Software.

6. Government End Users. If you are acquiring the Software and fonts on behalf of any unit or agency of the United States Government, the following provisions apply. The Government agrees: (i) if the Software and fonts are supplied to the Department of Defense (DoD), the Software and fonts are classified as "Commercial Computer Software" and the Government is acquiring only "restricted rights" in the Software, its documentation and fonts as that term is defined in Clause 252.227-7013(c)(1) of the DFARS; and (ii) if the Software and fonts are supplied to any unit or agency of the United States Government other than DoD, the Government's rights in the Software, its documentation and fonts will be as defined in Clause

Addison-Wesley warrants the enclosed disk to be free of defects in materials and faulty workmanship under normal use for a period of ninety days after purchase. If a defect is discovered in the disk during this warranty period, a replacement disk can be obtained at no charge by sending the defective disk, postage prepaid, with proof of purchase to:

Addison Wesley Longman
Developers Press
Editorial Department
One Jacob Way
Reading, MA 01867

After the ninety-day period, a replacement will be sent upon receipt of the defective disk and a check or money order for $10.00, payable to Addison-Wesley Publishing Company.

Addison-Wesley makes no warranty or representation, either express or implied, with respect to this software, its quality, performance, merchantability, or fitness for a particular purpose. In no event will Addison-Wesley, its distributors, or dealers be liable for direct, indirect, special, incidental, or consequential damages arising out of the use or inability to use the software. The exclusion of implied warranties is not permitted in some states. Therefore, the above exclusion may not apply to you. This warranty provides you with specific legal rights. There may be other rights that you may have that vary from state to state.

Software license

- XTND runtime files (Claris XTND System, contents of Claris Translators folder, XTNDInterfaceLib.o, XTNDInterfaceLib.*, XTND Power Enabler).

- MacODBC runtime files (ODBC Configuration Manager, ODBC Setup, ODBC Driver Manager).

- Serial Switch

- Thread Manager

- Sound and Sound Manager

- File System Manager

- Macintosh Drag and Drop, Clipping Extension, and Dragging Enabler, provided that the Licensee includes in a conspicuous place on the exterior of the packaging of the licensee programs, the following language:
  "Macintosh Drag and Drop included."

- MacApp provided that the Licensee includes in a conspicuous place on the exterior of the packaging of the licensee programs, the following language:
  "Macintosh Drag and Drop included."

- Apple Shared Library Manager files: Shared Library Manager and ASLM Resources

- AppleSearch Client, AppleSearch Authentication, AppleSearch Communication, and ASClientLib.o.

- Apple Guide

- UGLibrary.o (Appleshare API glue)

- Apple MIDI Driver and MIDI Manager

- Mathlib

- Telephone Manager and TelMgrGlue.o

- The following Communications Toolbox files: CTB Resources, CommToolboxExtensions.o, Apple Modem Tool, Text Tool, AppleTalk ADSP Tool, TTY Tool, XMODEM Tool, VT102 Tool, SerialTool, TTYFont, VT102Font, ADSP, AdminLAT, LAT, LAT Prep, and LAT Tool

- The following MacSNMP, MacTCP, and MacX25 files: SNMPLibrary.cln.o, SNMPLibrary.clf.o, LibraryManager.n.o, LibraryManager.o, LAP802.a.o, LAP802.c.o, LAP802Arp.c.o, LAP802Mdev.c.o, LAPAsmUtil.a.o, LAPloopBack.a.o, FSDES.o, IPCGlue.o, X25_Interface_Library.o

- The following Network Software Installer files: Apple Token Ring NB, AppleTalk, EtherTalk Phase 2, Network, Responder, Token Ring, TokenTalk Phase 2, and TokenTalk Prep

- The following MacTCP-related HyperCard XCMDs (built from the sample source code in the HyperCard MacTCP Toolkit folder): TCPActiveOpen, TCPCharsAvailable, TCPClose, TCPNameToAddr, TCPOverview, TCPPassiveOpen, TCPRecvChars, TCPRecvMsg, TCPRecvUpTo, TCPRelease, TCPSend, TCPState, and TCPVersion

For any additional information on Apple-licensed software contact Apple's
Software Licensing Department at the following address for further information:

Software Licensing Department
Apple Computer, Inc.
2420 Ridgepoint Drive, MS: 198-SWL
Austin, TX 78754
Telephone: (512) 919-2645
AppleLink: SW.LICENSE

For any additional information on Metrowerks-licensed software write or email to :

Metrowerks Corp.,
2201 Donley Drive, Suite 310
Austin TX 78758, USA.
attn: Warranty Information.
email: support@metrowerks.com

Free technical support from Metrowerks is provided by acquiring any of Metrowerks' commercial products. You can upgrade from this limited version of CodeWarrior to a commercial product and thereby benefit from this technical support. For more information, contact Metrowerks at (800) 377-5416, or via email at sales@metrowerks.com.